A DIFFICULT ROAD

A DIFFICULT ROAD

The Transition to Socialism in Mozambique

edited by John S. Saul

Monthly Review Press · New York

All photos by Stephanie Urdang, except p.35, courtesy of the United Nations/van Lierop; pp. 75 and 391, courtesy of Agência de Informação de Moçambique; and p. 279, courtesy of Barry Pinsky.

Library of Congress Cataloging in Publication Data
Main entry under title:

A Difficult road.

1. Socialism—Mozambique—Addresses, essays,
lectures.   2. Mozambique—Politics and government—
1975–   —Addresses, essays, lectures.   3. Mozambique—
Economic conditions—1975–   —Addresses, essays,
lectures.   4. Mozambique—Social conditions—
1975–   —Addresses, essays, lectures.   I. Saul,
John S.
HX449.A6D53   1985   335′.00967′9   85-7129
ISBN 0-85345-591-0
ISBN 0-85345-592-9 (pbk.)

Monthly Review Press
155 West 23rd Street
New York, N.Y. 10011

Manufactured in the United States of America

10 9 8 7 6 5 4 3 2 1

Contents

Acknowledgments

Too much time has elapsed between the first launching of this project and its final realization. Part of the reason for this lies in the rapid unfolding of events in southern Africa in general, and in Mozambique in particular, a reality that seemed to keep the prospect of a satisfactory rounding-off of a book of this nature just out of the reach of its authors. If, as a result, events have outstripped certain aspects of the accounts presented in some of the chapters, we trust the reader will feel that, because of their quality, all remain significant contributions to our knowledge about Mozambique.

Each author—all of whom have actually worked in Mozambique for extended periods in precisely the sector about which they write—has his or her own debts of gratitude for assistance received during the preparation of their chapters. This is a debt, in particular, to the many Mozambicans who have given generously of their time in making us more aware of the realities of their country. It would be invidious to single out individual names from the long list of those who have helped us in this way, although I feel there are special reasons for doing so in the case of Jorge Rebelo, formerly Minister of Information in the Mozambique government and now FRELIMO's Secretary of Ideological Work. He grasped from the outset the possible significance of this book and facilitated its preparation in innumerable ways—without in any way restricting the use to which we put the materials we collected. I can also speak for each of the authors of this book in thanking our editor, Susan Lowes of Monthly Review Press: as on three previous occasions she has nursed the present editor and his manuscript to press and has done so with a spirit of solidarity that rises far above the call of professional responsibility.

Speaking more personally, I would like to thank a number of *internacionalistas* who have aided in invaluable ways my own work on Mozambique and on the present book. They include, in addition to my fellow authors, Sam Barnes, Merle Bowen, Grete Brochmann, Alan Brooks, Colin Darch, Rob Davies, Bertil Egero, Polly Gaster, Ole Gjerstad, Wil van Gyn, David Hedges, Alan Isaacman, Don Kossick, Gary Littlejohn, Bridget O'Laughlin, Dan O'Meara,

7

Otto Roesch, Pat, Nick, and Jo Saul, David Sogge, Dave Wield, and Marc Wuyts. Nor is it coincidental that a number of the above-named have been, or continue to be, associated with Mozambique's African Studies Center; located at the University of Eduardo Mondlane in Maputo and under the directorship of Aquino da Bragança, the center has been an important touchstone for my own research work in Mozambique over the years. I am also grateful to Atkinson College, York University, Toronto, and in particular to the late Dean Harry Crowe and to Ron Bordessa, the present dean, for facilitating my work in and about Mozambique. Finally, special mention should be made of Barbara Barnes who played a vitally important role in the original conceptualization of this book and in the early stages of its preparation.

   Finally, with the full support of my fellow authors, I would like to dedicate this volume to Ruth First, friend and former colleague, to her pen and her presence, her formidable drive and her unflinching commitment, killed by the South African state while she was serving in the front lines of the struggle for a socialist Mozambique and a truly free southern Africa.

—John S. Saul

Toronto, Canada
January 1985

Introduction

In 1962 the Front for the Liberation of Mozambique—FRELIMO—was formed in Dar es Salaam and in 1964 it launched an armed struggle to liberate Mozambique from the grip of Portuguese colonialism. The success of that struggle was dramatic. By 1974 FRELIMO was undertaking successful military actions in the very center of the country, actions mounted not only from the movement's bases in neighboring countries but also, more dramatically, from those large and vibrant "liberated areas" which were by then well established within Mozambique itself. In turn, Portugal's losing hand in the battle for Mozambique, together with parallel difficulties in its other African colonies (Angola and Guinea-Bissau), had become the major cause of the officers' coup in Portugal in April 1974. This coup was ultimately to permit the winding-down of Portugal's overseas empire. After some further skirmishes between FRELIMO and the Portuguese, and a subsequent ten-month period of "transitional government," Mozambique became independent, under FRELIMO leadership, on June 25, 1975.

Equally important, and indeed a premise for military success, was the fact that FRELIMO had itself been radicalized as a movement in the course of the armed struggle. This is a process which has been well documented in the literature on Mozambique,[1] and we shall return to a consideration of it in Chapter 1 of the present volume. Nonetheless, the point may be put more briefly here. The intransigence of the Portuguese colonialists blocked, in Mozambique as in Angola and Guinea-Bissau, the kind of classic "neocolonial solution" to the decolonization process which had become so familiar in the British and French spheres of influence in Africa. In consequence, a different type of nationalist movement was necessary on the African side. Slowly but surely, the wing of FRELIMO which was prepared to forge the kind of close links with the mass of Mozambicans—rural dwellers in particular—required to ground a successful guerrilla war gained ascendancy within the movement. In the process, leaders had to learn to democratize their methods of work in order to really earn the popular support that was so necessary. They came, too, to commit themselves to people-relevant programs in all the spheres where developments in the liberated areas touched people's lives (education, health, and the like); they came to grasp the merits of collective solutions to economic problems, especially in the agricultural and distribution spheres. In sum, the foreshadowings of a socialist practice began to crystallize out of the struggle, and this was increasingly synthesized in an ideology at once socialist and anti-imperialist (a clear definition of the colonial enemy *and* of its Western capitalist allies becoming starkly more evident as the war progressed).

Not that FRELIMO itself romanticized this achievement. Thus Marcelino dos Santos, the movement's vice-president, was asked in 1972 how permanent these advances were likely to be. Was it the case, perhaps, that "in a war situation it is easier to get people to accept a certain type of communal effort even by those who are not ideologically committed to this as defining the form of the future society"? His reply:

> I accept that it is partly made easier by the demands of war. But does that mean that once we have independence the approach will be changed? In the particular conditions of fighting against Portuguese colonialism, revolutionary attitudes are not only possible but necessary. If we do not follow collectivist attitudes, we will not be able to face the enemy successfully. In this sense it is true to say that the internal dynamic of the struggle is such that the conditions generate collectivist thinking. But one should also say that even if the origins of such attitudes are partly pragmatic they can, nevertheless, provide the base for the growth of a real social revolution. There is certainly a strong possibility that in the course of collectivist effort a situation is created from which it will be difficult to withdraw.[2]

Dos Santos' hunch has proven to be correct. These kind of socialist roots in a popularly based liberation struggle did give Mozambique a running start on meeting the development challenges of the independence period. That the country has attempted to extend the achievements of its liberation phase into a set of bold and challenging present-day policies will be fully apparent in what follows. It will be equally apparent that efforts to do so are being carried out under the most difficult and challenging of conditions. As a result, from the vantage point of 1985 and ten years of independence we can see that problems far outweigh accomplishments in many, if not most, sectors. We intend to examine both problems and accomplishments in the present volume. Yet we would argue that the basic premise of the Mozambican revolution remains an exciting one: that the people as a whole can control their own production process, can control their own destiny, and that in doing so they can find and release energies—collective energies—for developing their own country. This process has borne, self-evidently, the promise of a development effort premised on a parallel process of socialist transformation. What does this latter phrase imply? An ongoing effort to repeal the most oppressive aspects of the law of the market (worldwide and local) in favor of planned development. An ongoing effort to expand democratic control by the "collective producer" over that planning process at all levels. An ongoing effort to ensure the betterment of the lot of the mass of the population (rather than advance the interests of any more privileged strata). It is because Mozambique has carried this process further than any other country in Africa so far that the experiment is worthy of particular attention. Though we will find good reasons for viewing Mozambique's "transition to socialism" circumspectly, the present authors do argue that a development project has been afoot in that country that must be taken very seriously indeed.

In 1962, the formation of FRELIMO; in 1964, the launching of the armed struggle; in 1975, the attaining of independence: to these dates must now be added March 16, 1984. On that date President Samora Machel publicly embraced South Africa's Prime Minister P. W. Botha and the Nkomati Accord between Mozambique and South Africa was given an official seal of approval by both parties. Defined as being a "non-aggression" and "good neighbor" pact between the two countries, it struck a particularly jarring note for all who have followed and applauded the Mozambican revolution. Some have even been tempted to strike an elegiac note, Rest in Peace socialist Mozambique, in the wake of Nkomati. We need not anticipate here the argument of the present book on this score, except to say that this is almost certainly an over-reaction. In any case, we will have much more to say, particularly in the final chapter, about Nkomati, the factors that lay behind it, and its implications for Mozambique's present and future. At this point, however, such dramatic recent developments can serve to remind us of a second powerful reason for taking seriously Mozambique's attempts to transform itself in socialist terms.

To understand this point fully we must adopt a regional perspective. For even in advance of Nkomati a mere glance at the map would have reminded us of the source of one of the most serious problems that confronts Mozambique: the country's location well within the battle lines of the continuing struggle for southern Africa. Mozambique's support for the guerrilla war that freed Zimbabwe from white-settler domination was a major factor in the war's successful outcome. Yet the costs for Mozambique were very high indeed, costs in terms of transportation link disrupted by the implementation of sanctions (and foreign exchange earnings lost), in terms of personnel and equipment diverted to meet military imperatives, and in terms of the sheer physical destruction of key sectors of the economy caused by brutal Rhodesian air raids. The war also provided the cover for Rhodesian sponsorship of armed groups that would attempt to subvert the Mozambican regime on the ground.

The independence of Zimbabwe promised, briefly, to provide Mozambique crucial breathing space. But it did not settle the battle for southern Africa, in the end merely shifting the main site of that battle deeper inside the belly of the beast, into South Africa itself. And South Africa, already implicated in earlier Rhodesian efforts to undermine independent Mozambique, lost no time in picking up the slack from its fallen ally. The attack on houses occupied by members of the African National Congress of South Africa in Matola (a Maputo suburb) in January 1981, the cowardly assassination of Ruth First at Eduardo Mondlane University in August 1982, and the killing and maiming of Mozambican civilians in the air raid of May 1983 are merely the most dramatic examples of South African aggression. Even more significant are Pretoria's systematic economic destabilization and its efforts to orchestrate and supply the further activities of the Mozambique National Resistance (MNR), a ruthless band of local renegades (intermingled with ex-Portuguese policemen, mercenaries, and South African advisers).

As mentioned, the MNR was originally of Rhodesian provenance, but now continues to harass Mozambique from the bush in various parts of the country, having clearly been nominated by South Africa to play the same kind of wrecker's role in Mozambique that Jonas Savimbi's UNITA has been helped to play in Angola—and with a significant measure of success, as witness Nkomati and its aftermath. Observers of the Mozambican revolution have long understood that an important part of what the future holds for Mozambique will hinge on the pace at which the struggle to overthrow South Africa's apartheid system advances. Such an understanding has often remained more notional than real, however, until recent events made it much more difficult to ignore the stark and chilling reality of this proposition. For the overthrow of the South African system will not occur overnight and Mozambique—still economically linked to South Africa in myriad ways but also committed to the cause of fundamental change there—has paid a very high price indeed for that commitment. Indeed, debate continues in some circles as to just how much of Mozambique's socialism remains after South Africa's onslaught of recent years. Clearly, in such a context the need for a better informed comprehension of developments in Mozambique and for a more alert network of support for that country seems especially pressing. And not just in light of South Africa's regional ravages: it is all the more the case when one considers the escalating attempts by various U.S. administrations (the Reagan team in particular has moved closer to Pretoria) to present progressive regimes throughout the world as "totalitarian" enemies or as mere cat's-paws of Soviet aggression. And to act against them accordingly!

Solidarity is imperative then, but at the same time there does exist the ever present danger of solidarity degenerating into apologetics. Fortunately, Mozambicans themselves have been well aware that any simpleminded spirit of "triumphalism" does not facilitate socialist endeavor: as one senior Mozambican leader once put the point to me, "Lies have short legs, they do not walk far." One of the most attractive aspects of Mozambique's attempted social revolution has been precisely the willingness to keep open many basic questions for further discussion and for possible change of direction. As we shall see in Chapter 2, this was most recently apparent at FRELIMO's important Fourth Congress, held in April 1983. Yet the same imperative of frank and honest inquiry also applies to the Western audience to whom this book is primarily addressed.

It is clearly late in the day to be presenting the quest for socialist reconstruction in the third world in uncritical terms. After all, how could such an undertaking ever be anything but problematic in the context of underdevelopment and "historical backwardness," and of a global capitalism spurred by its own crises to lash out more vindictively than ever at any challenge to its hegemony. Those sympathetic to socialism have probably done themselves and the revolutions they support a singular disservice when they have presented the processes involved in an unproblematic manner. As the rosy picture we have been tempted to paint—of Russia, of China, of Cuba, of Vietnam, of Tanzania, and the like—has proven to be a much more shaded one in reality, it has become apparent that a naive perspective virtually guarantees eventual disillusionment. Nor does a tone of unqualified adulation provide any real context within which the often singular accomplishments of such revolutions can stand out in bold relief—against the background, as it were, of the difficult sets of circumstances from which such accomplishments have been wrenched. Operating in such a manner, it is difficult indeed to expand sympathy and enlightened understanding beyond the circle of those who are already true believers. Yet Mozambique deserves support that runs deeper and flows more broadly than that.

Of course, by 1984 there seemed to be rather less risk of adulation of Mozambique than of premature and self-righteous dismissal of its efforts and its accomplishments. A combination of factors—South Africa's siege of the country not least among them—had combined to severely weaken the Mozambican economy, with the result that FRELIMO did not find itself bargaining with the apartheid regime from a position of very great strength. Any measure of "peace" that was purchased at Nkomati—and the auguries in this regard were still mixed as 1984 drew to a close—was at the expense of a further reintegration of the Mozambican economy into the circuits of Western capitalism and of a very considerable dilution of support for the African National Congress in its struggle to liberate South Africa. Despite this, we shall argue that an unsympathetic dismissal of FRELIMO's project in the wake of Nkomati is no better response than uncritical celebration of it. Nevertheless, any such argument also demands a realistic approach to the question of just how feasible, in an epoch of global economic crisis and resurgent and unapologetic counterrevolution, are socialist aspirations in the small peripheral economies of the world.

Fortunately the present authors' desire to present Mozambique's efforts more effectively and believably to a wider audience comes at a time when the general discussion of the "transition to socialism" has become more sophisticated—and more honest. It seems less necessary for sympathetic observers to link themselves slavishly to Soviet or Chinese models of development, for example, though they may continue to derive inspiration from some aspects of both experiences. And we find emphases in many recent analyses which seek more strenuously than ever to question the assumption that mere state ownership is a synonym for socialism. Nor need it be assumed that within the twin framework of state ownership and economic backwardness the key to the transition can lie simply in the "development of the productive forces"—with full-fledged socialism emerging more or less automatically at some point in the future in step with economic development and the more extended creation of a working class! There are also writings which question, in the absence of democratic processes available for effective use by the peasants and workers, the uncritical acceptance of self-proclaimed vanguards as manifestations of the "dictatorship of the proletariat." They question various mechanical versions of Marxism which allow little or no room for the creative and active role of these classes in socialist reconstruction. Such writings begin, instead, to highlight the importance of the emergence of new kinds of production relations and of genuine democratization during the actual transition period itself (the tragic failure of one kind of "socialism" in Poland being something that can only serve to reinforce such concerns in the future). In sum, they emphasize more openly than ever before the difficulties and the agonizing dilemmas attendant upon the attempt to consolidate a successful socialist project.

Indeed, one of the most eminent contemporary Marxists, Paul Sweezy, has taken the point so far as to argue of the various regimes presently claiming to be socialist that

> none of these "socialist" societies behave as Marx—and I think most Marxists up until quite recently—thought they would. They have not eliminated classes except in a purely verbal sense; and, except in the period of the Cultural Revolution in China, they have not attempted to follow a course which could have the long-run effect of eliminating classes. The state has not disappeared—no one would expect it to, except in a still distant future—but on the contrary has become more and more the central and dominant institution of society.

A sweeping comment indeed, one only notionally qualified by the subsequent statement (in which, significantly enough, no *specific* exceptions are identified) that "while I believe the Soviet Union [seen as manifesting the abovementioned weaknesses] to be a valid prototype of other presently existing revolutionary societies, I do not mean to preclude the possibility that some of them and others still to come are following or will follow a different road."[3] Even as the present authors prepare to affirm in what follows that Mozambique has indeed been attempting to follow "a different road," the forceful nature of Sweezy's warning underscores the necessity for us to keep our wits about us.

In fact, it is precisely by being sensitive to the difficulties of transition that we can best develop a range of questions likely to illuminate the achievements—and the continuing problems—of Mozambique's attempt at socialist reconstruction. The rest of this introduction seeks, briefly, to codify some of the questions which have guided us in our own work. Readers, in turn, will have an opportunity to judge for themselves which is the most prominent feature: the "difference" of the road Mozambique has chosen or the difficulties which the following of that road has presented. What may be worth mentioning here is that this is a matter of interpretation which has stimulated debate among the present authors themselves, a debate that has brought into question even the book's very title. So alive has Mozambique been to many of the problems of transition that when this volume was first conceived some years ago we thought to call the book "A Different Road," thus confronting quite self-consciously Sweezy's formulation. However, as the first draft was being brought together in 1983 the adjective "difficult" as qualifying Mozambique's "road" seemed at least equally appropriate and this remained all the more true in 1984, in the wake of Nkomati, as the book took its final form. In consequence, the book becomes, on publication, *A Difficult Road: The Transition to Socialism in Mozambique.* Yet both titles—"different" and "difficult"—continue to be apt. As does the subtitle: the notion of "transition to socialism" can still serve as a benchmark against which to measure Mozambique's efforts. It remains, in this introduction, to specify the principle themes that arise from such a notion and which will serve to structure our attempt to make sense of developments in Mozambique.

Class Struggle and "Undevelopment"

Despite continuing war and a crippling colonial inheritance, FRELIMO has never projected all its problems outward. During the period of the war of liberation, fierce internal struggles over the tactics and strategy to be adopted forced FRELIMO to confront head on the process of embryonic class formation which was occurring within the novel institutions of a Mozambique-in-the-making. As we shall see, those who won that struggle—the Mondlane/ Machel leadership team which still holds power—did so by grounding their activities ever more effectively in popular aspirations and popular assertions, linking up, in particular, with the mass of the peasant population. Nor was FRELIMO to lose hold of this insight in the post-independence period. For the danger existed that fresh life would be given to tendencies toward inequality by new aspirants to privilege *within* Mozambique's socialist structures. President Samora Machel himself emphasized this danger quite clearly in 1976:

> In 1964 and 1965 there was a great debate [in our movement] around the notion that there are no classes in Mozambique. And today, when we say that we are in a phase of class struggle, many ask: where are the classes in Mozambique? Why is it necessary to say that there is a class struggle in Mozambique? Now, without a class analysis, there can't be a struggle. Nor without a correct analysis of society.
>
> This, then, is the way we are analyzing our situation in Mozambique. We saw that exploitative classes present themselves in two forms. The first form: vestiges of feudal classes, with little economic and political strength, especially since the abolition of chieftaincy [*regulado*], but still retaining an important ideological and cultural

strength in rural areas. All peoples pass through this stage. To forget that is to forget everything, it is to forget our origins.

In the second place, the bourgeoisie manifests itself on two fronts: on the one hand, there is the colonial bourgeoisie en route to extinction, thanks to the flight from the country of its representatives; on the other hand, there is the internal bourgeoisie which is very weak economically, but with a strong presence in the apparatus of the state and in parastatal firms and benefitting from the cultural and ideological domination imposed by the colonial bourgeoisie. They assimilated a great many foreign values.

It is a question of doing away with this setup. This latter is, of course, a bourgeoisie that doesn't have its feet on the ground. It lives out there, in space. It's a question of this internal bourgeoisie trying to get its feet down on Mozambican soil. Its presence in the state apparatus, in state farms, its cultural and ideological dominance, and its alliance with imperialism (of which it is the representative inside the country) makes this class very dangerous.[4]

We shall have to look carefully at the ways in which this danger has been analyzed—and confronted—in contemporary Mozambique.

Marcelino dos Santos provided one early clue regarding FRELIMO's approach in the interview quoted above (see note 2) when he commented further on the possibility that the "collectivist effort" of the liberation period could be carried over into the new phase. At one level, he argued, "if our organization maintains a true revolutionary leadership, the special circumstances of our liberation open up real possibilities for an advance from liberation to revolution." "True revolutionary leadership," then, but in addition

the main defense must be to popularize the revolutionary aims and to create such a situation that if for one reason or another at some future time some people start trying to change these aims, they will meet with resistance from the masses.

We shall return to the question of what kind of interplay between leadership and mass action is necessary to underwrite a transition to socialism in a country like Mozambique. Here it bears noting that the possible consolidation of privileged class power in a third world setting can take diverse forms depending, in part, on the strength of other forces, worldwide and local, which are at work. Thus historical experience elsewhere suggests two possible blind alleys into which such a transition might be diverted.

On the one hand, there could be a collapse into mere *state capitalism,* a situation in which the state can continue to push itself into the economy, but primarily under the aegis of capital (again, worldwide and local). In this situation, the leadership, its membership—and its opportunities for self-aggrandizement—swollen precisely by the expansion of the state sector, can come to rest satisfied with its consolidation in power as a kind of bureaucratic middle-man for capital, a "bureaucratic bourgeoisie." This is particularly a danger in Africa perhaps, given the historic strength there of the networks of Western imperialism. Or, on the other hand, things could degenerate into what might be termed (for want of a better concept) *state collectivism.* This implies a situation in which the logic of the plan—not capitalist imperatives—remains central, but where the leadership becomes at best one whose impatience with the people leads it toward a hypercentralization of power and toward a self-defeating forcing of the pace of development. Moreover, there is a marked tendency for this kind of project to degenerate even further, the leadership stratum increasingly consolidating itself in power (as some have argued to be the case in Eastern Europe) as a "new class" in its own right.[5] If the trend toward either state capitalism or state collectivism were to become predominant in Mozambique, an initial index would be the cutting off of the leadership from precisely that popular base which had become its point of reference and inspiration during the armed struggle.

The existence of these twin dangers serves to define the principal terrain of class struggle in Mozambique. But this is not the sole problem which need be confronted. It is true that, too often, conventional "bourgeois" development theory has defined the problems of third world countries as being a matter of timing or phasing: the "advanced" societies are "somewhat ahead" of the most backward in what is, however, to be conceived of as a fairly linear global progression; a mere "gap" exists which can be closed with a bit of good will and effort on all sides. In contrast, a more illuminating approach to underdevelopment has come to underscore the importance of the *relationship,* a relationship of subordination, established historically—and reinforced contemporaneously—between the strong capitalist countries of the "center" on the one hand, and their weaker, but nevertheless class-structured, "dependencies" on the other. And this latter perspective undoubtedly does provide a much more accurate starting point for comprehending the situation of a country like Mozambique. It also brings into focus the question of practice, underscoring the importance of anti-imperialist strategies and domestic class struggle in breaking the links which lock backwardness into place.

Still, there is a danger of this approach degenerating in turn into a kind of ultraleft oversimplification, obscuring the kernel of truth which "modernization" theory does contain, however onesidedly. For third world countries are not only "*under*developed" (their potential for advance severely warped by imperialism and internal class formation), but "*un*developed" in an absolute sense as well. That is, they suffer from shortfalls in technical skills (which can be defined to include even such minimal basic requirements as fairly widespread literacy or numeracy), organizational competence, technological capacity, and the like.[6] Nor is the third world in general a specific enough referent. The reader more familiar with Latin America than with Africa, for example, will need to adjust his or her perspective to grasp the scope of this problem in the latter continent; moreover, it is a problem that presents an even more graphic challenge in Mozambique than in some other African countries, thanks to the particularly crippling legacy of Portugal's own backward version of colonialism (see Chapter 1). How is one to weight, in our explanation of what has happened during Mozambique's independence years, the fact that the rate of literacy in Mozambique in 1975 was less than 10 percent and that, of the one in ten who could read and write, very few had more than two to four years of primary schooling? How weight the fact that in a country of more than 12 million people there were only two agronomists and four architects? Such sobering examples could be multiplied almost indefinitely. Clearly such shortfalls must be dealt with in their own terms, with the release of popular political energies geared to challenging the class and imperial structures of underdevelopment to be complemented by programs that confront such relatively prosaic dimensions of the development challenge. Small wonder that, as Judith Marshall outlines below, FRELIMO has placed such a strong emphasis on education. But we shall see that the attempt simultaneously to overcome obstacles presented by underdevelopment and by "undevelopment" surfaces in every one of the subsequent chapters.

The Meeting of "Needs" and the Production Problem

The pattern of economic development chosen would seem to be one clear index of what class or classes are in charge: the international bourgeoisie, local entrepreneurial elements, bureaucratic strata, workers, peasants. Theoretically, servicing the needs of the mass of the population should lie somewhere near the core of the development process in third world countries. What is development about if it is not about that? Yet such an outcome is by no means an automatic one. Self-evidently, the definition of whose "needs" are to be front and center is a crucial focus of the class struggle that characterizes such countries.

In inheriting a classically distorted colonial-capitalist society, FRELIMO found itself confronting all those inequalities—class, racial, sexual, territorial—that define the structure of any such society and comprise a central part of the overall syndrome of under-development. As mentioned, during the period of armed struggle FRELIMO had developed a firm commitment to meeting the needs of ordinary Mozambicans rather than those of more privileged strata, a firm commitment, indeed, to empowering ordinary Mozambicans to meet their own needs! It will come as no surprise that concretizing this commitment by the upgrading of social services and other related policies has to date been the most successful aspect of the movement's practice in the post-independence period. Readers will be able to judge this for themselves in any event, for a number of the case studies that follow focus in on this reality in particular spheres: Carol Barker on the health sector, Judith Marshall on education, Barry Pinsky on urban development, Peter Sketchley on industrialization, and Stephanie Urdang on issues of sexual equality. Needless to say, the struggle to sustain an egalitarian thrust over a broad front of policy spheres remains an important key to the whole process of socialist development in Mozambique.

It may also be argued that putting the needs of the mass of the population front and center is not only good and humane politics but good socialist development economics as well. Put so strongly, this is a controversial point—and not so merely for orthodox economists. To be sure, the latter's fixation on the market mechanism encourages them uncritically to elide needs and "effective demand." Yet left to the whim of the market (and the biases inherent in an untransformed class structure), "consumer demand largely expresses the actual purchasing power in the possession of individuals" so that "when there are such distortions of the economic system as highly skewed income distribution, private ownership of the means of production, private appropriation of the social product, etc., demand in this sense will not always [sic] adequately express the needs of the people in that society." Genuinely socialist planning represents a smashing of the crippling logic of market limitations upon development; it must embody, in Clive Thomas's words, "the progressive convergence of the demand structure of the community and the needs of the population" and a firm rejection of marginalist orthodoxy.[7]

However, socialist economists have their own questionable orthodoxies as well. All too often the economics of socialist development in third world countries is presented as embodying a virtual contradiction in terms. A particularly stark—but not entirely atypical—formulation of the point is one advanced by Lucio Colletti:

To build a socialist society means to establish *socialist relations of production*. However one interprets it, this construction is inseparable from the development of *socialist democracy*, soviet government, or the self-government of the producers, in the real and not metaphorical sense of the word. On the other hand, and on the contrary, *accumulation* implies saving an extremely high quota of the national product for investment in industrial development; this means violently repressing mass consumption, violently restraining the needs of the population. It presupposes the precise opposite of democracy and of soviets: a coercive apparatus, charismatic leadership, and the *utilization* rather than the self-regulation of the masses. This is the problem with which Stalin was faced, or rather in the face of which the "situation" selected Stalin.[8]

Is "socialist accumulation" most accurately conceived in terms of this kind of zero-sum game? More convincing, perhaps, is an argument which sees accumulation and mass consumption as being much less contradictory than Colletti suggests: far from being opposites, one of them—accumulation—can be driven forward precisely by finding outlets for production in meeting the growing requirements, the needs, of the mass of the population. An effective industrialization strategy would thus base its "expanded reproduction" on ever increasing exchanges between city and country, between industry and agriculture, with food and raw materials moving to the cities, with consumer goods *and* producer goods (defined to include centrally such modest items as scythes, iron ploughs, hoes, axes, fertilizers, and the like) moving to the countryside. Collective saving geared to investment can then be seen as being drawn essentially, if not exclusively, from an expanding economic pool. Not that *self-willed* collective sacrifice is quite the impossibility that Colletti implies (which is just as well, since some necessary investments do not promise any instantaneous or direct payoffs for the populace). Nonetheless, the socialism of expanded reproduction does make the betterment of the people's lot a short-term rather than a long-term prospect. It thus promises a much sounder basis for an effective (rather than merely rhetorical) alliance of workers and peasants and for a democratic road to revolutionary socialism.

As we shall see, differing views as to the broad nature of the accumulation process and the imperatives to which it gives rise have been part of the debate—and part of the class struggle—in contemporary Mozambique. And such issues also overlap with other related themes. Within a few years of winning independence, the framework for a comprehensive planning process had begun to be put into place. However, by the time of FRELIMO's Fourth Congress in 1983 it had become evident that hypercentralization and excessive bureaucratization were dangers attendant upon this kind of planning and that a measure of devolution and a further democratization of economic decision-making, and even an extended utilization of the market mechanism, were in order. Similarly, in that congress it was argued that large-scale and "high-tech" projects had been unduly highlighted, at the expense of more modest, more local, more manageable ones. Applied quite specifically to the agricultural sphere, this latter critique underwrote a feeling that in concentrating too exclusively upon large-scale farms in the early years the government had granted much too low a priority to the peasant sector—and to the program of peasant-based cooperativization. Shifting resources to the peasant sector and revitalizing the network of commercialization, which is so critical as a stimulus to that sector, were now to become much more prominent features of development policy.

It will be apparent that the ongoing debate over the balances to be struck within Mozambique's development strategy reflects the complexities of any attempted transition to socialism. However, such complexities cannot be abstracted, as mere "technical questions," from the context of underdevelopment and "undevelopment" which frames them in a country like Mozambique. Underdevelopment? We have already suggested that class interests can impinge diversely upon the planning process—even within the framework of strong state ownership and control of major sectors of the economy. But we can also revert to our earlier mention of the "crippling logic of market limitations upon development" and remind ourselves that this "logic" has international dimensions as well.

For Mozambique's most dramatic inheritance from the Portuguese was an extreme form of economic subordination to the global capitalist economy. South Africa looms particularly large as, historically, a major source of foreign exchange earnings through returns from labor migration, from service charges linked to transportation, and the like. But historically Mozambique's economy was also warped by the Portuguese to assume the fragile posture of supplier of primary products to Western markets. These are not ties that are easily transformed and certainly not overnight. Thomas has suggested that the transition to socialism involves establishing "necessary and basic internal productive conditions [which] ensure that participation in the global capitalist international economy does not result in a global division of labor which works against the local community," but instead enables even exports increasingly to become an extension of production geared, first and foremost, to meeting domestic demand and domestic needs.[9] In this sphere, as in so many others, there is the continuing challenge to balance the apparent necessity of short-term compromises with the imperatives of the inherited situation (continuing economic ties with South Africa, for example, or concentration upon certain crops in international demand, the better to earn valuable foreign exchange) against the need to keep alive the long-term socialist goal of structural transformation. Returns garnered from such "compromises" would then be used to lay the basis for an economy structured along more self-centered, self-reliant lines.

Easier said than done, a conclusion that seems all the more true when one casts a realistic eye on the possible alternative of links to the Eastern bloc countries. The latter offer no panaceas, having severe limitations upon their capacity to help and, in any case, driving hard bargains of their own. Indeed, such ties do not always present themselves as offering any very substantial deviation from the norm of continued economic subordination to more advanced economies. "Undevelopment" takes its toll here too. The tremendous difficulty of finding in Mozambique the skills, the technical capacity, and the organizational means necessary to the tasks at hand makes everything that much more difficult. This is a point to which we will return again and again in subsequent chapters. Add to this the international dimension of this "undevelopment" which can, in its own way, make the long-term goal of "structural transformation" vulnerable. For the "necessary" reliance upon aid, expertise, equipment from abroad—whether from East or West—which undevelopment seems to dictate raises again the specter of "compromise" that threatens to get out of control, of compromise that finds the means coming to shape the ends rather than the opposite.

Does the prominence of economic and other linkages with the "socialist countries" pose the threat of a Stalinization of Mozambique's socialist experiment? Have attempts by Mozambique to lure foreign capital into joint participation with the state in certain fields marked a foreshadowing of the country's reabsorption into the Western capitalist fold? As we shall see, these are questions—particularly the latter—that have become all the more pressing as the Mozambican economy has entered into severe crisis in the 1980s, a crisis marked by increasing international debt and short-falls of production in virtually all sectors. As a result, the country has felt the need to seek economic succor from international capitalist sources with increased zeal (including, in late 1984, from the International Monetary Fund and the World Bank). At times the post-liberation Mozambican government has seemed master of such compromises rather than their victim, although recent economic maneuvers have had something more of a hint of desperation about them. Certainly the Mozambican case underscores the fact that the international terrain remains a treacherous one for a small and by no means powerful country attempting a transition to socialism. Indeed, the "production problem," a problem that spills over into so many other spheres, is perhaps the most intractable challenge confronting Mozambique.

The Leadership–Mass Action Dialectic

We shall discuss the "production problem" in what follows (in Chapter 2, for example, and in Peter Sketchley's case study of the industrial sphere and in Helena Dolny's of the process of collectivization in the countryside). But placing economic planning in the context of our earlier discussion of class struggle in Mozambique forces us back to those political questions which were also hinted at in that discussion. How to guarantee that the attempt to find socialist solutions to socioeconomic challenges—solutions which express and reflect the interests of workers and peasants—will be sustained? Marcelino dos Santos, quoted above, saw the answer to lie in some combination of "true revolutionary leadership" and effective mass action from below. What, we can now repeat, is the nature of the interplay between these two terms of the political equation in Mozambique?

Certainly, as noted, a major legacy of the armed struggle was precisely its combined emphasis upon strong leadership on the one hand and upon facilitating the democratic expression of the demands of workers and peasants on the other. After independence these two necessary elements were to intersect within the framework of a single-party system, FRELIMO having transformed itself in 1977 from liberation movement into self-described "vanguard party." To Mozambicans this was a logical development. During the war FRELIMO had come to give necessary focus to the liberation struggle and to exemplify the high degree of unity which was in the process of being achieved (among ethnic groups, regions, factions); that same highest common factor of unity which FRELIMO represented continues to seem a precious commodity, vigorously to be safeguarded. In addition, the FRELIMO leadership feels itself to be deeply rooted in and constantly learning from the popular classes. Beyond that it has, in its view, a sufficiently clear and coherent sense of the direction in which Mozambique must move that even when its policies run ahead of immediate popular demands, the vast mass of Mozambicans can be expected ultimately to comprehend and to embrace such policies as their own. This is the meaning of "vanguardism" in Mozambique and, given the high quality of the top leadership cadre there, the argument for it has strong appeal.

Of course, this kind of blending of leadership and popular democratic action is alien to many Western preconceptions. It is evident that a single-party system does structure political choice for people—though one may doubt whether it inherently structures choice in ways that are as limiting as in most multiparty systems. In the latter, the reduction of democratic involvement merely to periodic elections and the impact of economic power and media manipulation tend to negate the apparent openness of the political arena. Yet even if this is true, it does not quite resolve the matter. It remains the case that genuine popular control is fragile enough in *every* setting and the dangers of a collapse into authoritarianism which are present in a vanguard-party system are readily apparent.

Moreover, the socialist tradition is very far from having overcome this problem. Rosa Luxemburg saw the necessity for strong leadership in a revolutionary context:

> The Bolsheviks solved the famous problem of "winning a majority of the population," which problem has ever weighed on the German social democracy like a nightmare. As bred in the bone disciples of parliamentary cretinism the latter say: first let's become a "majority." The true dialectic of revolution, however, stands this wisdom of parliamentary moles on its head: not through a majority to revolutionary tactics, but through revolutionary tactics to a majority—that is the way the road runs!

Nonetheless, she advanced a sharp critique of what she saw to be the weaknesses of Lenin's vanguardist practices in the post-revolutionary period:

> Without general elections, without unrestricted freedom of press and assembly, without a free struggle of opinion, life dies out in every public institution, becomes a mere semblance of life, in which only the bureaucracy remains as an active element. Public life gradually falls asleep, a few dozen party leaders of inexhaustible energy and boundless experience direct and rule. Among them, only a dozen outstanding heads do the leading and an elite of the working class is invited from time to time to meetings where they are to applaud the speeches of the leaders and to approve proposed resolutions unanimously—at bottom, then, a clique affair—a dictatorship to be sure, not the dictatorship of the proletariat, however, but only the dictatorship of a handful of politicians, that is the dictatorship in the bourgeois sense, in the sense of the rule of the Jacobins.[10]

To his credit, Lenin himself agonized throughout his career over the nature of the dialectic to be established between leadership and mass action, moving from the stark formulations of *What Is to Be Done?* ("class political consciousness can be brought to workers only from without") in 1902 to some rather different observations in later years:

> History as a whole, and the history of revolutions in particular, is always richer in content, more varied, more multiform, more lively and ingenious than is imagined in even the best of parties, the most class conscious vanguards of the most advanced classes. . . .
> We do not cut ourselves off from the revolutionary people but submit to their judgment every step and decision we take. We rely fully and solely on the free initiative of the working masses themselves.[11]

Indeed, Lenin remained preoccupied with the tension between leadership and mass action within the socialist project until his death—without ever finding the means to resolve it in an entirely satisfactory manner. Yet the need to do so is no less pressing in Mozambique than it was in Lenin's Soviet Union, in Mao's China, or in any other setting where the most basic questions regarding the politics of the transition to socialism have been posed.

We are led, in consequence, to an evaluation of the manner in which the popular presence—the presence of the workers and peasants themselves—actually manifests itself within Mozambique's vanguard-party system. We have suggested that in the period of armed struggle the most effective cadres were those who struck roots among the people and elicited their voluntary engagement: the process of bringing the peasantry into the struggle was also the process of weeding out those leaders who could not make this transition to a people's politics. For the revolutionary direction which we saw FRELIMO attain during the war period was won only by dint of fierce contestation within the leadership, with those who were rooted in this kind of political process—representatives of the peasantry, in effect—carrying the day against more elitist politicans. The upshot was the balancing of a democratic style of work on the part of FRELIMO cadres against the development of a set of democratic expectations on the part of the people themselves. Moreover, there can be little doubt that the movement carried the precedent of this kind of dialectic with it into power as an inoculation against *both* kinds of potential degeneration of the socialist impulse: toward state capitalism, toward state collectivism.

Such a precedent does not bear fruit automatically, however. "Good reasons" for an extreme centralization of power and decision-making abound (the military threat, the apparent logic of "efficiency" and highly coordinated planning in a context of scarce resources, and the like), as do, potentially, bad ones (the crystallization in power of privileged strata of politicans and bureaucrats). Indeed, some of FRELIMO's practices in the political sphere since independence may appear to be subject to Luxemburg's strictures as quoted above. Yet an ongoing attempt to give institutional weight and substance to popular participation and popular control continues to be the key to many of the most positive features of the Mozambican experiment. In this volume both Peter Sketchley's investigation of popular participation in industry and Barry Pinsky's account of popular involvement in the redevelopment of urban neighborhoods suggest something of the democratization of various spheres of daily life which continues to be a central feature. As we shall also see (Chapter 2), the broader debate over development options touches as much upon the merits of popularizing the military struggle, of democratizing the development effort, of releasing the creative energies of workers and peasants and giving them scope to speak, as it does upon the merits of "rationalizing" military and development activities and rendering them more efficient in technical terms. From the ongoing efforts to deal with the tension between these two necessary sets of emphases something important can be learned concerning the creative potential of the Mozambican revolution.

The Ideological Front

One important index of the progress realized in any attempted transition to socialism will be the ideology which begins to crystallize out of the revolutionary process. Any collapse in the direction either of state capitalism or of state collectivism would be accompanied by the appearance of unsavory and mystifying ideological formulations as well. In the former case one might expect to find some bland form of "African socialism," say, to become a prominent rationale; in the latter case—if historical precedent is anything to go by—the result might be some dead and mechanical form of pseudo-Marxism. As will be discussed in succeeding chapters, Mozambicans have increasingly come to theorize their socialist goals and socialist practice in Marxist terms—or rather, in "Marxist-Leninist" terms, the latter being the formal designation of its ideology adopted by FRELIMO in 1977. In this way FRELIMO sought to draw out the logic of its revolutionary practice in an even more systematic manner, to develop and deepen it theoretically beyond the existing formulations of the leadership—brilliant though these have often been, as evidenced most prominently in the writings of Samora Machel[12]—and to give it increased weight and coherence as a scientific tool and as a pedagogy. This is undoubtedly a correct instinct, at once an index of the movement's clarity and a salutary antidote to the various narrowly Africanist definitions (e.g., Tanzania's "Ujamaa" and the "African socialism" of numerous other regimes) which have come to blur class struggles in Africa in the name of socialism. At the same time, it must be admitted that the project of specifying a brand of Marxism that will advance the Mozambican revolution is fraught with hazards. In this connection the important, even vital, links established with the "socialist countries" (as Eastern bloc countries are generally termed in Mozambique) have been of considerable importance. As in the liberation war period, the bottom line of defense against the inescapable reality of South African aggression has been military assistance from these countries (even if, in the end, such assistance has scarcely been adequate). And this link, in turn, has been complemented by others in the spheres of economic relations, technical agreements, and the like. No one who takes seriously the dangers of the southern African region to which Mozambique is exposed could wish such links away. At the same time, one can scarcely see in the kind of Marxism-Leninism proselytized by these countries any real intellectual key to a genuinely socialist practice. Quite the contrary, as we shall argue.

Of course, FRELIMO leaders have made it perfectly clear that their Marxism must be concretized in Mozambican terms:

> The historical experience of our people, of our party, constitutes a novel experience within the international communist movement which must be evaluated accordingly. . . . Marxism-Leninism sprang up among us as a product of our struggle and of the debates over ideas within FRELIMO itself. To underestimate this fact is to deprive Marxism-Leninism of the vital force which it possesses in Mozambique, it is to reduce it to clichés and abstract stereotypes, to pale copies of realities beyond our borders. "Historical materialism" must be studied with reference to the realities of Mozambican society and to the specific circumstances of its historical evolution. . . . [Such studies] are not to be made in an abstract manner, independently of Mozambican reality, or by treating Mozambican reality with merely passing references.[13]

Yet it must also be admitted that Mozambique has not avoided all the perils of mechanical Marxism and of *Diamat* ("Dialectical Materialism")—a set of ideological formulations which is very much on offer from its Eastern allies and one which has been a severe drag on socialist initiatives in other parts of the world (where it has often gone hand in glove with bureaucratic deformations and mass de-mobilization). We shall also return to this complex issue—and some more recent variations on it—in Chapter 2. Here we may merely anticipate the argument presented there: that on this front, too, and despite severe difficulties, Mozambique continues its efforts to find its own way forward, continues to inject the vitality of its own experience into the Marxist tradition, even as it draws upon that tradition's strengths.

The above areas all need to be explored if any kind of definitive balance sheet on the transition to socialism in Mozambique is to be drawn up, and certainly all will be focused on in what follows. Yet the aspiration of the present authors remains somewhat more modest than that of providing a definitive and exhaustive account. The two chapters in Part 1 attempt to sketch, in a preliminary manner, the broad outlines of a "political economy of Mozam-bique." But a major contribution of this book is to be found in the chapters of Part 2—sectoral studies rooted in the firsthand experi-ence of their authors, Western *cooperantes* who have themselves played an active role in the Mozambican development process. As on-the-ground, grass-roots explorations of key spheres within the overall project of socialist construction in Mozambique, these seek to demonstrate concretely both the strengths and weaknesses of the country's efforts to date, what has been done, and what remains to be done. In this way they may provide information from which readers can begin to form their own judgments regarding Mozam-bique's progress.

More generally, we hope that the book as a whole will serve to convey our own sense of what has been most important about the Mozambican experiment: that things have been in motion and ex-citing possibilities have been opened up; that a "transition to social-ism" has been placed on the agenda, even if formidable obstacles (not least South Africa's war) jeopardize the realization of a socialist outcome; that, despite such obstacles, the struggle continues, as Mozambicans themselves are fond of saying. If readers do not find any definitive balance sheet on the transition to socialism in Mo-zambique here, they will find some pointers toward such a balance sheet—just as, in the final chapter, they will find a preliminary account of Nkomati and its aftermath, this being much the most difficult moment that the Mozambican revolution has yet experi-enced. If they find some strong reasons for taking Mozambique's road as seriously as the present authors have felt moved to do, well and good. They will certainly find strong reasons for taking the difficulties which continue to stalk that road as challenges to be confronted not only by Mozambicans but by all of us who seek to support the struggle to transform the region of southern Africa.

Notes

1. See, *inter alia,* Eduardo Mondlane, *The Struggle for Mozambique* (Harmondsworth: Penguin Books, 1969; new edition, London: Zed Press, 1983); FRELIMO, *Central Committee Report to the Third Congress of FRELIMO* (London, 1978); Giovanni Arrighi and John S. Saul, *Essays on the Political Economy of Africa* (New York and London: Monthly Review Press, 1973), chap. 8; John S. Saul, *The State and Revolution in Eastern Africa* (New York: Monthly Review Press, 1979), chaps. 1–3; Allen Isaacman, *A Luta Continua: Creating a New Society in Mozambique* (Binghamton, N.Y.: Ferdnand Braudel Center, 1980); Edward Alpers, "The Struggle for Socialism in Mozambique, 1960–1972," in Carl G. Rosberg and Thomas M. Callaghy, eds., *Socialism in Sub-Saharan Africa: A New Assessment* (Berkeley: University of California Press, 1979); Barry Munslow, *Mozambique: The Revolution and Its Origins* (London: Longmans, 1983); Basil Davidson, "The Politics of Armed Struggle: National Liberation in the African Colonies of Portugal," in Basil Davidson, Joe Slovo, and Anthony R. Wilkinson, *Southern Africa: The New Politics of Revolution* (Harmondsworth: Penguin Books, 1976).
2. Interview with Marcelino dos Santos (conducted by Joe Slovo), "FRELIMO Faces the Future," *The African Communist,* no. 55 (1973).
3. Paul M. Sweezy, *Post-Revolutionary Society* (New York and London: Monthly Review Press, 1980), pp. 137–39.
4. Interview with Samora Machel, *Tempo* (Maputo), no. 325 (26 December 1976) (my translation).
5. For a fuller discussion of this distinction between state capitalism and state collectivism with reference to Africa, see John S. Saul, "The Nature of the Post-Colonial State: Further Reflections," paper presented to the panel on "Bureaucratic Bourgeoisie or Power Elite: On Power in Africa," African Studies Association, Philadelphia, Pa., October 1980.
6. It will be apparent that the global pattern of imperialism and underdevelopment has not been irrelevant to the creation of the condition of absolute "undevelopment." Though the impact of imperialism stimulated changes in the third world, the realities of subordination also found such imperialism freezing into place many attributes of "historical backwardness" in dependent countries for a period of centuries. Nonetheless, the distinction between two levels or aspects of "backwardness" which the distinction between underdevelopment and undevelopment seeks to encompass seems a useful one to make for some purposes.
7. Clive Y. Thomas, *Dependence and Transformation: The Economics of the Transition to Socialism* (New York: Monthly Review Press, 1974), p. 250.
8. Lucio Colletti, "The Question of Stalin," *New Left Review,* no. 61 (May–June 1970), p. 79.
9. Thomas, *Dependence and Transformation,* pp. 134–35.

10. Rosa Luxemburg, "The Russian Revolution," in Mary-Alice Waters, ed., *Rosa Luxemburg Speaks* (New York: Pathfinder Press, 1970), pp. 374.
11. Quotations from *"Left-Wing" Communism—An Infantile Disorder*, 1920, and "Our Tasks and the Soviet of Workers' Deputies," 1905; on this subject see Antonio Carlo, "Lenin on the Party," *Telos*, no. 17 (Fall 1973).
12. See, for example, Samora Machel, *Mozambique: Sowing the Seeds of Revolution* (London, 1974); *Establishing People's Power to Serve the Masses* (Toronto: Toronto Committee for the Liberation of Southern Africa, 1976); *Declaramos Guerra ao Inimigo Interno* (Maputo, 1980), among numerous other writings.
13. Samora Machel, "Dominar a Ciência e Arte Militares para Defender Conquistas da Revolução" (speech in Nampula on the opening of the Military School), *25 de Septembro* (Maputo), no. 88 (December 1979). (My translation).

PART I

Mozambique: An Overview

John S. Saul

1. The Context:
Colonialism and Revolution

An overview of Mozambique's post-liberation efforts to mount a socialist alternative to the inherited syndrome of underdevelopment is necessary at this point—the better to situate and give resonance to the sectoral studies found in subsequent chapters.[1] However, we must begin by placing this socialist project in its historical context. One relevant dimension is the incorporation of Mozambique's precapitalist societies into the global capitalist system, via the distinctive mechanism of Portuguese colonialism. A second is the struggle of Mozambicans to free themselves from that colonial stranglehold: a nationalist challenge which became, in turn, the chrysalis of a social revolution. We will explore both aspects in this chapter. Of course, with independence (June 25, 1975), the Front for the Liberation of Mozambique (FRELIMO) could bring the revolutionary project which it had generated through ten years of armed struggle more directly to bear upon the inherited socioeconomic structure of Mozambique. In consequence, the present chapter will also say something about the important initial years of transition from Portuguese colonial rule.

Yet it was only in 1977, with the holding of the Third Congress of FRELIMO, that the broad outlines of the party's post-independence project were spelled out with great clarity. Chapter 2 will seek, therefore, to specify the main characteristics—socioeconomic, political, ideological—of developments in Mozambique since the historic Third Congress. As we shall see, this process was ultimately to give rise, in 1983, to yet another important stock-taking, the party's Fourth Congress. But what of the years from 1977 to 1983? Steps along "a different road"? Steps in a "transition to socialism"? We begin to provide some of the evidence relevant to answering such questions in that chapter. First, as suggested, we must turn to the more distant past.

Portuguese Colonialism: Impact and Legacy

A detailed account of Mozambique's colonial experience is to be found in Part 1 of Eduardo Mondlane's book, *The Struggle for Mo-*

zambique. For this and other reasons the recent reissue of the 1969 study by FRELIMO's first president is required reading.[2] The present section will seek merely to outline some of the main characteristics of Portugal's colonial impact and the legacy for contemporary Mozambique of that experience.[3] What was happening, as noted above, was the incorporation of Mozambique's various precapitalist societies into the global system of imperialism, with distinctive new structures of economic exploitation and class formation emerging from this process. However, the fact that it was Portugal rather than some other European power which was the vector of this imperialist impact had a number of important and distinctive implications for Mozambique which also bear emphasizing. For Portugal itself remained only partially transformed by the development of capitalism in Europe and was thus relatively backward throughout the period of its rule in Mozambique. As a result, it was dependent upon other, stronger imperialist centers and, in part, its role in Africa became that of intermediary for these other centers.

Of course, the impact of Portugal—and, more generally, of imperialism—upon Mozambique changed in step with epochal changes in the global capitalist system itself. The first major steps toward incorporation of Mozambique's precapitalist societies into a broad mercantile system were linked to the impact of Asian trading networks in the Indian Ocean. Then, gradually, from the beginning of the sixteenth century, the Portuguese—attracted by the availability of gold—began themselves to enter into the picture and compete ruthlessly for control of that trade (circa 1505–1690s). Over time the focus of such trade shifted from gold to ivory (circa 1690s–1750) and ultimately to slaves (circa 1750–1840/60). Yet the logic of the economic structure so established remained much the same. At the base of the system of surplus extraction there was the reinforcement of what might be defined as a "tributary mode of production"—a reinforcement of the local king's power vis-à-vis the villages, for example—rather than its replacement by new relations of production. To be sure, there did come into existence some new forms of extracting the surplus. The *prazos,* vast "estates" under the domination of various freebooters, replaced certain indigenous kingdoms in the center of the country. Nonetheless, the relatively untransformed village remained at the core of the exploitative system. One can, of course, distinguish the slave trade from the trade in gold and ivory, for it was, self-evidently, infinitely more destructive than either of the latter in terms of its impact upon rural life. Still, it was not until the next phase of imperialist expansion that the most dramatic changes were to begin to occur in the productive process throughout the territory which now comprises Mozambique.

Portugal's status as a colonial power was confirmed at the Congress of Berlin (1885), but more as the result of the jockeying for position between Germany and Britain than because of its own independent strength. Rather than enter into a struggle over Mozambique, the more developed imperial powers would leave the colony to Portugal—in the knowledge that an economically backward Portugal would have to let others exploit it for them! Needless to say, the needs of a growing and industrializing European capitalism had developed far beyond luxury items and slaves. The periphery must now supply raw materials and foodstuffs, cheap labor, and profitable outlets for investment. And Mozambique was to be drawn into this global network, Portugal in effect playing the *rentier* role of leasing out its colony and its resources to various external interests, in particular to British capital.

This process took different forms in different parts of the country. In the south, from quite an early date, Portugal assumed the role of organizing the supply of Mozambican workers to the mines of South Africa. This was, in fact, to become a distinguishing feature of this region—and a major source of colonial revenue—up to the very end of Portugal's period of rule. To this was also added, as time went on, the function of servicing South Africa's trade via the port of Lourenço Marques—a further reinforcement of the colony's dependence upon South Africa. In other regions the primarily *intermediary* role of Portugal was even more evident. Vast sections of the country were simply turned over to large foreign companies—*companhias majestaticas*—to control politically and exploit economically, the colonial state receiving a percentage of the economic action thus generated in the form of taxes and fees. A particularly dramatic case in point was the Company of Niassa in the north; after playing a major role in "pacifying" that part of the country, the company limited its subsequent economic activities chiefly to organizing, by force, the African population for labor migration abroad (to Tanganyika, the Belgian Congo, Nyasaland, and the Rhodesias).

Some concessionaires in the center of the country mounted a similar kind of labor export business, but others developed there—particularly in the Zambesi Valley—a plantation economy which was to become of considerable importance. Sugar, sisal, copra, and, later, tea were prominent in this respect. These plantations were themselves dependent on cheap African labor, of course, as were such settler farmers as began to arrive (on the vast holdings of the

Mozambique Company, comprising all of the present-day provinces of Manica and Sofala, for example). Economic competition with the relatively high-paying South African mines was eventually limited by an agreement prohibiting labor recruitment for South Africa north of the River Save. Much of the center of the country thus became as much an *internal* labor reserve for the plantations as a source of labor export.

In sum, a significant measure of Mozambique's dependent economic structure was already in place by 1930, although the "economic nationalism" of Antonio Salazar's *Estado Novo* did, after that date, add novel dimensions. Indeed, with the Colonial Act of 1930, the colonies were now to have a more important role in facilitating the emergence of Portugal's own bourgeoisie and in solving, more directly, some of Portugal's own economic problems. In Salazar's words, the overseas territories were "a logical solution to Portugal's problem of overpopulation, to settle Portuguese nationals in the colonies and for the colonies to produce raw materials for the motherland in exchange for manufactured goods"! The *companhias majestaticas* were to lose their politico-administrative powers and the Portuguese state was to take charge. Of course, there were strict limits to this nationalism: the need for revenue dictated that the supply of migrant labor from southern Mozambique to South Africa and reliance on a high level of production from the externally owned plantations remain central to the economy. Nor were previous forced labor practices to be altered. On the contrary, as we shall see, they were merely rationalized and reinforced by the Salazarist system. The key to surplus extraction in Mozambique continued to be the extraction of *more work* from Africans, the extraction, in Marxist terms, of *absolute* surplus value!

What was more novel was forced cultivation of crops by Africans, especially of cotton to supply Portugal's fledgling textile industry (which in turn was destined to become that country's most important industrial sector by the 1950s). The impact of such cultivation in the north of Mozambique, in particular, was dramatic. New, too, was a very strong emphasis upon emigration to the colony, this being heavily subsidized by the Salazarist state with the intention both of providing a firmer political base for the colonial system and of helping legitimate the claim (made after World War II) that Mozambique was merely an overseas province of Portugal. After World War II as well, settlers on the land became important, especially in the Limpopo and Incomati valleys of the south, as suppliers of foodstuffs to the growing cities. And they provided some internal market for a slowly growing industrial sector, although it must be emphasized that severe limits were placed on this latter development by Portugal in order to protect the Mozambique market for its own domestic industries (e.g., in textiles).

In these ways new layers of dependency were being added to Mozambique's colonial economy. Moreover, with the coming of the 1960s a further dimension was introduced when Salazar reversed his policy of restricting new foreign investment in "Portuguese Africa" (other than that from Portugal) and of placing high tariffs on foreign imports. In contrast with this, the door was now thrown open to foreign capital, foreign firms being given guarantees— regarding the repatriation of capital, profits, and dividends, and customs exemption on plant and raw materials—even better than those for potential investors from Portugal itself. In part this was designed to tie these large foreign companies, and ultimately their home governments, into an even more vigorous defense of the Portuguese position in Africa—at a time when resistance to Portuguese colonialism was growing both in the colonies themselves and in the world at large.

As Marc Wuyts has recently argued, such resistance laid the groundwork for the re-entry of foreign capital in a second way as well.[4] For, under pressure, the Portuguese were forced in the early sixties to abandon some of the more obvious and extreme aspects of their forced labor system. With new limits thus set to the extraction of absolute surplus value, capital would have to rely more upon raising the productivity of Africans (upon the extraction of *relative* surplus value) by modernizing plant. Yet the Portuguese bourgeoisie, weak as it was, lacked the capacity to do this easily. Technology and "know-how" would have to come from foreign capital—this need arising at precisely the moment in the development of global capitalism when multinational enterprises, in their turn, were actively moving abroad with the intention of getting involved in import substitution industrialization and related developments on the periphery. In this way—and in the simultaneous opening up of mineral exploration to firms from Europe, North America, and South Africa—a group of new exploiters found their way to Mozambique in the 1960s. A list of these, to be found, for example, in Samora Machel's important pamphlet *O processo da revoluçâo democratica popular em Moçambique,* includes such familiar names as Anglo-American, Nestlé, Firestone, British Leyland, Lonrho, Bethlehem Steel, and the like.[5] And then, of course, there was the giant Cabora Bassa dam project, an especially graphic symbol of the attempted "modernization" of Portuguese colonialism, of the intensified involvement of international capitalism, *and* of the further integration of the southern African white redoubt (the power generated being planned primarily with South African consumption in mind!).

In this historical sketch we see the dependent economic structure of Mozambique taking shape, defining many of the challenges which FRELIMO would have to confront at independence. Its principal feature: a subordinate position within the international division of labor defined by imperialism, with this in turn compounded by Mozambique's very specific position of subordination vis-à-vis the major regional center of capital accumulation, South Africa. We will return to a discussion of the implications of this structure for post-liberation Mozambique later in the chapter. Here it is important to look more carefully at the impact of this evolving pattern of capitalist penetration upon the African population itself. It was noted earlier that the new demands which imperialism had placed upon Mozambique from the latter part of the nineteenth century began to transform the territory's precapitalist societies in a much more fundamental way than ever before. In fact these demands began to integrate Africans into a more clearly capitalist division of labor, undermining the prior internal logic of village life, dividing the people into new social classes, and yoking their labor to the global accumulation of capital. The primary mechanism was forced labor.

A statement by Marcelo Caetano in 1954 summarizes the fundamental Portuguese premise in this respect: "The natives of Africa must be directed and organized by Europeans but are indispensable as auxiliaries. The blacks must be seen as productive elements organized, or to be organized, in an economy directed by whites." But this was a note consistently struck in Portuguese policy from the very outset of effective occupation. Already, in 1875, an infamous decree defining labor policy was little more than an attempt to ensure the continued retention of the master-slave relationship despite the formal abolition of slavery. Antonio Enes' *Codigo de trabalho* of 1899 captured the characteristic tone of Portuguese legislation on the subject: "All natives of Portuguese overseas provinces are subject to the obligation, moral and legal, of attempting to obtain through work the means that they lack to subsist and to better their social conditions." As Enes himself further explained: "The state, not only as a sovereign of semi-barbarian populations but also as a depository of social authority, should have no scruple in *obliging* and if necessary *forcing* these rude Negroes in Africa, these ignorant Pariahs in Asia, these half-witted savages from Oceania, to work."

The systematic military conquest by the Portuguese of the African population—despite the latter's often impressive efforts to resist—was the first step in this regard. The system was then to be policed by the administrative apparatuses of the giant companies and the colonial state and by a network of nominated chiefs *(regulos)*. With this structure, and using such arbitrary means as the compulsory hut tax and directly forcible methods of recruitment of African workers (in the south, for example, *chibalo*—compulsory labor—came to complement migration to South Africa in order to guarantee the servicing of *local* labor requirements), the basic pattern of ensuring the colony's labor supply was established. As mentioned above, this pattern was merely streamlined by Salazar, with an even denser network of taxes, regulations, and administrative control being brought into play. A particularly graphic example of this was the notion of "obligatory labor" introduced in a government circular of 1947 and ordering all "natives" to work six months of the year for the state, a company, or an individual. Moreover, if such codes, and the tax system, did not drive people into the labor force, there was always "correctional labor," imposed instead of a prison sentence, sometimes for criminal activity but more often for breaking the terms of contract labor or nonpayment of tax. To this picture must also be added the aforementioned forced cultivation of cotton, rice, and other crops. While it is true that after 1960 some of the grossest aspects of this engine for extracting surplus value from the indigenous population were modified, many of these alterations were more of form than of substance and forced labor remained a crucial aspect of the colonial economy right up to the point of its collapse in the 1970s.

The impact of international capitalism—mediated primarily by this pattern of forced labor and forced cultivation—was crucial in its effects upon village life. Because of this process the vast majority of the Mozambican population was soon no longer living exclusively in the world of subsistence agriculture. They has become *peasants* and *workers* (albeit, as we shall see, often only "semi-proletarianized" workers) subordinated to the requirements of capital. In fact, such was the disruption in the villages that some Mozambicans fled to neighboring territories. For this disruption was often extremely dramatic and not merely in the south. Indeed, it could even sow some of the seeds of future disaster. To take merely one example: the forced cultivation of cash crops weakened, in certain areas, the production of food crops traditionally grown by the African population, thus actually exacerbating the fragility of local agricultural systems and their susceptibility to famine. It was Portugal's own lack of economic vitality that made forced labor a more ubiquitous and lasting dimension of its colonial project than was the case with powers like Britain and France. Yet even in a Portuguese colony, enforced involvement in the capitalist marketplace meant that goods purchased on the market slowly but surely became part of most Africans' very definition of subsistence as well as essential to the reproduction of their family agriculture (such goods including means of production—implements, for example—in addition to various consumer goods). Thus economic stimuli began to complement force in defining the economic activity of Mozambicans, even if subordination to external dictate remained the key to the process. Of course, what was emerging here was a peasantry different from that in some other parts of the world—without a quasi-feudal class of landlords directly oppressing it and without the same kind of land shortage as existed in Asia. Nonetheless, it will be clear that the subordinate position into which colonialism had forced Mozambican rural dwellers was comprehensible only in *class* terms and in terms of an understanding of the workings of imperialism.

This was one crucial dimension, a check upon any facile definition of the majority of Mozambicans as merely quasi-traditional subsistence agriculturalists. However, there was a second aspect as well. For the exploitative colonial system was structured in such a way as not only to extract labor and crops from Africans but also to keep the price of these things particularly low. What was the key to this? Paradoxically, it was the continuance of certain aspects of the rural subsistence economy. For this permitted a hidden subsidy to the accumulation of capital, underwriting the setting of wages and crop prices to Africans at levels even lower than might otherwise have been the case. In these several ways, then, it was precisely involvement in the capitalist world system that helped to keep much of Mozambican agriculture as backward as it was.

There were important regional variations in this pattern, to be sure. In some areas—the south, for example—migrant labor (largely male) was central, with women crucial, in consequence, to maintaining the quasi-subsistence rural base from which this migration came. In regions of forced cropping where, as suggested, low crop prices were premised on the subsistence dimensions of rural production, a broadly similar logic prevailed. Yet the difference between these two situations was important, too. Clearly, any post-independence policy of agricultural transformation would have to take into account the diversity of the "peasantries" with which such a program would be dealing. The nature of Mozambique's emerging proletariat was also affected by these realities. Under the circumstances, the pattern of migrant labor often resulted in a kind of "semiproletarianization," many workers remaining closely linked to their rural base. This probably helped to weaken the working class *qua* class during the colonial period; in any case it remained small because of the relatively underdeveloped nature of the economy. On the other hand, the action of the working class, especially in the ports, was to have considerable impact on a number of occasions: witness the strikes of 1947, 1954, and 1963, for example. Moreover, this working class would be of obvious significance when it came to advancing the struggle for socialism and defining the terms of the worker-peasant alliance in the post-liberation period.

Certain theorists have developed the notion of an "articulation of modes of production" to theorize the kind of interpenetration of capitalist and precapitalist patterns which has been alluded to above. For some aspects of preexisting production activities *and* social patterns were being conserved, even as much of their previous significance was being altered by the overall capitalist context in which they were enveloped. The result: in spite of the centrality of new economic involvements and of new capitalist-defined class structures in the rural areas, the interplay of old and new could often be formidably complex. If, for example, *lobolo* (bride-price) had now been commercialized by the impact of the cash economy, it still retained many quasi-traditional overtones which could not merely be thrown aside. Similarly, the implications of extended kinship relations might have been subtly altered but as long as these were conserved, not totally displaced, by capitalist transformation, the local social setting remained a rather complicated mix of ingredients. This kind of articulation also provided a basis for cultural differences—in terms of language, customs, and the like—to remain strong. Indeed, it was on this basis that the colonial government attempted to politicize such ethnic variations, manipulating anthropological studies to "resist the danger of detribalization," to reinforce "traditional law and customs," and to legitimate "tribal" residential patterns in the urban areas as part of a strategy of divide and rule. Clearly, awareness of such factors was another strong reason for a liberation movement or post-independence government to avoid generalizing about "the peasantry." What was necessary was a class analysis sufficiently subtle to permit comprehension of the complex realities of rural life created by a particular kind of capitalist development.

What of the state and ideology? The replacement of the companies and the intensification of the process of "peasantization" and "semiproletarianization" in the 1930s led to some streamlining of the state apparatus as well. True, Portugal's variant of the colonial state was to remain to the end of the colonial period even more labyrinthine and bureaucratized than its counterparts elsewhere in Africa—as befitted its quasi-feudal roots in a backward Portugal. Yet as it now began to collect taxes, undertake censuses of labor supplies, and enforce labor and cropping regulations, this state did move to centralize administration and establish a strong hierarchical network of control throughout the colony. The further reinforcement of the privileges and powers of the *regulos* was important, not least in contributing to the creation of a stratum of privileged Africans. More generally, however, the whole structure of the state was deeply scarred by the role defined for it as, in effect, the warden of a giant labor camp. And this role was reinforced in the last years of colonialism as the state became more and more militarized in defense of the old order. Small wonder that President Samora Machel could use the very moment of independence (in his speech in Machava Stadium on June 25, 1975) to define the problem of Mozambique's colonial state in the following terms:

> The State is not an eternal and immutable structure; the State is not the bureaucratic machinery of civil servants nor something abstract, nor a mere technical apparatus. The State is always the organized form through which a class takes power to fulfill its interests. The colonial State, an instrument of domination and exploitation by a foreign bourgeoisie and imperialism which has already been partially destroyed by the struggle, must be replaced by a people's State, forged through an alliance of workers and peasants, guided by FRELIMO and defended by the People's Forces for the Liberation of Mozambique, a State which wipes out exploitation and releases the creative initiative of the masses and the productive forces.
>
> In the phase of people's democracy in which we are now engaged as a phase of the Mozambican revolutionary process, our aim is to lay the material, ideological, administrative and social foundations of our State. We need to be aware that *the apparatus we are now inheriting is, in its nature, composition and methods, a profoundly retrograde and reactionary structure which has to be completely revolutionized in order to be put at the service of the masses. . . .* The new battle is only beginning.[6]

Nor were the mechanisms of colonial control strictly political. Particularly from the 1930s on there was a substantial ideological offensive designed, according to official documents, to win the hearts and minds (or at least the passivity) of the exploited themselves.[7] The chief mechanisms were the Catholic Church and, closely related to it, the educational system. Indeed, for the vast majority, whatever little education they received was designed quite self-consciously to fit them for a subordinate position in the colonial system. The 1930 rationale for the *ensino rudimentar* (basic education) which was to be the Africans' lot stated that it "had as its goal to guide the member of the indigenous population from a life of savagery to a civilized life, to furnish him with the consciousness of a Portuguese citizen, and to prepare him for life's struggle, making him more useful to society and to himself." Suspect enough even in these racist terms, no doubt. But when modest funding and reliance for its implementation upon so backward an institution as the Portuguese Catholic Church are added in, the *ensino rudimentar* can be seen even more clearly as a barrier to any real educational advance for the mass of Africans. For all Portugal's talk of a "civilizing mission," the end of her five hundred years of contact with Mozambique found more than 95 percent of the population illiterate. We have already observed the creation of those distortions in Mozambique's socioeconomic structures which came to define the territory's underdevelopment. In addition, Mozambique's "undevelopment"—its lack of "modern" skills and technical capacity relative to the most advanced economy—had been virtually frozen into place by the Portuguese presence.

It is true that a tiny minority of African children were enabled to receive primary education equal to that of the *colonos.* A much smaller minority was able to benefit from secondary, technical, and commercial education. (However, even when this was expanded after 1955 under pressure from the need for more highly skilled labor, it was intended principally for the children of those settlers whose number was then being swelled by Portugese emigration policies; the proportion of Africans benefitting from such "advanced education" was actually lower in 1960 than it had been in 1930.) Moreover, education for the "tiny minority" of Africans was lodged within the framework of a paternalistic ideology of "assimilation" designed to co-opt any Africans who did emerge from the system into the role of junior members of the privileged colonial petty bourgeoisie. In this regard such education actually proved to be a two-edged sword. So self-evidently exploitative and racially biased was the overall colonial structure that education helped to arm potential nationalist opponents of the colonial regime even as it created potential collaborators. Ironically, too, there was really very little room for maneuver opened up for such collaborators. At the very moment when their petty-bourgeois counterparts were coming to power elsewhere in Africa, these Mozambicans found the Portuguese turning their backs on neocolonialism and digging in their heels militarily against any such denouement to their rule.

Thus even if there were some Africans in the wings who might have been prepared to inherit political power on imperialist terms, "false decolonization" was not on the agenda. It is worth asking why, particularly in light of the decision by the English, French, and even the Belgians to substitute colonialism with neocolonialism. For Portugal's decision to grimly hang on to its colonies against the seeming tide of history and the mounting demands of the people in those colonies was crucially important in defining the nature of Mozambican resistance to colonialism. Ironically, it was primarily the need to fight for independence which provided Mozambique with an opportunity to build a radical alternative to the conventional syndrome of neocolonialism and underdevelopment— through the transformation, within the framework of a people's war, of FRELIMO.

No doubt the most important reason for Portugal's decision was its continuing economic weakness, a fact mentioned earlier. Other imperialist countries could hope to maintain their powerful voice in the affairs of their former colonies even after the granting of formal political independence. Yet, as William Minter has argued, "such influence depends on economic power, the ability to provide aid; to control enterprises through technicians as well as investment; to maintain good trade relationships by pressure on susceptible governments; to support with open or covert action the removal of governments that prove troublesome."[8] In contrast it was only the direct hold on the lever of power in the colonies, the direct hold on the colonial state, that enabled Portugal to profit from the economic exploitation of Angola, Mozambique, and Guinea—by claiming a percentage of the action, as it were. Even were a false decolonization to produce a very pliant government in Mozambique, such a government would most likely deal directly with the strongest of economic powers—with South Africa, the United States, West Germany, and the like—rather than with Portugal. Under such circumstances Portugal would be deprived of even those benefits attendant upon the middleman's role. In consequence, the granting of independence seemed a more costly option to Portugal's rulers than it did for other colonial powers.

In addition, there were other noneconomic factors which can be mentioned—the political realities of Portugal, for example. That country was an overtly authoritarian society. In consequence, not only was it difficult to theorize a logic of freedom for the colonies in black Africa, but it was also potentially dangerous to consider establishing a democratic precedent there: the Portuguese people might then have been encouraged to intensify their parallel demands for self-determination in Portugal itself. There was also a cultural-ideological factor. Authoritarian-cum-fascist regimes are particularly in need of myths to legitimize, both to themselves and to others, their continuing usurpation of power. Portugal's myth was empire and the colonial "mission." The constant reiteration of slogans related to this mission suggests the extent to which they provided a certain ideological glue for the system; such slogans could not, for that very reason, be readily brought into question by the powers-that-be. It is even possible that some of the rulers had come to believe them themselves.

Of course, the coup in Portugal has since demonstrated the importance of these latter points: the retreat from colonialism did indeed involve a complete overthrow of the fascist system in Portugal itself. But for a long time there was little reason to anticipate any such denouement. As the Mozambican liberation movement developed its critique of colonialism, it saw that in the immediate future Portuguese colonialism was not about to crack from within, or even to adapt its policies in any significant respect. It would be necessary to fight for freedom within Mozambique. To be sure, at the outset of the liberation struggle this pattern was not quite so clear-cut. Thus there were early indications that Western governments, perhaps even South Africa itself, might have accepted the notion of black governments coming to power in an independent Angola or Mozambique. Indeed the United States, particularly in the very earliest days of the Kennedy administration, seemed to be actively pressing for the decolonization of Portugal's colonies—this on the then current assumption that quite moderate and pliable black governments would inherit power.

It was the intransigence of the Portuguese which made any such smooth transition to neocolonialism impossible. It became necessary for the Kennedy team and subsequent American administrations—as well as the entire NATO alliance—to accommodate themselves to Portugal's position and even to cultivate an active economic-military partnership with that country (something which, as noted earlier, Portugal was increasingly inviting them to do in the 1960s in any case). And this arrangement became all the more attractive as the liberation movements in Portugal's African colonies were themselves radicalized and developed into much less certain guarantors of some future false decolonization. This meant, in turn, that more was soon at stake in Mozambique than a mere demand for national independence. The stage was being set for a genuine class struggle, for a genuine anti-imperialist struggle. As we shall see in the following section, it was being set for a social revolution.

Nationalism and Revolution

Here, again, Eduardo Mondlane's *The Struggle for Mozambique* is essential reading, important for exploring the roots of Mozambican nationalism, the formation of FRELIMO, and the pattern of the liberation movement's initial years. Mondlane's book illuminates both the important process of forging unity and laying the groundwork for the armed struggle *and* the beginnings of the parallel process which was to transform FRELIMO from a mere nationalist movement into the nucleus of a socialist party. Of course, there are some evident silences in his book. In spite of the fact that it was first published in 1969, it has little to say directly about the class struggle *within* the movement itself, the struggle which produced a severe internal crisis in 1968–1969 (and also laid the ground for Mondlane's own assassination in 1969). The timing of the preparation of his book helps explain these silences: the depth of the "struggle between the two lines" had not yet fully revealed itself. His book must therefore be complemented by such other sources as the account of FRELIMO's historical evolution which is to be found in the *Central Committee Report to the Third Congress of FRELIMO.*[9] In this section we will attempt merely to survey these various aspects of FRELIMO's development, introducing the reader to the history of popular struggle in Mozambique while also exploring the implications of that struggle for the present period.

The history of African resistance to the imposition of Portuguese rule is as old as the history of that rule itself. Such resistance was often fierce, and in fact Portugal cannot be said to have completely "pacified" all of the peoples under its sway until well into the present century. As one observer has noted, "the history of the wars of resistance is hardly more than two generations removed from the present liberation movement, and the memories are alive today."[10] Yet such struggles in the past remained localized, defining themselves primarily in regional and tribal terms; at their center, too, were often the class interests of dominant chieftain elements within the African tributary societies themselves. The crucial significance of the contemporary liberation movement was the new sense of territory-wide nationalism which it represented and its new class content; FRELIMO's project was to reflect a quite different moment in the integration of Mozambique into the global capitalist system.

The immediate protagonists of this new nationalism were men and women of the cities, employed near the center of the colonial system and often possessing at least some minimal level of formal education (yielded, albeit grudgingly, by colonialism). For these reasons they were better able to perceive the overall nature of the colonial system and to understand the means necessary for challenging it. At first their mode of challenge tended to be cultural, vaguely reformist, even elitist, only gradually taking on a more effective and broadly political expression as the pace of change in the rest of the continent picked up and as the full meaning of Portuguese colonialism was grasped. A detailed history of these stirrings would range from a discussion of such early initiatives as the Gremio Negrofilo, the Centro Associativo dos Negros de Moçambique, and the journal *Brado Africano* to the Nucleo dos Estudantes Secundarios Africanos de Moçambique (NESAM), the União Democratica Nacional de Moçambique (UDENAMO, founded in Bulawayo in 1960), and the Mozambique African National Union (MANU, with its base in Tanganyika but having close links with Cabo Delgado). But, as foreshadowed in the previous section, demands for reform were scotched by the Portuguese much more ruthlessly than by other colonial powers.

Moreover, when pressure for change from the broad mass of the population also began to surface, the Portuguese response was particularly brutal; thus, in 1959 at Mueda in northern Mozambique, six hundred Africans were shot down while peacefully protesting exploitative agricultural practices. This was precisely the point in the history of other colonialisms in Africa when the colonial power often chose to negotiate with the spokespersons of nationalism— gambling, in part, on the nascent elitism of this latter group to restrain any radicalization of nationalism and intending to co-opt them into a smoothly functioning system of continuing economic dependence. However, we have seen that the possibility of such a response was not open to the Portuguese. Turning a deaf ear to peaceful protest, the Portuguese chose instead to perpetuate and intensify the violence of their colonial presence. They thus forced the African population to take up arms to bring that presence to an end.

FRELIMO at its founding in 1962 represented a coming together of a number of nationalist organizations primarily operating in exile in neighboring African countries. The Portuguese met renewed demands for independence from this united movement with a severe crackdown on African activities, especially in the urban areas. The absolute necessity of military action became clear and FRELIMO prepared for this carefully, launching the fighting on September 25, 1964. As is well known, progress in the two northern provinces of Cabo Delgado and Niassa was sufficiently marked by 1968—with genuine "liberated areas" taking shape— that FRELIMO was able to launch armed struggle in a third key province, Tete, where once again the Portuguese were slowly but surely driven back. The year 1972 provided even more dramatic

evidence of progress, FRELIMO announcing the opening of a
front in the strategic and densely populated provinces of Manica
and Sofala in the very heart of Mozambique. Soon the war hovered
close to the important port of Beira and brought successful assaults
on Rhodesia's road and rail links to the sea; there were also attacks
on the pylons and transmission lines designed to carry Cabora
Bassa power to the south. In desperation, during this period the
Portuguese turned to strategic-hamlet campaigns, to fruitless but
damaging "great offensives" (for example, the much ballyhooed
"Operation Gordian Knot," involving the use of massive bombings,
napalm, herbicides, and other artifacts of counterinsurgency), and
the grossest kind of intimidation of the African population (for
example, the massacre at Wiriyamu of December 1972). Yet these
tactics all failed. A significant portion of the country, though not yet
the majority of it, could be said to have been effectively liberated by
the time of the coup. Moreover, it was FRELIMO's dramatic 1972
drive further south which, above all other factors, sapped the will
of the Portuguese army to continue the war.

   In sum, the military challenge to Portuguese rule was increasingly successful. However, it would be misleading to leave the discussion of the liberation struggle at this point. Developments in the
political and socioeconomic spheres were of at least equal importance and, in fact, help provide an explanation of the degree of
military success achieved. An instructive point of departure is a
comparison with the pattern of false decolonization which emerged
in much of the rest of Africa. As President Julius Nyerere of Tanzania once argued,[11] the nationalism which won independence in
Africa in the 1950s and 1960s was in some senses a relatively
superficial accomplishment. In its aftermath the leaders too easily
entrenched themselves as a new privileged class, and the mass of
Africans too easily lapsed back into cynicism and a feeling of help-
lessness. To obtain "real freedom" in all spheres of life and to claim
control over the productive forces, some form of "socialism" is
required, Nyerere stated; "to build real freedom" there must be, on
the part of the people, "a positive understanding and positive actions, not simply a rejection of colonialism and a willingness to
cooperate in non-cooperation." The striking feature of the kind of
struggle which the people were forced to undertake in Mozambique was that it began to reshape the conventional pattern of
African nationalism even before independence, demanding an attempt to restructure social, economic, and political relationships in
a fundamental way.

   As Marcelino dos Santos, FRELIMO's vice-president during the
war years, put the point at the time,

within almost every national movement there are different types of nationalism. There is the elementary, primary one—what is called primitive nationalism. But there is also revolutionary nationalism. Some people who take part in the struggle for independence do so not to realize or to satisfy the interests of the people as a whole but to satisfy the interests of a small group. They have a specific ideology which in general has a bourgeois national framework. In other words within a national movement there can be two general types of ideology—one which is bourgeois and one which is revolutionary.[12]

Inevitably some of the nationalists who emerged in Mozambique favored the familiar pattern of "primitive nationalism" which had rewarded their nationalist counterparts elsewhere in Africa. Conservatively they were prepared to pursue their own privileges as actively as they pursued independence, and to play down the importance of mass involvement, using vague appeals which asked no basic questions about the nature of the society that was to be brought into being. Unfortunately for them, in the context of Portuguese intransigence and the need for a genuine liberation struggle, this kind of nationalism did not work as it had for African leadership groups elsewhere on the continent. A successful liberation struggle had to become a *people's war;* it required that the energies of the people be released in a new way. The freedom fighters had to rely on the peasants as active partners in the struggle—to not betray them to the enemy, to help in carriage and supply of provisions, to serve as a source of recruits for the army and as a popular militia. Obviously these duties required more from the people than a mere "rejection of colonialism and a willingness to cooperate in non-cooperation." Instead they demanded "a positive understanding and positive actions," a level of popular consciousness and commitment unlikely to emerge unless the leadership had both forged a close, effective relationship with the broad mass of the people fighting for liberation *and* begun to demonstrate that the nature of the future society to be achieved seemed worth the risk involved.

As we shall see, this meant that genuinely *democratic* methods of political work were necessary to close any possible gap between leaders and people. In addition, the promise of the future had to be exemplified in entirely new programs and institutions in the liberated areas, programs and institutions which, in the spheres of health, education, production, and trade, visibly served the people's needs. In short, this involved embedding in the new society-in-the-making, from a very early date, certain central features of Clive Thomas' prescription for economic transformation, as sketched in our introduction. For in launching such novel activities

crucial choices were forced upon FRELIMO, choices which ultimately came to guarantee the further democratization and radicalization of the struggle. Thus new patterns of education had to be
developed which attacked elitism at the same time as they transmitted skills; similarly, collective practices generated in the economic
sphere—in marketing, distribution, consumption—served not
merely to pool popular energies but also to preempt any temptations toward entrepreneurial involvements on the part of the leadership. Nor is it surprising that in such a context some of the tough
problems linked to the liberation of Mozambican women were being confronted in an impressive manner. In the liberated areas a
new society was taking shape with institutions responsive, for the
first time in many generations, to the needs and desires of the
people themselves.

A reading of the wartime speeches of Samora Machel—dealing
with each of these themes in turn and conveniently collected in the
volume *Mozambique: Sowing the Seeds of Revolution*—will help illuminate this process. As Marcelino dos Santos, in turn, synthesized the
experience,

> In our case the necessity to define a revolutionary ideology with more
> precision emerged when we started to build up the liberated areas, to
> engage ourselves in national construction. As always, the task of
> building a society economically poses the problem of production and
> distribution, and especially who is going to benefit from what the
> society produces. This life process also raises more sharply than in the
> class room the deeper question of the type of ideology to embrace. So
> to summarize, there comes a stage when it becomes clear that the
> main aim of the struggle is to advance the interests of the working
> people. In the field of organizing the people we follow collectivist
> ways as is the case, for example, with our cooperative movement in
> the liberated areas.[13]

Moreover, the continuing confrontation with the Portuguese—and
with their Western allies, economic and military—also meant that
both leadership and people had an opportunity to become more
aware of the complicated network of external forces which locked
Portuguese colonial domination into place; the emergence of a
much more solidly anti-imperialist perspective was the result. In all
these ways, in short, the knot of neocolonialism was being untied at
an early moment in Mozambique. Consequently, it was soon apparent that more than a fight for independence was under way. Instead, as we have noted, there had emerged a genuine revolution,
one with great promise regarding the kind of post-independence
society which would eventually be built.

Such a pattern of development had one tremendously important corollary: the emergence of real contradictions within the nationalist movement itself. Basil Davidson, a noted commentator on the struggles in "Portugal's African colonies," summarized this point succinctly: "there is a general rule by which all movements of resistance produce and deepen conflicts within themselves as the reformists draw back from the revolutionaries and, in drawing back, fall victim to the game of the enemy regime."[14] For a movement like FRELIMO is, in reality, two entities for much of the early period of its existence: a conventional nationalist movement unable to secure an easy transition to power, and a revolutionary movement struggling to be born. Concretely, this dichotomy found expression in a struggle within the leadership—between those prepared and those not prepared to make the transition to revolutionary practice. Moreover, as the struggle developed, the broad mass of the people also came to play an important role in resolving such contradictions; for example, at the vitally important Second Congress of FRELIMO (held inside the liberated areas in 1968) delegates with firm links to the dramatic transformation taking place *inside* Mozambique were crucial in tilting the balance of power in favor of the progressive wing of the movement. It was this kind of "logic" of popularly based guerrilla struggle which made the process of FRELIMO's radicalization a cumulative one.

In fact, the seeds of the subsequent division within the nationalist movement were already present at the very first moment of effective unity, the founding of FRELIMO in June 1962. Thus it was a group of younger militants with more recent activist experience within Mozambique itself (NESAM, the student organization mentioned earlier, had been an important recruiting ground in this regard) which took a major part in drafting a fairly advanced program for the new front at its First Congress in September 1962. This happened "at the very moment when the established organizations (MANU, UDENAMO, and UNAMI) were hesitating to place their existing material possessions in a common pool for the benefit of the new movement," as the then existent situation was described in an editorial in *Mozambique Revolution,* FRELIMO's official organ, written on the occasion of the tenth anniversary of the founding. The editorial continued: "The causes which kept these organizations separate in the past—namely, tribalism, regionalism, lack of a clear and detailed set of goals and of agreed and relevant strategies—continued to exist. . . . The early days of FRELIMO were marred by mutual recriminations, expulsion, withdrawal, as between exile politicians who refused to give up the futile infighting of an irrelevant brand of nationalist politics."[15]

Many of the more conservative elements continued to be reluctant to embrace unequivocally the necessity of armed struggle. And even some who did so balked at the idea of "people's war," preferring terrorist tactics or the adventurist notion of a quick victory (or at least success sufficient to bring the Portuguese to the bargaining table!) by means of a direct confrontation with the colonial army. Slowly but surely, however, those who understood the necessity of a protracted struggle and a people's war consolidated their position within the movement.

Nonetheless, contradictions were to surface again within FRELIMO—the main points of conflict having important class content. One issue centered on the question of education and particularly on the danger of a proto-elite (or bureaucratic petty bourgeoisie) forming within the institutions of the new Mozambique-in-the-making. A key actor here was Father Mateus Gwenjere. Almost certainly an *agent provocateur* acting on behalf of the Portuguese, he succeeded in inflaming elitist sentiments, particularly within the Mozambique Institute in Dar es Salaam. Thus he encouraged students to expect scholarships for further studies and quite specifically advised that they resist the 1966 decision by FRELIMO's Central Committee that all such students spend a significant period inside Mozambique actively participating in the struggle after completing secondary school. Samora Machel was later to characterize this accurately as

> the idea that the army should be reserved for the "ignorant" while the "educated" ought to devote themselves to politics and administration. [This] epitomized profoundly reactionary notions about the role of the army and envisaged the creation, in the persons of the "educated," of a "leadership class" with an exploitative vocation and destined to substitute itself for the old exploitative class.[16]

Not surprisingly, an additional aspect of this kind of elitist project was the demand that the medium of instruction be English, not Portuguese (English being, in effect, the language of scholarships); manipulated equally demagogically was the demand that certain white teachers at the institute be sacked. This conflict escalated to the point of forcing temporary closure of the school. However, it also brought the censure of Gwenjere by FRELIMO in March 1968, and his eventual removal from the movement (though not before he had stirred up members of the long-standing community of non-FRELIMO Mozambicans in Dar es Salaam to stage a raid on the FRELIMO office during which a Central Committee member was killed). More importantly it led, in Mondlane's words, to "an even firmer and more realistic policy on education; to greater efforts at integrating studies with the struggle and at preventing in future the formation of groups who demand special privileges at the expense of the general population."[17]

A second countercurrent to FRELIMO's emerging revolutionary direction was personified by Lazaro Nkavandame. Here the danger lay in the kind of leader who pursued his self-interest in the private sector, and in the possible formation of a dominant "entrepreneurial petty bourgeoisie" within the movement. Unhappy with genuinely cooperative solutions to economic problems, Nkavandame sought to turn the new commercial structures of the liberated areas to his own use, skimming off large surpluses for himself and his immediate supporters. As he came under increasing pressure from other FRELIMO leaders, and from committed militants within his own area, he also sought to introduce the politics of tribalism, attempting to crystallize "Makonde consciousness" around his own person. He also actively looked for support for his intrigues among certain of the less progressive but strategically placed elements in the Tanzanian leadership. By 1968 he was prepared to make a bid for a separatist independence (along the lines of "false decolonization") for his province, to actively sabotage FRELIMO's military efforts, and, when finally balked and expelled from the movement in early 1969, to go over to the Portuguese and make public pronouncements on their behalf. However, it is important to note that long before this latter move Nkavandame had forfeited any claim to enjoy popular support. Just as the logic of the struggle had transcended Gwenjere and his elitism, so too it was moving beyond the economic self-interest and Africanized exploitative practices of such men as Nkavandame.

Thus by 1969 the existence of two different "lines" (as FRELIMO documents came increasingly to refer to the elements in conflict within the movement) was readily apparent. As Samora Machel once summarized the situation,

> Some Mozambicans conceived of independence as a simple change of personnel within the same colonial structure: having expelled the Portuguese Mozambicans would take their places, keeping intact the colonial political-administrative machinery. Exploitation and all the other negative aspects of the colonial system would then simply remain in place, run now by Mozambicans. Such an attitude was personified at the time [during the armed struggle] by Lazaro Nkavandame, allied with other elements within the organization who did not at first dare expose themselves so openly. Various notions linked to this . . . revealed themselves with the passage of time; for example, the elitism represented by Mateus Gwenjere who defended the creation of a group of intellectuals who would be spared the necessity to participate in the armed struggle and granted privileged

status and who, with the coming of independence, would move in as the leaders of Mozambique.[18]

And for a time the balance between the two lines was delicately poised. Thus, Samora Machel has more recently observed that

> if Marcelo Caetano, at the point our struggle began to take a revolutionary form in 1969–70, had agreed to enter into dialogue with us, to recognize the right of self-determination and independence and to enter into conversations with us . . . we weren't yet mature enough to resist. There wasn't ideological solidity or ideological clarity in the liberation movements. This was as true of MPLA [in Angola] and PAIGC [in Guinea-Bissau] as of FRELIMO. It would have been possible to construct neo-colonialism through the movements' own cadres![19]

Under such circumstances, it was also no accident that racism and "tribalism" became prominent aspects of the counterrevolutionary line within the movement. For definitions of the struggle in strictly racial terms served the interests of the aspirant petty bourgeoisie by tending to deflect attention away from the basic structural realities of socioeconomic dependence. And a politicization of ethnicity might help to blind the mass of the peasantry and working class to their economic class interests—once again to the benefit of their potential black exploiters, the petty bourgeoisie. Nor is it surprising that all these themes found expression in the ideological discourse of the man who came to focus the conservative backlash to FRELIMO's radicalization, Uriah Simango. Witness his support for Gwenjere and Nkavandame, his attack on the dominance of "southerners" in the movement, his attack on the presence of whites, his elitism, his hostility to "people's war." On every front he and his followers set themselves against the revolutionary process. As we now know, such differences could only be settled, in FRELIMO's words, by "a struggle . . . between the groups representing two lines" within the movement to clarify the class content of the process of liberation.

The interpretation of such developments presents a challenge. Clearly, as seen, a fierce struggle *within* the leadership itself was important. How was this leadership to be characterized in class terms? Some Marxist analysts have termed them "intellectuals" (following Gramsci), and indeed many of the leadership were distinguished by a measure of education beyond that of the mass of the African population. Certain of these intellectuals are then seen as having been assimilable into the imperialist network (by means of a false decolonization) while others were prepared to link themselves "organically" to the popular classes as a "revolutionary vanguard." Other Marxists have used the concept "petty bourgeoisie" to identify and analyze this group, seeing the petty bourgeoisie as a class caught between other classes more firmly rooted in the production process, the (international) bourgeoisie on the one hand, the workers and peasants on the other. In consequence, the members of the petty bourgeoisie are seen as being somewhat open in their potentialities, capable of identifying upward (with the bourgeoisie) or downward (with the popular classes) as the struggle progresses. Thus some could opt for bureaucratic privilege and entrepreneurial advantage (like Gwenjere, Nkavandame, and Simango) while others, in the words of Amilcar Cabral, could choose to "commit suicide as a class in order to be reborn as revolutionary workers, completely identified with the deepest aspirations of the people to which they belong."

But this is not the end of the story. Whatever the terms in which we interpret this "choice" and the struggle within the leadership which it produced, it will be clear that the definition of direction was not occurring in a socioeconomic vacuum. It was framed by strong pressures which sprang from the actions of other classes with a stake in things. On the one hand, as already seen, the strategies and tactics of the Portuguese ruling class and its imperial allies—in this case, their very lack of flexibility—made a significant difference, narrowing the options available to the movement's leadership by closing the door to false decolonization. On the other hand, we have already alluded to the important impact upon the movement of the popular classes, especially the peasantry. Of the peasantry's significance in the struggle there can be no doubt. As Mondlane put the point:

> Both the agitation of the intellectuals and the strikes of the urban labour force were doomed to failure because in both cases it was the action only of a tiny isolated group. For a government like Portugal's which has set its face against democracy and is prepared to use extremes of brutality to crush opposition, it is easy to deal with such isolated pockets of resistance. It was the very failure of such attempts, however, and the fierce repression which followed, that made this clear and prepared the ground for more widely based action. The urban population of Mozambique amounts altogether to less than half a million. A nationalist movement without firm roots in the countryside could never hope to succeed.[20]

Perhaps the peasantry in Mozambique was not quite the quasi-spontaneous revolutionary force which some believe the peasantry in, say, China to have been. Yet, as seen in the previous section, its grievances against the exploitative reality of Portuguese colonialism were real and pressing, providing a firm basis for its mobilization into the struggle. Marcelino dos Santos underscored this point at the time, stressing that overemphasis upon the distinction between a capitalist sector of Mozambican society and a "traditional" sector ("a sort of subsistence economy") would not illuminate the objective situation created by capitalist penetration:

> the two [sectors] do not exist in isolation from one another; they are entirely linked. Why? Where do these people who work on the plantations come from? All those people who work within the capitalist sector come from the traditional sector. And most of them do not remain permanently outside the traditional sector because, for instance, many of them go to work on the plantations for a maximum of two years and they then come back to the village and to the traditional system. So that is the main link—going back and forth. Then there are those people who do not become absorbed into the capitalist system but who are nonetheless related to it. For instance, the people who produce for themselves must sell their produce on the market, mainly food like grain, cashew nuts. They are forced into the market system to find cash for colonial-imposed taxes and to purchase commodities which they do not produce themselves. So these two societies are linked and on many levels the people comprising them are the same.[21]

Indeed, as argued in the previous section, the very idea that there existed "two societies" or "two sectors" seems a questionable one in light of the advanced kind of "articulation" between capitalism and the peasantry which dos Santos himself describes. Thus his analysis underscores, once again, the "availability" of both peasantry and semiproletarianized workers (self-evidently the dividing line is not a clean one) for revolutionary purposes.

In fact, as seen, the attachment of the peasantry to the struggle was an obvious requirement for military success. Nor was it a merely passive element in the radicalization of that struggle. Of course, the leadership role of FRELIMO was important: organizing the war effort, raising national and class consciousness. Yet the interaction between the leadership on the one hand and mass/class action on the other was one which helped, in turn, to determine the outcome of the confrontation within the leadership and to force the movement to the left. We have noted the importance of delegates from within the liberated areas—as well as from the military—in determining the outcome of the crucial Second Congress of FRELIMO in 1968. Also to be noted is the Congress's decision that the Central Committee include representatives elected from the provinces and the mass organizations, an important factor as the struggle over FRELIMO's direction shifted from the Congress to the Central Committee during the next few years. We will return to this theme in the third section of this chapter. Here we may merely recall from our introduction the answers given by Marcelino dos Santos to questions about the role of the popular classes in both the liberation *and* the post-independence phases of the struggle. It was seen as necessary for a committed leadership to carry such classes with it, both during the war of liberation and in the effort to construct socialism. But it was also deemed necessary that the popular classes, those who had most to gain from the socialist option, themselves act to safeguard that goal against bureaucratization and other dangers. As dos Santos' words suggest, a sensitivity to the importance of establishing a genuinely dialectical relationship between leadership and mass action was to be a major legacy of the armed struggle:

> the main defense [of a genuinely revolutionary denouement to the liberation struggle] must be to popularize the revolutionary aims and to create such a situation that if for one reason or another at some future time some people start trying to change these aims, they will meet with resistance from the masses.

Finally, it bears noting that the radicalization of FRELIMO's practice was beginning to be consolidated in the ideological sphere as well. We have seen in the liberated areas the emphasis upon the meeting of popular needs and upon collective solutions in the spheres of production and services. Yet in a whole range of related policy areas the FRELIMO counterrevolutionaries had favored policies which advanced primarily their own interests. And in their political practice they relied, like Chief Nkavandame in the rural areas of Cabo Delgado, on the support of a hierarchical network of local notables and would-be entrepreneurs or, like Father Gwenjere and his students, on an elitist and self-servingly racist definition of the nationalist movement and its post-independence project. From such experiences the progressive wing of FRELIMO reaped not merely the seeds of the socialist economic programs of the post-1975 period, but also a sharpened sense of the extent to which the alternative to mass action was class consolidation of the petty bourgeoisie. Increasingly "the masses" were conceptualized as *classes* in their own right, as "the workers" and "the peasants." A firm step had been taken away from the universe of discourse of manipulative populism and of "African socialism" and toward FRELIMO's Third Congress in 1977 when the movement would formally recognize Marxism as its ideological framework for action and analysis.

Moreover, we know that the kind of "internal" learning experience which thus drew the movement onto the terrain of Marxism was paralleled by its gradually deepening understanding of the external enemy: narrowly nationalist and/or racist definitions of that enemy gave way to revolutionary nationalist and anti-imperialist perspectives as the war progressed. Small wonder that after the Second Congress and only weeks before his assassination, Eduardo Mondlane could argue:

> I am now convinced that FRELIMO has a clearer political line than ever before. . . . The common basis which we all had when we formed FRELIMO was hatred of colonialism and the belief in the necessity to destroy the colonial structure and to establish a new social structure. But what type of social structure, what type of organization we would have, no one knew. No, some did know, some did have ideas, but even they had rather theoretical notions which were themselves trans-formed by the struggle. Now, however, there is a qualitative trans-formation in thinking which has emerged during the past six years which permits me to conclude that at present FRELIMO is much more socialist, revolutionary, and progressive than ever and that the line, the tendency, is now more and more in the direction of socialism of the Marxist-Leninist variety. Why? Because the conditions of life in Mozambique, the type of enemy which we have, does not give us any other alternative. I do think that, without compromising FRELIMO, which still has not made an official announcement declaring itself Marxist-Leninist, I can say that FRELIMO is inclining itself more and more in this direction because the conditions in which we struggle and work demand it.[22]

In Mondlane's view, it would be "impossible to create a capitalist Mozambique. . . . It would be ridiculous to struggle—for the people to struggle—to destroy the economic structure of the enemy and then reconstitute it in such a way as to serve the enemy," and he stressed as well the importance of learning from the "concrete experience, including the errors, of the socialist countries which since 1917 have worked and lived the socialist experience." This, then, was the emerging perspective of the movement which came to confront the legacy of Portuguese colonialism—and, as we shall now see, the *collapse* of the colonial economy—at the moment of independence.

Independence and the New Terrain of Class Struggle

When, with independence, FRELIMO came to power in all of Mozambique, it was faced with a grim inheritance: not only with the structure of an economy warped by Portugal's impact upon the territory, but with the *crisis* of that colonial economy, indeed, its near collapse.[23] Thus FRELIMO confronted a paradoxical task: keeping some aspects of the colonial economy functioning in the short term so as to avoid economic catastrophe, while simultaneously laying the groundwork for the long-term structural transformation of that distorted economy. Of course, the main tool was to be the primacy of state planning rather than the market. This basic premise was already quite explicit in the practice of the liberated areas and was quickly reaffirmed by the nationalizations which occurred shortly after independence, first of land, education, health, legal, and medical practice, then of vital productive sectors, abandoned industries, rental housing, and the like. Yet acceptance of this premise did not, by any means, eliminate all problems. Not only were there difficult economic questions to deal with but also questions linked to defining the terms of class struggle in the new phase and the nature of the political structures which could best advance that struggle on a new, territory-wide basis.

We have already noted, in the first section of this chapter, the inherited structure of the colonial economy: Mozambique's integration into the worldwide imperialist division of labor and into the southern Africa capitalist subsystem. At independence, we find 78 percent of the economy's exports to be primary agricultural products (with cashew nuts, cotton, sugar and groundnuts comprising 65 percent and tea, sisal, and wood another 13 percent) and 85 percent of imports to be manufactured goods! We have also noted how important to the colonial economy was the servicing of transportation links geared to the requirements of South Africa, Rhodesia, and Malawi, how crucially important, too, the movement of migrant labor, especially from the south of the country to the mines of South Africa. (The fact that the deferred payment of wages to such migrants had passed through the hands of the colonial state at a high fixed gold price added to the importance of this economic connection, of course.) These central features of the economy defined its dependent status; these features were also to be placed in jeopardy by the economic crisis of the colonial economy at war's end.

The structure of rural production on the ground, as sketched above, was also important. In certain crucial sectors it was premised on the exploitation of land alienated to either plantation owners or *latifundarios* (settler farmers), these profiting from the external market for such products as sugar and tea and the internal urban market for foodstuffs. (Needless to say, these enterprises also profited from the availability of cheap labor.) Thus the four central provinces produced about 40 percent of the country's agricultural output—sugar, copra, tea, rice, maize—and of this the plantation sector produced about 60 percent. The three southern provinces produced about 20 percent of the nation's output—rice, vegetables, cashews, maize, groundnuts (and, beyond these figures, a substantial percentage of dairy and beef production as well), with about 40 percent of this coming from the capitalist *latifundios* of the Limpopo Valley and elsewhere. In the north the picture was different again, with fully 40 percent of agricultural output coming from Nampula, Niassa, and Cabo Delgado—cassava, groundnuts, cashews, cotton—but almost 90 percent of this from small peasant farmers. The crisis of the colonial economy, while a general phenomenon, obviously had quite different attributes in these different regional settings.

There was also in the later stages of colonial rule increased industrial activity, mainly concentrated in Maputo and Beira. This involved, on the one hand, industries devoted to intermediate processing of cotton, sugar, cashews, copra, and tea geared to export and, on the other hand, what were often merely assembly and packaging plants. These latter, producing finished goods for the Mozambican market, tended to be dependent on imported raw materials and machinery and to be controlled from South Africa, Portugal, or elsewhere. Dependence is the key word here, dependence on foreign capital and technology, but also dependence, as in so many other sectors in colonial Mozambique, on foreign (generally Portuguese) personnel in technical and managerial positions. Indeed, the Portuguese colonial strategy of promoting further European immigration in the 1960s and 1970s served to reinforce this pattern, with African labor, unskilled, cheap, and tightly controlled, thus serving merely as a base for extracting considerable surplus value. Clearly this African labor force—in industry, but also in such crucial sectors as the docks and transport—had its full share of grievances and long-bottled-up demands. These would necessarily come to the surface with the collapse of colonialism and a new revolutionary alliance of workers and peasants would have to deal sensitively with this legacy of colonial superexploitation. Then, too, the impact of the crisis of the colonial economy upon the Mozambican peasantry—trapped by the logic of colonial capitalism in a twilight zone between "modern" and "traditional" economic activities—was also to present serious challenges to the FRELIMO leadership. To these related issues we shall return.

But first, the crisis. The most visible initial index of this was the flight of the colonists, those who had kept virtually all technical training and managerial expertise to themselves and now saw their claim to privileged status in the society jeopardized by egalitarianism. By the end of 1976 about 90 percent of the approximately quarter of a million Portuguese had left. The result? The departure of petty capitalists—shop and transport owners—undermined the trading network of the country, and departure of the *latifundarios* threatened to destroy such crucial activities as the supply of foodstuffs to the towns. The departure of skilled workers and managers in industry, communications, public works, and other services opened up equally gaping holes in the economy. The full implications of Mozambique's condition of "undevelopment"—the "historical backwardness" that had been frozen by colonial Mozambique's structure of dependence and underdevelopment—became painfully apparent when the stratum of colonists disappeared. Moreover, the whole process was accompanied by an extremely costly (and often quite vindictive) wave of sabotage and by a flight of capital. Witness the export of vehicles and wrecking of machinery, building, and livestock by the departing Portuguese and the diverting of funds and incurring of new debts abroad. Much of this latter activity was crudely done; some of it was accomplished more subtly (as in the case of the running down of capital stock and shifting of debt by Sena Sugar Estates in the period after independence and prior to its nationalization).

There were other aspects of the post-independence situation which contributed to economic difficulties. For example, there was the movement of migrant labor to South Africa. Though wanting eventually to phase out this aspect of its dependent position, FRELIMO felt that only limited adjustments could be made in this regard until the distorted rural economy of the south was sufficiently transformed to permit absorption of the miners.* Yet after an initial period it was South Africa itself which cut drastically the number of Mozambican workers going there (1977) and also ended the practice of deferred gold payments at a fixed price rather than market price; these actions exacerbated Mozambique's balance of payments difficulties and its unemployment problem.[24] Then, too, there were the costs of continuing war, now focused on Rhodesia. Supporting ZANU and upholding international economic sanctions meant foregoing earnings from road and rail transport to Rhodesia and reducing employment opportunities both in the Mozambican entrepôt of Beira and in Rhodesia itself. And the war brought refugees to be fed—at the same time as Rhodesian aggression was disrupting agricultural production and other activities in the affected areas of Mozambique.

---

*Other aspects of Mozambique's dependence on South Africa had also to be accepted in the short run in a similar spirit (servicing that country's transportation links and supplying Cabora Bassa power, for example) while keeping a way open toward future transformation.

Obviously FRELIMO had the long-term intention of transforming the structure of production so as to serve the needs of the Mozambican people rather than those of the beneficiaries of the colonial economic structure and global accumulation of capital. However, in the short run, production was declining in all sectors and emergency action was necessary. This was particularly true of the rural areas and there, most pressingly, in the large farm rather than peasant sector. Particularly dramatic in this regard was the abandonment by the Portuguese of about four-thousand settler farms, especially in the Limpopo Valley. Yet, as noted, these farms were the main suppliers of foodstuffs to the cities. Urban catastrophe and/or vast expenditure on imported foodstuffs were the likely outcome of failure to deal with this sector. Small wonder that the "state farms" established on these *latifundios* were so important an aspect of agricultural policy in these first years. Yet this was also a sector with a very highly developed level of technology and scientific management (irrigation, tractors, and the like). Considerable investment had to be given over to it, and a great concentration of expertise (both Mozambican and that of expatriate *cooperantes*) dedicated to it.

This necessity to concentrate on the state farms also meant less immediate emphasis on the peasant sector. Yet, in the long run, the latter is of at least equal importance—and was at least as negatively affected by the crisis. It is true that the subsistence-producing capacity of peasant agriculture (where this had been partially preserved rather than undermined by colonial capitalism) meant that many peasants could hope to ride out the crisis in some way even if deprived of other economic stimuli. Yet this also meant economic activity at a very low level rather than any kind of economic development. What was the problem? In the first place, with the removal of colonial compulsion the peasant would now produce only as it seemed worthwhile for him/her to do so. Yet this situation emerged at the very moment when, as seen, the marketing and transport networks fell into disarray. This created difficulties in selling crops on the one hand and in purchasing agricultural inputs and consumer goods on the other. Not surprisingly, the marketing—and actual production!—of such export crops as cashews and cotton and of such food crops as rice, maize, and groundnuts began to fall precipitously.

The network of commercialization would have eventually to be resurrected. And cooperativization in the countryside, seen as a key to revitalizing the peasant economy and raising the level of peasant life (while also reabsorbing migrant labor), would have to be given a real push. However, with state farms so dominant a preoccupation of agricultural policy in the early years, the careful planning and the funding necessary to carry forward a policy of peasant-sector cooperativization was not forthcoming; unfortunately the more spontaneous efforts which occurred instead often produced negative results. Here, clearly, challenges remain which continue to be at the center of policy debate up to the present moment. Yet in the meantime one more source of export earnings was soon performing well below par. Moreover, the urgency of regaining the former level of production of the various crops concerned loomed large. In consequence, actually remodeling the overall pattern of agricultural production so as to establish a new, more autocentric economic logic for the country was not seen as quite so pressing a consideration.

In the industrial sphere, where foreign managerial and technical skills were an even more prominent feature prior to liberation, the flight of the Portuguese combined with an extremely high degree of economic sabotage to produce equally devastating effects. Tea, cashew and sugar processing, cement manufacturing, steel production, and other activities were soon lagging very far behind previous levels of production; production at CIFEL, the steel mill, fell by 45,000 tons to an output of 5,000 tons between 1975 and 1978, for example. Of course, it represented a considerable accomplishment—often the direct accomplishment of the workers themselves (though often, too, sustained by state intervention and administration)—merely to keep such industrial undertakings afloat. Moreover, the active role taken by the workers was extremely suggestive of the kind of relations of production which might become part and parcel of Mozambique's transition to socialism. Most immediately, however, the difficulty of producing manufactured goods and the shortages which ensued reinforced the problem of establishing fruitful exchanges between city and countryside, between industry and agriculture, of the kind which would stimulate further development in both these sectors. And there were even more basic questions to confront. Merely getting the old colonial industrial structure back on a productive basis would not be sufficient in and of itself. In this sphere, too, it was going to be necessary to plan toward a new internal logic for the economy, toward new kinds of exchanges between sectors, and the like. Fortunately, with FRELIMO's Third Congress in 1977, discussion of these and other issues in the economic realm was to be carried forward. We shall explore this discussion and its concrete results in the chapter that follows.

Economic challenges also highlighted issues linked to Mozambique's class structure. The need to get some kind of immediate handle on the socioeconomic situation made it necessary to take hold of many of the structures of the established state and use them—just as it had proven necessary to use some of the structures of the established economy. Despite President Machel's Independence Day warning (quoted above), it was not easy to "smash the colonial state" all at once. True, the work of structuring new ministries and restructuring old ones did begin. But the extreme shortfall of trained personnel dictated the necessity of entrusting responsibilities to members of a petty bourgeoisie of whose "class suicide" the leadership could not be entirely confident. The President did speak directly to this issue not long after independence.

> There are maneuvers of the local bourgeoisie which have already failed. Thus, some of that group had thought that after the takeover of power, and after a period of time had elapsed, FRELIMO would have a great need for qualified personnel and that it would be among the "*évolués*" that we would be obliged to look for such personnel. They thought in this way to lay hold of the state apparatus and to block or distort our projects.
>
> But we haven't such an overwhelming need for technicians and administrative personnel (of which the bourgeoisie has many more than FRELIMO). We aren't afraid, in the first phase, of making the state a little less efficient, in order that it can safeguard its popular inspiration and its popular character. This is always preferable to having a state which is efficient in theory but entirely in the hands of the petty bourgeoisie because in the latter case we would find ourselves completely dependent upon our class enemy. How many African countries have experienced this phenomenon and thus fallen into the hands of privileged classes!
>
> We will destroy all the structures and tendencies which are characteristic of the capitalist system. It's the people who must take over everything since the only ones "qualified" in our country are the people, the people who have struggled for liberation.[25]

Yet Machel's prognosis was rather too optimistic, the problem of the "efficiency" of the state apparatus much less straightforward. Even with many of the "petty bourgeoisie" kept on the job (and numerous "cooperants" from abroad added as well), problems of inefficiency continued. "Historical backwardness" thus exacted a heavy price from Mozambique's socialist development effort and came to reinforce the importance of those with some degree of training. At the same time, the President's fears were not ill founded; the mechanisms for winning and holding the petty bourgeoisie to the revolution have not always been easy to come by. Clearly, a major dilemma seemed to be surfacing here. Moreover, it was a dilemma to be further complicated by the fact that even political cadres were not immune to the allure of petty-bourgeois privileges and complacency in the post-independence period.

In part the answer to the problem of "historical backwardness" and "undevelopment" is to seek an advance in the *overall* level of education: literacy, numeracy, technical training, what Lenin called a "cultural revolution." We have suggested that this fact helps explain the centrality of a focus on education in FRELIMO's development project. But FRELIMO also made it clear from the outset that the key to avoiding bureaucratization and a petty-bourgeois takeover of the structures of newly independent Mozambique was to be *class struggle.* And crucial, in turn, to this class struggle was to be *people's power,* exercised both by FRELIMO as tribune of the people *and* by the people acting directly through popularly based mass organizations. We shall see that realizing an effective balance between FRELIMO leadership on the one hand and action by the popular classes on the other has remained the most central theme of Mozambican politics to the present. However, there can be no doubt that the desire to empower the people, so deeply grounded in the wartime experience, was ripe to be carried over into the period of transitional government. For, in the liberated areas, there had developed a range of institutions designed to facilitate mass action. Most characteristic, if least formally structured, were the regular community-wide mass meetings *(reunões)* which FRELIMO personnel facilitated from an early date and which were designed to engage all members of a particular community or sector in frank discussion of problems and prospects.

In addition, a more formalized committee structure was also emerging to complement and focus the political energy stirring in such meetings. This involved the establishment of an elected committee (and, more often than not, a local militia unit) at the *circulo* or locality level. True, the exact format of this basic institution varied somewhat from place to place since, in Mondlane's words, "existing parapolitical structures, traditional and modern, have been incorporated in the structure of the liberation movement." Slowly, too, a more dense political network built up from this base, elected representatives from the *circulo* going to the district level councils, thence to provincial councils and, finally, to the national Congress of the movement. At this stage in the development of a new Mozambique the movement was, of course, party, state administration, and representative institution all in one, an intertwining of threads which were slowly to be disentangled and rationalized after the winning of independence. In consequence, the precise nature of the balance struck at that time between central guidance and initiative from below is a bit difficult to specify. However, the general spirit in which these institutions operated was spelled out in Samora Machel's important document of the period, *Establishing People's Power to Serve the Masses.*[26]

This document was prepared in 1971 in the wake of the leadership crisis within FRELIMO in order to underwrite an "offensive of reorganization." In it there is no apologizing for the centrality of the leadership function, necessary for raising the class consciousness of a scattered peasantry, for focusing the national consciousness of a divided people, and for exemplifying to Mozambicans their own potential efficacy as historical actors after centuries of disfranchisement. Thus the document states that the movement's task "is definitely to lead, organize, guide, and educate the masses," to lead and guide "the reorganization of the life of the masses and national reconstruction just as it guides and leads the army, setting the goals to be achieved and heightening political consciousness." Yet this is only one side of the coin. There is also

the tendency of certain comrades to conceal especially the mistakes of responsibles from the masses, [which] reflects a lack of political democracy and lack of confidence in the masses. Power belongs to the working people. The political line reflects the interests of the labouring masses and discipline is the watchdog which defends the line. It is therefore clear that the defence of our line and discipline is first and foremost the task of the masses of the people, since this defence is the defence of their lives.

As the argument continues:

The process and experience of democracy are new in our country. Because they have always lived under the domination of various exploiting classes, our people have never known real democracy. . . . From the circle to the locality, and from the district to the national level, for the first time in our history the people have their own power which they do not feel to be something alien to which they are subject. . . .

. . . the Revolution has brought democracy which is already being asserted at several levels: political, economic, and military. It is also exercised within the framework of the Organization. In the present phase it is vital to broaden its field of application, thereby even further putting into practice the principle that power belongs to the working masses. . . . In this context an important requirement, corresponding to the consolidation of power in the liberated areas, is to progressively extend the system of elections, starting at the lowest levels, from the appointment of responsibles from among the people, creating truly democratic base structures of administrative power. . . .

. . . Our decisions must always be democratic in content and form. "Content" means that they must reflect the real interests of the masses. "Form" means that the broad masses must take part in the decision, feeling that it is theirs, and not something imposed from above. . . . However good in content, a bureaucratic decision runs the risk of being unrelated to the masses' level of understanding; in other words, it may be unrealistic and create a contradiction which would have been avoided if discussion had taken place. . . .

What, then, of leadership? At no time does the document lose sight of that parallel requirement, thus bringing the argument full circle:

> It is obvious, however, that elections cannot be anarchic but must be oriented in such a way that the choice of the masses falls on those who have internalized the Party line, both conceptually and in their behaviour, and who have initiative and organizing ability. . . . It is therefore important to show great vigilance in preventing the election of people with exploitative tendencies, even though they may enjoy some popularity, either for subjective reasons or because of demagogic activity.

Obviously there are complexities here. We shall examine the ongoing dialectic between leadership and mass action in the post-independence period in the following chapter. However, enough has been said to show why establishing a political process embodying this dialectic was to become the chief focus of policy-making and FRELIMO activity during the initial period of its nationwide rule, a moment in the Mozambican revolutionary process to which we now turn.

In April 1974 came the coup in Portugal, a direct outgrowth of the victories of the people in Mozambique, Angola, and Guinea-Bissau. The new Portuguese government, particularly for so long as Antonio de Spinola was prominent within it, tried to retain control over the decolonization process. But FRELIMO continued fighting until, in the wake of Spinola's departure, a genuine handing-over of power could take place. By September Portugal had capitulated and the agreement then signed in Lusaka determined that during a ten-month transition period FRELIMO would have a free hand in fashioning Mozambique's new nationwide institutions as it thought fit. In the period of the "Transitional Government" running up to Independence Day, June 25, 1975, it was to do precisely that.

As suggested above, FRELIMO had realized that it must carry the people with it into the next round of the struggle. Indeed, the Central Committee of FRELIMO was to reaffirm in 1977 that democratization, the structuring of the political process, the grounding of "people's power" as "People's Democracy" en route to the consolidation of a socialist society, had been its top priority during the transitional period. The movement's experience of the war had suggested both that this was possible *and* that it was necessary. As Sebastiao Mabote, a senior FRELIMO leader, once commented to me, "the atomic bomb in this war is the people's consciousness." The people's consciousness was seen as the key to winning the peace as well.

Yet it was still a relatively small percentage of the population which had experienced the lessons of the liberated areas at first hand. Thus the primary task FRELIMO confronted was to find a novel means whereby people elsewhere in the country could, in effect, partake of that experience. The answer was the "dynamizing group" (*grupo dinamizadore* or GD)—this to be twinned in turn with the familar mechanism of the mass meeting *(reunião)*. Mounted in both residential areas and workplaces (including factories and state offices) the GDs were committees of eight to twelve "responsibles" *(responsaveis)*, usually elected by public meetings of everyone involved in the locale concerned and charged with the task of stimulating and coordinating the activities of that locale in a wide range of spheres.

The watchword of their catalyzing activities became "Unity, Work, Vigilance," but the spheres of health and community development, political education, literacy, women's emancipation, and work-related problems all fell within the GDs' purview. Like the committees in the liberated areas before them, they were somewhat unstructured and variable in form, and of course their success record also varied. Nonetheless, there can be no doubt that their import was considerable. Within these *grupos* the two aspects of FRELIMO's politics—leadership and mass action—once again came together. Though all activists within them did not have to be FRELIMO members, the GDs were plugged into the FRELIMO hierarchy above them, to be stimulated (and supervised) by it. At the same time, the GDs' links to the mass base (leading it, but being controlled by it, with criticism and self-criticism the order of the day) through the mass meeting were often very vibrant.[27]

It might have been sufficient, in a context where democratic expression had long been crushed by a particularly brutal colonialism, that this process began to create (in the words of Marcelino dos Santos) "a new sense of confidence in the oppressed masses and . . . helped to convince them that they had the capacity to transform Mozambique, [this being] the very essence of People's Power." But, as alluded to above, the GDs were also a framework for advancing the development effort—and the class struggle. In particular, their economic significance was often crucial, as when they provided an institutional focus for the efforts by workers to check the economic sabotage of departing Portuguese and keep abandoned factories and settler farms going; they were also a framework for some of the first moves by peasants toward more collective forms of agricultural involvement. The successful vaccination campaigns in the early post-independence years are another example of the capacity of this network to engage people massively in their own liberation. Moreover, as we shall see, such a mobilizing role was to be enormously important as Mozambique began to move into a fresh political phase. As new forms of popular participation were articulated—the selection, in 1977–1978, both of popular assemblies and of members of the new political party then in formation—the GDs provided an essential mechanism for facilitating such developments.

Of course, the latter point also serves to remind us that the political process—and the class struggle—in Mozambique did not come to rest at the stage encapsulated by the universalization of the *grupo dinamizadore*. The latter's role had been significant, nonetheless. For it had been necessary to incorporate working class and peasantry actively into the revolutionary process on a countrywide basis. The working class, for example, did have genuine grievances, grievances now unleashed from the tight controls imposed by the Portugese (and even fanned to some extent by the departing Portuguese). It was important that these grievances (including wage demands) be met, but important, too, that they be met within the framework of the new national priorities in the process of formation. It was equally necessary that the energies of both peasants and workers be released and, simultaneously, focused toward the new goals of economic liberation and development. In the event, there was an apparent fit between the framework provided by the *grupo dinamizadore* (including the broader structure of FRELIMO polity and ideology within which that mechanism was located) and popular action. And this, in turn, allowed the new FRELIMO-sponsored system to slide comfortably into place, allowed it to be embraced by the popular classes as an acceptable means for their political expression. Indeed, it is not fanciful to see the establishment and relative effectiveness of the GDs as a kind of referendum for FRELIMO, a referendum that the movement won. It was this success, above all others, which enabled FRELIMO to relocate its struggle effectively on the new terrain of independence. It is to a more detailed analysis of the struggle on that terrain which we now turn.

Notes

1. The present essay seeks to locate the issues identified in the introduction within the context of a broad overview of Mozambican historical

development. In consequence, the chapter is designed especially for readers with little prior knowledge of the Mozambican revolution and the existing literature on it. I have therefore taken the liberty— especially in the section on "Nationalism and Revolution"—of incorporating into the text several passages originally published in my earlier essays on the development of FRELIMO's liberation struggle, especially chap. 7 in Giovanni Arrighi and John S. Saul, *Essays on the Political Economy of Africa* (New York and London: Monthly Review Press, 1973) and several chapters in my *The State and Revolution in Eastern Africa* (New York and London: Monthly Review Press, 1979).

2. Eduardo Mondlane, *The Struggle for Mozambique* (Harmondsworth: Penguin Books, 1969; republished, London: Zed Press, 1983, with an introduction by the present editor and a biographical essay by Herb Shore).

3. Of particular importance in the writing of this section have been two published essays by Marc Wuyts, "Peasants and Rural Economy in Mozambique," discussion paper of the Centro dos Estudos Africanos (Maputo: Eduardo Mondlane University, August 1976) and "Economia politica do colonialismo em Moçambique," *Estudos Moçambicanos* (Maputo) 1, no. 9 (1980); two collections by the Department of History, Eduardo Mondlane, University: *Historia de Moçambique*, vol. 1, *Primeiras sociedades sedentarias e impacto dos mercadores (200/300–1886)* (Maputo, 1982) and *Cadernos de historia de Moçambique*, published in *Tempo* (Maputo) between September 1981 and March 1982; and several unpublished essays by David Hedges of the abovementioned Department of History.

4. Wuyts, "Economia Politica do Colonialismo em Moçambique."

5. Samora Machel, *O processo da revolução democratica popular em Moçambique* (Maputo, 1976).

6. Samora Machel, "The People's Republic of Mozambique: The Struggle Continues," *Review of African Political Economy*, no. 4 (November 1975).

7. The following two paragraphs draw on David Hedges, "Education, Missions and the Political Ideology of Assimilation, 1930–1960," unpublished manuscript.

8. William Minter, *Portuguese Africa and the West* (New York: Monthly Review Press, 1973).

9. See my introduction to the new edition of Mondlane, *The Struggle for Mozambique*, for an elaboration of this point. For other materials relevant to this section, including the *Central Committee Report*, see Introduction (to this book), fn. 1.

10. Minter, *Portuguese Africa and the West.*

11. Julius Nyerere, "Introduction" to his *Freedom and Socialism* (London and New York: Oxford University Press, 1968).

12. Interview with Marcelino dos Santos (by Joe Slovo), "FRELIMO Faces the Future," *The African Communist*, no. 55 (1973).

13. Ibid. The reference to Samora Machel is to his *Mozambique: Sowing the Seeds of Revolution* (London, 1974). My own firsthand observations of

74   *A Difficult Road*

the guerrilla struggle, which bear out the emphases of dos Santos and Machel, are to be found in my essay "Inside Mozambique" in *The State and Revolution in Eastern Africa*.

14. Basil Davidson, *In the Eye of the Storm* (New York: Doubleday, 1972).
15. "25th of June—The Starting Point," *Mozambique Revolution* (Dar es Salaam), no. 51 (May–June 1972).
16. Samora Machel, cited in CEDIMO, *Documento Informativo* (Maputo, 1978), p. 10.
17. Mondlane, *The Struggle for Mozambique*.
18. Machel, in *Documento Informativo*.
19. "Doa a quem doer, nós somos moçambicanos," interview with Samora Machel in *Expresso* (Lisbon), 24 December 1980.
20. Mondlane, *The Struggle for Mozambique*.
21. Dos Santos, "FRELIMO Faces the Future."
22. I have transcribed and translated this statement by Eduardo Mondlane from a tape in the possession of Aquino da Bragança, who conducted the interview and was kind enough to lend me the tape.
23. In the first part of this section I have drawn extensively on notes prepared by David Hedges (in typescript under the title "National Independence, 1975–1980") and am grateful for his permission to do so. On the subject matter of this section see also Allen F. Isaacman, *A Luta Continua: Creating a New Society in Mozambique* (Binghamton: Ferdnand Braudel Center, 1978) and David Wield, "Mozambique—Late Colonialism and Early Problems of Transition," in Institute of Development Studies (Sussex), *Revolutionary Socialist Development in the Third World* (Brighton: Harvester Press, 1983).
24. On this subject see the material presented by the late Ruth First and her colleagues at the Center of African Studies, Eduardo Mondlane University, in *Black Gold* (Brighton, Sussex: Harvester Press, 1982).
25. "Nôtre tâche principale: Bâtir une société nouvelle," interview with Samora Machel, *Afrique-Asie*, no. 109 (17–30 May 1976).
26. Samora Machel, *Establishing People's Power to Serve the Masses* (Toronto: Toronto Committee for the Liberation of Southern Africa, 1976).
27. As I was to witness for myself at the time of the independence celebrations, this pattern was already well developed by the end of the formal transition period (see my "Free Mozambique" in *The State and Revolution in Eastern Africa*). And it was to be deepened and extended in the immediately succeeding period.

John S. Saul

2. The Content:
A Transition to Socialism?

Having achieved this transitional goal—the relocating of its struggle on the terrain of independence—FRELIMO found the stage set for a new period of political creativity. We may take this fresh phase as beginning with FRELIMO's Third Congress in 1977 and will explore this political process in the first section of the present chapter. At the same time it must be emphasized that political creativity is not sufficient in and of itself; political and economic transformation must go hand in hand. Thus political transformation—the advance of the class struggle, the consolidation of viable national institutions, the empowering of the popular classes and release of their popular energies—can facilitate economic transformation. But economic advance is also necessary to underwrite political change and deepen popular commitment to a revolutionary project. A positive, and dialectical, relationship between changes in the forces of production and changes in the relations of production (broadly conceived) is crucial to a transition to socialism. Clearly, the economics of socialist development in Mozambique is a theme to which we must also turn, as we will in the second section of this chapter.

Advances and setbacks are etched in practice and we will be reviewing Mozambican practice in this chapter, as well as in the sectoral studies that follow. But ideology can be studied, too, as a kind of litmus test of the degree of advance or retreat. Indeed, ideology is more than some mere passive reflex of developments in other spheres. An emergent ideological line, in its strengths and weaknesses, can also push a situation forward positively or freeze and reproduce its negative aspects. Ideology has functioned in both ways in Mozambique as FRELIMO has sought to define a Marxist orientation suitable to its revolutionary project. In consequence, a third section of this chapter will survey the terrain of *ideological class struggle* in present-day Mozambique. Here, too, I will be able to draw most directly on my own experience of working in Mozambique. As noted in the introduction, all of the case studies that follow in Part II reflect the firsthand work experience of their authors. I myself have made a number of research trips to Mozambique: once to the liberated areas in 1972, once to join in the independence celebrations in 1975, and twice after independence, in 1978 and 1979. But in 1981–1982 I also had the opportunity to work within the Mozambican structures, in both the FRELIMO Party School in Maputo and the Faculty of Marxism-Leninism at the University of Eduardo Mondlane, where my work consisted of reviewing and critiquing existing syllabi and teaching materials in the area of Marxist studies, helping to prepare new ones, and presenting such new materials in the classroom. My discussion of ideological class struggle in Mozambique has the benefit of that firsthand experience.

The Politics of Socialism

As suggested, the Third Congress of FRELIMO in February 1977 may be taken as the benchmark for a new phase in the Mozambican revolution in the political, economic, and ideological spheres. Certainly this was the case in the development of the country's distinctive political process, giving this latter new focus and institutional expression. The *grupos dinamizadores* (GDs) had indeed served the function of generalizing participation and concretizing an important measure of democracy. But it was felt that they could no longer play the central role if further progress was to be made. In essence, they were just a shade too unstructured and amorphous to be an adequate expression of FRELIMO's politics at the base. Specifically, this had permitted, upon occasion, their infiltration and manipulation by elements deemed questionable and opportunist. More generally, by blending within themselves both political movement *and* mass action, they had begun to blur a distinction which FRELIMO felt its experience in the liberated areas had proven to be important: the distinction between cadre and populace, between vanguard and mass, between party and class base. Progress would come from maintaining, even underscoring, these distinctions and allowing the creative tension, the dialectic, between leadership on the one hand and mass action on the other to drive the revolution forward.

This meant, in the first place, that the role of the cadre was to be given a much more explicitly defined place within the political process as FRELIMO transformed itself, formally, from movement to party. The immediate task in this regard became the establishment of party cells—and the selection of their members—within the various sectors which had up to that time grounded the GDs. Secondly, if the GDs were to lose their quasi-party status, it was clear that they would also be too loose and transitional a structure to focus adequately the "mass action" aspect of FRELIMO's politics. The creation of production councils within the factories in late 1976 had already suggested that this was seen to be the case. Even though the *grupos* were to continue to play a role as the basis of neighborhood organization, a variety of other structures of mass action were now to be developed in order to further consolidate "People's Democracy."

The intended vanguard nature of FRELIMO is clearly enunciated in the important *Central Committee Report to the Third Congress:*

> The party's historic mission is to lead, organize, orientate and educate the masses, thus transforming the popular mass movement into a powerful instrument for the destruction of capitalism and the construction of socialism.[1]

The class basis for this is also quite specifically stated: an alliance of workers ("the leading force") and peasants ("the principal force"), attended by "the progressive elements of other labouring classes." (Moreover, as we shall discuss below, this alliance was to be sealed by the self-conscious adoption of Marxism-Leninism, "the scientific ideology of the proletariat," as the intellectual premise of FRELIMO's vanguard role.) More concretely, the emphasis of the *Report,* and subsequent Congress resolutions, implied a vigorous effort to "structure" the new party. As an official account of the campaign to do this was to comment somewhat later,

> the basis for the party already existed, but the new situation demanded more than this. It demanded the party's presence throughout the country, in the factories, the cooperatives, the offices, military and para-military bodies, within the state apparatus, and in the villages.[2]

How was this presence to be guaranteed? The first efforts to build up the party after the Congress were not notably successful, as Oscar Monteiro, the new party's Secretary for Organization, was to admit. But a much more concerted effort came with the launching of the "Campaign for Structuring the Party" in February of the following year (1978).

Significantly, the populace as a whole was now to participate in the selection process for new party members, as organizing brigades fanned out into the various workplaces and neighborhoods, collecting applications at general meetings of all workers or residents, discussing them with the GDs, production councils, and other organizations, and then presenting the candidates to a second general meeting for open debate on their suitability for party roles. Like the similarly structured elections for national and local assemblies the year before, this process was generally an open and lively one, although, unlike in the assembly elections, the party itself made the final decisions regarding admission. It was these admittees who now formed the party cells within the various institutions and locales touched by the campaign. They were to join the ranks of cadres, the definition of whose responsibilities was a particularly rigorous one and to whose upgrading by means of political and other training the party now pledged itself. For, the *Central Committee Report* noted,

> the leading activity of FRELIMO depends, in the final analysis, on the political activity which its militants carry out among the labouring masses. Our Party must concern itself with the political, ideological and cultural training of its members, inasmuch as it will be through them that we will raise the revolutionary consciousness of the masses, their level of organization, and their will and ability to build the New Society.[3]

Thus 1977 saw the culmination of a trend which had begun in the early 1970s with the formation, in the army, of the first cells of this party-in-the-making and had continued with the establishment, in January 1974, of what was, in essence, a party training school. Now the party's role as vanguard, as guide and catalyst of mass action, was confirmed. But what of the control of this party, in turn, by the popular classes themselves? As seen above, there was genuine mass involvement in the selection of party members and, of course, the door was to remain open to continued recruitment, especially from these popular classes. Beyond this, "democratic centralism"—defined in contradistinction both to "the relaxation of discipline, anarchy or lack of forethought" on the one hand and to "bureaucratic centralization, which sterilizes and impedes any task" on the other—was to be the official designation of the party's internal practice. And as we shall see—the Fouth Congress of FRELIMO in 1983 provides a striking case in point—FRELIMO's structure has permitted a measure of openness to debate and feedback throughout its existence. At the same time, it also seems fair to say that there has continued to be rather more centralism than formal democracy within FRELIMO, at least below the level of the Central Committee. It might therefore be argued that the main guarantor of the democratic term in the Mozambique political equation must arise from the interaction between the party and the people.

In this regard, one check against an easy collapse into authoritarianism has come from the party's perspective on political methods of work, a perspective first defined in the liberated areas. For throughout the war period the political onus had been placed on the cadre to succeed in mobilizing the people, rather than assuming the onus to be upon the people to respond. This was a distinction, subtle but important, often repeated by FRELIMO personnel over the years and one firmly institutionalized in the movement's practice. Its meaning: if communication breaks down, query the quality of leadership, the quality of the "vanguard," first. The populace thus had at least a *negative* check upon the movement's activities, and this in turn represented a kind of vaccination, internalized by FRELIMO, against the day when bureaucratically minded cadres might try to put forward the notion that the people had failed them and that tougher, more Stalinist notions of "mobilization" were in order. In fact, cadres who did not make this interaction with the people work could thus be weeded out, the movement in this way "learning from the people." It was no accident that the new party now defined its methods of work vis-à-vis the people in closely related terms: "it is not enough to proclaim the leading role of the party—this must be won in practice."

Equally important in this context, however, was the active, *positive* role to be played by the workers and peasants through their "democratic mass organizations." As the *Central Committee Report* put the point, these

> constitute the fundamental means of broadening and consolidating on a national level the wide-ranging popular anti-imperialist front: they are the school of democratic life and organized participation by the people in social life. They enable FRELIMO to feel and to know at every moment the problems, needs, opinions, criticisms and suggestions of the various sections of the population.

As noted, one relevant set of institutions which began to take shape in the wake of the Third Congress—and of its resolution calling for general elections within a year—were the People's Assemblies, chosen in late 1977. These thus antedated the mass involvement, mentioned earlier, in the selection of party members and also represented the first Mozambican election ever held on the basis of universal adult suffrage. The vibrancy of the public meetings which considered the merits of various nominated candidates to local assemblies and then voted upon them was notable; the same vibrancy characterized these assemblies when they sat to consider nominees for the district assembly and when the latter in turn selected nominees to the provincial bodies. Though the selection process for the National Assembly was much more controlled from above, all these assemblies were granted responsibilities which held out the prospect of politically significant activity for them as their members became more confident in their roles.

In time, too, there were to be other complementary consultative processes. Thus in the areas of urban planning (1978–1979) and collective rural development (1979–1980), for example, there were built up, beginning with seminars in the urban *bairros* and communal villages themselves and thence in district and regional gatherings, national planning meetings regarding these policy areas. Also of great importance (partly realized, partly in potential) in the sphere of popular action were a variety of more constituency-specific "democratic mass organizations"—the Organization of Mozambican Women (OMM) and the Organization of Mozambican Youth (OJM), for example. Then, too, there was the institutionalization of village committees and village meetings, linked when possible to the ongoing formation of communal villages *(aldeias comunais)* and agricultural cooperatives, which provided the infrastructure for politics and planning at the very base of the system, in the rural areas.

The opportunities for participation and self-expression which such institutions opened up to Mozambicans should not be underestimated, whatever the shortfalls and setbacks which continued to accompany their development. Perhaps special mention should be made of the Production Councils, however, especially in light of the primary importance which FRELIMO has granted the working class within Mozambique's revolutionary class alliance. As noted earlier, this institution had already begun to be defined even in advance of the party congress, the initiative to launch such councils having been formally announced in a presidential speech in October 1976. President Machel decried the fact that "authoritarian labour relations remain intact within firms and hinder the creative initiative of the working class"; he looked to a situation in which "the relations of production would be dominated by the working class." Concretely, the Production Councils were to play a role in such spheres as planning production, facilitating worker self-discipline, and advancing health and safety concerns. More broadly,

> the Production Councils are, above all, a weapon which will lead to the destruction of the old capitalist relations of production. It will be through this new structure that the workers will participate in an active, collective and conscious manner in the discussion and solution of problems, and will plan and control production. To sum up, they will dominate the production process and participate in the direction of the economy.[4]

FRELIMO also saw these councils as potential building blocks for trade union development, though any further definition of what such unions might look like within the FRELIMO framework and what the line of march toward them might be was slow in coming.

For our purposes what is important to note is that, as party cells replaced GDs, it was mass organizations like the Production Councils with which party cells were expected to interact in order to play their role as catalysts of class action from below. In fact, it is in regard to precisely this process that Peter Sketchley's chapter in this volume provides extremely useful documentation.

There can be no doubt that these various institutional innova tions made a significant difference to Mozambican political life and that important foundations had thus been laid for sustaining the effective dialectic between leadership and mass action so necessary for the successful construction of socialism. Yet much remained to be accomplished. Indeed, by the end of 1979 it had become apparent that there were serious flaws in what had already been done. Signs of bureaucratic inefficiency and corruption, and even of worker indifference, were to be seen. And in the rural areas political dynamism seemed to have slackened off in a number of places (a point to be emphasized the following March at the abovementioned national meeting of communal villages). There were excuses enough for this. As we have seen, the disruption caused by the abrupt departure of the Portuguese had been considerable and the shortage of trained cadres had made itself painfully apparent as FRELIMO sought to spread its structures from the liberated zones across the country as a whole. Moreover, the Rhodesian war had taken a distressingly heavy toll on resources, on personnel, and on attention. Still, it was characteristic of FRELIMO that it did not seek such excuses but chose instead to confront matters head-on, taking responsibility for its own errors and moving to correct them. This is a process which is continuing.

The first sign that something new was afoot came in early December 1979, when Samora Machel spoke to a meeting of health service personnel in Maputo.[5] In his speech he condemned indiscipline, slovenliness, and lack of hygiene in the medical sector, with the emphasis clearly upon the first word, "indiscipline." His apparent solution: a reinforcement of the hierarchical structure of the hospital in order to create a clear line of command and a clear delineation of responsibilities. Even the too promiscuous use of the word "comrade" was banned as having become an excuse for lack of order and efficiency, exemplifying "petty-bourgeois egalitarianism, populism, and ultra-leftism." Indeed, the President took this attack on populism and the evasion of the necessary division of labor and responsibility to the point of querying, by way of illustration, whether the wife of a minister should be expected to share the same hospital ward as the wife of a cook! As a first approach by

President Machel to a real problem there were things in this speech which might be questioned, not least this last point. Certainly one could see what the President was driving at; in some ways it was a harking back to a key feature of the liberated areas, the model of military command. But there was also some risk here that a legitimate concern with increased efficiency might lapse into technocratic and bureaucratic solutions.

There was a risk, too, that this initiative might not merely reinforce bureaucratic hierarchization in some narrowly institutional sense but might also help to consolidate those at the top of the hierarchy into a quasi-class. Of course Mozambicans have been preoccupied with this possibility, as noted in our introductory chapter when we cited an extended statement, circa 1976, by Samora Machel regarding precisely this danger; moreover, further evidence of this concern on FRELIMO's part was cited in Chapter 1. It is also true that some outside observers have expressed parallel concerns in a rather exaggerated manner on the basis of their extremely abstract overviews of the Mozambican situation and in apparent ignorance of FRELIMO's active efforts to deal with the dangers involved.[6] But those Angolans who warned recently of an authoritarian bureaucracy in their own country "becoming a privileged counter-revolutionary class, and conscious of the fact" have something important to say to Mozambicans, as they also do when they underscore the resultant "danger of falling, in the best of cases into a state bureaucracy, and in the worst, a capitalist type society, with an 'intermezzo' of 'African socialism.' "[7] It is significant, therefore, that Machel continued the statement just alluded to with some further thoughts on how to avoid any such denouement, harking back as he did so to the experience of the liberated areas:

> It's a question of completely modifying existing conceptions and this implies: first, recruiting the civil service by and large from among the working class and the peasantry; secondly, instilling in workers in the civil service the attitude of serving the labouring classes; thirdly, collectivizing at all levels the methods of administration; fourthly, democratizing executive structures at all levels through assemblies elected democratically by the labouring classes; and, fifthly, introducing our revolutionary legislation, thereby abolishing colonial-bourgeois legislation which only services the interests of capitalism. It's here that we will be able to link up with our previous experience in the liberated zones, although it is this theme which seems to worry many of our friends. Why do we talk so much about the liberated areas? It is because we are the products of those liberated areas. We created the liberated areas and they in turn produced us. Thus when we speak of extrapolating into the present the experience of the liberated areas, we can do so precisely because it was in those areas that we had

already established the embryo of the kind of state apparatus which would serve our purposes, in line with the five norms which we have just mentioned.

One important aspect of this concerns the state enterprises. . . . It is important to ensure that the working class exercises power not only within the state apparatus but also in the organization of the operation of state enterprises, and that it participates actively in the organization and control of other enterprises as well. There's a lack of trained cadres, of forged cadres. Struggle was a forge for us and . . . as in the armed struggle the forge for us today is the class struggle. . . . At present we still talk about the situation in the liberated zones and how the exploiters appeared [from within our ranks], of the struggle in which we engaged to block them from seizing power. And many did not understand this process, even our friends. How was it possible to unleash this process: to carry on the armed struggle and, at the same time, the class struggle against the new exploiters?[8]

We have examined the process to which Machel refers—the blending of national liberation struggle and social revolution—in Chapter 1. But we must say something more about the possible ways in which lessons from that phase were now to be transferred onto new terrain. How was the present struggle for economic development to be blended with the class struggle against a second wave of "new exploiters" which the leadership saw stalking the Mozambican revolution in the post-independence period? For it soon became apparent that the hospital speech was merely the opening shot in what became, in the new year, a full-scale "Political and Organizational Offensive." On January 17, 1980, in an important speech in Beira, the President rounded on the very hierarchy which he had apparently defended in the hospital speech, pointing out the extent to which many government institutions had been turned against the interests of the people by those Mozambicans who had come to occupy positions of authority. Back in Maputo he made a dramatic round of surprise visits to state enterprises and facilities, uncovering concrete evidence of incompetence, corruption, and the like. The underlying motifs of the President's crusade, and the need to move beyond the President's personal intervention, were eventually summarized in a speech to a huge rally in Maputo:

On September 25, 1964, we declared war on the foreign enemy—Portuguese colonialism. Here today, March 18, 1980, we declare war on the internal enemy. . . . It is a battle in the class struggle . . . to open and consolidate the wide road to socialism. . . . Our state is a workers' and peasants' state. It is not a state of the useless, the lazy and the reactionary.[9]

As he added in response to a query from the crowd on another occasion: "We placed those who studied in charge to use their knowledge for your [the people's] good. But some of them are using it against you."[10]

The speech of March 18 was important, yet it pointed in two different directions, directions which were potentially compatible but not automatically so. One lay in its emphasis on "iron discipline" and reiteration of a theme related to that of the hospital speech: the central importance of "management," of the "concentration of power," of the clarification of responsibility. As noted, this was certainly understandable enough at one level. Yet where were the Production Councils, pushing from below to guarantee the commitment to revolutionary practices by administrative and political "responsibles"? And where were the party cells in facilitating such a push from below? True, Machel did speak forcefully of the need to revitalize this other term of the leadership–mass action dialectic:

> The people have the task of participating in this cleaning up. The people are once more the filter, as in the elections for the People's Assemblies, as in the structuring of the Party. The people must denounce infiltrators, point out the undisciplined, unmask the incompetent, attack the arrogant, and drive out the villains. We will create conditions for the people to take part in this task.

But the instruments were to be newly created Offices of Control and Discipline headed by the minister in each ministry—to take initiatives and to receive complaints directly from citizens—and special brigades designed to launch the same processes in the provincial governments. However important such initiatives might be, these measures indicated that established institutions of popular control had not been doing the job they were established to do.

Of course, the speech did suggest one specific opening for revitalization of established political structures in order to underwrite the offensive: the fresh round of elections for the People's Assemblies—at district, locality, and city level—already in prospect for the following months of 1980. As the President said:

> Let us make the elections a time for giving account, a time for the engagement of our deputies, an offensive in organization, and an offensive against irresponsibility, routine and disorganization.

And this is what did begin to happen, to a considerable extent, as preliminary meetings were held in the localities to review the work, since 1977, both of the assemblies themselves and of the individual representatives to them. Then, in a second round of meetings, elections were held. Moreover, as the new assemblies met, it was clear that they would now have rather clearer guidelines as to their duties and responsibilities, to facilitate their role in keeping the state apparatus under scrutiny; this was also a task with which the deputies to the National Assembly charged themselves at the meeting of the latter body in July. Such developments carried the promise of the further strengthening of the role of these institutions.

Even more significantly, however, the offensive was also to be carried in the direction of the party itself. At the beginning of April, in the immediate aftermath of the President's speech, Marcelino dos Santos and Jorge Rebelo were relieved of their ministerial assignments in order to concentrate exclusively on their party responsibilities (in "economic policy" and "ideological work" respectively). What was intended by this and other moves was a *strengthening* of the party and a *repoliticization* of the development process. This reflected, on the one hand, a growing feeling that the line between party and state had become too blurred, that, in allowing itself to be absorbed into the state, the party had begun to cede far too much of its vocation as guardian of the ideological integrity of the bureaucratic stratum and guarantor of the long-term goals of the revolution.* As we shall see, further self-criticism along these lines was to surface again at FRELIMO's Fourth Congress.

But what, on the other hand, of "repoliticization"? Almost immediately a campaign was launched to breathe new life into the party cells "so that the party can exercise its leading role in the state apparatus and business enterprises." As Jorge Rebelo stated in a Maputo speech to party cell secretaries, "During the nationwide political and organizational offensive . . . it had been observed that there had been a decrease in dynamic action by the party structures." What was needed was "greater awareness of the people's

---

*A dramatic early statement of the problem was made by Oscar Monteiro, then Minister of State in the President's Office, in opening the First National Conference on the State Apparatus in October 1976: "In his message to the nation at the swearing in of the Transitional Government, Comrade President Samora defined it as the first government which represented the mass of the people, and as the executive arm of FRELIMO. He attributed the following tasks to it: to decolonize structures and mentalities; to extend people's democratic power to the whole country; to function in close liaison with the workers. We can see now that instead of communicating our experience to the entire country, instead of impressing upon the state apparatus throughout Mozambique the popular and revolutionary character that it had assumed in the liberated areas, we were swamped by the administrative machinery left behind by colonialism. Instead of giving direction, we were controlled and directed." ("The State Apparatus of Civil Servants," conference speech by José Oscar Monteiro, in *Principles of Revolutionary Justice: The Constitution and other documents on Law and State from the People's Republic of Mozambique* [London, 1979].)

problems" and greater efforts "to fight against bureaucracy at all
levels," and Rebelo promised much better backup from provincial
and national bodies to enable grass-roots party organs to do this
work.[11]

However, Rebelo's remarks were merely a prelude to what was to
come at the meeting of FRELIMO's Central Committee in July
1980. Here the theme was self-criticism by the leadership, and it
cut quite deeply. In the words of the final resolution from that
meeting:

> The Central Committee criticizes itself for neglecting to pay due at-
> tention to strengthening party machinery. The Central Committee
> paid more attention to the state machinery than to the party ma-
> chinery.
>
> It was an incorrect attitude because it is by strengthening the party
> machinery and the party's leading role that the task of destroying the
> old state machinery and building a new socialist state can be carried
> out. . . . This error meant that the leading structures of the party, both
> at central and local level, were not filled, that party work was carried
> out as a secondary task and that the party did not concentrate on the
> principal task, the economic battle. Consequently the work of the
> party cells was weakened, and militants frequently remained without
> tasks.[12]

This was now to be rectified and the party reinforced in a number
of ways to provide more effective control over the state machinery;
the party would lead the state in a very concrete manner, critiquing
its inadequacies while also ensuring, from "outside" as it were, that
the drive toward Mozambique's long-term socialist development
goals was not preempted by a bureaucratic petty bourgeoisie.

The concrete proposals which were made to achieve this end
were familiar ones, but important nonetheless. The party was now
to be strengthened in terms of the cadres available to it, of cadre
training (literacy, political education, and the like), and of a clearer
definition of cadre responsibilities. Without this, the revitalization
of party supremacy vis-à-vis the state would be impossible. But
building up the party apparatus was important for another reason
as well: the Central Committee affirmed the importance of the
offensive in strengthening "the unity between the party and the
people," and this too had to be consolidated.

With this we come to the final link in the chain of the Political
and Organizational Offensive. For one of the deepest currents
within FRELIMO at the time of this Central Committee meeting
was a feeling that the movement risked forgetting some of the most
important lessons learned in the liberated areas (some of those
referred to by Samora Machel, as cited above, for example), in

particular the continuing need "to learn from the people." Moreover, it was impossible to assume that the petty bourgeoisie would not attempt to penetrate the party itself, thus creating the danger of bureaucratization and pursuit of personal self-aggrandizement there, too. In consequence, one clear instruction in the Central Committee resolutions was to intensify the program of building party cells in the various workplaces and localities while also drawing in new members and generally revivifying those cells already in place. And, with such cells, to intensify "the class struggle" by further reinforcing the "class consciousness" and subsequent activism of the popular classes themselves through the organizational mechanisms—the "democratic mass organizations"—available to them. What was being stressed here, in short, was the "mass action" pendant to the emphasis upon "leadership" and "discipline" with which the offensive had first been launched.

It was precisely this dialectic between leadership and mass action which continued to be at the core of Mozambican politics up to the very moment of FRELIMO's Fourth Congress. Up to the Congress—and beyond. On one important front, however, a further specification of the Political and Organizational Offensive was put on the agenda more or less immediately. Thus, the "Legality Offensive" was announced in a strong, and quite concrete, speech by the President on November 5, 1981, its target being abuses of power by the military, security forces, and police.[13] This offensive was to involve strenuous efforts within these various structures to put their houses in order, but also the further opening up of political channels from below to facilitate popular criticism and control (including the creation of specially constituted "work teams" within the People's Assemblies to deal with the issue, for example). As with the Political and Organizational Offensive itself, these intentions would be easier to announce in principle than to realize in practice. Yet the intention was a serious one: a "law and order" campaign directed not at the populace but at ensuring that the law enforcement agencies themselves were keeping to the straight and narrow.

The year 1982 saw other important political events exemplifying the attempt to revitalize the development process, events which, in retrospect, clearly set the tone for the Fourth Congress to follow. When FRELIMO came to power in 1974–1975 it had publicly identified those Mozambicans who had collaborated most actively with the Portuguese colonialists, especially during the final years of the war. Of course, those involved in the most heinous crimes tended to flee, though some were captured and imprisoned. The rest, labeled *comprometidos,* were in effect placed on a kind of political probation (their pictures posted in their workplaces for all to see, for example, and some record kept of their comportment). In May 1982, that period of probation came to an end and a televised meeting, stretching over a period of some days, was held between these *comprometidos* and Samora Machel. It was an extraordinary event, becoming, as the former discussed frankly their own pasts and their changing sentiments in the period since independence, a moving public reflection on the historical reality and meaning of colonial domination. It was also a process which culminated in the pardon of almost all of those involved and their reincorporation into the mainstream of society. In this way FRELIMO was clearly reaching out to embrace the full diversity of Mozambican society, an effort which also led to its meeting, toward the end of the year, with representatives of all the major religious denominations in the country. The atmosphere was one of genuine give and take. Though still concerned about the institutional role of the Catholic Church, a role which had been so important within the armory of colonial domination and which encouraged a certain arrogance on the part of a few Catholic representatives even in the meeting itself, the basic message was one of openness on the part of the regime to freedom in the spiritual realm.

Perhaps the most significant of such meetings, however, was the one held in Beira in June, a reunion of all those who had fought in the liberation struggle. Here, as the history and lessons of that period were once more reviewed, the *antigos combatentes* had a range of sharp criticisms to make regarding not only errors of economic planning but the breakdown of many of the links binding party to people since independence; many also criticized what they felt to be their own marginalization in the ongoing revolutionary process. Such criticisms were taken seriously, as we shall see, but it becomes important here to put them in the context of South Africa's continuing war against Mozambique. For throughout this period the war had a role to play in sharpening FRELIMO's awareness of the challenge which confronted it in the political sphere. Some further background regarding that war may therefore be in order. Direct attacks by South Africa have had a role to play here but, as noted in our introduction, most important has been the Mozambique National Resistance (MNR).[14] First created by the Rhodesians, this was given a fresh lease on life by the South Africans in 1980–1981 and continues to be the latter's cat's-paw, effective primarily because of the training, provisioning, and logistical support South Africa provides. Indeed, what is particularly striking is how little the MNR's activities have been grounded in anything like a strategy of mobilizing political support.

Its primary goal has been destruction, the destruction of as much as possible of the infrastructure of national development in Mozambique, thus making it as difficult as possible for Mozambique to exemplify—on the borders of apartheid South Africa—the full promise of a socialist future for the region. (Not coincidentally, this also constitutes an upping of the ante for any Mozambican support of the African National Congress of South Africa, one more example of South Africa seeking to export its own domestic contradictions into the region. For this and other reasons South Africa may have much less interest in "winning" the war—and then confronting the difficult problem of restabilizing a defeated Mozambique along lines more favorable to itself—than merely keeping Mozambique as much off balance as possible.) Moreover, the attack on such infrastructure (and in particular on transportation and communication links) is also an attack on the Southern African Development Coordination Conference (SADCC), i.e. on the attempt by the black-majority-ruled states of the region which SADCC represents to establish an alternative economic network outside the orbit of South Africa's historically established regional economic hegemony.

To this theme we will return. More immediately important here are not merely the obvious economic costs to Mozambican development activities but also the stark human costs of MNR destructiveness. As stated, the MNR has made little effort to ground its counterrevolutionary version of "guerrilla warfare" in a popular base. There have been occasional rhetorical bursts of anticommunism and some attempt to mobilize ethnic resentments. But the basic tactic is the intimidation of local populations, often carried out with almost unimaginable bestiality, and the forced seizure of what little the peasants do have in order to sustain the *bandidos* themselves. Perhaps the only positive aspect of this is what it tells us about FRELIMO's continuing legitimacy: the MNR apparently sees little point in challenging it head-on in political terms. We shall argue that FRELIMO's inability to deliver on much of the economic promise of independence and socialism has indeed eclipsed some of the popular enthusiasm which accompanied it into power. However, despite its difficulties, FRELIMO's government has been anything but a venal one; FRELIMO retains a substantial popular base upon which to build, something which the MNR knows perfectly well.

FRELIMO knows this, too, and fortunately, recent developments in its military strategy have come to reflect, more effectively, such awareness. The MNR's success to date in disrupting Mozambique springs most directly, as we have said, from South Africa's very strong support for it. Yet FRELIMO's own military policies did give some opening to the MNR. Thus, with independence, FRELIMO shifted too readily from its own distinctive, popularly based guerrilla warfare model to the model of a more "modern" standing army. Partly this reflected the movement's hunch that the main threat to a free Mozambique lay in a direct invasion by Rhodesia or South Africa, not in some bastard version of guerrilla war. This shift may also have reflected an initial temptation, perceptible across the board in post-liberation Mozambican policies, to look to modern, high-tech, large-scale solutions to development challenges of all kinds. On a slightly different tack, it might also be suggested that FRELIMO—no doubt understandably—let down its guard a little too far after the defeat of the Rhodesians in 1980, too eagerly seizing upon the first hint of peace the country had known in almost twenty years.

Yet FRELIMO did begin to bounce back, part of the reason for its resilience having been, as hinted above, its recovery of the secret of its original success—the politicization and popularization of the armed struggle. In the past two years the military structure has been decentralized to a greater degree, and new, more flexible regional armies have emerged with closer links to provincial political structures. And not just to the provincial hierarchy but to the people themselves. Interestingly, a number of those *combatentes* who had spoken up in Beira were brought back into the military, carrying with them, as was expected, the old methodology of popular war which had once been so effective. Soon a program of organizing and arming local militias had begun to surface as an effective complement to the reorganization of the armed forces themselves. In a number of provinces the MNR's ability to move up from small marauding bands to ever more dangerous concentrations of troops was cut back and some of the enemy's effectiveness thus reduced.

Despite these advances Mozambique has continued to pay the price of South Africa's war, up to and even after the signing of the Nkomati Accord in early 1984. The apartheid state has been a ruthless antagonist and the MNR still exacts a heavy toll. There are also negatives enough in the economic situation. Interestingly, however, the very depth of the economic crisis in which FRELIMO finds itself has—like the military crisis—helped to reinforce an awareness of the necessity to return to some of the first principles developed during the armed struggle. In the next section we will explore in more detail the kind of repopularization of economic strategy that has paralleled the repopularization of the ongoing armed struggle (although we will also have to assess some of the ambiguities that arise from the simultaneous reemphasis upon privatization and the more extended use of the market mechanism). It can be noted, however, that the most important arena for such economic developments was 1983's Fourth Congress, mentioned several times above but to a discussion of which we can now turn. For in that Congress the economic and political threads of the Mozambican revolution came together in a tight weave and between them clearly defined the challenges that now confronted the revolution. In the remainder of this section we shall focus primarily on the political implications of the Congress.

In fact, the Congress had been seen from quite an early date as providing, in and of itself, a focus for the reinvigoration of the political process, especially at the grass-roots level. Abstract insistence upon increased "mobilization" was correctly seen as being counterproductive; mobilization would have to have real content. And that content was, at least in part, to be supplied by the undertaking of a "broad national debate," stretching down to the very base of the party and culminating in the Fourth Congress itself. This process had begun in March 1982 with a hitherto unprecedented event, the calling together of the first National Conference of the Party, an assembly of party members from across the country charged with elaborating the ways in which to give the Fourth Congress the desired resonance. In particular, a set of major themes was identified—several of which, especially those dealing with economic strategies, were of very special significance—and these in turn led to the elaboration by the party leadership of a set of eight "Draft Theses" designed to focus and to anchor the intended nationwide debate.

> Preparation of our party's Fourth Congress was a process that aimed to maintain, in form and content, the popular, democratic tradition that we have followed since the armed struggle for national liberation . . . [We] sought to set in motion a process that would involve the entire Mozambican people, from the Rovuma to the Maputo, in the course of which every militant and every citizen would be encouraged to express freely his ideas, his concerns, his criticisms—in a word, his concept of our current difficulties and the way to overcome them. The aim was in this way to make the preparatory phase of the Congress one of broad national debate on our current situation, the problems we encounter, the priorities before us. It was hoped through this process to develop and deepen democracy within the Party and throughout Mozambican society as a whole.[15]

A range of evidence suggests this to have been a successful exercise, even though its impact necessarily varied from area to area. It had clear implications for the political structures themselves: "it was impossible in fact to prepare the Congress properly while there was the situation that then obtained of total or partial stagnation of many party cells. The revitalization of the cells had, therefore, high priority and importance in preparing for the Congress." But in much of the country the exercise also had the effect of facilitating considerable popular input into the decision-making process. Indeed, the impact may have gone beyond what was foreseen by the drafters of the Theses. Although the Theses contained much of importance regarding political, economic, and international matters, the generality of their formulation rendered some of the content rather bland. Debates at the grass-roots level, whether within party cells or in the more broadly based mass meetings called to discuss the Theses, were often far from bland, however. With the Theses as a jumping-off place, sharp criticism of established practices surfaced in many of these meetings, thereby communicating upwards popular demands (especially from the rural areas) for more effective and immediately visible solutions to the country's economic problems. There can be no doubt that these demands oriented the perceptions of the Congress delegations elected from the provinces. They also doubtless had a crucial impact on the tone and content of the key document of that Congress, the *Central Committee Report*.

Certainly, this "return to the grass-roots" helped underwrite the emphasis upon intra-Mozambican class struggle which came centrally to preoccupy the Congress. One "class enemy" was those black marketeers who had begun to stalk the Mozambican economy in recent years. In the considerable public education effort which has gone into mobilization for the ongoing war, they have been identified as the "internal enemy," the domestic counterpart of the "external enemy," those "armed bandits" who are South Africa's proxies. True, the term "internal enemy" too uncritically lumped together those with the most marginal involvements in illicit marketing (those for whom such activity was primarily a "survival strategy" in the context of severe economic crisis and collapse of the formal network of commercialization) and others who were much more dangerous large-scale operators. Nonetheless, the class categorization of the latter elements as a bourgeoisie-in-the-making, working the marketplace against the grain of Mozambique's socialist intentions, was usefully made:

> The internal bourgeoisie now has more economic power than it held immediately after independence. It has infiltrated the trade circuits and the state apparatus. Hence the blackmarket is not essentially an effect of economic difficulties and low production. As comments in

the study of the Theses indicated, it is above all the action of the class enemy.[16]*

Perhaps even more striking was the linking of this group, analytically, to a second set of "aspirants to the bourgeoisie" (a term introduced by the President in an important speech of 1982 and echoed in the central Fourth Congress documents). The reference to the "state apparatus" in the quotation in the preceding paragraph is the tipoff here, for the danger of "bureaucratization" was specifically linked to a process of class formation. The Congress documents thus reflected the fact that, as both leadership and populace cast a critical eye on the economic policy options pursued since independence, a pattern began to emerge. If too much had been made of "high-tech" solutions and big projects at the expense of projects scaled down to local capabilities and peasant requirements, if decision-making had been allowed to become too highly centralized, these things were not to be interpreted as mere errors in development strategy:

> Our country has a social stratum that enjoys levels of consumption unavailable to the overwhelming majority of the people. From the social point of view, it consists chiefly of citizens originating from the social strata that were already privileged in the colonial period. Politically, this social stratum is opportunist, elitist, unscientific and hopeful of transforming itself into an authentic bourgeoisie. All it admires in the bourgeoisie is its corrupt consumerist nature.
>
> From the cultural standpoint, aspirants to the bourgeoisie are alienated and estranged. They are unaware, or pretend to be unaware, of the value of Mozambican culture and they spurn the people's wisdom and knowledge. These individuals are slaves to everything that comes from Europe, and particularly from the West. *For this reason, they try to distort the class character of our revolution by transforming it into a technocratic process through which they can control power.*
>
> This social stratum actively opposes any measures that aim at simplifying organization and methods, democratizing leadership or increasing the workers' share in planning and controlling production. Because of their book-learning, aspirants to the bourgeoisie despise

---

*As we shall see in the following section on the economic sphere, when discussing the situation of severe economic crisis in Mozambique in the 1980s this kind of formulation, presenting the problem of the blackmarket in strictly class terms, has its weak as well as its strong side. In stressing the point that the blackmarket is "not essentially an effect of economic difficulties," it runs the risk of merely reducing the problem, undialectically, to a resultant of "the action of the class enemy—" "the internal bourgeoisie." To which formulation the response must be: yes . . . and no. Fortunately, other Mozambican theorizations of the problem of the blackmarket tend to be more balanced and nuanced than this.

solutions from the people. They are unable to learn from the people. So they reject the experience of the liberated areas. They reject the small-scale projects that require the intelligence, sensitivity and understanding of the people and prefer the projects that come ready made from abroad.

The characteristics of aspirants to the bourgeoisie make this social stratum vulnerable to the insidious action of the enemy. Strict class vigilance must be exercised over these individuals.[17]

One of the most dramatic moments in the Congress itself occurred precisely around this kind of definition of the ongoing class struggle in Mozambique. One ex-combatant, now managing a sugar estate in Sofala Province, concluded a formal address on the efforts his estate had made in combatting the MNR. He then went on more informally to note that he, like many others, well remembered the struggle which had taken place against the "class enemy" within FRELIMO during the days of armed struggle. But now he feared the possibility that that enemy was seizing power once again, *within* the structures of FRELIMO and the state! Such a bombshell was apparently unexpected but it was seized upon immediately by Machel, who reflected on the possible corrupting influences of power and "comfort" on the movement and on the danger of bureaucratization which had begun to carry the movement away from its base. Indeed, in the work of the Congress, and in various initiatives which followed hard on its heels, reorganization of the state apparatus and decentralization of decision-making (including the posting of many of the "experts" themselves to rural locales) became a central theme. Moreover, when the Congress selected the new party Central Committee which was to serve until the next Congress, something of a sea-change was apparent. Expanded in numbers from fifty-four members to one hundred twenty-eight, it was now to include a far higher proportion of workers, peasants, and *antigos combatentes* drawn from all over the country than had the much more technocratically oriented Central Committee chosen at the Third Congress in 1977.

There are in these aspects of the Congress—and also in the economic-policy content of the Congress's proposals which we will examine in the next section—indications that the democratic pull of FRELIMO's revolutionary tradition remains very much alive and that popular power is sufficiently institutionalized to have real significance. In addition, the revolutionary process is, at its best, permeated by an intangible atmosphere of real contact between leadership and mass which is difficult to capture in words but quite evident to any who have lived on the spot. Perhaps this aspect of things is best exemplified in the populist style of the President himself, who seems, in an almost uncanny way, to link popular preoccupations to government decision-making. Indeed, the commitment of the President, and of the leadership team which emerged with him out of the armed struggle, to popularly grounded socialist policies remains very strong. And it would be naive to underestimate the importance of this fact for guaranteeing the present integrity of Mozambique's development project. This is not to fall into some kind of fetishization of "wise leaders," a highly suspect basis for socialist transition in the long run; it is merely to underscore a factor of considerable weight in the Mozambican equation at the present moment.

In the meantime, the pursuit of new ways to institutionalize a positive dialectic between this leadership and mass action continues, the most recent step, presaged in the Congress and acted upon before the end of 1983, being the transformation of the Production Councils into full-fledged trade unions. This was to involve the strengthening of the former and their integration into a new nationwide network. In the formulations put forward there was certainly an emphasis upon the role these unions should play in "the battle against negligence, apathy, theft, corruption and bureaucracy" in the economic sphere, and an emphasis, too, upon the democratization of these unions' own internal structures. Of course, as with other "mass organizations," the role they would play was to be firmly situated within the overall framework of party guidance. Yet perhaps less was heard than might have been expected about the possible role of the unions as instruments of working-class control over potentially emergent "aspirants to the bourgeoisie." Instead, the need to fight against the danger of "populism" and of acting along "Western lines" (e.g., by pressing wage claims) was strongly emphasized by the President in a key speech to the founding convention of the unions in October 1983: "Given the class nature of our party and our state, the socialist trade unions are not an instrument of confrontation. Their role lies in the realization of the fundamental interests of the worker-peasant alliance, pressing for the correct application of party policy." In this regard the emphasis would have to be upon "raising the technical and scientific capacity of the workers" and upon their "organization and work discipline" in the interests of development.[18]

There are grounds for unease with these formulations—and grounds for accepting their logic. They encapsulate, in fact, some of the most searing contradictions of socialist transition under Mozambique-like conditions. Opinions will differ as to how best to seek to resolve such contradictions in an effective and ongoing manner. Barry Munslow, alluding to Mozambique, has recently written forcefully on this issue, responding to Trotskyist writers who criticize (among other aspects of "third world socialisms") the "political movement for encouraging discipline and imposing production norms on the working class." He suggests that such criticism puts the movement in a "no-win situation":

> Our rejoinder would be that running an economy without skilled manpower, with an illiterate working class lacking experience of trade-union struggles and without a developed class consciousness, with an inherited dependence on the world market, and faced with armed intervention by external forces ready to take advantage of economic collapse, all mean that the measures being condemned are in fact indispensable.
>
> The class-conscious workers prior to a revolutionary takeover are the ones who lead the strikes, the everyday mass resistance in form of go-slows, etc. After the takeover, the class-conscious worker is the one who is actively involved in the reorganization of new social production relations and in increasing productivity above set targets.[19]

In fact, given the fragmented nature of the working class and its lack of class and democratic consciousness, "The aim of the vanguard party, by controlling the state, is to create not only the conditions for the development of class consciousness but also to create the classes necessary for effective socialist development. A working class must be built up as a conscious strategy to provide an essential material foundation for the transition to socialism." Munslow would no doubt see the new trade union structure in Mozambique in precisely this positive light.

Munslow's is a good answer, one that some might feel tempted to apply even more confidently to the peasant sector. There, it could be argued, the historical legacy of "traditionalism" and "obscurantism," the economic reality of "individualism," the extremely low level of literacy and numeracy, and the absence of an historical experience of self-organization and democratic assertion undermine even more effectively the possibility of any very spontaneous class action from below in the short and medium run. However we must also query the extent to which it is an adequate answer. Doesn't it, in the industrial sphere, slide a bit too easily into the old "transmission belt" theory of trade unions under socialism, blurring, in the process, the question of the *two-way flow* of power and control which might be thought essential to a socialist transition? Isn't it, more generally, just a bit too comfortable a formulation for leaders to adopt, quite possibly serving as a mere rationalization to further persuade them of their own indispensability? Before pursuing such questions further, however, we should note in passing two very concrete steps taken in Mozambique in recent years that have also stirred up controversy.

One of these, a source of considerable consternation—at least in Western support circles—has been the reintroduction of both capital and corporate punishment. True, these innovations have been introduced against the backdrop of an ongoing, even quite dramatic, attempt to democratize the judicial system by means of a novel system of people's tribunals. Nonetheless, such measures have seemed to many to stand in stark contrast to FRELIMO's historic emphasis upon re-education rather than retribution in the penal sphere. These moves have been defended, in part, in populist terms, the argument being that the populace itself has demanded that justice be seen to be done much more visibly, not only vis-à-vis common criminals but, even more importantly, vis-à-vis the most bloodthirsty of the captured *bandidos* and the black-marketeers. At the same time some leaders have suggested that such measures are temporary, and indeed it is hard not to see them as representing, if not a growing feeling of desperation, at least a hardening of approach which springs from the reality of siege and the desperate difficulties which have appeared in the economic sphere.

FRELIMO has also taken a rather hard line in implementing another set of policies pursued in the immediate wake of the Fourth Congress: "Operação Produção." This has involved the forced removal from the cities of large numbers of unemployed to the rural areas, most often to the underpopulated areas in the north. Certainly urban overcrowding, especially in the capital of Maputo, has been a major problem, exacerbated by the economic difficulties, drought, and enemy attack in the countryside. And in principle these unemployed are being plugged into ongoing rural development projects in their transfer areas which may ultimately carry the promise of a better life for them. Moreover, it seems clear that the original "invasion" of Maputo was much more the symptom than the cause of structural problems in the economy. Any critical evaluation of "Operação Produção" must therefore be qualified by the fact that the question of more long-term solutions to such structural questions had been addressed quite centrally at the Fourth Congress only a few weeks earlier. Still, it is the case that the administration of this undertaking left much to be desired (even though some of the initial arbitrariness and insensitivity of its application was soon to be corrected through the self-criticism which emerged during the campaign). For many observers, as well, the campaign had the air of a mere "gut-response" to a situation of crisis, serving in this way to underscore the difficult nature of the period through which Mozambique was then passing.

We can conclude this section by viewing the political situation and the terrain of class struggle in Mozambique from a broader perspective, referring back in so doing to some of the preoccupations that were sounded in our introduction, preoccupations that have also pushed their way to the surface in the present chapter. Despite what has been said about the ongoing effort to strike an effective balance between leadership and mass action within the Mozambican revolutionary process, it would be wise not to romanticize the degree of accomplishment in this sphere. There can be little doubt, for example, that the leadership term in this equation is still very much the more weighty. This is an imbalance which, as we have seen, Munslow and others argue to be a legitimate one. Moreover, it is the case that, given the conditions of severe economic distortion and backwardness, underdeveloped popular-class consciousness, fragile unity, and vicious external attack, some recent criticisms of Mozambique have sounded much too shrill, insensitive to the complexities of the situation there, at best churlish, at worst hopelessly academic. They are all the more likely to appear so when one takes serious note of the positive political developments that we have elaborated on in the preceding pages.

Yet, as suggested, there are also certain very real problems with what has transpired in Mozambique politically. The words of Rosa Luxemburg, quoted in our introduction, must continue to haunt any attempted transition to socialism, including that in Mozambique. In much the same spirit Ralph Miliband has invoked the "visionary" emphasis upon the radical democratization of the transition process to be found in Lenin's *The State and Revolution* as an "overestimation" which may be, nonetheless, "the necessary condition for the transcendence of the grey and bureaucratic 'practicality' which has so deeply infected the socialist experience in the last half-century,"[20] while Norman Geras has recently questioned whether the existence of at least one opposition party is not a necessary precondition for a successful transition.[21] One need not go so far, perhaps. Advocating the creation of an "official opposition" in Mozambique, even if it appeared to be a "good idea" in terms of the "health of the revolution," would be a fairly arbitrary and ahistorical undertaking. Perhaps a stronger case could be made, however, for a greater measure of autonomy for organizations of workers, of women, of peasants and the like to develop and press their own demands. Nor can even the most sympathetic observers be entirely complacent about the kind of nervous uniformity that sometimes characterizes the state-controlled media in Mozambique; in this sphere one suspects that some further pluralism of opinion would have its benefits.

Nor is this all. Anyone who seeks to evaluate such matters in Mozambique must also be alert to the possibility that bad reasons can come to complement good ones in supporting tendencies to overcentralization of power. There are those who argue, for example, that even if such emphases as found expression in the 1979 hospital speech (cited above) did have some justification, they have had the negative effect, in certain spheres, of privileging hierarchy at the expense of the "people's power" which was carried over from the liberated areas. In this regard, a comparison is often made with an earlier presidential "hospital speech," that of 1976, which gave pride of place to "hospital ward councils" as guaranteeing control from below. Any snapping of the tension between leadership and mass action in such spheres could well prove to be in the *class* interests of the "qualified" and the relatively privileged, thus suppressing those qualms about the possible logic of bureaucratization which the Fourth Congress sought to bring into focus. There is also a second, somewhat different, reason to scrutinize carefully any signs of apparent authoritarian "closure" of the Mozambican political system, one reflecting a tendency only superficially more "progressive" than that just mentioned. Thus, there exists the possibility (we shall discuss this in more detail later in this chapter) that one wing of the left leadership of FRELIMO might present its commitment to popularly oriented and/or developmentalist policies as legitimating quasi-Stalinist methods. More than an abstract possibility, in fact: to take one example, there is evidence that in some Mozambican districts "rural mobilization" has occasionally degenerated into a practice of enforced villagization. Following further along such a route would be another way in which the Mozambican revolution might lose its way.

Such factors are important and developments in Mozambique must be interrogated with them front and center. Yet interpretations that explore things in terms simply of these factors—the consolidation of a parasitic state class, the burgeoning of neo-Stalinism—oversimplify some of the country's most profound complexities. Ironically, the good reasons have probably outweighed the bad for the hyper-centralization of the revolutionary process in Mozambique. Nor have the results of this been entirely negative. As noted above, even if the strength, the coherence, and the commitment of the leadership team forged during the armed struggle does not provide the sole explanation for the positive direction

Mozambique has taken, it has nonetheless had a disproportionate impact in this regard. Moreover, the confidence which many observers still feel compelled to vest in the strength of that team is perhaps the main reason such observers have not despaired of Mozambique's revolutionary process in the present very difficult period. Still, it cannot be argued that even such an exemplary leadership has been entirely successful in striking the proper balance between leadership and mass action—despite the efforts to do so noted in the present chapter. Indeed, at the risk of overstating the case, one might argue that the revolution has become weaker rather than stronger at the base in the years since independence. FRELIMO has, quite simply, failed to institutionalize "people's power" to anything like the degree which its experience and its ideology might suggest to have been its goal.

As Munslow has warned us, it would be unwise to overestimate the extent to which workers and peasants have been prepared spontaneously to deepen the democratization of the revolution, to seize power "on their own behalf" and exercise it effectively. If there is criticism to be made regarding the leadership FRELIMO has provided in the political sphere, it may be less a criticism of its stifling of popular action than of its failing to find the means to stimulate it, of failing to find the means to *empower* the people effectively. But why has it proven difficult to transplant the methods which seemed so effective in resolving contradictions between leadership and mass action in the war period to the post-independence terrain? Put simply, the politics of national liberation appear in retrospect to have been far more straightforward than those of the current phase. There were contradictions then, as we have seen, but the goals were nonetheless clearer, the means more straightforward, the scale smaller, and the pace of the expansion of that scale more comfortably under FRELIMO control. After independence the scale became infinitely vaster, the stratum of middle-level cadres too thin on the ground and too ill-trained, the challenges—not least South Africa's ongoing war—literally overwhelming in their scope and variety. We shall add to what has already been said above in this regard when we explore, in the following section, the causes and character of the economic crisis in which Mozambique has found itself and its profoundly demobilizing impact. Not surprisingly, even the most solid of senior leaders have been reduced under such circumstances to fire-fighting a seemingly endless series of emergencies rather than finding time to concentrate on the slow, patient, ongoing political work which would serve to consolidate a firmer political basis for the revolution.

The result? The leadership's "correct line" on "popular power" has not always given rise to vibrant political life at the base. Perhaps, too, we should add—albeit much more tentatively—one further consideration: a query regarding the degree of "correctness" of the line itself. Has FRELIMO's own project been sufficiently clear in this sphere? True, as we have seen, it has often reiterated the premise that "the vanguard party leads the working masses, but cannot substitute itself for them, and neither can it act instead of the working masses. It is the people and the people alone who build history."* But has the party taken sufficiently to heart dos Santos' dictum, cited in the introduction, regarding the possible benefits that would flow from further empowering the people—empowering them to control, even to resist, their leaders more aggressively, more legitimately? Given the complex, contradictory nature of development issues, has sufficient space been granted, in the workplace, in the village, elsewhere, for people to criticize, to debate, to make demands, to learn, to learn even by making mistakes? Can "political revitalization" take place without granting more real power at the base? It might even be argued that the Fourth Congress, impressive as we have argued it to be, still retained too many elements of stage management about it, that the person of the President, very much front and center in the proceedings, loomed just a little too large for the Congress to provide

---

*This particular formulation appears in an official commentary on the Fourth Thesis to the Third Congress of FRELIMO, a commentary serialized in *Noticias* in April–May 1977; it is quoted in Center of African Studies, "FRELIMO from Front to Party: Revolutionary Transformation" (Maputo: Eduardo Mondlane University, n.d.). The original document continues: "The vanguard is not an elite. An elite is a gang of bourgeois intellectuals who consider themselves superior to the working masses and are contemptuous of them. It is that class that Joana Simeao [a defector from FRELIMO] called 'the thinking class,' thereby saying that society is divided into two groups: a minority . . . who are born to govern and decide everything and a majority, incapable of thinking, made to obey and work under the orders and in favor of the minority. . . . [In contrast] the vanguard is born from the working masses, lives in the middle of the masses, learns from the working masses." The Center of African Studies paper also cites an editorial in *Mozambique Revolution*, dating from as early as 1966, to similar effect. Discussing Nkrumah's overthrow, the editorial, entitled "The African Lesson," argues that "fundamentally it is necessary to encourage the people to participate in the political life of the country; further, it is necessary to reject a concept in which the Revolution is built by an active nucleus of leaders who think, create, and give everything, and who are followed by a passive mass, who limit themselves to receiving and executing. This concept is the result of a weak political conscience and expresses lack of confidence in the fighting and revolutionary capacity of the people." A strong formulation, though we should note, if only in passing, that there is a possible difference of some significance between the concepts of "popular participation" on the one hand and "popular control" on the other.

an unequivocally promising model for the future. In Mozambique, in short, the very best of the leadership has sometimes seemed a little too reluctant to risk "too much democracy"—with the notion of "too much" taking on, simultaneously, rather too expansive a definition. Something I once wrote with reference to Zimbabwe (albeit in a different context and about a situation much less promising for socialist advance than that in Mozambique) may have relevance for the question of the pace and character of any more ample democratization of the Mozambican revolution:

> There is a very real possibility of becoming *trapped* on the terrain of short-run calculation, circumstances never quite so ripe for socialist change as to make realization of such change a straightforward exercise. Then, with powerful forces . . . [reinforcing] pragmatism and caution, long-term goals of transformation may, without ever having been quite "ripe," merely wither on the vine! For a transition to socialism is never risk-free; the deftest (and most successful) of revolutionaries have been those who have pushed carefully but creatively at the margin of risk.[22]

Can we conclude that too often, even in Mozambique, the comforting nostrums of a certain brand of Leninism have served to paper over challenges that require even more creative responses than the ones we have been examining in this section? Perhaps, but we must quickly add that what has been done does have considerable resonance in its own right. We need not be surprised that in Mozambique political contradictions and political miscalculations, class struggle and ideological contestation, form a crucial part of the transition process. Nor that the crushing weight of "historical backwardness" and "imperialist encirclement" under which Mozambique labors has given the country shockingly little room for maneuver. All the more impressive—especially when comparisons are made with a number of other attempted transitions to socialism—that in Mozambique so many important tensions and contradictions have at least been kept alive and that there is some ongoing effort to resolve them, rather than merely to suppress them. Though much remains to be accomplished in the political sphere, enough has been attempted in Mozambique to give the revolution serious claim to our attention.

The Economic Sphere

The previous chapter itemized the economic problems which confronted FRELIMO in the first years of independence, problems defined both by the inherited economy and by the *crisis* of the economy so structured which was produced by FRELIMO's victory.

Moreover, the productive base was to be placed in further jeopardy
not only by the ongoing war against Rhodesia but also by the destructiveness of South Africa's own proxy war against Mozambique
and by a staggering range of natural disasters (the floods of 1976–
1978, the catastrophic drought of the past few years). As seen, the
costs of closing the Rhodesian border shortly after independence
and of supporting ZANU's liberation struggle were enormous,
both directly (in terms of lost revenues from returns on transit and
port facilities, tourism, and the movement of migrant labor) and
indirectly (in terms of defense requirements, the feeding of large
numbers of refugees, and the willful destruction caused by the
Rhodesians inside Mozambique). More recently, as we have also
seen, the central South African/MNR goal has continued to be "the
maximum possible damage of the Mozambican economy." The
damage caused by the Limpopo and Zambezi floods was great in
terms of crop destruction and the displacement of hundreds of
thousands of peasants, but much less serious, nonetheless, than the
subsequent two-year drought which affected some four million
people, with 15,000 cattle dying off every month, and food production in the south reduced by at least 70 percent in 1982, including
90 percent of the maize crop lost and nearly 100 percent of the
rice.[23]

Against the broad backdrop of dependency, underdevelopment,
and "undevelopment," faced with such realities as war and natural
disaster, FRELIMO has tried to pick its way forward on the economic front. As noted earlier, the task has been a paradoxical one:
attempting to keep the inherited structure sufficiently in operation
to sustain a viable level of economic life while, at the same time,
beginning to lay the groundwork for a new economic structure.
The new structure would be a socialist one. It did not take long for
the new state to establish a predominant position within the economy. Bertil Egero and Jens-Erik Torp have summarized this accomplishment in the following terms:

> To fulfil its functions, the state needed restructuring and extended
> control over strategic sectors of society. [With] independence, all land,
> health and medical activities and education were nationalized, and
> private legal and medical service abolished. Strategic sectors of the
> economy, such as banks, insurance, rented buildings, main industrial
> units and large-scale agricultural units were also brought under the
> control of the state. Gradually, other abandoned or seriously mis-
> managed production units were added, until today at least three
> quarters of all production—outside the peasant sector—is function-
> ing in accordance with state plans. Practically speaking, this implies

that production goals are fixed for the planned sectors, and that they receive resources, i.e. imported raw materials, spare parts, transport and technicians accordingly.[24]

And, in the rural sector, not only was there the state sector, created in this manner, but there was also envisaged a major trans-formation of the peasant economy in the direction of cooperative production units.

The restructured economy was seen as being, ultimately, both a much more industrial economy and a much more autocentric one. As detailed in the preceding chapter, the latter goal could not be realized at once. The inherited economic structure, including its established external linkages, would have to be used in order to shift the logic of the economy inward. Retention of economic links with South Africa is perhaps the most striking case in point in this regard. Services, especially vis-à-vis South Africa, had been the major source of foreign exchange for Portugal in Mozambique, and certainly traffic to and from South Africa was to remain a crucial element in the economic viability of the important port facilities of Maputo. Moreover, as seen, large numbers of workers still move to South Africa from southern Mozambique, as does the vast percentage of Cabora Bassa power. Add to this Mozambique's inherited emphasis on such agricultural exports as cotton, copra, cashews, tea, and sugar in its primary role as supplier of raw mate-rials within the Eurocentric global division of labor. Not a role to be abandoned overnight, unfortunately.

We should note that even the attempt to profit from these neces-sary compromises with Mozambique's inherited economic struc-ture and global economic location has not been an entirely straightforward exercise. Certainly South Africa has not hesitated, upon occasion, to crack the economic whip it holds over the Mozambican economy; thus it has reduced the migrant labor quota offered to Mozambique and, more recently, has diverted more traffic than might have been anticipated away from Maputo and to the new facilities at Richard's Bay within South Africa itself. There have been problems for Mozambique in following the primary product export route as well. One of these was underscored in an important study pamphlet widely distributed by FRELIMO in 1981, *The Present Situation in Our Country,* concerning the extent to which Mozambique, as exporter, remained at the mercy of negative trends in the international terms of trade:

> From what can be seen in the accompanying tables, it is apparent that in order to import the same quantity of goods which we imported in 1975 we have to export almost two times, in some cases three times, as

much. This is the case because we are still an underdeveloped country which produces mainly agricultural products and produces few industrial products. This is the meaning of economic dependence.[25]

In this regard, the rising cost of oil was of particular importance, though not the only cause of the imbalance.

The study pamphlet tended to ignore a second, equally important, dimension of the problem, one also noted in the previous chapter. For a sharp decline in the *absolute* amount of such primary products exported has itself contributed greatly to balance of payment difficulties. Thus "exports of the main cash crop, cashew nuts, fell from an annual average of some 75,000 tons (after shelling) in the early 1970s to less than 10,000 tons in the last season (1983)";[26] copra fell from 70,000 tons in 1970 to 29,000 in 1980; sugar fell from 265,000 tons in 1974 to 177,700 in 1981; only tea exceeded its preindependence level of production over a similar period, although ultimately it, too, was badly hit as the MNR began to step up its activities in Zambezia Province during the past year or two. In addition, many food crops experienced similar shortfalls, leading at times to a necessity to import foodstuffs and a consequent drain on foreign exchange. As noted, such production problems have been cruelly exacerbated by external attack and natural disasters—as well as other causes, as we shall discuss shortly.

Yet even if the pattern of compromise with Mozambique's established (albeit shaky) economic structure were eventually to prove more successful, it would still only make sense if surpluses so earned were to be used to transform that structure and to further the promise of bettering people's lives. It will come as no surprise that this was precisely the note struck at the Third Congress of FRELIMO which began the task of outlining a socialist development strategy for Mozambique. The premises of that strategy bear repeating here. The goal:

> the fundamental aim of social and economic development is the building of the scientific and technical base for the transition to socialism. In carrying out this aim we shall have to engage in a long and difficult battle for the effective conquest of economic power. This will gradually make it possible to raise our people's material, social and cultural living standards.[27]

The means? On the one hand, "our strategy for development rests on agricultural production. The communal villages are the fundamental lever for liberating the people in the rural areas." On the other, "industry is the dynamizing factor for economic development. The construction of heavy industry constitutes the decisive factor for our total independence, enabling us to break from our integration into the imperialist system."

And the mechanism? "The building of socialism demands that the economy is centrally planned and directed by the state. Planned management is one of its basic characteristics." The President was later to express a number of the same points in a speech entitled "Let Us Make 1980–1990 the Decade of Victory over Underdevelopment," August 4, 1979:

> We said, and it is correct, that agriculture constitutes the basis of our development and industry its dynamizing factor, with heavy industry its decisive factor. We're not dealing here with either merely off-handed remarks or with a copying of models. This is a pronouncement based on the scientific analysis of our reality, one which has as its objective the permanent raising of the level of well-being of our working classes, the creators of socialist societies, of all wealth and of history.[28]

The strong commitment to putting popular needs, not "effective demand" (worldwide and local), increasingly at the center of Mozambican socioeconomic development will be evident from these citations. In subsequent chapters we will see how this important premise of Mozambique's revolutionary practice has worked itself out in a number of important service spheres—in education, health, and urban development, for example. And we will have more to say about this premise here as we examine the debate about Mozambique's economic strategy more broadly defined. For the moment it is important also to take note of the strong emphasis which is placed upon stepping up the country's pace of industrialization as key to structural transformation and to bringing into more effective play Mozambique's valuable endowment of energy resources and mineral and agricultural potential.

As seen, FRELIMO is careful to talk about industry and agriculture being closely interrelated. But the precise nature of that interrelationship has been subject to considerable debate within Mozambican decision-making circles. Thus, upon occasion, heavy industry as "decisive factor" has seemed to take pride of place. Some FRELIMO pronouncements have even suggested that the country has launched its "development decade" with almost reckless boldness, with heady visions of the mechanization of agriculture, the electrification of the countryside, and the establishment of a range of heavy industries. So great was the sense of urgency that sometimes the "big project" seemed to be the only way to make up for lost time. Here was where foreign exchange earnings would be expected to play their most crucial role, with *accumulation* becoming the centerpiece of transformation. The abovementioned pamphlet, *The Present Situation in Our Country,* put this point as follows: "We can now cite some examples of what is proposed in order to change the structure of our economy and to produce what colonialism never wanted us to produce. We are going to speak of the big projects which we expect will contribute decisively to the resolution of our problems." The pendant to this formulation is equally interesting:

> [Such projects] involve the expenditure of enormous sums by the state, sums which could be used instead to purchase rice—we have a shortage of rice—sugar, milk powder, meat, etc. But here there is a question of choice. If we buy those products which we need (it's true, we need them), then the money we spend is merely used up and is not going to be productive.
>
> If, on the contrary, we make a sacrifice in this phase, such that instead of buying rice, meat, fish, flour we use that money for the construction of factories, then four or five years down the road the sacrifice we're making today is going to permit the production of all the material goods that we have mentioned. We think that to escape from poverty and underdevelopment, such sacrifice is necessary.[29]

Perhaps it is such emphases that has led at least one commentator to stress the parallels between Mozambican intentions and what he calls the "Stalinist development formula"![30]

However, the fact of the matter is that FRELIMO's economic thinking has generally tended to be much more nuanced than this. Thus even the Third Congress document which laid such a strong emphasis upon heavy industry had, at base, a much more subtle picture of the interplay, over time, between industry and agriculture, one more subtle certainly than the *Present Situation* pamphlet. For the Third Congress, the "priority task" of the agricultural sector is "the satisfaction of the country's food needs" and provision of "the necessary raw materials for manufacturing industry," although, needless to say, "increased exports of agricultural goods, and the resulting revenue" are also necessary "for developing our industrialization process." As for industry, "the industrial sectors which supply the people's basic needs assume an immediate importance. So, factories producing foodstuffs, clothing, footwear, etc., should be organized around the real needs of the working masses, converting production lines that were designed for the luxury consumption of the colonial elites." Moreover, "we must develop industries that support production, particularly engineering, cement, fuels, fertilizers and the packing industries. Upon them depends the reactivation of other economic sectors, particularly agriculture. . . ." On the other hand, "the process of building heavy

industry is lengthy," however important to the efforts of "our country . . . to ensure control of the productive process, free itself from
dependence and increase its economic capacity decisively."[31] Here,
already, we find a pull toward that model of "expanded socialist
reproduction" which we discussed in our introductory chapter. We
shall see this emphasis surfacing even more forcefully in the period
leading up to, and including, the Fourth Congress.

This is just as well. The Mozambican economy has been in
sufficiently desperate straits that centering the discussion of economic development around the theme of further "sacrifice" would
be disastrous. To understand why this is so we must look briefly at
the crisis of production which currently stalks the Mozambican
countryside. Momentarily bracketing off, as suggested earlier, such
relevant factors as external attack and natural disaster, we can see
that declining production also reflects both the difficulties peasants
have had in marketing their produce *and* the severe scarcity of
items (be they consumer goods or productive inputs) which they
can purchase with such earnings as they might receive. This, in
turn, reflects in considerable measure the collapse of the network
of commercialization mentioned above. But it also reflects the slow
rate of recovery and transformation of Mozambique's industrial
sector. Quite simply, the latter has not been able to produce the
goods necessary to such urban-rural, industry-agriculture exchanges as could stimulate, in turn, agricultural production. Faced
with such a situation, many Mozambican peasants simply retreat
back to subsistence agriculture (when they cannot enter the black
market!). To talk of sacrifice as the key to development and of the
further one-sided extraction of surpluses from the peasantry
under such circumstances would be to ensure the latter's further
retreat (or else to contemplate the reintroduction of Portuguese-
style forced cultivation, an option at worst impossible and at best
self-defeating).

Of course, the mere awareness of these facts does not, in and of
itself, remove the many "vicious circles" which scar the Mozambican economy. We have mentioned the tailspin into which Mozambican industry fell at independence. Why was it so difficult to revive
and restructure this sector? There has certainly been the problem
of "know-how," the fact of "undevelopment" rearing its ugly head
in the wake of the Portuguese exodus. But equally important has
been the absence of foreign exchange, exacerbating those shortages of spare-parts, raw materials and plant and machinery which
help keep industrial output low. The result, as Hodges points out,
is that "many industries are operating at only 20–40% of capacity. . . . Cement production, which had totalled 465,000 tons in

1974, amounted to only 270,000 tons in 1982, according to Helder Rodrigues, the director-general of Cimentos de Moçambique. . . . [T]he breweries . . . turned out 51.1m litres of beer in 1982, as against 80.8m litres in 1981, and have a target of 45m litres this year."[32] Examples could be multiplied, yet without the industrial output of consumer goods and light producer goods, where are the items which are required to stimulate the production of export crops and food crops necessary to earn or to conserve foreign exchange? A vicious circle indeed.

Furthermore, apparent awareness of some of the imperatives of "expanded socialist reproduction" has too often tended to be honored in the breach rather than in the observance. As noted by Egero and Torp,

> FRELIMO sees its political base as being an alliance between the workers and peasantry, and the question of securing a material content to this alliance is a question of practical policy. . . . [A] certain degree of processing of agricultural raw materials already exists in the industrial sector. But the industrial sector in its turn historically produced only a limited quantity . . . of products of direct use for the peasantry. Although a reorientation of production is underway, the transformation of the existing economy and the erection of new projects geared towards the needs of the peasantry is still in its initial stages.[33]

Indeed, a rather onesided "primitive socialist accumulation" still seemed, on balance, to lie at the heart of so important a policy initiative as the ten-year economic plan which emerged at the end of the 1970s (the "Plano Prospectivo Indicativo para 1981–1990" or "PPI," an undertaking which represented the first overall planning exercise entered into by the Mozambican government). Not all details of this plan were made public. Nonetheless one can get the flavor of it from a key document of the time entitled *Linhas fundamentais do plano prospectivo indicativo para 1981–1990*.[34] Thus, even if questions of agricultural-industrial linkage are not altogether ignored in that document, there can be little doubt that for both the agricultural and the industrial sectors the planners' chief emphasis was on "large projects" *(os grandes projectos)*. In the agricultural section of the *Linhas* a long shopping list of such large projects is presented, such projects to receive 75 percent of all agricultural investment; as for industry, the "fundamental strategic importance" of "heavy industry" for changing "our economic structure" is stressed, as is the crucial role of large projects—iron, steel, chemical and petrol-based industries, for example—to any such goal of heavy industrialization.

Still, it is significant that only a year or so after the completion of this planning exercise—and even before the powerful expression of peasant demands had placed the necessity of response to immediate economic crisis firmly on the agenda for the Fourth Congress—the leadership itself had begun to raise some serious questions about the plan's apparent approach. In his speech of May 1, 1981, the President suggested that self-criticism was in order in this regard:

> We must fight against the tendency to identify the Development Decade only with big projects. The battle begins with the creation of essential goods, those which we need in daily life. They appear to be small things—but how can we develop without guaranteeing their production?
> What are essential goods? In the first place it's necessary for us to produce what's necessary to kill the hunger which in turn threatens to kill us. It's necessary to produce maize; it's necessary to produce rice; it's necessary to produce potatoes and sweet potatoes; it's necessary to produce fruits, and necessary to produce chickens and eggs; it's necessary to raise goats; and ducks; and rabbits.
> It's necessary for us to produce things for daily use: the fork, the spoon, the knife, the cup, the pot, the shirt, the suit, the blouse, the skirt, the slippers, the shoes, the work-boots.[35]

By early 1982 the continuing search for a more balanced approach to designing the country's overall economic strategy was defined as being of crucial importance to the work of the forthcoming Fourth Congress. In March 1982, as mentioned earlier, an unprecedented National Conference of the Party was held with the specific object of setting the agenda for the national debate which would lead up to the Congress itself. Significantly, one of the points made most forcefully was just how crucial it was that

> the mass of workers be fully aware that it is not large projects by themselves which are going to transform our life.
> The large projects take time to bear fruit. They require vast technical and financial inputs, they require many trained personnel. They are necessary to guarantee our future, they are seeds planted in the present that will germinate in the future. But we have also to consider our present situation and begin to improve it too.
> A correct solution is a combination of large, centrally initiated projects with small projects initiated at the local level and drawing on local resources. Small projects create new bases for production. This implies moving on from the hoe to the plough by using the returns generated by employing the hoe and in the same way having the plough lay the groundwork for the eventual introduction of the tractor.[36]

More than a discussion of the relative merits of large and small projects was at stake here, important as that discussion was in its own right. For under very real pressure from the peasantry itself the party was also inching its way toward a greater acceptance of the "economics of expanded socialist reproduction" as key to defining other aspects of the industrial mix, in particular the balance between heavy industrial and infrastructural development on the one hand and consumer goods industries on the other. As already noted, the context within which peasant demands made themselves felt was the nationwide debate over the Draft Theses prepared for the Fourth Congress. What that debate brought into focus was the peasants' concern that the economics of Mozambican development begin to mean something far more tangible in terms of the betterment of their own standard of living. In particular, they argued, a much wider range of goods—once again, consumer goods and light producer goods—should be made available. The FRELIMO leadership could readily grasp that meeting such needs made eminently good political sense. Fortunately, as has been argued above, it can be an important premise of good socialist development economics as well, something the leadership also had begun to comprehend more clearly.

In April 1983, at the Congress itself, the report of the Central Committee of FRELIMO to the Congress (entitled *Out of Underdevelopment to Socialism*) synthesized the position at which the party had now arrived.[37] Its premise: "Today the agrarian question appears as one of the fundamental questions of economic and social development and for the consolidation of the Mozambican revolution." Yet "rural development has not reached the high level of mobilization necessary. It has still not galvanized the enthusiasm and creativity of the peasantry and all the people of our country." Why? Because the peasantry, "the family sector," has been "relegated to a secondary position." Yet to the production of many food crops and many important export crops this sector is crucial. Moreover, "the importance of the family sector is not limited to the quantities it produces. In it we find millions of citizens. They are the most numerous base of our power." Unfortunately, "in practice support for the family sector was virtually nonexistent, particularly in terms of factors of production. All these facts were analyzed at the fourth meeting of the Central Committee [1978]; however, little was done." Clearly, this situation now had to change.

A second Congress document, one summarizing, quite specifically, the results of the months of debate over the Theses *(Building Socialism: The People's Answer—Report on the Preparation of the Congress)*, gave this point even greater focus. "At the Third Congress we defined industry as the dynamizing factor for economic development. Today we are detailing the role that falls to each branch of industry by specifying that light industry answers present needs, namely socialization of the countryside, and that heavy industry is to build a future free from underdevelopment." Present needs?

> It was stressed [in the public meetings held to discuss the Theses] that we often gave more attention to technical factors than to the human and to the creative initiative of the people. We are not bothering about manufacturing the hoe because we are awaiting the arrival of the tractor we must import. We are distributing tinned beans, that cost foreign exchange, in a communal village that produces beans and from where no one has bothered to collect surplus production. We overload the peasant with items he does not use but do not provide him with a lamp, cloth, a file or a hammer. Nonetheless we expect him to exchange his production for goods he does not need.
>
> It was pointed out likewise that the failure to support small-scale projects and local initiative has the effect of demobilizing the people. They make great sacrifices to make large-scale projects possible, but they do not feel the support of state structures in improved living standards and in the fight against hunger.[38]

As we shall see, other themes surfacing in the Congress reinforced these emphases, not least the considerable stress placed upon the activating of internal networks of commercialization—trading centers, transport, and the like—as a necessary pendant to any such adjustment in industrial strategy. These emphases bore the promise—other things being equal—of closing crucial gaps in FRELIMO's post-independence economic policies. Moreover, this was a promise which built upon historic precedent: the precedent of FRELIMO's close links with the peasantry, links which had premised the movement's victory in the guerrilla war. For anyone in attendance at the Fourth Congress it was hard to escape the feeling that a fundamental aspect of FRELIMO's practice was reasserting itself.

Not that putting such guidelines into practice is any easy matter, especially under conditions of continuing war; other things have scarcely been equal in contemporary Mozambique. But war aside, their implementation involves the making of tough, concrete decisions which would be difficult enough even if all Mozambicans were agreed on the broad premises of development policy. How decide, for example, how much of the surplus should be skimmed away from the economy for long-term investment purposes, how much ploughed back more directly to permit the economy's day-to-day expansion? And such decisions are all the more difficult when even the premises themselves may not be entirely agreed upon. Thus at the Congress itself some FRELIMO activists—the speech

by Sergio Vieira, then Minister of Agriculture, provided one notable example—seemed to see the new departures more as reflecting
short-term tactical retreats than as representing a positive, long-
term adjustment in strategic thinking. Even one of the central
party documents presented at the Congress *(Building Socialism: The
People's Answer—Report from the Economic and Social Directives Commission)* seemed to have a slightly different tone regarding these
issues than other of the documents quoted above:

> The objectives laid down in the Prospective Indicative Plan for the
> decade (PPI) for the elimination of underdevelopment likewise re-
> main valid although the current demands of the fight against the
> enemy lead us to adopt less rapid growth rates and to postpone im-
> plementation of some of the new investments that had been planned.
>
> The Economic and Social Directives we are now presenting set out
> short- and medium-term actions to overcome current difficulties in
> our development process.[39]

Perhaps we should avoid reading too much between the lines of
such documents. Nonetheless, on the ground one had the distinct
impression that differences of opinion about development strategy
stirred beneath the surface, an impression that the "primitive
socialist accumulation" emphasis continues to have its supporters.
For many of the latter such an emphasis may continue to make
good sense theoretically—even if Mozambique's lack of organizational skills, capital, and foreign exchange mean that their more
grandiose plans must be modified. Mark Wuyts has argued that
another questionable premise may underlie this approach as well, a
kind of "dualist perspective" regarding the peasantry;[40] such a perspective tends to contrast a "progressive," "modern" sector with
what it views as the extreme social and economic backwardness of
Mozambican peasant society. Yet, Wuyts argues, this underestimates the extent to which Mozambique's rural areas had been
"mobilized" economically by even the backward form of colonialism which Portugal had to offer, and underestimates, too, the
peasantry's historically conditioned responsiveness to economic incentives. Wuyts thus sees the burgeoning of the black market in
Mozambique in recent years as evidence not merely of the goods
shortage which Mozambique's difficult economic situation has
given rise to. It is also striking evidence of peasant responsiveness,
a responsiveness which a strategy of "expanded socialist reproduction" could build upon in order to transform Mozambique's productive base.

We discussed some of the possible sources of such thinking in the
first section of this chapter. There it was suggested that part of the
difficulty is ideological: a rather rigid definition of Marxism, one

which all too readily identifies Marxist truth with Soviet, even Stalinist, historical practice, has not been entirely absent from Mozambican debates and this has given some added weight to "primitive accumulationist" thinking. We should also recall, from the same section, the paragraph quoted from the *Central Committee Report to the Fourth Congress* which stressed the possible *class interest* of a bureaucratic stratum in overvaluing the merits of the top-down, big-project, heavy-investment line of thinking. Yet, in the end, the prominence of such factors merely makes all the more striking the fact that peasant-centered preoccupations were so prominent in the Fourth Congress. Indeed, the apparent victory for this line was, in economic terms, probably the most important single aspect of the Congress.

Not that this victory need be interpreted strictly in factional terms, as the outcome of a struggle between the "primitive accumulationists" and the "socialist reproductionists." There have been, and continue to be, elements of class struggle in the debate over the "party line" regarding economic development and very probably some pushing and pulling within the party as well, on ideological and other grounds. However, it is equally likely that the tension exists *within* many of the protagonists of Mozambican politics themselves as they wrestle with the conflicting claims of alternative development emphases. It must also be stressed that the novel emphasis which we have been discussing has distinct ambiguities of its own. For example, the precise manner in which the peasantry is now to be drawn into a more active role in the economic transformation of Mozambique remains less than clear. Consequently, we have to examine the extent to which the notion of facilitating a pattern of more flexible interchange between town and country, industry and agriculture, has simultaneously implied a release of market forces which has an antisocialist logic of its own. Where does FRELIMO's stated goal of rural collectivization stand in such a context? Or, to examine a different aspect, what more detailed policies follow from an awareness that the process of accumulation and industrialization is far less straightforward than the model of some once-for-all, big-push breakthrough could foresee, and that the goals of accumulation and industrialization must be more carefully tailored to fit Mozambique's needs and its capacities? Ironically, as we shall see, the move toward a "socialism of expanded reproduction" has had the practical result of moving Mozambique toward a more benign view of the role that international capital can play in helping close some of the gaps in Mozambique's internal economic circuits. Obviously this view, as well as the policies which follow from it, needs to be scanned very carefully as well.

As stated, the question of the precise relationship which is to be established between industry and agriculture cannot be separated from the question of how best to transform the agricultural sector itself. Building on the experiences of the liberated areas, FRELIMO has looked to collectivization as the means both of raising agricultural productivity and of preempting the emergence of a counterrevolutionary pattern of class formation. Yet there have been real differences of opinion as to how any such collective solution in the rural areas might best be achieved. Central to rural planning has been the idea of forming *aldeias comunais* (communal villages), such villages conceived, minimally, as being nucleated settlements where services could be concentrated and political structures developed. Beyond the issue of settlement pattern, however, have lain more controversial questions regarding the precise nature of the productive base for Mozambique's rural economy which was to be facilitated.

A subsequent chapter by Helena Dolny will have more to say on this and other related issues. Briefly put, two main models of collective production suggested themselves: the state farm on the one hand, the peasant-based production cooperative on the other. As noted in the previous chapter, the food crisis of the first years of independence led to primary emphasis being placed on the state farm sector. This was virtually inevitable under the circumstances and, indeed, undertakings in this sector have continued to be of crucial importance. However, there were costs to this emphasis as well, most notably the exaggerated concentration of government personnel and scarce resources upon this sector, with correspondingly much less support for the peasant sector and for the program to advance its cooperativization.

There was some tendency within the FRELIMO leadership to conceive the distinction between state farm and cooperative in other terms as well, terms which, in effect, served to make a considerable virtue of the necessity of concentrating on the state farm sector. Partially this reflected some of the second thoughts about the revolutionary vocation of the peasantry referred to above. Thus a certain kind of Marxism may have encouraged the granting of greater importance to those rural dwellers who worked on state farms—primarily because they were at least partially proletarianized. State farms also fit more neatly into the narrowly accumulationist and technocratic preoccupations of certain planners. In 1982, for example, I attended a meeting at which the senior governmental planner suggested a distinction which should be made between the two sectors. For him, state farms were to be defined first and foremost as an "investment question" (with the issue of technical inputs to raise productivity therefore central). In contrast, the peasant-based cooperatives were defined as primarily an "organizational question," a matter of "mobilization," a front to be left, in effect, to party workers and not economic planners.*

This distinction between spheres of "investment" and spheres of "organization" is a revealing one, the limitations of which will be readily apparent in light of our previous argument. In particular, the definition of investment which was at play here had the effect of casting thinking about agricultural development far too exclusively in terms of fairly advanced and mechanized technology. This had the direct result of underplaying the kind of investment required in the family-cum-cooperative sector if that sector, too, were to become increasingly productive and rewarding to the peasant. As President Machel was ultimately to make so clear, the fact that in the latter sector we are talking about such modest items as the hoe and the plough, seeds and fertilizers, does not make such inputs any the less important—nor are they any the less to be considered "investment." Small wonder that such planners as the one cited above have had difficulty in conceiving, let alone specifying, an adequately balanced industrial strategy. How difficult for them, too, to confront creatively, in the context of Mozambique's broader economic crisis, the "crisis of reproduction" which has confronted the peasant household at the level of its own agricultural undertakings.

Significantly, technocratic thinking has had its costs in the state farm sector as well as in the peasant sector. When, for example, state farms were defined primarily in terms of "investment," there was a tendency to privilege technique and hierarchical control at the expense of an equal concern for participation by, and release of the creative energies of, the workers themselves. Needless to say, this is a more general question—a question of the balance to be struck between administrative hierarchy and technical expertise on the one hand and genuine workers' participation on the other—

---

*Ironically, the technocratic bias which thus downplayed the economics of peasant mobilization *complemented* an opposite tendency on the part of some FRELIMO leaders, precisely those who were in fact least affected by any such bias or, indeed, by any stereotype of the "backward peasant" which might arise from too rigid a set of quasi-Marxist categories. In their enthusiasm to apply the successful model of political mobilization of the peasantry generated in the days of armed struggle to the complex problems of rural economic transformation, such cadres were tempted, for their own good reasons, to underestimate the importance of investment and incentives in the peasant sector. In short, even FRELIMO's best instincts had to be disciplined by further reflection on the harsh subtleties of economic calculation. Fortunately, as we have seen, the Fourth Congress demonstrated this kind of reflection to be well advanced.

which has run well beyond the state farm sector, a general problem to be discussed by Peter Sketchley in a subsequent chapter. What is important to note here is that it was the failure to avoid bureaucratic and technocratic methods in the rural sphere which was the main charge made by FRELIMO's Central Committee against Mozambique's first Minister of Agriculture, Joaquim de Carvalho, when the latter was dismissed from his post in 1978. His conception of development was seen to have been wrong and "in contradiction to the process of advancing socialism. . . . In essence he does not place trust in the people, he does not consider man as the determining element of development."[41] It was felt that this latter tendency had also led him to downgrade the policy of cooperativization of the peasant sector; as a result, "he refused to implement the priority defined by the leading bodies in relation to communal villages." No doubt this latter reference was to the strong statement made in the *Central Committee Report to the Third Congress* to the effect that

> the [producers'] cooperative movement under the leadership of the Party constitutes a huge mobilization of the great masses of peasants for organized, conscious and planned participation in the socialist development of the whole country. . . . Agricultural and livestock cooperatives are . . . a major form of organizing work, fundamental for the socialization of our agriculture. They allow direct control by the peasants over production which is decisive for the increasing growth of their social and political awareness and of their scientific and technical knowledge.[42]

The need to give life to the cooperativization program was a theme to which FRELIMO kept returning forcefully in subsequent years. It bears noting that Carvalho was sacked at precisely that Central Committee meeting cited self-critically in the Fourth Congress document quoted above: "All these facts were analyzed at the IVth meeting of the Central Committee; however, little was done." Again, Helena Dolny's chapter in the present volume analyzes the reasons why so little subsequent progress was made and why only a tiny percentage of peasants found themselves in producer cooperatives by the time of that Fourth Congress (perhaps as few as 70,000 out of 10 million people in the peasant sector!). However, it is also true that by the time of the period leading up to the Congress such failures had become an even more pressing preoccupation. Marcelino dos Santos, the party's influential Secretary of Economic Affairs, headed up a series of teams designed to give new life to the program at the district level. And the aforementioned National Conference of the Party placed this issue, too, firmly on the agenda of the Fourth Congress.

In spite of the large number of communal villages and the fact that more than a million peasants live in them, the communal villages still do not have a basis in collective production. The cooperative movement has not kept pace with the growth of villagization. The cooperative is not considered the principal source of peasant income. In many cases the cooperative is considered merely as a farm which is worked collectively and whose returns are used exclusively to pay for social services and administrative costs.

A producers' cooperative should be central to its members' way of life and be their main activity. It is run by bodies elected by the members. The returns from production go to the members. Central and local state structures as well as the state farms should support the cooperatives, helping them to raise their scientific and technical capacities, aiding them in the obtaining of factors of production and in marketing their production. In this respect, cooperatives and state farms ought to link themselves together contractually. The cooperatives should have priority in the distribution of scarce goods.

The importance of the socialization of the countryside demands that its implementation be the focus of a great national effort. It is fundamental that every citizen be conscious of his or her responsibility in this regard. The role of members of the party and of members of popular assemblies is decisive. They should receive scientific and technical training linked to their facilitating cooperative development.

The socialization of the countryside is the fundamental requirement for our victory over underdevelopment and for the construction of socialism in our country.[43]

This was not so exclusively the tone of the Congress documents and Congress debates which followed, however. The peasant sector was to be given a new centrality in state planning, that much was clear. But the question which we posed earlier remained: what mode of peasant production was in fact to be facilitated within the novel framework of a revitalized system of urban-rural exchanges? And in this regard as much was heard at the Congress about "the family sector" (itself not distinguished with absolute clarity from "the private sector") as about the cooperatives; it was clear to all that a much more overt and unapologetic focus upon the individual smallholder and upon his/her involvement in the market was front and center.

We must, then, act in such a way as to transform the instruments of trade into real class instruments. All our people must participate enthusiastically in this combat. The priority is to stimulate marketing in the rural zones, ensuring the sale of necessary agricultural tools and consumer goods. Extending the trading network to the countryside is essential for supplying the peasants and for agricultural marketing itself. The state must encourage traders who seek to establish them-

selves in areas poorly served by commerce, giving them the necessary support. . . .
Pricing policy should encourage production of crops for the market in the family sector. It should stimulate productivity in factories by linking prices to the normal costs of production and encouraging greater efficiency in factories. The state should encourage production in the cooperative and private sectors through pricing policy and the contract system, establishing the necessary machinery. *Prices should be conceived as a factor to stimulate commercial exchanges and to reestablish the market economy.*[44]

As in Russia in the 1920s, the market was being looked to as a mechanism for reactivating economic activity (and/or drawing it out of the circuits of the black market and back into the public realm!). Yet no more than Lenin in the 1920s had the Mozambican leadership lost sight of its long-term goal of rural cooperativization. As seen, the latter program had never had widespread success, at least not after an initial spurt of rather spontaneous enthusiasm for it in the first post-independence years. Now FRELIMO seemed to be arguing that if its own version of the "New Economic Policy" were to begin to bear fruit, then a revitalized economy would merely provide a much more viable terrain upon which to demonstrate to peasants the value of collective solutions. And it would be advances in the struggle for collectivization which would, in turn, combat such trends toward class formation as are a potential outgrowth of increased reliance on market forces. In the FRELIMO view, "the movement for communal villages and agricultural producer cooperatives—despite the scanty and uneven support given them—has scored some success, due mainly to the commitment of the peasants. . . . Their [slow] growth, however, raises problems that need consideration, particularly the question of *strengthening their economic base.*"[45] Then, as Lenin himself had put the point regarding the contradictory potential of the Soviet Union's NEP, "we must win the competition against the ordinary shop assistant, the ordinary capitalist, the merchant who will go to the peasant without arguing about communism. . . . Either we pass this test in competition with private capital or we fail completely."[46]

Interestingly, something of the same spirit can be found in Marx's writings:

> either the peasant hinders every workers' revolution and causes it to fail, as it has done in France up to now; or the proletariat (for the landowning peasantry does not belong to the proletariat and even when his own position causes him to belong to it, he does not *think* he belongs to it) must as a government inaugurate measures which directly improve the situation and win him for the revolution; measures

which in essence facilitate the transition from private to collective property in land so that the peasant himself is converted for economic reasons.[47]

More direct state support would be necessary in Mozambique, it was seen: "The meager development of the cooperative sector reflects the low level of priority given to it in practice and the inadequate support given by the state structures. Of the investments made in agriculture between 1977 and 1981, only 2 percent went to the cooperative sector." Now more effort, albeit effort of a much more nuanced sort, would be put into the program:

> With regard to development of the *socialization of the countryside* it is necessary to concentrate state support for the cooperative movement in the priority districts, to ensure the viability and operation of the pilot cooperatives as development poles of the cooperative movement. It is also necessary to give priority in the formation of cooperatives to poor peasants who will draw immediate benefits and to develop the cooperative movement in the light of the specific circumstances of each region. Realistic stages up to the stage of the socialist cooperative must be defined, from the starting point of elementary producers' associations and with due regard for the wishes, experience, and needs of the peasant.[48]

Nor, self-evidently, was the state farm sector to be abandoned. Its centrality to a range of major productive activities is patent and, in addition, the government had already formally committed itself to a number of further such undertakings, often with international partners. Yet it was apparent that some of the most important of these farms had fallen on very hard times. Of none was this more true than the mammoth Limpopo Agro-Industrial Complex (CAIL)—and its administrative structure, the Secretariat of State for the Limpopo and Incomati Region (SERLI)—an enterprise crucial to Mozambican rice production. Indeed, the kind of dramatic inefficiency revealed in such a project was one of the factors pushing, where appropriate, toward more of an emphasis on small manageable projects—built to Mozambican scale, as it were. Once again, the *Central Committee Report to the Fourth Congress* gave something of the flavor of these preoccupations:

> The transition from the hoe to the plough, and from the plough to the tractor and the combine harvester are both a result and a factor of the development of the productive forces; their use must be guaranteed by correct operation and maintenance. The transition from the hoe to the plough, and from the plough to the tractor and the combine harvester must be accompanied by a higher level of organization of work and of production and by an increase in the skills of those who have to use them. When this does not happen, modern factors of

production are not properly used, and the best results are not obtained from them. . . . Production technology based on imported factors is still not mastered by those who have to apply it. This occurs because the technology demands a high level of organization and strict regard for extremely complex rules of agronomy.

Small-scale projects in the agricultural sector are the answer to this crucial question of development. In the short to medium term they correspond to the immediate needs of the population. They awaken the people's creativity, develop the principle of self-reliance and enable the enthusiastic participation of the masses. In the period from now until the Fifth Congress, actions to promote rural development must, therefore, be based on wide-ranging support to the cooperative, private and family sectors and on reorganization and consolidation of the state agricultural sector.[49]

In the case of CAIL, such "reorganization and consolidation of the state agricultural sector" was to mean, immediately, its breakup into a number of smaller, potentially more manageable units, with further changes in the offing.

Clearly, then, Mozambique has not avoided mistakes in dealing with the staggering range of economic problems which have confronted it. More striking, however, has been the continuing ability of party and government to rethink various problems—as at the Fourth Congress—and to return, when necessary, to first principles. Promising, too, was the attempt to establish a much firmer basis upon which to undertake such rethinking, a basis to be rooted in the increased capacity to *plan* economic life. Very far from being a complete success, as we shall see, this planning exercise nonetheless represented a significant attempt to inch away from the near chaos of the immediate post-independence economic situation. With the Third Congress serving to epitomize the consolidation of control over that situation, the stage was set for a more coherent effort at sustained coordination of the economy and for an ongoing process of reflection regarding the range of development options which might be pursued. As Mark Wuyts has put the point,

> The hierarchical subordination of economic ministries to the National Planning Commission and of state enterprises to their respective ministries, the nationalization and restructuring of the banking system, the reorganization of the state budget, the nationalization of the key sectors of the economy and the formation of state enterprises—all were different aspects of the move to establish the foundation of a planned economy.[50]

The creation of the National Planning Commission in 1978 was key here, its first efforts involving primarily the "coordinating of various bottom-up production plans"; the more prominent assertion of centrally defined global criteria as a basis for planning emerged only after the first year or two. The first state plan, the aforementioned PPI, "was born," in the words of Samora Machel, "in August of 1979 during a meeting of the Council of Ministers, when we launched the challenge of making this decade the decade of victory against underdevelopment." Moreover, "annual plans have since been available to direct government action and economic development." No small accomplishment, as stated, and the Mozambican leadership has made much of it, most notably in the 1981 speech by Machel entitled, significantly, "Our Plan Is the Key to Economic Victory":

> [T]he PPI must constitute a source of national pride. It is not the mechanical transposition of any model, neither is it the fruit of voluntarism, even well-intentioned voluntarism. The PPI is a Mozambican model, the project of Mozambican intelligence, of the character of the Mozambican people. In this Decade there will be born new heroes of labour, heroes of the victory of the PPI, heroes of the great victory against underdevelopment.[51]

The accomplishment was more than merely verbal, of course. In theory, upward of "75 percent of the economy is organized and administered according to annual state plans." We shall see that there are grounds to question the practical content of such an assertion, but there can be no doubt that the establishment of this planning process has provided the essential precondition for Mozambicans to face up more coherently to the complexities of their economy and to inch their way forward; workers in most government ministries and enterprises would testify to the new sense of coherence and discipline which accompanied the increased saliency of these planning mechanisms. For a time, too, economic progress was being made. "With respect to 1977 (the bottom point in production in the immediate aftermath of the production crisis of 1974–77) the global material product (= gross value of material output) rose 12 percent by 1981, of which agricultural production by 9 percent and industrial output by 14 percent. This amounts to average annual growth rates of respectively, 2.9 percent, 2 percent and 3.3 percent." Not spectacular, to be sure, but strong in comparison with what was to follow:

> The drought and escalation of the war contributed considerably to the worsening of the situation since 1981. In 1982 production (= the global material product) went down by 7 percent relative to 1981 and this trend continued the year after. The supply of commodities on the market went down 8 percent in 1981 relative to 1980, the reduction being 6 percent in food and nearly 17 percent in other products (the

major drop being in textiles). In 1982 supplies went down a further 8 percent (relative to 1981) and this specifically with respect to textiles, vegetable oils, beans, wheat flour and some other products. This situation continued into 1983 when the food situation became highly critical and famine widespread, especially in the regions affected by the actions of the MNR. Hence in the latter two years the gains achieved in the recovery of production were wiped out by the effect of the drought but much more so by the impact of the escalating war, which caused a widespread disruption over the country.[52]

War and drought: it is well to keep reminding ourselves of these essential factors. But we have also seen that the substance of Mozambican economic planning left something to be desired in terms of facilitating the clarification and choice of strategic options. Thus the paper by Wuyts from which we have quoted extensively above suggests that the linking of what we have here called "accumulationist" and "technocratic" tendencies lent to the planning process per se certain negative tendencies, tendencies which served to balance off some of that process's more positive attributes. Recall our qualification of the phrase "organized and administered according to annual state plans" in the immediately preceding paragraph. In the opinion of Wuyts and a number of other observers, much of that "administering" was far more notional than real. The passing down of unrealistic output targets to various production units was commonplace, insufficient sensitivity being shown to the broader economic problem of what conditions—beyond mere fiat—would be necessary in order to facilitate an expansion of production; in this sense, more traces of "voluntarism" may have attached to the planning process than Samora Machel suspected when giving the speech quoted above. Not coincidentally, the planning model under discussion had potentially quite negative implications for the possibility of active participation by workers and peasants in the setting of their own production norms.

Interestingly, a number of rural delegates, speaking from the floor at the Fourth Congress, criticized the abstract nature of the production targets delivered from the center to the rural districts and thence to the localities and the communal villages. The point was taken very seriously by all those assembled. As one senior government minister and Central Committee member admitted candidly to a group of foreign delegates at the Congress, this problem had very deep roots indeed. He suggested that these lay in FRELIMO's adoption, at the Third Congress and in its immediate aftermath, of too oversimplified a picture of what planning in post-independence Mozambique was all about. Though he, too, stressed the dangers of bureaucratic class formation and of class interest asserting itself and distorting policy within the state apparatus, he argued that within FRELIMO the culprit was less technocratic bias than the surfacing, in the first flush of victory over the Portuguese, of an overweening self-confidence. Tribalisms and regionalisms and other divisions had been vanquished, along with the Portuguese, in the armed struggle: surely this meant that a united Mozambique could be planned—uniformly. Moreover, with unity of purpose ensured, the development process could be planned both apolitically and—why not, since it seemed so rational—centrally. Only slowly did the majority of FRELIMO leaders begin to sense that a far too uncritical belief in the efficacy of "the state" and "the plan" had begun to "block local initiative," "alienate local leadership from the state planning structure," and bottle up popular energies. It was also seen that, in a related manner, such methods had tended to blur, for planning purposes, concrete development problems in what were, in fact, very different areas of the country, geographically and socially. For these reasons, the minister was tempted to see the question of planning as "the big issue of the Congress."[53]

We can return to a quotation from the key Congress document to get a further clue to this "big issue." For the Congress's emphasis on smaller, more decentralized projects was not only an attempt to gear Mozambique's undertakings to its real capabilities. Recall that decentralization would also "awaken the people's creativity, develop the principle of self-reliance and enable the enthusiastic participation of the masses." It remained to be seen how all this would be put into practice, but some of the initial signs were positive. As regards the bureaucracy itself, the emphasis in the period immediately after the Congress was on moving many more cadres out of Maputo into roles much closer to the base. Just how the planning process would come to meld into itself the reinvigorated flow of "planning from below" that the Congress seemed to call for also remained to be seen, however.

A very different kind of decentralization of decision-making is implied by the promised reliance on the increased use of market mechanisms, especially in the rural areas. Not that this was something entirely new. The Third Congress directives had themselves allowed for the continuation of private sector activity. An even more positive approach to that sector was taken after the failure of the government's early attempts to have state-run "people's stores" *(lojas do povo)* fill the yawning gap left in the marketing sphere by the flight of the commercial class after independence. Although cooperative marketing ventures have had somewhat more success, especially in urban settings, by 1980 the FRELIMO leadership was inviting back private traders to take up some of the slack in the country's battered network of commercialization. As the President put the point in an important speech, "Private enterprise has an important role to play in our country. . . . The state cannot continue to be involved in hundreds of people's shops. The state is going to create conditions to help private traders, farmers and manufacturers whose activity is within the framework of our objectives."[54] And, on another occasion: "Marxism has nothing to do with selling eggs or tomatoes. The state cannot set up to sell cigarettes or run garages. It must simply supervise the economy's primary sectors."[55]

The first of these quotations indicates that the embracing of the private trader was paralleled by an outreach to the private investor in other spheres. We shall explore this aspect of Mozambican policy more thoroughly below. However, we have already noted the extent to which, in the view of the Fourth Congress, market mechanisms had to be exploited in order to help revive the shattered rural economy and—by extension—the economy as a whole. There are those who will argue that this is, in any case, the only "feasible socialism," feasible in economic terms, feasible, as well, in the sense of reducing the danger of creating mere "state collectivism," rule by a bureaucratic class, in the name of socialism. Yet it is also the case that class formation of a more conventionally capitalist kind can be spurred on by the market and is also self-evidently a danger to socialist aspirations; the logic of planning must ultimately override the logic of the market if socialism is to have any meaning at all; democratic structures and popular class action rather than market constraints must, ultimately, be the primary means of constraining an overweening bureaucracy. The Mozambican leadership has shown itself to be very much aware of these latter points, too. This gives some grounds for optimism regarding Mozambique's future as the leadership attempts to steer between the Scylla of state collectivism and the Charybdis of state capitalism.

It will be apparent by now that any such attempt is taking place upon difficult terrain and this fact becomes even clearer as we turn, once again, to locate Mozambique in its international environment. As seen, Mozambique's strategic vulnerability has been a major factor contributing to its economic weakness. In a document delivered on February 2, 1984, to the embassies of its creditor countries explaining its request to reschedule its growing foreign debt, Mozambique itemized some of the more visible costs of South Africa's aggression via the MNR: the destruction of 900 rural shops, 490 primary schools, 86 health posts, and 140 communal villages in 1982 and 1983.[56] But the cost of diverting scarce domestic (as well as foreign exchange) resources to military purposes has been even greater than this (29 percent of total expenditure allocation in the 1982 budget, and growing), as is the invisible cost of vital trading, transport, and communication networks and the like destroyed. Yet it is also the case that Mozambique's economic weaknesses make it, in turn, all the more vulnerable.

We noted at the outset of this section some of the economic trump cards which South Africa inherited from the Portuguese and which have now been available to play against Mozambique. Indeed, in the above mentioned note to its creditors Mozambique speaks at length about South Africa's "boycott" of the Mozambican economy—as evidenced by such things as the fall in labor recruitment and the avoidance of Mozambique's port. Of course, other costs, such as those linked to implementing sanctions against Rhodesia, to floods (1977 and 1978) and drought (1982 and 1983), and to deteriorating terms of trade, are also mentioned, though the growing need to import food and thus add to the growing trade deficit is not. As Hodges notes,

> the balance of payments deficit on current account was already running at about $175–200m a year in 1977–81. Foreign exchange reserves were being run down, and the government was forced to borrow from abroad. The external public debt was $445m by the end of 1980 and $539m a year later. But with the balance of payments deteriorating further over the past two years, "there are reasons to believe that the real figures now could be four times as high," contends a recent report prepared jointly by embassies of EEC countries here.[57]

To be sure, the attendant collapse of Mozambique's credit rating is very recent; moreover, its "debt crisis" is far less dramatic than that of many other third world countries. Yet it hampers economic development, constraining import of necessary inputs, for example. And, to repeat, it makes Mozambique more vulnerable to outside pressures.

Most recently, Mozambique has startled many outside observers by turning dramatically toward the international capitalist system itself (and even toward South Africa!) in order to find a way out of its difficulties. We will return to an analysis of these developments shortly. But other alternatives have also been canvased, notably links to the "socialist countries" on the one hand and to its regional neighbors—via the Southern African Development Coordination Conference (SADCC)—on the other. We will look briefly at each of these fronts in turn. Although Mozambique has consistently repeated its adherence to the principle of "nonalignment" in foreign policy, it has been equally adamant in emphasizing both its "anti-imperialist" position and its particularly strong affinity for those states which it defines as being "socialist countries." It is worth underscoring the fact that in the latter category are to be found not only the Soviet Union, Eastern European countries, Cuba, Korea, and Vietnam but also China. Mozambique has refused to compromise on the principle of nonalignment within the socialist camp itself, even though there have been moments of strain—caused, for example, by China's championing of extremely suspect "liberation movements" in southern Africa, apparently on no better grounds than that they did not enjoy Soviet support. As we shall see, a common adherence to "Marxism-Leninism" has been one of the terms in which this affinity has come to be cast. But it has had a solid material basis as well.

The crucial link has been military, again from the earliest days of the armed struggle. The Organization of African Unity provided some assistance in this respect, but, in essence, Mozambique could only look east if it was to obtain the weaponry necessary to advance its cause. Moreover, the bottom line of military backup in the ongoing war against first Rhodesia and then South Africa which FRELIMO has been forced to wage since independence remains the Eastern bloc countries, even though Mozambique has continued to receive African assistance (notably from Tanzania and Zimbabwe) in recent years and has also sought to obtain Western European backing. Not that Mozambicans have always found the assistance of the Soviet Union and its allies to be as extensive—or nearly as cheap—as they might have liked. But it has been crucially important nonetheless. Meanwhile, on other fronts,

Economic support from the socialist nations in the form of direct aid and capital investment has been far less significant than their military assistance. Nevertheless, through barter agreements Mozambique has acquired heavy industrial equipment, trucks, tools and badly needed spare parts in exchange for deliveries of cashew nuts, citrus fruits, coal, cotton, sisal, shrimps and fish. Details of the financing are secret, but the agreements transform Mozambique's annual deficits from these exchanges into long-term, hard currency loans at rates somewhat below international levels. This strategy, beneficial to the Eastern European countries as well, has enabled Mozambique to acquire badly needed capital goods without having to utilize its limited hard currency, has provided it with new markets, and has helped Mozambique to reduce, if not reverse, its dependency on South Africa. Whereas in 1975 trade with the Warsaw nations was negligible, in 1979 it accounted for approximately 15 percent of Mozambican commerce and by 1982 East Germany had become Mozambique's fourth largest trading partner.[58]

Moreover,

since 1980 the USSR and East Germany have increased non-military aid to Mozambique, which was negligible up to that point. Both have helped to fund mineral exploration, Mozambique's fledgling textile industry, and some heavy industry including a truck and tractor assembly plant. . . . [In addition], technical assistance from the socialist countries is quite substantial in comparison to direct financial support.

Of course, the Soviet Union and its allies are hard bargainers, economically and politically. Mozambique seems to have succeeded in steering carefully around most of the pitfalls and quid pro quos, gaining some important room for internal economic maneuver in the process although finding no panacea for its problems in the East. In fact it bears noting that, contrary to Western mythology, the Soviet Union is not as eager to enter into commitments abroad, particularly of an economic nature, as might be expected. Witness the reluctance to countenance readily Mozambique's entry into COMECON despite Mozambique's apparent eagerness to do so. Moreover, even if greater Eastern commitment were there, the fact is that these countries simply do not have the wherewithal—the capital, the technology, the personnel—to become a crucial flywheel for putting the Mozambican economy into gear. Or such, at least, is the conclusion to which Mozambicans have come.

Development of a regional economic network has been another front to which Mozambique has looked for economic succor. SADCC was founded in Lusaka in 1980, with Mozambique among its most enthusiastic advocates. Although building on the experience of the "front-line states," it embraced a quite eclectic membership, ranging from Malawi and Swaziland on the one hand to Mozambique and Angola on the other. In effect, it was to provide an alternative to South Africa's own proposed "constellation of states," the latter a mechanism designed to institutionalize South Africa's economic hegemony in the region. Many hoped that in the long run SADCC would structure an economic grid that could sustain economic and other exchanges outside South Africa's orbit, gradually acquiring an independent regional logic of its own (at least until such time as South Africa itself was transformed by revolution). Its eclectic membership and its brief existence to date have placed limits on its accomplishments, of course, but progress has been made, particularly in the coordination of transportation and communications (and some external assistance—geared specifically to SADCC undertakings—has been brought in that might otherwise not have been forthcoming). Sufficient progress, in fact, for South Africa to make transportation and other linkages which fall under the SADCC aegis privileged targets of the extensive sabotage that has accompanied its destabilization efforts in the region; this has been especially true of MNR activities in Mozambique. Not that SADCC could be central to resolving Mozambique's short-term problems in any case. But as an earnest of what a southern Africa finally at peace might look like, it has its importance.

More recently, Mozambique has felt compelled to reach out to a powerful global capitalism somewhat more invitingly in order to mend its tattered economy. To be sure, it has done so in some degree right from the very first days of Mozambican independence; we have seen that FRELIMO had little initial choice but to retain many of the ties which subordinated it to South Africa and to the imperial marketplace beyond. (It has been estimated that 80 percent of Mozambique's main exports go to the United States and Western Europe.) For these ties gave Mozambique's economy a good portion of such life as it had. Even the country's extensive nationalizations of productive enterprises in the early days took place at a far more dramatic rate than FRELIMO might otherwise have chosen for itself. But the wave of abandonment of factories and farms and the extensive sabotage which followed the movement's ascension to power forced its hand. Thus it was not entirely inconsistent, if nonetheless somewhat surprising, that in 1979 and 1980 the party signaled with sharp clarity its eagerness to cooperate with Western capital. As the Isaacmans have written,

> Mozambique's leaders have sought investment capital from a wide variety of sources, both in the West and in the socialist countries. This policy is based on their assessment that the socialist countries were unable or unwilling to provide the necessary capital, that Western countries had greater available investment capital and technological superiority in certain strategic sectors, and that the potential advantages of entering into agreements with capitalist countries and multinational corporations outweighed the necessary risks. "We are open to mutually advantageous cooperation with firms from other countries," announced the Council of Ministers in 1979. "As a socialist country we do not fear [such] cooperation. . . . We need technology. We need finance."

But, they add, Mozambique stipulated that "foreign investments would be approved only if they furthered Mozambique's economic plan, ensured an appropriate transfer of technology, guaranteed the training of Mozambican workers, and permitted nationalization at the end of a specified time written into the initial contract." And they quote a strong statement by Samora Machel to a 1980 meeting with prospective Western investors (a meeting organized by the consulting firm Business International) to the effect that "We do not intend to become perpetual suppliers of raw materials. We intend to develop our industry and agriculture. We intend to participate in the international division of labour in a position of equality."[59]

Other statements were more inviting. As Sergio Vieira, then governor of the Bank of Mozambique, put the point to London's *Financial Times*, "We want to cooperate on the basis of mutual advantage and non-interference. There are no abstract principles. We are concerned to define what is the most profitable basis for both sides."[60] And the business press took note: "A Marxist State Tilts Profitably to the West," headlined *Business Week* in December 1979; "Winds of Change: Mozambique Warms Towards Capitalism," wrote Bridget Bloom in the *Financial Times* in April 1980. But Mozambique was indeed intent upon driving a hard bargain: witness, some months later, a headline in the *Wall Street Journal* (December 30, 1980), "African Maneuver: Mozambique Woos Foreign Investor but Keeps Socialism." Too hard a bargain for businessmen, perhaps, the government even refusing to publish a general investment code, preferring hard bargaining on a case by case basis. Not that foreign investment was entirely absent in these years. The General Tire and Rubber Company, for example, was linked by a supervisory contract into the tire business, and the Isaacmans list a growing number of firms from a wide range of countries which had begun to move in. But it was scarcely a flood, and unlikely quickly to become one in the opinion of Bloom and others in articles in the business journals listed above.

Whatever the results, the initiatives of 1979–1980 demonstrate that an "opening to the West" has long been part of FRELIMO strategy. However, the deepening of the NEP orientation of the party's strategic thinking combined powerfully in the past few years with the increasingly desperate nature of the economic situation in which Mozambique increasingly found itself. As a result, the country began to push this "opening" even more aggressively in the wake of the Fourth Congress. It is true that the key document at that Congress had been unequivocal in its analysis of "the international economic situation":

> The difficult situation we face is aggravated by the effects of the current international crisis on underdeveloped countries. The most serious factors affecting our countries are imported inflation, protectionist measures, deteriorating terms of trade and rising interest rates. Food scarcity and increasing technological and scientific dependence make the situation more dramatic.

The tendency on the part of the imperialist powers to use coercive economic measures to gain certain political ends is becoming common practice. Thus, underdeveloped countries become subject to pressure from international financial institutions. The economic measures that are imposed on these countries are ruinous to the interest of their peoples. The present international economic order is characterized by flagrantly unjust relationships resulting from ties of dependence. This situation is leading to a growth of consciousness among the countries who are the greatest sufferers. In international institutions, anti-imperialist feeling is growing, and the will to find alternatives to the present situation is being strengthened. In underdeveloped countries there is an increasing conviction that only socialism can bring the total independence and social and economic progress that lead to justice, freedom and prosperity.[61]

Yet the fall of 1983 found President Machel in Europe making a further spirited bid to attract foreign private investment to Mozambique. This bid was tied to attempts to secure military cooperation as well, and one may suspect that both initiatives were also designed to win friends in Europe, the better to focus international pressure on South Africa to cease its aggression against Mozambique. But Mozambican leaders made no excuses regarding the economics of their outreach to global capitalism. Indeed, quite the opposite was true of the tone of speeches Machel made to Portuguese businessmen in Lisbon and Porto and of his statements in other European capitals.* Moreover, when early the next year (March 1984) Mozambique came to sign a "nonaggression pact" with South Africa, one aspect of the resultant Nkomati Accord was to add even South African businessmen to the list of possible investors in that country.

We shall discuss the Nkomati Accord more fully in the concluding chapter of this volume. Here we must focus on what seems to be the underlying premise of FRELIMO's thinking regarding the economics of this "opening to the West," a premise which seems clear enough, however controversial it may be. It is that international capital is to provide the necessary "flywheel" for Mozambican development of which we spoke earlier. This would be especially true with regard to that key blockage to "expanded socialist repro-

---

*While in Europe, Samora Machel also signaled a new willingness to link Mozambique to the European Economic Community via the Lomé Convention; discussions with both the International Monetary Fund and the World Bank suggested an increasingly debt-ridden Mozambique to be on the verge of linking itself to these two pillars of the international capitalist system as well—and indeed this was soon to occur.

duction" which we have identified and where foreign investment might be expected to play a role: the consumer and light producer goods sector. But the same medicine is apparently thought to be promising for certain agricultural and mining activities whose increased production might help confront other crucial bottlenecks: food shortages and limited foreign exchange earnings. Whether this gambit will work or not, even in narrowly economic terms, remains an open question. A *Financial Times* correspondent visiting Maputo in April 1984 found some evidence that it might:

> . . . on the economic front, say officials, there is substantial progress. "We discovered that if we provided £50,000 worth of spare-parts," said one visiting chairman of a detergent company, "we could revive a factory worthy ten times that amount." A South African freight company is discussing investment in Maputo port: "We will provide equipment such as fork-lift trucks in return for rebates on our South African traffic," says one director. "For the first time in years our Maputo office could make a profit."

But he also found contradictory evidence as well:

> "[The Mozambicans] overestimate the appeal of Mozambique to Western businessmen," said one diplomat. "Tiny Rowland jetted in, committed Lonrho to agricultural ventures, and continued on his African rounds. But there aren't many Tiny Rowlands in the West." "The infrastructure is poor, skills are scarce, and the currency is massively overvalued," he continued.[62]

In fact, it is too early to say anything with very great confidence regarding such developments. Investment prospects will also depend, as we shall see, on the degree to which Mozambique and South Africa can, between them, wind down the MNR's destructive campaign inside Mozambique. It is also too early to tell how clearly and effectively Mozambique will seek to guide such investment as may be forthcoming into areas which represent priorities within its own long-term strategy of transformation. The degree of day-to-day control which will be maintained over private investors in the running of their businesses remains a question mark. The extent of one kind of control will not be apparent until we see the terms of the investment code which Mozambique has finally agreed to draw up—under some pressure from its potential new partners in development; one fears, however, that Mozambique may be in an even less effective position to bargain than it was in 1979–1980. And what of workers' control? Would a much greater influx of foreign capital put greater pressure on party and government to use the structures of "worker's participation" to control the workers rather than facilitate their action from below?

Time alone will tell. Certainly some Mozambican public state-

ments seem almost willfully naive about the risks to Mozambican
socialism which are involved. Thus Jacinto Veloso, a senior economic minister in the President's office, comments on the new
investment code by saying, "We will be very flexible. We understand that a businessman will want to repatriate capital to amortize
his investment as quickly as possible. . . . Capital is capital, investment is investment. If someone invests capital he wants a return on
it, whether he is a private entrepreneur or the head of a state
enterprise."[63] An editorial from the official Mozambican Information Agency (AIM) takes a rather different tone, a tone one might
have expected to hear more of from the FRELIMO leadership,
given its track record, during this difficult period. It bears quoting
at length.

> The Nkomati Accord between Mozambique and South Africa closes a
> cycle of twenty years of military aggression against Mozambique. It
> sets up the conditions for a lasting peace inside the country's borders
> after the final elimination of the bandit gangs who call themselves the
> "National Resistance."
>   But, on the other hand, the accord opens up other areas of strug-
> gle. One of these areas, perhaps the most important one, is that of
> foreign investments.
>   Because of the war situation that Mozambique had to confront,
> many financial institutions and multinational companies suspended
> their investments in Mozambique. These investments will now return,
> and, as banditry is eliminated throughout the country, they will in-
> crease.
>   The basic truth of the past nine years is that imperialism failed to
> destroy socialism in Mozambique by military means. A second truth is
> that it will now try to do so via economic means. This is perfectly
> normal and logical—it is in the nature of imperialism to try to domi-
> nate, to take out minerals and leave behind empty holes, to take out
> profits from industrial enterprises and leave behind the same level of
> ignorance that existed before these enterprises were set up. Its prac-
> tice is to train some technicians, but afterwards persuade them to
> abandon the country where investment was made. It accumulates
> capital and leaves behind governments and petty bourgeoisies com-
> pletely corrupted by the scraps from the neocolonial banquet.
>   In this struggle it is up to Mozambique to avoid domination, to raise
> the level of expertise constantly of its technicians; to search for new
> and better sources of raw material inside its own territory; to learn to
> master the transition from the mere extraction of raw materials to
> their transformation in manufacturing industry; to fight against cor-
> ruption.
>   And once again, Mozambicans will apply their heritage from
> twenty years of armed struggle: analyzing each success and each fail-

ure, instead of taking the mediocre way out, namely that of just hurl-
ing accusations against imperialism.

... Today ... many people are frightened by the thought of foreign
investment. Some are preparing for battle with a feeling that they are
already defeated. They overestimate the strength of imperialist
capital and they underestimate the capacities of the Mozambican people....

Given our state of economic and technical backwardness, this struggle will be, without doubt, the longest that Mozambicans have
launched to date. To defend socialism in Mozambique from the inroads of capital will not be easy. But either we confront the enemy in
this field and learn to handle the weapons of economic liberation ...
or we will forever, as a people and as a nation, be chained to misery,
backwardness, and mediocrity.

Today we are saying to foreign capital "Come here." And we will
have to fight this battle, too, with appropriate weapons—the defense
of our national interests in each contract that is signed, professional
training, study, quality in production, the use of other socialist countries as a firm rearguard, and many other weapons that we will only
learn to use in so far as we undertake the struggle.

This is the wider context of the Nkomati Accord, its strategic dimension. Not to understand this, to see in the accord only its tactical
aspects, is like refusing to see in the years at the end of one century,
the beginnings of the century that is to follow. Indeed this economic
struggle will be the main arena in which Mozambique will have to
fight in the first decades of the twenty-first century.[64]

This is a disarming presentation, though not a surprising one, and
we shall return to it in our final chapter. One question we will have
to ask at that point is whether Mozambique has had any choice but
to follow this hazardous road; another question is whether its
socialism is likely to survive the journey. It would be wise to avoid
dogmatism about such questions, perhaps, although it must be admitted that the prospect for any third world country, socialist or
otherwise, judiciously manipulating international capitalism in
such a way that the latter comes to negate itself is not self-evidently
a promising one. This struggle may indeed prove to be "the longest
that Mozambicans have launched to date." Undoubtedly it will test
the strength of the analogy with the days of armed struggle which
provides the basis for the AIM document we have been quoting
from.

Twenty years ago, those half-dozen Mozambicans [who decided to
take up arms to struggle against Portuguese colonialism] did not have
an exact plan of how they were going to struggle in the months and
years to follow. They learned how to struggle by struggling, but always with a solid base of self-confidence and a clear strategic objec-

tive: total and complete independence. Today there is no detailed map of the future. But again, there is a clear strategic objective: the economic independence of Mozambique. And today, just as twenty years ago, there is a full awareness of the strength of the enemy. Once again it is fundamental to be aware of why the struggle is necessary and to have confidence in Mozambicans—in short to set out for battle with a feeling that victory is possible.[65]

The Ideological Front

In our introduction we suggested that the complex sphere of ideology has provided both opportunities and distinctive challenges to Mozambique's socialist project. Thus FRELIMO has increasingly availed itself of the strengths of the Marxist tradition, but has also had to struggle to minimize the costs of certain of the weaknesses of that tradition. The present section will address itself in more detail to this issue. Of course, we have already traced (in Chapter 1) the manner in which FRELIMO moved, during its long years of struggle, onto the terrain of Marxism. In addition to Mondlane (as quoted earlier), other FRELIMO members have emphasized the kind of "elective affinity" which began to establish itself between the maturing practices of the movement and the Marxist tradition. In the words of Oscar Monteiro, presently a member of FRELIMO's Political Bureau, "It is our experience which led us toward Marxism-Leninism. We have spontaneously demonstrated its universal character. We have, on the basis of our practice, drawn theoretical lessons."[66] So, too, Samora Machel:

> Ideas come from practice. When we set out, all those years ago, we wanted to liberate our people; and we found that people have to liberate themselves if the thing is to be real. We found that people could not liberate themselves unless they were active participants in the process of liberation. And so, little by little, we applied a revolutionary practice . . . [that] enabled this indispensable participation, this mass participation—political and social, cultural, and military—to begin to grow and develop itself. We learned much, we made mistakes and saw how to correct them. In doing so, we evolved a theory out of our practice; and we found that this theory of ours, evolving out of our practice, had already acquired a theorization under different circumstances, elsewhere, in different times and places. This theory and theorization is Marxism-Leninism.[67]

The sense that Marxism-Leninism would enable Mozambicans to systematize the lessons of their previous practice more coherently, thereby helping to transform their "practical ideology" into a more effective method of work and a more effective pedagogy, was given formal recognition in 1977. The key document of FRELIMO's Third Congress in that year announced the following:

> If it is to be a real vanguard force of the laboring classes, our Party must be armed with a revolutionary theory which enables its members to understand exactly the laws of social development and of the Revolution. Without this ideological and theoretical basis, the Party is not in a position to direct and lead the struggle of the laboring masses. This ideological and theoretical basis is Marxism-Leninism or Scientific Socialism. Marxism-Leninism is the theoretical synthesis of the rich experiences of oppressed classes and peoples throughout the world, in their age-old struggle against the exploiters for the establishment of the new Power. Applied and developed creatively in the process of our struggle, it is a powerful beacon which lights the way that the laboring classes must follow in the process of constructing the new society. Scientific Socialism is not a static doctrine; it is a science that is continually enriched by the daily experiences of mass struggle. The Party will always apply the universal principles of Marxism-Leninism, taking into account the concrete conditions in which the class struggle develops in our country. In this way, what our party and our people do will continue to contribute to the development and enrichment of the scientific ideology of the proletariat.[68]

This was a development of truly continental significance, of course. True, a number of other sub-Saharan African states have begun to portray themselves publically in Marxist-Leninist terms, thus sparking a flurry of books and articles in Western circles on "Afro-Communism" and "Afro-Marxism."[69] Yet Mozambique has seemed to be pursuing this course on a firmer basis and with a clearer and more committed sense of what they are about.[70] The break with the nostrums of "African Socialism" which had passed for quasiprogressive discourse in ruling circles in the early post-colonial period could not have been sharper. Note Samora Machel's response when asked a question regarding FRELIMO's use of the adjective "scientific" instead of "African" in front of the word "socialism":

> We refuse the idea of "African socialism" because then there would have to be a European socialism, an Asian socialism, an American socialism. How many socialisms would there have to be? Socialism is a science . . . the result of hard work and the development of that science by the workers. And that's where we have the key, where we find the spinal column of struggle in the world—in the class struggle. If we want to launch a serious combat, if we want to develop our country in a balanced, clear, organized way, only science will serve. And science is in the hands of the workers. . . . Our strategy for struggle is very simple: to define correctly our enemy and to define correctly our objectives. And it is for this reason that we use the term "scientific socialist" analysis.[71]

At the same time, Machel did not apologize for the fact that this Marxist perspective was to be concretized with clear reference to local realities—not a "Mozambican Marxism" to be sure, but certainly a Marxism firmly cast by Mozambicans in Mozambique's own terms. We cited one important statement by Samora Machel to this effect in our introductory chapter but it is a recurring theme of his: "Africans must use Marxism, but Marxism cannot be allowed to use Africans," as he once put the point in my presence. This is also a time-honored theme, of course, despite the difficulties some Western commentators seem to have had in comprehending the point. Indeed, in calling for a Marxism-Leninism developed with reference to Mozambique's own realities, Machel is unconsciously echoing Lenin himself who had once argued that

> we do not regard Marx's theory as something complete and inviolable; on the contrary, we are convinced that it has only laid the foundation stone of the science which socialists *must* develop in all directions if they wish to keep pace with life. We think that an *independent* elaboration of Marx's theory is essential for Russian socialists; for this theory provides only general *guiding* principles, which, *in particular,* are applied in England differently than in France, in France differently than in Germany, and in Germany differently than in Russia.[72]

It must be admitted, however, that such subtlety in defining FRELIMO's ideological project has not always proven to be so easy to exemplify. The ideological terrain remains a contested one in its own right, as we shall now see.

In part this has sprung from the fact that one particular definition of what is at the core of Marxism did initially have a very strong impact upon this new, more formalized ideological option: this was the orthodox Soviet definition. The costs of this impact were high—and the reasons for it numerous. The Soviet Union and the other countries of Eastern Europe had played a very positive role in supporting the armed struggle and were therefore already trusted allies. Moreover, as we have seen, they have continued to provide an important bottom-line of support for defense purposes and to provide, as well, a range of other kinds of assistance. And they were Marxists to boot, Marxists who also had a readily available, pre-packaged (in Portuguese as in other languages) Marxist-Leninist pedagogy which could be slotted into place quickly whenever the occasion arose. With so few trained and politically tested people within its own ranks (and given the wide range of tasks which had to be undertaken at independence), FRELIMO was tempted to cede part of the job of filling in the blanks in its more systematic statement of Marxism to Eastern

European "experts." This occurred most notably throughout the
education system, where the need to make FRELIMO's historic
practice accessible as a coherent pedagogy and a method of work
was particularly pressing for those many Mozambicans who did not
have the direct experience of the guerrilla war to draw upon.

There was a second reason of at least equal importance for what
might appear to have been the undue prominence of "Soviet Marxism" in Mozambique. For some of the negative aspects of Soviet
Marxism actually fit the Mozambican situation all too neatly; it
served, in effect, to sanction certain negative tendencies within
Mozambique's attempted transition to socialism, tendencies which
had other structural foundations beyond the strictly ideological. To
elaborate this point we must underscore the fact that, as a model of
socialist construction, the Soviet Union leaves a great deal to be
desired. Moreover, the weaknesses in its socialist practice are entirely congruent with weaknesses in its ideological formulations. Its
Marxism has come to serve far more as a rationalization and legiti-
mation of a bureaucratic, technocratic, and authoritarian status
quo than as a growing body of scientific knowledge, as an intellectual instrument of emancipation or a guide to ongoing class struggle in the post-revolutionary phase. The most revealing indication
that this is a "frozen Marxism" is its loss of a sense of the *dialectical*
relationship between elements. For example, the "productive
forces" are generally conceived as being "determinant" in a very
onesided way, and the importance of changes in the relations of
production and of an ongoing class struggle during the period of
socialist construction played down. The potential linkage between
this kind of theoretical problematic on the one hand and, on the
other, bureaucratic and technocratic definitions of what socialist
construction must involve in practice will be clear. In a similar
manner, onesided definitions of the "vanguard party," the "dictatorship of the proletariat," and "democratic centralism" can also
begin with such an undialectical starting point. And these are
definitions which, in their blunting of a sense of the two-way relationship that must necessarily exist between leadership and mass
action, can also have bureaucratic and authoritarian implications.

In Mozambique, too, there have been strong pressures toward a
high degree of centralization (the apparent imperatives of mobilization for a seemingly unending war, the "logic" of economic planning and the like). At the extreme, such pressures have threatened
to freeze up the vibrant links between mass action and progressive
leadership which lay at the heart of the successful armed struggle.
In consequence, there (as in the Soviet Union) mechanical and
unproblematic definitions of "vanguard" and "dictatorship of the

proletariat" could serve merely to lock such a negative tendency into place. Fortunately, as argued earlier, FRELIMO has struggled to avoid any such denouement to its ongoing struggle. Not that it offers any apology for the vanguard model it has adopted, nor for the fact that it sees itself as having a crucial role to play in giving shape and direction to the assertions of the popular classes as these latter grow into their power. But neither has it allowed dubiously Marxist precedent to freeze the positive potential of that concept; instead FRELIMO has remained sensitive to the need to keep the leadership–mass action dialectic alive and has refused, as well, to blur the continuing need for class struggle.

Indeed, as Sonia Kruks has observed, FRELIMO was even prepared to seize hold of another staple concept of orthodox Marxism-Leninism and use it creatively in the effort to deepen its own revolutionary practice.[73] The concept was that of "popular-democratic revolution" or "popular democracy," a self-definition Mozambique formally embraced for itself over an extended period. A FRELIMO presentation to an international congress of Communist parties in Bulgaria in 1978 catches the tone:

> The program of our party makes it clear that the stage of popular democracy is the historic period in which the process of eliminating all forms of foreign domination over our country is completed; in which we deepen the process of eliminating vestiges of traditional-feudal and colonial-capitalist society, developing a new culture, strengthening the power of workers and peasants over the society and creating the armed forces for defense of the Revolution; in which we develop the economy, satisfying the social needs of the people and instituting socialist relations of production. In sum, it is the stage in which we construct the bases for the passing over into a Socialist Revolution.[74]

Such a concept implies the necessity in an underdeveloped society to create a set of preconditions before socialism (let alone communism) can really be placed on the agenda. One precondition which is so identified is the mobilization of mass participation in the development process. As seen, this notion is not something foreign to FRELIMO's own historical experience. In fact, it was precisely here that the party has been able to breathe life into orthodoxy, allowing this concept to help it theorize in more resonant terms its various efforts to translate the institutions of "people's power" from the liberated areas into a democratization of post-independence Mozambique.

This is only one side of the story, however. Many Mozambicans chafed at the concept's implicit sub-text—that they were not quite ready for socialism—a reading borne home by the fact that it was applied to Mozambique with a somewhat patronizing air by many Eastern European politicians and intellectuals. Already at a major conference in Berlin held in 1980 less was heard in the Mozambican presentation about "popular democracy" and more about the "passage from colonialism to socialism," a subtle but real shift of emphasis which some Eastern Europeans fielded with more good grace than others.[75] Yet that said, it must be admitted that the emphasis upon "backwardness" which gives the notion of a necessary popular-democratic phase such coherence as it has had does have some resonance in Mozambique. There is just enough truth in this emphasis to strengthen some Mozambican leaders in an exaggerated suspicion of the revolutionary vocation, in the post-independence phase, of the peasantry, for example, and to confirm them, too, in a certain hesitancy about the efficacy of a more full-blown commitment to "people's power"—in the "absence" of a "developed proletariat." In this kind of "class analysis" might lie some of the ingredients for crystallization of a much more negative brand of vanguardism, one which would, in Kruks' phrase, make "people's democracy" an "increasingly empty rhetoric."

We have seen the way in which any downgrading of the peasant role in the Mozambican revolution could also have negative consequences for socialist economic strategy. But this is merely one aspect of a much broader point that must be made concerning the relevance of ideology to economic practice. There is an almost universal temptation for third world countries to look for shortcuts in order to bridge the economic development gap, shortcuts which tend to be conceived in terms of "high-tech" and "large-scale" solutions. As we have seen, Mozambican planners experienced this temptation as well, thus running the risk of costs on two fronts. Firstly, the need to maintain a delicate balance between the claims of such "modernization" on the one hand and mass involvement in the development process on the other can sometimes get lost in the shuffle. Secondly, the presumed imperatives of "accumulation" can take undue precedence over the logic of "expanded socialist reproduction." Here, too, the neo-Stalinist version of Marxism-Leninism can sanction such one-sided tendencies. The chief reason for this was mentioned earlier: it lies in the economistic and undialectical privileging of changes in the forces of production as being more fundamental than any simultaneous changes in the relations of production. Ergo, "backwardness" dictates accumulation. Nothing much is possible in more expansively socialist terms without industrial transformation (and without the proletariat that will emerge alongside that kind of transformation of the forces of production). From such a perspective undue preoccupation with socialist relations of production and with democratization can be deemed unseemly; certainly these are not to take precedence over the claims of "centralization," "planning," and efficiency.* A comforting thought for technocrats, certainly. There can be little doubt that, whatever its other merits, Eastern European assistance in various key economic sectors has facilitated such thinking. To take merely one of the most obvious examples, the prominent role taken by Bulgarian (and other) experts in the state farm sector helped both to reinforce an unhealthy bureaucratization of that sector itself and to reinforce the unbalanced approach which unduly privileged that sector over and against the claims of the peasantry and of the cooperativization program. It is no doubt significant, in a similar fashion, that many of the most influential technical planners in post-independence Mozambique—and some of those most responsible for the onesided emphases discussed above—have been young Mozambicans, often white, whose initial radical formation took place not in the ranks of FRELIMO but in circles much more closely associated, in both Lourenço Marques and Portugal, with the Portuguese Communist Party (e.g., the Associação Academico). Perhaps it is also this group, and others like it to whom Samora Machel was referring when he was cited recently to the effect that "cooperation with China," to take one example, "had experienced some difficulties owing to the introduction of certain themes alien to FRELIMO's philosophy":

> Thus with independence there began to appear pro-Soviet and pro-Chinese lines, introducing into Mozambique a conflict which opposed the USSR and China. . . . Samora Machel had to intervene on various occasions. He explained to us that this kind of thinking came from outside, especially from intellectuals returning from Portugal. It represented a kind of rootless intellectualism.[76]

Of course, some senior leaders have also been subject to some of these temptations. Yet our examination of post-independence developments in this chapter has shown that FRELIMO has not, on the whole, rested content with the seductive formulae of orthodoxy. It has, among other things, continued to air its own vanguardism, to seek out possible class contradictions, and to critique onesidedly "accumulationist" prescriptions. Here is considerable evidence both as to the *independence* of Mozambique's Marxism and the *creative* manner in which FRELIMO has been attempting to

---

*An undialectical conception of the "primacy of the productive forces" can have other costs as well, one of the most important being a possible facilitating of an economistic and reductionist approach to gender oppression. However, I will not anticipate here the more detailed remarks on this theme which are to be found in Stephanie Urdang's chapter in the present volume.

develop such an independent elaboration of Marxist theory and pratice. But FRELIMO has also turned an increasingly critical and creative eye on the actual process of ideological elaboration and propagation itself. For the party has become increasingly conscious of serious problems in this regard, problems which are to be seen in the formal education system, in the university, even in the party's own cadre training schools. Central here has been a disturbing gap between the "practical Marxism" which has characterized FRELIMO's own developing ideology and the more theoretically elaborated framework taken over (somewhat uncritically) from Eastern European textbooks and teachers in the post-independence years. The uneasiness of this mix was soon manifest in the pedagogical programs themselves, in their formidable degree of abstraction, and in the mechanical and lifeless (in fact, undialectical) manner in which they sought to explain social interconnections.

The growing complaint was that the resulting programs did not facilitate the student's gaining any more enlightened comprehension of Mozambican realities and therefore did not provide an adequate guide to action. Reiteration of the so-called laws of the dialectic and of other such dubious formulations tended to take pride of place over developing an analysis of Mozambican realities in Marxist-Leninist terms. The result? In the formal school system it was more the political demobilization of the students than it was the reverse. Before long most of the programs in the schools had actually disappeared, although subject to ongoing efforts to revive them. At the university students took to calling the Department of Dialectical and Historical Materialism, charged with providing political-cum-social science courses to all faculties, the "Department of Diabolical and Hysterical Materialism." Ultimately, at a disputatious public meeting at the university in 1980, resistance boiled over into open and pointed critique of what was being taught in the name of Marxism; moreover, it was painfully apparent that student scepticism regarding the courses under debate was by no means coming from the right (despite efforts by some faculty members, local and expatriate, to so portray it).[77] Shortly after the old Department of Dialectical and Historical Materialism became the new Faculty of Marxism-Leninism it was specifically ordered by the party's Department of Ideological Work (DTI) to develop much more creative and innovative syllabi.

Even in the party schools all was not well. There cadres were more diligently attentive to what was being taught, but there was sharp self-criticism nonetheless from those involved in mounting the programs in the schools. For even when students succeeded in mastering the slogans which were too often taught in the name of

Marxism-Leninism, it was apparent to party structures that they had been given little in the way of *analytical tools* with which they could grapple with concrete realities in the field. Changes were in order. As it happens, in 1981–1982 I myself worked in the FRELIMO party school in Maputo and in the Faculty of Marxism-Leninism at the university, participating in the attempt to develop new curricula in both institutions that it was hoped would begin to overcome some of these limitations. Progress was not easily realized in practice. At the university the innovative efforts of the new director of the faculty, a Mozambican, were actively undermined in the classroom and elsewhere by the still primarily Eastern European teaching faculty; moreover, the negative efforts of the latter group tended to be supported by a party branch on the campus that was itself of orthodox cast. In the party, too, progress was slow, if only because in the sphere of ideological elaboration, as in so many other technical spheres, the lack of trained person-power was painfully apparent.

So slow was progress, in fact, that by early 1983, in a dramatic move, it was decided to close down all party schools, as well as the Faculty of Marxism-Leninism at the university, for a period. These institutions were to reopen only when stronger curricula, more firmly rooted in a Mozambique-relevant Marxism, were available. But what would a Mozambique-relevant Marxism look like? From the very outset of the process of rethinking the sphere of "ideological work," self-criticism had tended to define the problem as being primarily a lack of Mazambican *content* in the teaching programs in Marxism-Leninism. The party Secretary of Ideological Work set the tone in an important meeting in early 1981: this work "must not be overburdened with abstract materials. It must base itself . . . in the tasks, the problems, and the questions directly linked to the process of development in Mozambique itself."[78] A few months later a national meeting of the party's DTI also spoke of the dangers of a "revolutionary verbalism" that did not "clarify the real explanation for the situation which presently exists in our country."[79]

This was a theme I was to hear often when working in the ideological sector in Mozambique; not surprisingly, the need to develop a Marxism more sensitive to Mozambican realities was also underscored at the Fourth Congress:

> Practical training is not enough for the needs of the class struggle. Theoretical training is an indispensable part of the preparation of a revolutionary cadre able to understand reality and act to transform it.
> Cadres must master the FRELIMO party's political line, which means they must master Marxism-Leninism. Theoretical training programs are useful when the syllabus is rooted in the heritage of our

militants' experience and culture. We understand and assimilate Marxism-Leninism when it is possible to relate it to our militants' experience, our traditions, our culture, the environment in which we live, and the class struggle in our country.

Marxism-Leninism, therefore, is an effective weapon for the Mozambican working class and peasantry when it is applied and enriched from the starting point of our national reality. Revolutionary theory and revolutionary practice are always intimately linked. Revolutionary theory without practical examples of its practical application with reference to our country cannot be properly useful to party militants. This reflection has led the Central Committee to decide on a sweeping reorganization of the program for teaching Marxism-Leninism at all levels.[80]

This theme was picked up by a number of Central Committee members with whom I discussed such matters at the time of the Congress. Indeed, one of them, speaking informally to a group of invited foreign guests, suggested that the abstract nature of Mozambique's brand of Marxism complemented all too neatly the empty formalism which had infected the planning process itself.[81] He made a number of suggestive points in this regard, one of which has particular relevance in the present context. Having playfully likened the top-heavy philosophical cast of what has sometimes passed for Marxism-Leninism in Maputo to yet another "big project," he underscored the fact that this particular big project tended to steamroller specificity and to reinforce a misleading sense of national uniformity in the planning process. Such a sense of uniformity had been "at the expense of an understanding of our people," he said, blocking a comprehension of the socioeconomic and cultural complexity of diverse local settings. Yet the subtlety of its comprehension in this respect had been one of FRELIMO's hallmarks in the period of armed struggle. A Marxism which was not concrete, manageable, and "decentralized" in the same manner had ill-served present-day cadres attempting to work creatively at the local level.*

Rediscovering in this way the need to concretize Marxism is one important vaccination against becoming prisoner of a dead and

---

*On a closely related front, a serviceable, concrete Marxism would have to help more than it had to comprehend effectively other aspects of Mozambican society, aspects also freshly emphasized by the Fourth Congress: "Among us there is a tendency to think that in Mozambican society tribalism, regionalism, and racism have already been finally eradicated. It is a triumphalist tendency that can only have the effect of disarming us and demobilizing us in denouncing and resisting those divisive phenomena that still exist in our society." This diversity, too, was not to be steamrolled by theoretical fiat!

ultimately counterproductive variant of that tradition. Moreover, there have been signs that an even more profound point is beginning to be made by Mozambicans. This reflects a growing awareness that not only must Marxist theory, to be useful, be applied creatively to the concrete realities of Africa but that it is, in and of itself, a *contested* theory. As suggested earlier, it is not accidental that "Soviet Marxism" has such difficulty in illuminating concrete situations, clarifying existing contradictions, and advancing class struggle. The kind of creativity which might enable it to do so was drained away from it long ago as it became more and more an "ideology" in the negative sense—as it became, in effect, a legitimating rationale for holders of power. Fortunately, Mozambicans have a strong sense of the legitimacy of theoretical contestation, a sense that Marxism is alive in their hands and that they have the capacity to innovate on its terrain. In this regard, I recall the openness and frankness with which I was able to discuss first principles with leading party cadres in the Department of Ideological Work during my own tenure in Mozambique. I recall, too, the self-conscious irony with which Samora Machel once said in my presence that "some people seem to think that the development of Marxism ended in October 1917."

Nonetheless, to consistently pursue the question of Marxism back to theoretical first principles around which different conceptualizations form is a contentious undertaking, however much it may be a necessary one. To begin with, it could seem inadvisable to do so overtly for reasons of diplomacy: the Eastern European countries are valued allies. In addition, there could well be real differences of emphasis over such questions within the Mozambican leadership itself, differences which are not worth bringing to the surface and pushing to the limit. In discussions with a number of FRELIMO leaders at the time of the Fourth Congress, I also sensed that, in any case, some of the felt need for the theoretical innovation that underpins the emergent critique of Marxism-Leninism in Mozambique is still more implicit than fully realized. As I scanned proposed new syllabi scheduled for use in the party schools when they eventually reopened I could see that the all-too-familiar litany of "dialectical materialism–historical materialism" was being pushed into an increasingly smaller corner of the syllabus as more empirically focused Mozambican preoccupations took pride of place. But much of what passed for theory was still to be found in that corner. Moreover, the party cadre in charge of this revision of the course structure spoke to me frankly of the difficulty he and his colleagues had had, given the limitations of their own training, in really critiquing and innovating with regard to that section of the syllabus.

This is not necessarily so great a weakness as it may seem: the importance of theoretical first principles can be overstated by pedants of all political hue. For example, there has probably been more genuine Marxist analysis of Mozambican society in some of Samora Machel's most informal speeches than in most of the syllabi on "dialectical and historical materialism" produced by "advisors on ideology" to the Mozambican government. It is fortunate that many Mozambicans seem well aware of that fact. Surely the spirit of innovation (in a range of policy spheres) that we have traced elsewhere in this chapter bears eloquent testimony to this. Nonetheless, one must hope that the gap between theory and "ideological practice" which does exist in Mozambique will be filled even more creatively with the passage of time. After all, a mere concretization of Marxism, if cut off from the recasting of theory which should premise it, runs the risk of collapsing into a kind of pragmatism, however enlightened and revolutionary it may be. It runs the risk of becoming not so much a Marxism firmly rooted in Mozambican realities as a "Mozambican Marxism," with many of the negative connotations Samora Machel saw such a conceptualization to imply. For the less progressive this could be an invitation to a brand of atheoretical nationalism, cast in Marxist terms but rationalizing every opportunistic turn of the party line on both the international and domestic fronts, a kind of "African socialism revisited." For the more progressive the costs could be equally serious: they would be cut off, over time, from the full range of creative intellectual resources which the Marxist tradition at its best can offer those who seek to undertake a transition to socialism. In short, "ideological class struggle" is one more front upon which the broader struggle against the potent combination of underdevelopment and undevelopment continues in Mozambique. On past experience, however, it would be unwise not to expect further creativity, in this and in other spheres, from the Mozambican revolution.

Notes

1. FRELIMO, *Central Committee Report to the Third Congress of FRELIMO* (London, 1978), p. 35.
2. Article entitled "The Building of Mozambique's Marxist-Leninist Party," Mozambique Information Agency (AIM), *AIM Information Bulletin* 27 (September 1978).
3. This quotation as well as several others noted in succeeding paragraphs are also drawn from the document cited in n. 1 above.
4. The quotations from Samora Machel's speech cited in this paragraph are drawn from David Wield, "Mozambique—From Late Colonialism to Socialist Transformation," in Gordon White, et al., eds., *Revolu-*

148   A Difficult Road

tionary Socialist Development in the Third World (Brighton: Harvester Press, 1983).

5. See "President Spearheads Drive Against Negligence," *AIM Information Bulletin* 42 (December 1979).
6. For an example of this genre see Peter Meyns, "Liberation Ideology and National Development Strategy in Mozambique," *Review of African Political Economy* 22 (October–December 1981): 42–64.
7. Ronaldo Munck, citing *Novembro* 33 (June 1980) in his "Angola: Results and Prospects," *Critique* 15 (1981).
8. Interview with Samora Machel, *Tempo* (Maputo), no. 325 (26 December 1976).
9. Samora Machel, "Speech in Maputo on 18 March 1980," *AIM Information Bulletin* 45 (March 1980). See also Bertil Egero, "The Political Offensive 1980–81 in Mozambique," unpublished paper (November 1981).
10. Quoted in Roberta Washington, "Getting Hold of the Lion's Tail: The Campaign Against Bureaucracy," *Southern Africa* (June 1980).
11. Quoted in the article entitled "Campaign to Revitalize FRELIMO," *AIM Information Bulletin* 47 (May 1980).
12. "FRELIMO Central Committee Meets," *AIM Information Bulletin* 49 (July 1980).
13. See Samora Machel, "The Offensive Reaches the Defence and Security Forces," *AIM Information Bulletin* 65 (Supplement) (1981).
14. See, among other sources, Allen Isaacman and Barbara Isaacman, "South Africa's Hidden War," *Africa Report* 27, no. 6 (November–December 1982), and Paul Fauvet and Alves Gomes, "The Mozambique National Resistance," *AIM Information Bulletin* 69 (Supplement).
15. *Report on the Preparation of the Congress*, in FRELIMO, *Building Socialism: The People's Answer* (Maputo, 1983), p. 8.
16. Ibid., p. 25.
17. Central Committee of FRELIMO, *Out of Underdevelopment to Socialism*, (Maputo, 1983), pp. 71–72.
18. Samora Machel as quoted in the article "Founding Conference of Trade Union Organization," in Mozambique Information Office (MIO), *News Review* 17 (17 November 1983). Machel continues: "The task of our socialist trade unions is not to make wage claims. The living conditions of our workers improve in step with the growth of production, in step with the development of our economy."
19. Barry Munslow, "Is Socialism Possible in the Periphery?" *Monthly Review* 35, no. 1 (May 1983): 36.
20. Ralph Miliband, "Lenin's *The State and Revolution*" in Ralph Miliband and John Saville, eds., *The Socialist Register 1970* (London, 1970), p. 319.
21. Norman Geras, "Classical Marxism and Proletarian Representation," *New Left Review* 125 (January–February 1981): 75–89.
22. John S. Saul, "Zimbabwe: The Next Round," in Ralph Miliband and John Saville, eds., *The Socialist Register 1980* (London, 1980), p. 183.
23. See Tony Hodges, "Mozambique Emergency," *Africa Business* (Decem-

ber 1983); reproduced in *Facts and Reports* (Amsterdam) 13, no. 2 (23 December, 1983), 20–2.

24. Bertil Egero and Jens-Erik Torp, "Country Case Study on Mozambique," paper presented to conference on "Africa: Which Way Out of the Recession?" (Uppsala, September 1983), p. 7.
25. FRELIMO, *A situaçao actual no nosso pais*, as printed in *Noticias* (Maputo), 3 February 1982.
26. Hodges, "Mozambique Emergency," p. 21.
27. *Central Committee Report to the Third Congress of FRELIMO*, p. 43.
28. Samora Machel, "Façamos de 1980–1990 a década da vitoria sobre o subdesenvolvimento," closing speech to the Enlarged Session of the Council of Ministers, Maputo, 4 August 1979, reprinted in CEDIMO, *Discursos de Samora Moises Machel* 5 (Maputo, 1979): 97.
29. FRELIMO, *A situação actual no nosso pais*, as printed in *Noticias* (Maputo), 5 February 1982.
30. Nicos Zafiris, "The People's Republic of Mozambique: Pragmatic Socialism," in Peter Wiles, ed., *The New Communist Third World* (New York: St. Martins Press, 1982), p. 129.
31. *Central Committee Report to the Third Congress of FRELIMO*, pp. 46–48.
32. Hodges, "Mozambique Emergency," p. 21.
33. Egero and Torp, "Country Case Study," p. 18.
34. *Linhas fundamentais do plano prospectivo indicativo para 1981–1990* (Maputo: Imprensa Nacional de Moçambique, n.d.).
35. Samora Machel, speech of 1 May 1981, printed in *Noticias* (Maputo), 2 May 1981.
36. FRELIMO, *Premeira Conferência Nacional do Partido FRELIMO—Documento Final, Março, 1982* (Maputo, 1982), p. 23.
37. Central Committee, *Out of Underdevelopment to Socialism*, pp. 28–29.
38. *Report on the Preparation of the Congress*, pp. 24–25.
39. "Report from the Economic and Social Directives Commission," in FRELIMO, *Building Socialism: The People's Answer* (Maputo, 1983), p. 42.
40. Marc Wuyts, "Money in the Context of Socialist Transformation: A Case Study of the Mozambican Experience," unpublished paper, 1984, pp. 20–21.
41. Mozambique Information Agency, *Dossier: Fourth Session of the Central Committee of FRELIMO* (Maputo, 1978), p. 3.
42. *Central Committee Report to the Third Congress*, p. 46.
43. FRELIMO, *Premeira Conferência*, pp. 24–25.
44. Central Committee, *Out of Underdevelopment to Socialism*, pp. 44, 61.
45. Ibid., p. 28.
46. Lenin to the Eleventh Party Congress, 1922, as quoted in Charles Bettelheim, *Class Struggles in the USSR: Second Period: 1923–30* (New York: Monthly Review Press, 1978), p. 210.
47. From Karl Marx, "Marx on Bakunin," cited in David McLellan, *The Thought of Karl Marx* (New York, 1971), p. 210.
48. Central Committee, *Out of Underdevelopment to Socialism*, pp. 28, 59.
49. Ibid., pp. 29–30.

150   *A Difficult Road*

50. Wuyts, "Money in the Context of Socialist Transformation," p. 13.
51. Samora Machel, "Our Plan Is the Key to Economic Victory," speech in Maputo, 6 October 1981, reprinted in *AIM Information Bulletin* 64 (Supplement) (1981): 10.
52. This and the immediately following quotation are from Wuyts, "Money in the Context of Socialist Transformation," p. 10.
53. Interview with Minister of Information, Jose Luis Cabaço, Maputo, April 1983.
54. Samora Machel, "Speech at a Mass Rally in Maputo on March 18, 1980," *AIM Information Bulletin* 45 (Supplement) (1980).
55. Samora Machel, as quoted in Jean-Pierre Langellier, "Africa's El Dorado: Mozambique Five Years After," in the *Le Monde* section, *The Guardian Weekly,* 4 January 1981.
56. National Planning Commission, *People's Republic of Mozambique—Economic Report* (Maputo, January 1984).
57. Hodges, "Mozambique Emergency," p. 21.
58. Allen Isaacman and Barbara Isaacman, *Mozambique: From Colonialism to Revolution, 1900–1982* (Boulder, CO: Westview, 1983), p. 182; see also Jean-Pierre Langellier, "Machel's Uneasy Partnership with the East," in the *Le Monde* section, *The Guardian Weekly,* 11 January 1981.
59. Isaacman and Isaacman, ibid., pp. 163–64.
60. Quoted in Quentin Peel, "Links with South Africa Likely to Increase," *Financial Times,* "Survey—Mozambique" (8 December 1980): 25.
61. Central Committee, *Out of Underdevelopment to Socialism,* p. 157.
62. Michael Holman, "Why Wooing the West: Mozambique's Economic Crisis," *Financial Times,* 24 April 1984.
63. Quoted in Alister Sparks, "Mozambique, South Africa Seek Wide-Ranging Economic Links," *Washington Post,* 7 June 1984.
64. Mozambique Information Agency, "Peace Is a Struggle," reprinted in Mozambique Information Office, *News Review* 27 (12 April 1984).
65. Ibid.
66. Oscar Monteiro, quoted in Augusta Conchiglia, "FRELIMO: un rôle capital," *Afrique-Asie* 217 (7–20 July 1980): xiii (Special: *Mozambique: une décennie pour vaincre le sous-développement*).
67. Samora Machel in conversation with Basil Davidson, as quoted in the latter's "The Revolution of People's Power: Notes on Mozambique, 1979," *Monthly Review* 32, no. 3 (July–August 1980): 77–78.
68. *Central Committee Report to the Third Congress,* p. 35.
69. See, among other sources, Crawford Young, *Ideology and Development in Africa* (New Haven: Yale University Press, 1982), especially chap. 2, "The Rise of the Afro-Marxist Regime"; and David and Marina Ottaway, *Afro-Communism* (New York: Africana Publishing House, 1981). For a survey of these and other much less savory writings see my chapter "Ideology in Africa: Decomposition and Recomposition," in Gwendolyn Carter and Patrick O'Meara, eds., *African Independence: The First 25 Years* (Bloomington: Indiana University Press, 1985).
70. My chapter in ibid. elaborates on this point and in doing so overlaps with some of the material presented here.

71. Interview with Samora Machel, *Tempo* (Maputo) 325 (26 December 1976).
72. V. I. Lenin, *Collected Works* (Moscow: Foreign Languages Publishing House, 1960–70), vol. 4, pp. 211–212.
73. Sonia Kruks, "From Nationalism to Marxism: The Ideological History of FRELIMO, 1962–1977," unpublished paper, n. d. See also Edward Alpers, "The Struggle for Socialism in Mozambique, 1960–1972," in Carl G. Rosberg and Thomas M. Callaghy, eds., *Socialism in Sub-Saharan Africa: A New Assessment* (Berkeley: University of California Press, 1979).
74. FRELIMO, "A contribuçao do nosso partido para o enriquecimento do Marxismo-Leninismo," presented to the seminar on "The Construction of Socialism and Communism and World Development," Sofia, Bulgaria, 1978, and published in *Voz da Revoluçao* (Maputo) 70 (November 1979).
75. FRELIMO, "Construimos o socialismo na nossa patria," presented to the International Scientific Conference on the Joint Struggle of the Workers' Movement and Movement for National Liberation Against Imperialism and for Social Progress, Berlin, October 1980, and reprinted in *Voz da Revoluçao* 72 (December 1980).
76. Quoted in Augusto de Carvalho, "Samora Machel: historias para um retrato," *Expresso* (Lisbon), 8 October 1983.
77. Some of the documentation from this debate can be found in Luis de Brito, ed., *Dossier sobre o ensino do Marxismo-Leninismo na Universidade Eduardo Mondlane* (Maputo: Faculdade do Marxismo-Leninismo, 1981).
78. Jorge Rebelo, "Vamos fazer de cumprimento do PEC o ponto central do nosso trabalho," presentation to the Interprovincial Seminar on Party Mobilization and Propaganda, reprinted in *Noticias,* 22 January 1981.
79. Department of Ideological Work, "Resoluçao do trabalho ideologico do partido sobre estilo e métodos de actuaçao," July 1981, reprinted in *Noticias,* 6 July 1981.
80. Central Committee, *Out of Underdevelopment to Socialism,* pp. 93–94.
81. Interview with Minister of Information José Luis Cabaço, Maputo, April 1983.

PART II

Case Studies

Judith Marshall

3. Making Education
Revolutionary

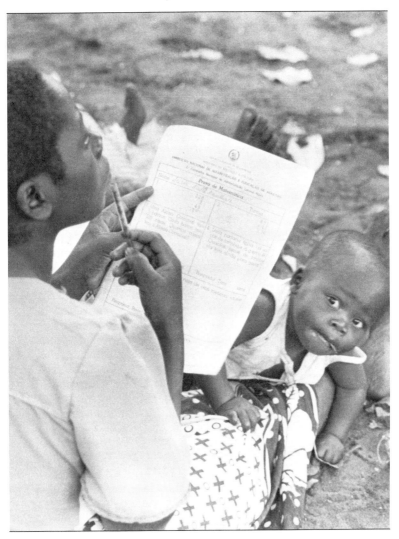

The notion of "education" in post-independence Mozambique has been very broadly defined. During the years of armed struggle the revolutionary process itself was often referred to by FRELIMO as a "school," and something of the same spirit has continued to frame a wide range of educational experiences in the years since independence: the discussion groups in workplace and community organized by the GDs and dealing with everything from nationalizations and South African attacks to neighborhood security and clean-up campaigns; the run-up to the two FRELIMO party congresses (of 1977 and 1983) which included debates throughout the country on the main theses of the congresses; the information and mobilization sessions for such events as the vaccination campaign, the census, the introduction of the new National Education System (NES); the mass rallies and demonstrations characterized by dialogue with the assembled crowds; the electoral process, including as it did local level meetings to discuss each candidate's qualifications. There have been cultural activities ranging from local people's history projects to impressive dance and song festivals at district, provincial, and national levels. There have been efforts to transform the media, to create through radio, print, photography, billboards, and records social images relevant to the struggles of the day. Indeed, an adequate list of examples of Mozambican education broadly defined would have to include the State Cotton Secretariat's puppet shows for peasant producers, the comic books prepared for railway and port workers, and the popular theater productions designed to bring health issues into focus!

Such developments provide a rich backdrop for Judith Marshall's chapter, which focuses forcefully and in exemplary detail on the more formal aspects of education in Mozambique, on the national education system itself. In that sphere, too, the struggle to consolidate real advances continues, the National Education System discussed by Marshall having been duly launched by the

This chapter originated as a joint project with Barbara Barnes, who worked in the field of cultural studies in Mozambique in the first years of the post-independence period. I acknowledge with much gratitude her collaboration on early drafts of the chapter; in particular, the section on general education draws extensively on her work.

end of 1984. But the broader context outlined in Chapter 2—drought, armed bandits, the foreign exchange crisis—has also continued to take its toll. In 1982 489 schools were closed down because of enemy attacks and this pattern has not been reversed; Inhambane Province, traditionally a province with dynamic literacy campaigns and impressive results, has had its program dwindle to nothing, for example, doubly hit by drought and the MNR. Moreover, the first year of the NES has been fraught with logistical difficulties: in getting such new materials as are available out to the schools and literacy centers, in preparing other materials, in training teachers in the new programs. By mid-1984, it is true, the Ministry of Education and Culture had been pared down and reorganized, becoming, simply, the Ministry of Education (with both culture and technical education now to enjoy structural autonomy as state secretariats). But the educational challenge, in a country of 13 million, where 7 out of 10 are still illiterate, would remain a daunting one even in conditions less turbulent and less fraught with danger than those which a Mozambique under siege has to face.

> Let's make the entire country a school in which
> everybody learns and everybody teaches.
> —Samora Machel[1]

When I arrived in Mozambique in 1977 the education cadres whom I met were working out of a small three-story apartment building overlooking the entrance to Maputo harbor, and included some of the same people I had encountered in the FRELIMO education department in Tanzania prior to independence. There they had been working to build primary schools, literacy programs, and teacher-training courses in the liberated areas, all in the midst of the war and with an almost complete lack of facilities and materials. But now the task had changed: these cadres no longer had to build up new forms starting from scratch, but instead had to bind together several distinct systems of education into one coherent national education service. At the same time, the newly formed Ministry of Education and Culture had to encourage and support new forms of informal education and cultural activities. With regard to schools per se, the national education service had to bring together the FRELIMO system that had emerged in the liberated areas, the small, elite system inherited from the colonial state (largely urban and catering to settlers' children, Asians, and a few "assimilated") and the sprawling network of rural mission schools (largely Roman Catholic) that offered primary education to indigenous children.

In my discussions with the education cadres about the new system to be created, they repeatedly mentioned what an important instrument education had been for building up the colonial state. Perhaps they, as I, felt the weight of this more strongly because we were viewing it from within the old colonial capital with its imposing university and secondary schools. My apartment overlooked the old Liceu Salazar, which had been the colonial establishment's top secondary school. Here settlers' children had been groomed for their continued role as rulers. The name "Salazar" in large letters was still faintly visible over the front door despite efforts to paint it out when the school was renamed Josina Machel Secondary School, after an important heroine of the liberation struggle.

During my seven years in the Ministry of Education and Culture that tension between "Salazar," erased but still tangible, and "Josina," symbol of the best that was born in the liberation struggle but was still to be consolidated, was constantly there. In this chapter I shall try to present something of the texture of that process of consolidation, beginning with a brief look at both the colonial education system and that of the liberated areas as the key points of reference in the struggle to transform education. I will then sketch the main features of education in the immediate post-independence period and discuss some of the contradictions inherent in its rapid growth, followed by a more detailed description of the general education, adult education, and technical education systems. The concluding section will discuss perspectives for the future within the context of the new national education system, the first phase of which was introduced in 1983.

Education Under Colonialism and in the Liberated Areas

The colonial state in effect sponsored a dual educational system, one part of which was to reproduce the rulers and the other to reproduce the ruled; one part was provided directly by the state for the settlers' children and the other part was provided by the Roman Catholic Church, with state authorization and supervision, for the African population.

During the early years of Portuguese colonialism there was some argument about how the school system was to function. In the brief era of liberal government in Portugal (1834–1910), a single system of public schooling equally accessible to Europeans and Africans was established, but settler protest prevailed and by 1868 mission-based schools for Africans were once again in operation. They were few in number, however, and even by 1910 there were only 54 primary schools in all, 6 of which were for girls, with a total enrolment of 1,195 African and mulatto pupils.

Schooling as an important site of ideological contestation was evident, however. On the one hand, Mouzinho de Albuquerque, a colonial official writing at the turn of the century, was blunt in putting forward the colonialist perspective:

> As far as I am concerned, what we have to do to educate and civilize the "indigena" is to develop his aptitude for manual labor in a practical way and take advantage of him for the exploitation of the province.[2]

On the other hand, the potential of education to question the prevailing colonial ideology was clearly recognized. By the late 1920s a study of the labor force in Homoine district of Inhambane Province in southern Mozambique questioned the expectations created by education:

> In the province of Mozambique . . . we continue to make the same mistake—the old system of assimilation. Because of this, there is already a superabundance of schooled natives in all the districts—the assimilated—who, not all being able to be responded to in their demand for the right to be considered educated and nominated for public positions, already are trying to organize into class groupings and found newspapers to attack the duly constituted powers. Not far away is the demand for the right to carry out nationalist political propaganda, attacking and injuring the European race, similar to what has been happening and is growing in the neighboring English colonies.[3]

When Salazar came to power in Portugal in 1928, a "Regime do Indigenato" was established in the colonies which set out a series of state-regulated racial and ethnic distinctions that bound Africans into subordinate positions, although theoretically they were citizens with the rights and duties of all citizens and the privileges of the white population.[4]

Although *assimilado* status was ostensibly attainable to all, few Africans could pass the multiple hurdles of literacy *and* paid employment, and by 1961 only 1 percent of the African population had been legally assimilated. Indeed, part of the ideological work of the state was precisely to legitimate the meager success of the assimilation policy. Minister of Colonies Armindo Monteiro put it this way in 1935:

> We do not believe that a rapid passage from their African superstitions to our civilization is possible. For us to have arrived where we are presently, hundreds of generations before us fought, suffered, and learned, minute by minute, the intimate secrets of the fountain of life. It is impossible for them to traverse this distance of centuries in a single jump.[5]

The lived experience of the African population was one of harsh colonial exploitation, in large part engendered by Portugal's own economic weakness. The labor process was characterized by a systematic subordination of the African worker through state legislation, including land expropriation, hut taxes, no right to employ labor, no access to credit, no right to trade or set up shops, and extremely low prices for cash crops—all this in addition to the broader legislation that locked into place systems of migrant labor, forced labor, and forced cultivation. This multiplicity of state practices was categorized by the colonial state as evidence of the natural condition of the *indigena*—brutish, idle, and stupid.

Schooling for Africans was almost totally neglected. Few even got the opportunity to attend, and in 1958 the illiteracy rate was estimated at 98 percent.[6] In 1960 there were only 361,966 pupils registered in the schools for Africans—out of a population of more than 11 million.[7]

Although the missions were authorized to offer schooling, the actual funds for the physical plant—for church buildings, staff housing, classrooms, workshops, and transport—were not provided by the state. Instead, the state sanctioned close collaboration between the missions and local officials, who made land and labor available in abundance:

> Pupils came to be used as a free source of labor for agricultural production, especially rice and cotton, subsequently sold to improve mission finances. This form of exploitation, a kind of forced labor extracted by the missions in the guise of payment for education—despite the difficulties and costs—came to be known as *xipadre* (*xibalo* in the mission fields.) Often parents had to supply the hoes of their children so exploited, and in addition contribute sacks of maize or beans—also supposedly in payment for the education received, but in reality a tithe on agricultural production which the mission could dispose of for profit as it saw fit. The close collaboration of church and local administration was shown in the disposal of *xibalo* and prison labor; the Catholic missions received *xibalo* for their farms, and on the other hand allowed "recruitment" of older pupils by the administration before their dispersal home.[8]

In the period from 1940 to 1960 the Catholic missions expanded dramatically, from 296 in 1940 to 2000 in 1960. During the same period foreign missions not receiving state support decreased from 41 to 27.[9]

The school system for Africans has been described in detail by Eduardo Mondlane.[10] It consisted of three years of "rudimentary education" whose objective was "gradually to lead the 'indigenous' from savage life to civilization . . . making him conscious of himself as a Portuguese citizen and preparing him for life's battles, making him more useful to society and to himself."[11] Language studies, the geography and history of Portugal, and moral education all were aimed at fostering a love for Portugal and pride in having been born in a Portuguese territory. This education was entirely in Portuguese, with the exception of the catechism which was taught in the children's mother tongue (which varied from one region to another). Given the difficulties suffered by inadequately trained teachers trying to teach in a language not spoken by the children, it is not surprising that the syllabus was often neglected while the teachers contented themselves with filling classroom time with rote learning of the catechism.

The process of schooling was portrayed as the way to resolve the "problem" of being "indigenous." But the bureaucratic and administrative hurdles made this an almost insurmountable task, since a series of age restrictions made it virtually impossible for Africans to proceed upward in the system: by the time a student learned enough Portuguese to pass the necessary exams, he or she was too old for that level of education. Students were thus examined and declared failures in large numbers, and perceived their failure as being due to their own inadequacies and those of the indigenous community as a whole.

And the failure rates were staggering:

Table 1
Enrollment and Pass Rates, 1940–1960

	1940	1950	1960
Total enrollment	50,000	232,923	379,060
Passes	1,844	2,985	10,448

Source: David Hedges, *Education, Missions, and the Political Ideology of Assimilation, 1930–1960* (Maputo: Eduardo Mondlane University, 1982), mimeo, p. 5.

If these figures are accurate, they show clearly how literacy can be used as a means of social control: the schools worked to make it impossible for those who entered to succeed, while at the same time holding up education itself as the only legitimate channel for evaluating worth and certifying qualification for advancement. Thus although critics of the colonial education system now tend to see it as a failure, it was in fact highly successful in terms of its "hidden agenda" of forming a "nation," destroying a class, and creating the notion of individual failure. And of course its "failures" became skilled forced laborers on the large agricultural holdings and on state projects, creating a very efficient system for supplying needed workers.

Few indeed were the Mozambicans who were able to penetrate the upper echelons of the system: by 1950 only one black Mozambican had completed the fifth and final year of upper secondary school. A Mozambican who managed to reach secondary or higher education "did so at the cost of turning himself into a little black Portuguese, the docile instrument of colonialism, whose ambition was to live like a settler, in whose image he was created," according to a Mozambican document submitted to UNESCO shortly after independence.[12]

By the mid-1960s, however, internal and international protest, and the opening of the colony to multinational capital, had begun to bring about changes. With new demands for a skilled labor force, and with the need to avoid exposure of Portugal's totally retrograde colonial policies as the liberation movement advanced, the general secondary schools and technical schools began to enroll black Mozambicans, albeit still extremely slowly. The "indigenous" status was abolished, and with it went the special mission schools for the "indigenous." Table 2 shows the extent of the advance.

Table 2
Primary School Enrollment 1934–1974

	Public	Private	Mission (Protestant)	Mission (Roman Catholic)	Total
1934	3,505	372	493	49,263	53,633
1944	4,019	862	4,149	102,953	111,983
1954	8,683	1,130	6,797	220,799	237,389
1964	27,904	2,451	14,370	373,587	418,312
1974	623,771	13,053	—	—	636,824

Source: Adapted from Ministry of Education and Culture, "Education Systems in Mozambique," 1980.

This, then, was the colonial system that was functioning in September 1974 when the Lusaka Accords were signed. It was ridden with class, race, regional, and gender divisions, obsolete in its stress on religion to the detriment of science, imbued with the self-reproducing colonial ideology of European superiority and African inferiority and a fantasy of a Lusitanian destiny in Africa—a system as backward, in fact, as fascist Portugal itself.

New Practices in Education Growing Out of the War of Liberation

I had had the chance, during visits to Tanzania, to see FRELIMO's own educational policies developing in the period of the armed struggle. "Educate man to win the war, create a new society, and develop our country" had been an important FRELIMO slogan during the ten-year war of liberation. Once the northern part of Mozambique was free of Portuguese control, FRELIMO had begun a new kind of education, one that was in sharp contrast to the colonial past.

The new system was arrived at only after sharp conflict within FRELIMO itself about education's relation to the goals that the liberation forces had come to espouse. Two distinct positions on the aim of the overall struggle had gradually emerged. One, eventually rejected, defined it simply as eliminating colonial political domination, without changing the social and economic structures supporting it. The other, more sweeping, proposed to create a society free from exploitation, which required a new economic and social system directly reflecting the interests of the masses of working people. Thus the goal, according to the dominant and victorious view, was not to Mozambicanize existing institutions—which would have left intact a social system of class and privilege, replacing one set of exploiters with another—but to take power in order to destroy that set of social relationships.

In education, this conflict erupted most dramatically at the FRELIMO secondary school in Dar es Salaam, which had been established in the early 1960s for Mozambican refugee students. FRELIMO had looked to this school for trained cadres, yet most of the students had never been in the liberated areas or close to the war itself. After completing their high school program, many wanted to continue their education abroad, ostensibly to prepare themselves for high-level government posts after independence. FRELIMO, however, wanted them to participate in the liberation struggle and did not believe that releasing them for further study was in the interests of either the liberation movement or of ordinary Mozambicans prepared to put their own lives on the line for independence.

The conflict resulted in the closing of the school for two years and led to a clear statement on the role of education as a primary tool for serving the people—knowledge had to be used to benefit others. At the second national conference of the Department of Education and Culture in 1970, President Samora Machel explained FRELIMO's position:

To us education does not mean teaching how to read and write, creating an elite group of graduates, with no direct relationship to our objectives. . . . Just as one can wage an armed struggle without carrying out a revolution, one can also learn without educating oneself in a revolutionary way.[13]

A new FRELIMO secondary school opened in Bagamoyo, Tanzania, in 1970, and when I visited it the principles of the educational program had been clearly worked out. "The aim of the school is the same as for all education within FRELIMO," reported the director, Mario Sive. It is "to serve the people and the liberation work. The studies are not part of individual careers but are intended to fill the needs of the organization in all phases of its work."[14] In addition to formal classroom work in such standard subjects as language and mathematics, students spent a considerable amount of time in activities that both supported the operation of the school in a material way and helped to break down colonial ideas about distinctions between mental and manual labor. The students worked in the fields to produce food for the school community and did cleaning and construction tasks to maintain and build up the school compound. They returned to the liberated areas for some portion of each year so that they could contribute directly to the war effort and experience the realities of life there. According to the 1976 document cited earlier:

When everyone participates in productive work on the basis of complete equality, each learns from the other and the barriers between the intellectual and the illiterate, between teacher and pupil, are removed by the hoe and the shovel. We all put our knowledge to practical test, make mistakes, and learn from them. In the revolution, manual work is praised, not despised, for it helps us to develop our sense of class, it makes us more aware of the class we come from and represent; and by working together we get to know each other, contributing to our greater unity. It is also the practical and effective manifestation of our spirit of self-reliance.[15]

Teachers at the Bagamoyo school included both Mozambicans and foreigners sympathetic to FRELIMO's goals. I had the opportunity of hearing firsthand about the workings of the school, both from my Mozambican hosts and from two American friends teaching there. One of their tasks was to develop curriculum materials suitable to the liberation struggle and to life in the liberated areas, for use not only in the Bagamoyo school but in the many primary schools and literacy centers established in FRELIMO-controlled zones. The new materials attempted to develop political awareness along with skills. An example was the literacy manual, where the letter *X*, a complicated sound in Portuguese, with several pronunciations and tones depending on its context, was compared with imperialism:

> *X* is like imperialism. Imperialism always hides from the eyes of the people and appears in many different forms. Sometimes it is colonialism, then it changes form and appears as neocolonialism. Neocolonialism is a sly way of tricking the people of Africa, Asia, and Latin America. *X* also changes many times. It is like a chameleon; sometimes it is read "sh," sometimes "ks," sometimes "ss," and finally "eis." But the people always manage to discover and conquer imperialism, by struggling a lot. We too will be careful. We will study and we will discover the values of *X*.[16]

In addition to developing new curriculum content and making manual work a constant and accepted part of the school program for both teachers and students, a new democratic organizational structure within and between schools was also formed:

> Our schools are democratic centers, structured in such a way as to incorporate all school workers—pupils, teachers, and ancillary staff—in running the school together. The base units are study groups which form sections which make up one class. Running vertical[ly] through the school are activity sections covering cultural activities, production, hygiene and so on, which send representatives to a managerial committee which works with the headmaster. It is through the practice of assuming responsibility that our young people learn to assume responsibility and develop their creative initiative. It is also the means whereby we learn to develop new relations of mutual respect, assistance, and confidence. These relations are supported by a constant process of criticism and self-criticism, in which we learn to recognize our errors and those of others.[17]

I was told that on an inter-school level, teachers periodically came together during the war to share information and to exchange experiences, planning the curriculum for the future.

The importance of creating a new role for teachers and the difficulties which had to be surmounted in order to do so had been stressed by Samora Machel during the second national conference of the Department of Education and Culture:

> [T]he task of teachers and cadres in education is an extraordinarily delicate one, because like us, they grew up and were formed in the old world and carry within them many bad habits, and defects, a lot of individualism and ambition, many corrupt and superstitious attitudes which are harmful and might contaminate the new generation.
>
> Teachers and cadres must behave like the doctor who, before approaching the patient in the operating theater, disinfects and sterilizes himself so as not to infect the patient. Through constant meetings, through continual criticism and self-criticism, teachers and education

cadres must eliminate old ideas and tastes, so as to be able to acquire the new mentality and pass it on to the next generation.[18]

When I was at Bagamoyo in 1970 I discussed the new roles for students that were being worked out through trial and error in the course of the armed struggle, including democratic participation in the running of the schools, physical work together with other members of the school and surrounding community, and collective study. The conclusion of those I spoke with was unanimous: a dozen pupils with adequate marks who have a concern about the school community and who study collectively are worth much more than one genius who works on his or her own.

Many of the students I met were also teachers. Having progressed through the first year, they would then teach that year's material to others as they continued with the second year, and so on up the educational ladder. By the time of the Lusaka Accords in September 1974, more than 30,000 Mozambicans had received primary-level or literacy training inside liberated Mozambique.

When I talked to veteran education cadres in 1977, they felt that perhaps more important than the academic achievement of the schools in the liberated areas was the experience gained in training personnel and in testing new values and goals for education in a new society. No one would claim that the process had been completed, but the experience did mean that when FRELIMO formed a government in 1975, it could draw on the education policies, programs, and practices of the liberated areas, and also on a group of experienced educators.

The transitional government installed after the Lusaka Accords set many changes in motion. A key event was the Beira seminar on education held in January 1975. It brought together, for the first time, primary and secondary teachers from all of Mozambique's schools and FRELIMO cadres experienced in education for an intense ten days of study and discussion. People I talked to a year later, during my first visit after independence, still spoke of the meeting with emotion, recalling how shocking the FRELIMO work methods of discussion and participation were to teachers coming from the almost entirely closed colonial system. Out of this seminar came the decision to discard the entire colonial syllabus and all of the textbooks that had been in use. New programs for the first to eleventh grades were to be drawn up. Political education was to be introduced into the schools, as were new courses in Mozambican history and geography and new cultural activities that would initiate a process of reconstructing and affirming the Mozambican personality. Special attention was to be given to manual work as a means of linking study and production, theory and practice. Teachers themselves were to undertake political study.

At the same time that these radical changes were being instituted in the general and technical schools, a major effort was also made to tackle the question of adult education. The recently created *grupos dinamizadores* or dynamizing groups (GDs) had been given the task of encouraging literacy activities in the workplace and at the community level. A broad mass movement emerged, involving students, workers, priests, plus a hodgepodge of other volunteers. This burst of energy and enthusiasm resulted in some 500,000 Mozambicans becoming literate.

Just a month after the independence celebrations of June 25, 1975, came the nationalizations—land, health services, funeral and legal services, and of course, education. One of my colleagues in the International Cooperation Secretariat had been part of a team of education cadres sent to the town of Namaacha, center of many mission schools. She recounted her part in the very complex process of taking over the more than one thousand regular and mission schools that were nationalized. "You wouldn't have believed the tricks and maneuvers of some staff members," she said. "Equipment was hidden or destroyed. There were attempts at hasty exits into Swaziland with school property." All in all the nationalization of education involved intense political work, interpreting the decision to workers in the schools and the population in general, carrying out a rapid inventory of school property in order to prevent sabotage, and, most difficult of all, coping with what overnight was an enormous education service with few people to direct and staff it. As Graça Machel, the present Minister of Education, reflected later:

> If, on the one hand, the nationalization signified a major victory, on the other hand the effective and immediate control of the education process necessitated enormous efforts for which we had insufficient resources, either human or material.[19]

The initial actions of the Ministry of Education and Culture were indicative of its broader strategy for transforming education. The urgency of training teachers who would be both pedagogically and politically well grounded was of paramount importance and ten provincial training centers for primary teachers were opened in 1975. By the end of that year the First National Seminar on Technical Education had been organized and a Technical Education Commission had been appointed. By 1976 a full-fledged National Directorate of Literacy and Adult Education was in place. The education sector had some presence at the provincial level through ten provincial commissions of education and culture.

The Third Congress of FRELIMO, held in February 1977, gave further shape and clarity to the emerging education system by defining the following general goals: (1) organization of an education system that ensures access at all levels to workers and their children; (2) consolidation of a system of education at the service of socioeconomic development and the worker-peasant alliance; (3) transformation of the schools into revolutionary bases in the midst of society, guaranteeing a constant link with the life and struggles of working people; (4) intensification of political and ideological training of teachers and students; (5) linking of study with production and theory with practice; and (6) planning of education to guarantee the realization of all these objectives.

On March 8, 1977, Samora Machel met with students to explain the Third Congress directives and to interpret politically the strategy adopted to deal with the enormous shortages of trained people and the urgency of placing students at the service of the working class. Tenth- and eleventh-grade graduates were to interrupt their studies and move directly into teaching or defense. Others were to take up higher level technical training (especially in agriculture) and intensive pre-university training. In future, all ninth-grade graduates would be placed according to immediate economic and social priorities.

By 1978 significant steps had been taken to implement the Congress's directives in relation to adult education. The first national literacy campaign was launched, with the target of making literate 100,000 women and men in key sectors of organized production throughout the country. I had the sense of being part of a tremendously important moment as I watched the flurry of last-minute preparations for the campaign in a huge assembly hall at CFM, the state railway in Maputo. Railways had symbolized colonialism; for decades they had taken Mozambican workers to South Africa's mines, and the rail lines had been developed to service the expanding economies of Mozambique's racist neighbors, South Africa and Rhodesia. But they were also the symbol of worker resistance, and so it seemed very appropriate that the campaign should start there. We education workers had arrived early and watched with concern the flurry of last minute preparations. The huge banner proclaiming the battle against illiteracy persisted in falling down!

When President Machel arrived, he almost danced into the hall, concentrating in his person an amazing energy, commitment, and excitement, which were also communicated in his speech to open the campaign:

> The national literacy campaign begins today. We have come to CFM to launch a new and major battle within the working class. It is a major battle because our entire development—political, economic, cultural, social, and ideological—depends definitively on our victory

in this battle. . . . If we are not able to win this battle that we are launching today, we will live in poverty and misery, we will remain dependent on imperialism. This battle, then, demands energy, intelligence, and effort. In particular, it demands patience.[20]

We all left the hall ready to commit our energies to carrying out the marching orders that summed up the speech—"Let's make the entire country a school in which everybody learns and everybody teaches!"

Post-literacy training was also seen as vitally important from the outset. Even prior to the mass post-literacy campaigns which began in 1980, accelerated programs of adult primary education were set up for key workers from industry and state farms and those in important leadership positions. Women and men with only second-grade education were given the opportunity to do accelerated six-month residential courses to reach the equivalent of fourth grade. In 1979 I visited the center for the northern provinces, located in an abandoned military barracks an hour's drive east of Nampula, the old military capital. There I met a group of workers who were determined not only to do two years of primary school in six months but to salvage the twisted, rusty metal in old bed frames and lockers and chairs in order to put their dormitories, classrooms, and dining hall into working order. They also had plans for agricultural production, including an orchard. All of this was in addition to an incredibly full schedule of courses in math, geography, history, Portuguese, political education, and basic health and hygiene, as they resumed a life of study many years distance from their first two grades under the colonial regime.

In the field of higher education, the first efforts were being made to transform the university. In 1974 the student body of 3000 consisted basically of those being groomed for power in the colonial settler regime. By 1976 the student body was reduced to 699, 150 of whom were not Mozambican. Within the student body, some 75 percent were worker-students, carrying heavy responsibilities in their workplaces and also a full load of studies. After an evaluation of the existing curricula in the light of the country's socioeconomic needs, the courses of study were reduced to agronomy, medicine, veterinary science, engineering, education, law, and economics. The economics faculty, waiving the normal entrance requirements, developed a special accelerated program for workers in key leadership positions in the workplace. The education faculty undertook the training of all secondary school teachers.

Such moves were aimed at linking the university more closely with socioeconomic development priorities, but progress was slow and uneven. It was impeded by the weight of old attitudes of intellectual arrogance on the part of both teachers and students, and by the inability to create viable plans for collaboration, even on the part of the socioeconomic sectors most urgently needing it. Furthermore, given the acute shortage of trained cadres, even those students most anxious to put their new training into practice at the base, or at least at the provincial level, often found themselves in ministry jobs at the national level instead.

Rapid Expansion at the Base

There was a veritable explosion in education as the system broadened out dramatically to encompass men, women, and children who had previously had no access to education. The elitist, restrictive character of colonial education gave way to democratization, reflected in a burst of high enrollments and in community initiatives to build new schools and adult education centers, set up night school programs, and the like. The fruits of independence were becoming very tangible indeed.

In the primary schools, the first five years of independence saw an increase from 695,885 to 1,494,729 in student enrollment, while teachers increased from 10,281 to 16,810. From 1975 to 1979 the number of secondary schools increased from 33 to 104, with student enrollment jumping from 23,980 to 92,815. Most of the primary school teachers, however, were only minimally equipped to teach. The majority had been monitors in the old mission schools, with no training and with the responsibility for rote learning of the catechism as their main task. Many had completed only second grade themselves. The ratio of students to teachers in the primary schools was estimated to be about 88:1 in 1978, with many teachers in rural schools having classes of a hundred lively little bodies in cramped, hot classrooms without enough desks, pencils, notebooks, or texts. Experienced teachers were scarcer by the month in those early years as the massive outflow of the Portuguese settler population continued.

The five national directorates that made up the Ministry of Education and Culture—general education, adult education, technical education, physical education, and culture—were increasingly hard pressed to keep up with the rapidly growing numbers crowding into the schools and literacy centers. Many of the schools were, in fact, little more than rudimentary structures in remote villages with two or three first- and second-grade classes, mainly reflecting the enormous desire of the villagers to have a school. There was little or no notion of a school as meaning trained teachers, text-

Table 3
Expansion of the Education System, 1975–1980

Number	1974/75	1976	1977	1978	1979	1980
Primary schools						
Students	695,885	1,276,500	1,334,742	1,462,282	1,494,729	1,387,192[a]
Teachers	10,281	15,000	16,142	16,308	16,810	17,030[a]
Schools	5,235	5,853	7,076	7,104	7,170	5,730[a]
General secondary schools						
Students	23,980	37,255	47,877	67,416	92,815	90,950
Teachers	?	?	1,872	1,853	2,479[b]	2,087
Schools	33	65	93	95	104[c]	104
Technical secondary schools						
Students	10,297	9,401	9,423	10,676	12,448	12,704
Teachers	?	?	597	633	673	680
Schools	34	34	34	41	32	31

[a]Consolidation of scattered rural schools offering only two years of primary schooling into complete schools offering the four-year program.
[b]Includes night-school teachers.
[c]Increase refers to technical schools with a general course.

Source: Adapted from Anton Johnston, *Education in Mozambique, 1975–1984*, Education Division Document No. 15, Swedish International Development Authority, May 1984.

books, syllabi, equipment, exams, and some links to a broader system of administrative and pedagogical supports and controls. Nevertheless, expansion was the reality, however much it outpaced the needed administrative and pedagogical backup. Adult education burgeoned. By the end of 1979 there were 243,500 adults registered in the literacy campaigns, and 4 accelerated training centers for workers. The southern region center offered the equivalent of fifth and sixth grade in six months, while the other three continued to provide the equivalent of fourth grade.

The number of worker-students mushroomed. The situation in my own workplace, the International Cooperation Secretariat, was not uncommon. Two colleagues worked only half-days and carried a full university program. Two taught history five nights a week at the nearby Josina Machel Secondary School and I myself taught five nights a week at the language institute. Four were enrolled as students in full secondary school programs at night and had a daily work schedule which involved getting up to catch the 5 A.M. bus to work, working from 7:30 A.M. to 5 P.M., interrupted by a two-hour lunch break (during which they ate at best a sandwich), after which they proceeded to night school classes that ran from 6:30 to 11 P.M. They arrived home sometime around midnight, only to start again the next morning at 5.

The technical education system, too, expanded dramatically. During my first visit after independence in 1976 I had discussed projects in technical education with a tiny group of eight dedicated cadres working in two small rooms. They were responsible for developing an entire technical education system. By 1979 the new National Directorate of Technical Education was a functioning reality, although its formal creation took place only in 1980. Plans and actions were under way to establish fully staffed and equipped agricultural, industrial, and commercial schools at all levels; these would become key components in developing a trained labor force and empowering workers with the technical knowledge and political consciousness to take control over production. The enrollment drop after independence from 15,000 students in 1973/74 to 9,401 in 1976 was staunched and by 1980 some 12,704 students were registered, with a teacher training institute and three other intermediate-level institutes functioning in addition to the thirty-one secondary schools.

New Textbooks

One of the boldest decisions taken at the Beira conference in 1975 had been to discard all the existing textbooks and start fresh.

The first new texts began to appear the next year. First there were new readers for grades 1–8, a celebration of images of the "New Mozambican" and the new society in prose, poetry, and graphics. Then came a primary school syllabus, a history book for fifth and sixth grades, followed by new geography and biology texts. Later a political education book and teacher's manual appeared, as did an English book for the seventh grade. Only in 1980 were language and arithmetic workbooks for primary students introduced. For basic literacy, a student text and teacher's manual were produced rapidly. Later, a revised and much simplified manual and textbooks for post-literacy training were introduced.

The decision to produce the books in Mozambique was an audacious one. The story of the small and not so small acts of heroism required to get the new texts written, printed, and into the schools would fill a chapter in itself. For the fledgling writers, the time and courage required to produce a manuscript while at the same time carrying on other Ministry of Education work reflected deep commitment. For the newly nationalized graphics industry, the 1976 printing of the first-grade reader marked the longest press run on record for a book published in Mozambique. The decision to have children purchase the texts at a nominal price so that families would have one or two books in their homes meant producing every book for every person in the education system every year, although by 1979 the first experiments in treating texts as school property had begun. Distribution, given the poor transport system, was yet another drama, with everything from floods to Rhodesian military aggression delaying the arrival of the books in the hands of the students.

Despite heroic efforts, however, the writing, production, and distribution of schoolbooks comprised one of the country's most problematic tasks during the first years after independence. The ambitious yearly plans for new texts were consistently unrealized and this, aggravated by the organizational bottlenecks in importing science and technical books (and, indeed, all texts for the intermediate and secondary levels), meant that teachers and students had to depend on their own resources, individual and collective, with students spending a disproportionate amount of classroom time copying text materials from the blackboard. While this was a tolerable situation during the first two or three years after independence, the book shortage seemed less explicable by 1980. It was the subject of much debate in ministry meetings and a favorite topic of concerned parents on social occasions when I identified myself as a Ministry of Education worker.

Similar minidramas attended the supply of basic school materials—notebooks, ballpoint pens, pencils, and erasers—a situation hard to imagine for those of us accustomed to the availability of consumer goods in Europe or North America. The whole process of acquiring these materials, through local production, importation, or international grants, and their storage, distribution, and sale at the schools and literacy centers in 115 districts severely taxed already scarce ministry resources. Of course, there were recurrent delays in the arrival of imported supplies and not enough trucks to transport them. There were also serious organizational hitches at the school level itself; the limited and seasonal cash incomes of rural parents made selling on credit a necessity, posing problems of financial control for fledgling faculty who, with minimal administrative experience, had to function as bookkeepers.

Thus despite the enormous progress made during the early period, the material base for education during the first five years was extremely precarious and was recognized as a major constraint upon the quality of education in independent Mozambique.

Contradictions of Rapid Expansion

By mid-1979 officials were speaking openly of the deficiencies of the education being offered. The Minister of Education, Graça Machel, addressed these problems at the third national meeting of the Ministry of Education and Culture:

> It has not been possible from the beginning to establish a mechanism to integrate popular initiatives at the local level with the national plan, in which enrollments could be duly linked to the capacities of the Ministry of Education and Culture to train teachers and supply the necessary school materials. . . . If we add to these objective difficulties the insufficient general education and training of the great majority of our teachers, we can understand the low level of results that we find in the schools.[21]

Discussions also took place in the national People's Assembly concerning the need to control enrollment and guarantee a higher quality of education. The deputies took on the task of working at the district level to decrease the dropout rate, to actively encourage the enrollment and continuation of girl students, and to interpret to the local communities why more new schools could not be opened without first training more teachers.

Many of the difficulties were seen as inevitable, given the enormous broadening of the system and the need to put into place basic pedagogical and administrative structures staffed by new, inexperienced personnel at the provincial and district levels. In fact, new programs and structures were created in abundance, and directives on all manner of activities bombarded provincial and district education offices on a regular basis. These offices, however, lacked the capacity to implement them. The shortage of trained and experienced cadres was felt acutely at all levels. Many of the key education cadres from the era of the armed struggle were now in other sectors. It was not uncommon to find people in their late teens and early twenties functioning as principals of large, urban secondary schools with a full schedule of day and evening classes, in which many of the students were the same age (if not older) than the principals. I visited the Polana Lower Secondary School in Maputo where the twenty-year-old principal had responsibility for a staff of about sixty teachers and workers and three programs enrolling some 1,700 students, whose ages ranged from eleven to forty-five. One of my colleagues in the International Cooperation Secretariat had just come from five years as director of education in Tete Province, a position she had assumed after independence at age nineteen, fresh from a two-year teacher-training program which followed ninth grade.

The few mature and experienced people in the education system were terribly overextended and had beneath them ranks of minimally trained and inexperienced people, albeit with a real willingness to take hold of the new and rapidly evolving situations presented to them. In my own work, in visits to schools, and in endless talks with *cooperantes* in other ministries, I often tried to imagine myself in the position of these young cadres, particularly at moments when they were visibly feeling overwhelmed at how little real knowledge and experience they had to draw upon. Burnout because of being given too much responsibility too soon was a major occupational hazard of the first years after independence.

Inexperience and lack of training also had a negative impact on the democratization of decision-making. The work methods advocated to guarantee genuine participation—regular meetings with subordinates, organization of work collectives at each level, and regular meetings for criticism/self-criticism—were avoided as too threatening. To call a meeting was to reveal just how uncertain you were yourself about how to tackle a given problem. So while the party and state at top levels advocated broad participation, mass democracy was often shunned, even if unconsciously, in favor of centralism.

The capacity to integrate effectively the non-Mozambicans who brought the technical knowledge and experience so desperately lacking was another much discussed point among both senior cadres and the *cooperantes* themselves. The national director of technical education, Andre Carvalho, posed the problem very straightforwardly to a visiting delegation working out programs of cooperation within that sector:

> The very weaknesses that make us need your assistance in the first place mean that we won't be able to use either the people or the materials and equipment you send us to maximum effectiveness. This is our reality, the reality of underdevelopment. There will be consultants underutilized and teachers with work undefined. There will be extensive equipment left too long in the ports and warehouses or not set up for lack of the technicians or wiring or cement to do so. If you want to work with us to overcome these problems, you are welcome. But we warn you that such problems are a real and unavoidable part of the present phase.[22]

The New Schools—Centers of People's Power

> To effect these changes in the minds and lives of their students, the schools in Mozambique have generated structures that are still only dreams in the minds of progressive teachers in western Europe. Because the schools must be a "base for the people to take power," they must facilitate the participation and mobilization of all the productive energies of their students.
>
> —Chris Searle, *cooperante* teacher in Nampula, 1977–1979[23]

All of us who taught or were close to the daily life of the schools were caught up in alternative periods of elation and despair as we joined in the work to create the "new school." The experiences of schools in the liberated areas were instructive, but the dynamic of the war situation itself had been a critical factor in making these structures function; thus the struggle to create similar structures in all of the schools after independence was fraught with difficulties, with dramatic successes and equally dramatic failures.[24]

The "new school" was to be characterized by:

• its links with the productive sector;
• its links with the community;
• its function as a center of active democracy;
• its new teacher-student relationships;
• its polytechnic character.

The schools in the liberated areas had played an active role in production and in general played a very dynamic role in community activities. Serious efforts were made to generalize this experience throughout the inherited system. As one of their obligatory tasks, the schools did indeed produce, but the quality of the experience varied widely. In the years immediately after independence there was a flourish of production everywhere; city GDs organized vacant-lot vegetable gardens and civil servants spent a day a month working on nearby state farms. The schools too had a burst of energy directed toward agricultural activities and other kinds of production. But by 1978 the high energy was less widespread and the schools had settled into a variety of patterns. Some Maputo high schools had not moved beyond a token vegetable plot in the school yard, clearly not anybody's idea of a way to link students with genuine work and workers and therefore the subject of much critical discussion at school meetings. Yet when I visited Llanguene High School in the periurban area of Maputo, I found its students working in regular two-week half-day shifts at nearby textile and box factories and at the local hospital. In return, the hospital staff offered a first aid course in the school and the factories helped out with transport for weekend sports outings and study visits.

It was by no means a static situation. A School Production Service was created in 1980 to support activities in the many residential schools that had substantial productive capacity—for example, saw-mills, carpentry or auto repair workshops, or large landholdings with hundreds of fruit trees. Plans were moving ahead for an even closer and, in fact, structural integration of agricultural and indus-trial schools with nearby production units. Schools were also begin-ning to be integrated into the provincial agricultural production plan, which meant that they had to take production targets very seriously and were also receiving more systematic support from provincial structures, including mechanized services and supplies of seeds, fertilizers, and the like. And everywhere token produc-tion was ridiculed as meaningless.

Vacation activities provided an important new dynamic in the life of the school and community. The long vacations of the colonial era had reinforced the idea that students were privileged. A new ap-proach was taken in which only one month during the December to mid-February break was for actual vacations with families; the rest of the period was reserved for special activities, which ranged from painting and repairing the schools themselves to forming brigades to participate in national events such as the literacy and vaccination campaigns or, in 1980, the national census. Periods in the produc-tive sector were also common, with student groups working on state farms or in cooperatives. From discussions with students at the Namaacha Agricultural School, an hour's drive west of Maputo on the Swaziland border, I got enthusiastic accounts of the 1979 vacation activities: brigades of students had worked in the school's piggery and poultry units or on repairing the school buildings.

Others had been assigned to the nearby Moamba State Farm or to literacy work. Some had done a stint with district-level party structures.

The effort to make the schools centers of democracy were both exhilarating and frustrating. One was struck time and time again by the fact that structural change in progressive directions was not enough. When all was said and done, each student individually had to come to terms with what it meant to participate and to take on the new values.

At the classroom level, new organizational structures similar to those in the liberated-zone schools were already in place. In all general and technical schools and in the teacher training centers work groups of three to eight students were the basic unit. Each class numbered between thirty-five and sixty students who stayed together for all subjects and contained a number of these groups. Every group and every class selected a leader, and these comprised a class council. In addition, every class elected "activists" to each of the eight committees or sections that ran the school: pedagogy, administration, information, social and disciplinary affairs, health and hygiene, production, culture, and sports. From time to time committees were formed to deal with specific issues, such as school-community relations, and these also had representatives from each class.

Each school had a director appointed by the provincial education directorate; he or she was the senior official in the school, with both administrative and political accountability. The director had two assistants, one for administration and the other for pedagogical matters. Each teacher generally was in charge of a class, and was also part of a subject-area group if in a secondary school, or of a year group if in a primary school. Each such group nominated a "responsible," who had to be accepted by the school director. The groups held weekly meetings to plan lessons, share ideas, and discuss teaching problems. Usually teachers were required to sit in on one class a week taught by another teacher in order to broaden their understanding of the teaching process and participate more fully in their groups. All education personnel in the schools taught and participated through committee membership in running the school. For those with the heaviest administrative duties, the weekly teaching load was reduced.

Through these structures, students, teachers, and workers were expected to participate fully and actively in all facets of the life of the school. A new kind of student-teacher relationship could emerge in this context. In some cases, students participated in grading via exam councils which evaluated each student not just on test performance but on participation in the life and work of the school. There were also full discussions of the teachers in the spirit of criticism/self-criticism, many of which were constructive, although some were devastating to the inexperienced teacher struggling merely to maintain order in the classroom.

Within the small student work groups, students were encouraged to reason out problems themselves and to look to their peers and not just to the teacher for solutions. By design, each group contained both strong and weak students and also a mix of social backgrounds, for the groups were viewed as important political tools for breaking down class barriers and instilling cooperative work methods. From a British *cooperant* working in Nampula Province I heard particularly vivid examples of how the groups functioned to bring about change. Early in the year, she had had great problems trying to convince Luisa, an academically gifted student from an Indian shopkeeper's family, to work with Mussavele, a young man fresh from a peasant background. At first Luisa was reluctant to have anything to do with the less academically oriented Mussavele, saying he could never learn and expressing her resentment at having to waste her time on him. Her small group discussed her individualism and lack of concern for someone of a different class background. Over time Luisa's attitude did change and before the year was over she was helping Mussavele outside the class with his Portuguese and English. This process of discussion, criticism, and struggle, multiplied manyfold, was fundamental to the development of the new school and the "New Mozambican."

The work groups certainly had their shortcomings, however. Study in groups often prevented or de-emphasized individual mastery of concepts and materials. At times the brighter students had little notion of pedagogy and virtually did the work for their weaker colleagues. But by and large the new structures for participation and decision-making brought important gains in developing the students' critical capacities and involving them in the broader process of socioeconomic change.

The notion of polytechnic education was perhaps the least concretely conceived feature of the new school. The intention was to link education with the production process so as to create people capable not only of doing productive work but of actually controlling production and running the society. The need was to educate workers and their children to see beyond the limited horizon of their own immediate workplace or professional training, and to furnish them with a broad understanding of the technological, economic, and political relationships governing production and society, so they could defend themselves against class domination and play their vanguard role.

In practice, however, the new school did little to demystify the workings of the economy and the society. Clearly, given Mozambique's underdevelopment, the productive forces had to be developed swiftly. In the transitional phase it was necessary to set up rapid-training schemes to create cadres with a solid technical and political base, while at the same time raising the cultural level of the general population to prevent their being mystified by "expertise." In a situation of such widespread backwardness, where six years of schooling already guaranteed a place in a privileged sector of the workforce, it was difficult to develop the students' critical faculties concerning various technologies and their implications or to give them a full grasp of the technological, political, and economic relationships between a specific workplace and the whole system of social production in Mozambique.

Students, whether young people taking day classes or adults in night schools, tended toward a very naive acceptance of what the "engineer" or "technician" proposed; they had little notion of alternative options and even less understanding of how to control the one that was chosen. Traditional technology was considered to be of little value; the "big," the "mechanized," was automatically seen as the path into the future. Discussion of technology in relation to rural transformation was rare, and in many situations dramatic leaps were made from one level of technology to another, without any of the interpretive work en route which could have enabled the users to understand and begin to dominate the new techniques.

A New View of the World: Curriculum and Textbooks

The commitment to develop the school as a place not simply to transmit knowledge but also to equip ordinary people to take power in their workplaces and communities led to dramatic changes in both the process and the content of education. Among the most important was the introduction of Mozambican history and geography, as well as political education. The new geography texts did not merely replace the map of Portugal with that of Mozambique; they presented a fundamentally different view of the world, in which human beings interact dynamically with nature to create history. Similarly, the new history program did not merely replace a chronology of colonial conquest with a record of African resistance; it tried to present history as an ongoing struggle of opposing class forces. Far from romanticizing traditional African society, it analyzed both its positive and its negative aspects. The veneration of age to the point of stifling initiative, for example, and the relegation of women to an inferior position were shown as extremely negative. There was also a clear depiction of the exploitive aspects of the ancient African kingdoms. Moreover, the new texts explicitly identified the African intermediaries who collaborated with Portugal to give colonialism its entry into the interior of Mozambique; this countered the notion of a classless Africa and challenged simplistic racial definitions of the enemy.

Political studies were introduced for the first time into the school program. The textbook prepared for the lower grades combined elements of civics with a brief history of colonialism, FRELIMO, the armed struggle, the history of women's emancipation, and other important themes. The secondary schools and institutes drew on basic Marxist texts and current policy documents. With the paucity of both texts and teachers who felt themselves capable of teaching political studies, the experiences in many of the schools were somewhat less than positive, with a tendency to use dictated texts and rigid teaching methods rather than create a real dialogue with the students that would begin to develop a capacity to read Marxism as Mozambicans and read Mozambique as Marxists. An effort to introduce current issues into the political studies program was made, and by 1981 there were brief texts on racism, the African National Congress of South Africa, and apartheid available for use at the secondary school level.

Undoubtedly more important than the content of the courses, however, was the transformed nature of the school itself, both in terms of joint decision-making by teachers, students, and workers on all questions related to the internal workings of the school, and in terms of the role of the school in the broader political process. Students were active participants in all political activities. Each campaign that emerged—for vaccinations, literacy, or the census—each public demonstration—for May Day or against an attack by the Rhodesian or South African regime—included mobilization of young people through the schools.

Cultural activities and sports took on a new significance. Dance groups were formed, specializing in the traditional Mozambican dances. These traditional dances were already being transformed in the broader community to include social and political themes ranging from the vaccination campaign to polemics against the illegal Rhodesian regime and "Smitty, the tobacconist," Mozambique's derisive name for Ian Smith. Choral singing, drama, poetry—all became popular activities in the schools. Although the struggle to win the young away from the culture of tight jeans and pop stars was often difficult, particularly in the big city high schools where it historically had the strongest hold and where students of petty-bourgeois class origin were still concentrated, elsewhere there was significant success in planting the seeds of an alternative culture.

Teachers have been encouraged to break out of the old molds of teacher-as-lecturer and to move away from reliance on the rote learning and theoretical, bookish approaches that had been so central to colonial education. Teacher training schools now devote more time to practice teaching, technical schools to laboratory and workshop activities, literacy centers to oral methods and workbook exercises. All education centers have been encouraged to increase field trips and study visits, and in general work toward more interactive teaching methods.

It has not been an easy process to transform authoritarian classrooms into participatory ones. In the technical schools, the lack of workshop and lab equipment created a built-in bias for the continuation of a very theoretical approach. There were no simple solutions, however, since the arrival of large quantities of equipment for science laboratories and carpentry and mechanics workshops, beginning in 1978, simply brought into sharp relief the related difficulties of training teachers to use and maintain the new equipment and of modifying schools to install it, at times including the supplying of power and water to make it usable. Installation, storage, maintenance, and use required new budget outlays as well, for everything from sheet metal and lumber to chemicals, lubricating oil, and projector bulbs. The strain on the education system was enormous.

In some projects there were dramatic successes, such as in the people's history groups in the Nampula secondary schools. Here students and teachers made contact with the local population and began to transcribe oral histories, piecing together a significant series of local events related to early resistance to colonialism. Having gradually won the trust of the rural population, they were shown the grave of a local leader, Khapula. Here they discovered that at independence a monument had been raised by the local people to Khapula, depicting clearly the strong link in the minds of the local population between the early resistance to Portuguese occupation at the beginning of the century and the later resistance through the war of national liberation. Other schools had similar successes, often based on the initiatives of individual staff members.

The struggle to transform teaching methods was a long and slow one, however, and for every situation like that of the Nampula people's history groups there were still many classrooms with rote learning via dictated notes, to be duly regurgitated on the day of the final exam. Critical discussion of such tendencies was constant, however, and inroads against them were slowly being made in a variety of ways, including better training and improved programs and textbooks.

The New Teacher

> The great family from the Rovuma [river] to the Maputo [river] has chosen you as agents at the base of this transformation, and the principal object is to make the students begin to live a different type of life, a life in society in which we all live through the same problems, and we all collaborate on their solutions.
>
> —Minister of Education Graça Machel[25]

> Well, as for me, I can say that I found it difficult when I was given this task [primary-school teacher training]. But now I am convinced that I can do it well. Yes, with difficulties, but now I am interested in doing it. As to where, well I am from Zambezia and hope to go back there.
>
> —Deolinda, seventeen-year-old newly trained teacher[26]

Historically the role of teacher in the liberated areas was an important one—indeed, it was a key role for a FRELIMO militant because it guaranteed the formation of *continuadores,* those who would carry on the fight against Portuguese colonialism when the then current generation died. These cadres rapidly came to play a part in school and community life that was vital to the political and socioeconomic development of the liberated zones. An area which had a school and a teacher possessed a strong center for mobilization and the dissemination of new ideas.

The task after independence, of course, was to propagate the best of the tradition of the teacher-militant in an entirely new situation which inherited a large number of teachers, particularly at primary level, who had not shared that experience. Thus a main task of all of the teacher training programs was ideological transformation, to enable the future teachers to recognize and surmount the distorted views of themselves and the world which the colonial education system had engendered. Without the spur of the war situation, it was a more difficult process, albeit one with significant successes. In terms of the general system, by 1978 the

ten primary teacher training centers set up in 1975 had trained
some 3,400 teachers in courses lasting for seven months. By 1979
the courses had been extended to ten months with forty-five hours
of observing and practice teaching in primary schools annexed to
the centers and seven weeks of practice teaching in district schools,
including seventy hours supervised by an instructor.

The four regional refresher-course centers opened in 1979 extended the earlier five-week vacation courses into a full four-month
program, which during that year provided training for 11,176
teachers. The plan was to continue at the rate of 1,280 new
teachers every four months.

A more advanced-level teacher training center opened a two-
year program with an entrance requirement of ninth grade, designed to train teachers for grades 1–6. By 1980 the first refresher
courses for fifth- and sixth-grade teachers were housed in a permanent center near Chokwe and plans were proceeding for the opening of a second advanced-level center near Maputo. By 1982 there
were 3,517 teachers trained for secondary and post-secondary
levels, while the total enrollment in the teacher-training colleges
was 6,300.

In 1978 the university was assigned the task of setting up a
teacher training program for grades 5 and 6 and later for grades
7–11. With the decision to channel all ninth-grade graduates into
key sectors, the university received its first teacher trainees. But
they were only a small fraction of the new teachers needed, for the
total number of ninth-grade graduates in 1978 was well under a
thousand and they were sent into defense, agriculture, and industry, as well as education.

Winning over these new recruits to a commitment to teaching
was a struggle. To be an engineer or a doctor or even an airline
hostess was to be something—to be a teacher was tantamount to
admitting failure. Such was the prevailing attitude. The salaries
were extremely low compared to those in other sectors and there
were no established promotion patterns or career paths. A new
national salary policy introduced in 1980 promised to alter some of
the inequities of the old system. In addition, steps were taken toward launching a national teachers' journal and setting up a national organization for teachers, all in the context of making the
teaching profession attractive.

Other problems besides recruitment had to be dealt with. Material conditions in the teacher-training programs not only affected
how much the trainees learned but also communicated a message
about the importance of the task. The centers were located in
buildings formerly used for other purposes, many of them by the

church. Frequently these had been vandalized at independence; in other cases, periods of disuse or use without proper maintenance had taken their toll. Many teacher trainees had to spend much precious time walking to streams to fetch water or had to cope with cold nights on cement floors without mattresses or blankets. In many centers, all evening activities were effectively ruled out for lack of light.

Equipping the centers with such items as dishes, mattresses, and blackboards, whether supplied through international cooperation or purchased locally through the ministry budget, was a battle in itself, one to which much of my time was devoted in terms of organizing external funding. On top of scarcity and lack of funds there were difficulties with transport and installation, and these were compounded by organizational weaknesses in the ministry. Had the surprise warehouse visits made by the President during 1980 included the storage centers of the Ministry of Education and Culture, that ministry would also have been criticized for the quantities of material stockpiled for months on end, material urgently needed to resolve critical problems in the schools and teacher training centers.

Undoubtedly the central challenge of teacher training was the struggle to lift off the dead weight of colonial pedagogy. Rote learning had prevailed, reflecting the concept of education as transmitting a determined body of knowledge to be "deposited" in the mind of the student where, safely "banked," it could be "withdrawn" at a later date for exams. Education as problem-posing, as knowledge derived from real interaction between the learner and his or her environment—all this was new.

Here also was the key to giving continuity to the liberated areas' tradition of the teacher as political cadre, a dynamic force for action and transformation. To the degree that the teacher training process was characterized by active, participatory teaching methods, a strong insertion into the local community, and a set of work methods that made the time in the teacher training center one in which the trainees actually experienced face-to-face democracy, there was some hope that the ideological transformation of the teacher could begin.

The teacher training centers I visited over the years were making halting progress in this regard. The instructors were young, inexperienced, and faced with daunting physical conditions and logistical problems just to keep the centers functioning with minimal food and water—none of which helped overcome the initial resistance to the idea of teacher training that many trainees brought with them. These conditions put issues of authority/subordination on the agenda in the teacher training centers in a very crucial way, making it even more difficult to take the risks that go with active participation and decentralization. A related difficulty was the amorphousness of the vision of teacher as community activist. Although the teacher was supposed to be a dynamic agent of change, particularly in the rural areas, the program to train primary school teachers did not touch on the real problems of the transition from individual peasant production to cooperatives. Nothing situated the primary school teachers as part of a team of front-line workers, along with their colleagues in agriculture and health, in the battle against underdevelopment.

This problem was recognized by the teacher training department, and in 1982 a request was made to the Center of African Studies at the university to study the primary teacher training program in order to introduce activities that would equip the primary school teacher to take on a more active role in the community. A report was submitted to the ministry in 1984.[27]

The problem of merely changing the content, without a radical transformation of form, was discussed at length. A speech to the second national meeting of the Ministry of Education and Culture by Sérgio Vieira, veteran FRELIMO militant and then head of the Bank of Mozambique, alluded to the problem of confusing rote learning with revolutionary education. When a child is taught to dutifully recite "Long live Marxism-Leninism,"

> the child is saying something he does not understand. He is learning a habit. And we who are adults, when we look back and remember the time when we were forced to say "Hail Mary, full of grace," we become angry, we become revolted. And this child may also have the same reaction tomorrow.
>
> To acquire the new mentality is to learn new habits, to have a new relationship between people. For example, it is the responsibility this three-year-old child will have toward his friend who is crying. . . . When the child worries about his friend, he is acquiring a sense of responsibility, a sense of collectiveness.[28]

Yet despite all the difficulties, from the sometimes involuntary enrollment and poor material conditions to the weight of colonial pedagogy, one had only to visit the centers to recognize that a real process of transformation was taking place, however haltingly. Deolinda, a seventeen-year-old student from Zambezia who found herself suddenly whisked off to the Namaacha primary teacher training center, had this to say of her year of training:

> I think that traditional education played an important role in forming women's attitudes, giving us a certain propensity to be timid and various other complexes as well. I can now see in practice how the

directive to involve women in different roles is being carried out. Women are becoming active in all fields that men are active in. But it's hard to move quickly from one set of attitudes to another. I've seen that here at the center. Some of us arrived with a lot of timidity and a notion of inferiority. We've changed since coming. Now we have good relations with the male students and we've lost these attitudes of inferiority and timidity. For example, we used to avoid participating in sports because of these attitudes. Now we've very active participants in sports and in all other activities.[29]

There can be no question that the role of the teacher in the schools has been altered in profound ways by the new structures. New teachers in particular find their roles in today's schools quite normal. "I can't imagine preparing a lesson all by myself and not showing it to the other teachers in my subject-area group," a Nampula teacher told me. Another recalled an incident in which the biology group was having trouble putting together a model unit for the fifth-grade students. When it was suggested that one teacher do it alone so that the task would be finished on schedule, the others would not hear of it. Teachers seem proud of their collective work methods and the results. "I may start with an idea which is not very well formulated. Another teacher can develop it, and when we have formed the idea completely, it is much more than any one of us could have created individually," explained another teacher in the same school.

These new work methods do not always come easily, particularly for teachers trained to function in the highly individual manner of the old system. While many of the teachers I met had gone through profound personal and political changes to transform their self-images as teachers, others had left the country.

Education for Adults, Too!

> I wanted to continue to study but I didn't have the chance to do so because the Portuguese colonial regime didn't let adults study. This year the GD in our community came to my rescue because they encouraged me to enroll in secondary school. It really helped me in my work, especially mathematics and Portuguese.
>
> —Eugénio Bahane, 51, hospital records clerk, Mavalane Hospital[30]

The idea of education as a fundamental right for all women and men, and of adult education as a vital component of the education system, was gradually consolidated during the time I was in Mozambique. Education was viewed as the means to equip more and more workers and peasants to play conscious and decisive roles in the development of their country. Literacy was clearly the beginning point, but only that, for there were plans to develop an adult basic education system that could guarantee advance to higher levels.

The 1977 survey done by the newly formed National Directorate of Literacy and Adult Education led to the ineluctable conclusion that the eradication of illiteracy in Mozambique would have to be carried out in phases. With an illiteracy rate estimated at 85 percent of the population above age fifteen, and the need to use available cadres to at least hold the line if not advance on other key fronts (such as defense and production), the objective conditions for the kind of dramatic, all-out literacy campaign that had taken place in countries starting from a higher level of socioeconomic development and with a high proportion of the population literate— such as Cuba or, more recently, Nicaragua—simply did not exist.

Literacy was where it all began. As noted earlier, the GDs had already tackled the problem in the immediate post-independence period with decentralized literacy efforts. It is estimated that more than 500,000 people became literate between 1975 and 1977.[31] The first national literacy campaign targeted 100,000 women and men in key sectors. These included workers in industrial and agricultural enterprises, cooperatives and communal villages, soldiers, party members, and leadership cadres from the mass organizations, particularly the Organization of Mozambican Women (OMM). The campaign actually registered 130,000 in the targeted sectors and another 110,000 in nonpriority sectors, mainly at the community level. Of the 240,000 enrolled in the campaign, 140,000 passed the final test.

The methodology used in the campaign was based on the experiences of literacy training during both the armed struggle and the period of the transitional government, along with a careful study of the experiences of other countries. The national primer consisted of ten lessons, each with a theme highlighted in an illustration, a key phrase, and a key word. The themes were designed to promote active discussion on important socioeconomic topics. Far from being narrowly functional and/or purely work-oriented, they ranged from concrete aspects of the armed struggle to broader concepts of cultural affirmation. The manual for literacy teachers suggested the use of the illustrations in the students' book, a song, an object brought into the classroom, or a national event to spark these discussions. In the Mozambican context, the discussion method had the additional aim of introducing and consolidating oral skills,

Table 4
Literacy Enrollment and Pass Rate, 1978–1982

	1978/79	1980	1981	1982
Enrolled	more than 260,000	324,000	310,000	200,000
Successfully completed course	140,000	120,000	60,000	40,000

Source: Rui Fonseca, "Information on the Development of Literacy Programs in Mozambique," paper presented to an international symposium on Cooperating for Literacy, Berlin, October 1983, p. 7.

since for the great majority literacy also meant learning to speak a new language. Some of the specific lesson themes were "The people's war is just," "The school belongs to the people," and "Defending health is a duty of the people." From the key phrase, a key word was selected which was then divided into syllables. The learners were then encouraged to make new words from the various syllables, with writing exercises and recognition exercises to help the participants identify the syllables as phonic units.

Many lessons were drawn from the first campaign. The director of the Literacy Monitor Training Center for Maputo Province, José Machado, contrasting the training and pedagogical support for the first campaign with that of the second, commented that "Really, the first campaign was more like a dress rehearsal for us."

The second national literacy campaign was launched on February 16, 1980, and had as its goal making literate 200,000 women and men, including permanent workers in industrial and agricultural production units, party members, deputies to the national, provincial, and district People's Assemblies, and leadership cadres of mass organizations. In this campaign, 324,000 were enrolled and 120,000 passed the final test successfully (see Table 4).

As for post-literacy, two approaches were taken. Mass campaigns were launched from 1980 onward that gave workers the equivalent of fourth grade in the general system. Three Accelerated Training Centers for Workers developed new approaches for covering the third and fourth grades in a six-month intensive course. The participants were workers from key sectors. From the outset, these centers had in mind a teaching program that would combine formal disciplines and skills training. The main critique of the first courses was that they erred on the side of bookishness; students were barraged with classes in mathematics, Portuguese, hygiene, geography, history, and political education, a very intensive regime which was both very theoretical and very teacher-centered. During the second year the courses were divided into half-days of classes in formal disciplines and half-days of production and other activities in order to teach concrete skills. Students were taught how to make building blocks, from which they built a refectory in the Makubulane center; in Namialo, near Nampula, students made exemplary efforts to refurbish the old military barracks and to build up agricultural production.

The centers are decidedly experimental and play an important additional role as a training ground for the adult instructors from the working class who will be needed to guarantee adult education in their workplaces in the future. The Makubulane center in the southern region had already offered a first intensive course for the fifth and sixth grades by July 1979. The idea of offering places to talented literacy teachers who could benefit from more study was well established. Inhambane Province took the initiative and opened its center well ahead of the targeted date in 1980, and by July 1979 a first intensive course for Inhambane Province party members and deputies, mainly from the communal villages, was in progress.

The establishment of a functioning program of adult education from top to base, starting from zero, all within the very brief span of two years, was a remarkable achievement. And yet measured against the enormous needs of Mozambican workers to break out of centuries of ignorance and passivity to confront the technology and organization of new production processes, and measured against their need to take commanding roles in running the economy and society, the results, both quantitatively and qualitatively, were meager.

The concrete problems of the campaigns were, of course, innumerable. A central and perhaps surprising one was the lack of proper involvement of other sectors, from the party and the mass organizations to the enterprise managers. Literacy commissions were created from the national to the district level, in which party, ministries, and mass organizations like OMM were represented, in order to underscore that literacy was a national task and not simply another educational service. By 1981 the joint roles of the Ministry of Education and Culture, the party, and the workplace or community authorities had been formalized in Law 1/81 of the Council of Ministers, which made it obligatory for the workplace to guarantee literacy and post-literacy training for its workers, with annual plans having to include not only production targets but also education targets for literacy, adult basic education, and vocational training. The law did not resolve the problems, however, and there were huge discrepancies from one workplace to another, basically turning on whether literacy was understood to be a fundamentally political activity or was turned into one on which administrative categories and solutions could be imposed. There were still factory managers, even some in state enterprises, who were themselves party cadres and who, while willing to grant space for a literacy center, were resistant to adjusting work schedules and saw little or no reason to include adult education targets as part of their production plans.

As the yearly campaigns continued, the commissions proved rather ineffective tools for the constant mobilization and organization necessary to guarantee each phase. Party and ministry representatives on the commission tended to play somewhat passive roles, overburdened with other problems and understaffed even in their own fields. Often there was no continuity in representation from one meeting to the next, the underlying assumption being that literacy was a task of the education sector. Even in 1980, at the end of two mass campaigns, the director of the Literacy Monitor Training Center in Maputo Province still spoke of factory managers resistant to the presence of literary instructors as an ongoing problem. In some factories, of course, management was totally cooperative, organizing the two-hour literacy classes each day to include one hour of work time and one hour of voluntary time. Others made use of seasonal lulls to schedule extra time for more intensive literary activities, as was the case in Maputo cashew-processing plants during 1979.

Adult education did become rooted in some workplaces and communities, regardless of support, or the lack thereof, from outside. I spent holidays on the tiny resort island of Santa Caroline in Inhambane Province, which had an adult education center for the resort's sixty-five workers, none of whom had gone beyond the fourth grade. There, the three-member party cell held a meeting just prior to the launching of the third national literacy campaign and decided that, despite a total lack of communication from the district literacy office about how to proceed, it had best take the initiative in response to radio announcements that the date for resuming literacy and post-literacy classes was near. I was invited to meet with the cell, one of whose members was also a deputy in the district People's Assembly, the literacy teacher and representatives from the hotel management and the Production Council, to help organize festivities marking the campaign's start. With the entire island community and guests staying at the hotel, the third campaign was duly christened with speeches, songs, and dances, and another year's teaching and learning began.

Another fundamental difficulty of the literacy campaigns was the language problem. For the vast majority, literacy meant not only learning to read and write, but doing so in a second language which they first had to learn how to speak! The first literacy surveys did not take even a rough sampling of oral capacities and thus the proportion of adults who did (or do) not speak Portuguese was not known. One has to assume, however, that this language problem will become even more acute as succeeding campaigns reach beyond workers in centers of organized production, where minimal knowledge of Portuguese can be assumed, into the heart of the rural areas.

There is no doubt whatever that tackling literacy in a second language complicates the process enormously, from methodology to teacher training, from textbooks to evaluation methods. Thus, as might be expected, the question of whether illiteracy should be tackled in local languages was a recurrent one. To do so would require developing materials, training monitors, and administering evaluations for a number of major language groupings, some of which are only minimally systematized, and it would also carry the seeds of political division. Moreover, since Portuguese is the language of work and of political mobilization, and since people in rural communities encounter Portuguese to the degree that they have access to radio and/or are integrated into a larger process of community life (health campaigns, agricultural extension courses, people's tribunals, the OMM, cooperatives, and political rallies), one can assume that there will be a growing exposure to Portuguese, and a positive one, too, as the language related to the combat against underdevelopment.

A third major difficulty for the literacy campaigns was the meager training of the literacy monitors themselves. The first campaign trained some 3,000 monitors just for the priority centers. For the second campaign, basic training and refresher courses were given to about 18,000 more. The monitors themselves were primarily drawn from the workplace. The first training courses were models of suspect pedagogy, since the twenty-one days were used for a barrage of lectures on a range of subjects—from history to how to build latrines, from mathematics to the link between agriculture and industry. While raising the general level and establishing from the outset that literacy was not narrowly linked to language and counting skills were undeniably correct objectives, the courses did little to instruct monitors in how to teach adults to read and count, and how to overcome shyness and break out of the colonial classroom model of passive students parroting the words of teachers who lectured incessantly. The first visits to monitors in classroom situations after their training showed all too well the inadequacy of the approach, and its weaknesses were exacerbated by the complex and confusing first edition of the manual for monitors. Rote learning prevailed, and many students finished the course with the literacy book memorized perfectly and no capacity whatsoever to read.

By the second campaign, a much simpler manual had been developed with more clearly defined lesson plans and monthly schemes. Perhaps most important, a whole structure of pedagogical support was in place. With a vehicle for each of the ten provinces and a motorcycle for each of the more than one hundred districts to guarantee mobility for the pedagogical support teams, the staff of six instructors from the provincial office, linked with the three district-level instructors, were able to make more regular visits to the literacy centers. Despite some heavyhanded instructors who turned such visits into inspections that left the monitors and students demoralized, and despite provincial officials who latched onto the pedagogical support vehicle as the only functioning transport for the entire province, there was more frequent contact with the centers.

Clearly measures such as simplifying the manual and organizing support teams helped, but the level of the monitors continued to be an obstacle. The materials had to be geared more to their capacity to teach than to the illiterates' capacity to learn. In late 1980 I visited a class where the monitor was still drilling her class in the phrase, "Long live the independence of the people of Mozambique." Student after student parroted the phrase; there was no discussion of meaning, no application to real life situations. Everything was committed to memory; the students were not learning to link sound and written symbol. The importance of June 25, the anniversary of independence, was recited like a catechism, with no reference to the rich experiences of these adults in fighting to make independence a reality.

By contrast, in the hands of a skilled and confident teacher with a minimal level of general knowledge, a song, a poster, a news event, a national celebration, or an item brought to class could become a jumping-off point for discussion of the lesson's theme, thereby developing oral skills, out of which came detailed work on the key phrase and key word, and the discovery of a capacity to create other words. In the hands of a minimally trained monitor, with lesson plans and pedagogical support, it was still a manageable method, though less rich and flexible. In the hands of poorly trained or untrained monitors, abandoned to their own devices and falling back on their own primary schooling under colonialism as their only effective model, the theme-centered lessons dwindled into drills and exact hand-copying of the primer.

And yet even with all the difficulties, the students were obviously learning. In the working-class ward of Hulene, I talked to two men, Raul Chilave and Eugenio Bahane, whom colonialism had robbed of access to an education and who were eager to talk about their experience of going back to school. They had found a chance to resume their studies in a lower secondary school organized by the community, and were convinced that their new knowledge and skills had a direct positive effect on their lives, both at work and in the community.

Raul Chilave was a forty-nine-year-old customs agent at CFM, the state railway and port authority, who had worked as a domestic servant and as a messenger and junior clerk in various firms under colonialism before starting to work with the railway. When asked why he resumed his studies at such an age, he said:

> I came back to school to learn more and to be more sure of my job because what I knew wasn't enough for my work. At the port, as a worker in the customs clearing section, I sometimes get goods from various countries, and I have to know the major ports of these countries. Also I have to make conversions from other currencies to Mozambican currency, and this takes some know-how.

Eugenio Bahane, a fifty-one-year-old hospital records clerk, was equally enthusiastic: "At Mavalane Hospital where I work, I have a lot of responsibility since I'm in a section that deals with the public. Portuguese, both spoken and written, helped me most and mathematics was the most difficult."[32]

Eugenio Bahane's sons were so enthusiastic about their father's return to his studies that they regularly scrutinized his notebooks to make sure that everything was being properly understood!

Certainly in the minds of the adults of this community, as in countless others, there was no doubt that adult education had come to stay, and that they would be able to reach higher and higher levels.

Technical Education: A Prerequisite for Tackling Underdevelopment

> Our struggle to build socialism depends on the gradual building up of technical, scientific, and political knowledge in our working class, in order for it to play the leading role defined for it.
>
> —Andre Carvalho, National Director of Technical Education

The concern to build up a subsystem of technical education was made concrete at a very early stage. The first National Seminar on Technical Education had already taken place by December 1975. During my first visit in June 1976 its conclusions were important reference points in discussions about possible areas of cooperation between agricultural and industrial schools. An in-depth analysis had been made of technical education as it had functioned in the colonial era and as it needed to function to make the transition from being a backward, underdeveloped country to one in which the forces of production, including skilled labor, were developed rapidly. From the outset there was a clear recognition that technical education had to be geared closely to socioeconomic development and thus to manpower planning and the larger questions of vocational training and professional upgrading for adults already in the workforce.

The discriminatory character of the prevailing system had been duly noted. The existing schools, mainly commercial and industrial, were located primarily in colonial population centers, i.e., the provincial capitals. A few black Mozambicans had been permitted to enter these schools in response to external pressures in the late 1960s. The classic neocolonial option would have seen the creation of a black petty bourgeoisie and a skilled black workforce ready to enter into a partnership with the former colonial power, still dominating the economy from a distance but now in league with the multinational corporations as well. Portugal's weakness as a colonial power, however, and the delusions of its settler population, who were lost in a dream of a Lusitanian Africa, resulted in an inability to create any kind of decolonization process able to withstand the growing nationalist pressures. Thus in Mozambique there was a brake on the process of education for the African population which had been so characteristic of other African colonies in the later phases of decolonization. Even at a time when the opening up of the colony to the multinationals should have dictated much greater educational opportunities for black Mozambicans, in order to create a more skilled workforce for the expanding economy, such opportunities were severely limited.

If commercial and industrial schools were scarce, agricultural schools were almost nonexistent. What did exist in some quantity were trade schools, many of which included an agricultural course. They offered three-year programs for students who had completed the fourth grade. At independence there were fourteen trade schools, and four more under construction, and eleven elementary agricultural schools. One of the standard "perks" of office for the *regulos,* the local-level administrators in the colonial apparatus, was to send their sons (not their daughters!) to these

Table 5
Enrollment in Technical Education under Colonialism

	1950	1960	1970	1971
Primary				
Trade	—	270	308	306
Elementary Agriculture	—	—	44	55
Secondary (grades 7–9)				
Commercial	524	1,530	6,125	5,951
Industrial	428	1,664	4,344	4,509
Agricultural	—	—	68	33
Intermediate (grades 11–13)				
Industrial institute	—	—	503	548
Commercial institute	—	—	546	629
Agricultural institute	—	—	131	208

Source: "Systems of Education in Mozambique," Ministry of Education and Culture, 1980.

residential trade schools, many of which had been built in the early 1970s as showpieces in the face of international protest about Portuguese failure to educate black Mozambicans.

The number of black Mozambicans in these schools was very small indeed, and even as more entered in the final years before the collapse of the colonial regime, they encountered a system geared not to developing their full capacities but merely to training them to perform certain limited tasks more efficiently, as called for by a changing economic situation.

From 1975 on, however, technical education underwent a major transformation to meet the need for a working class capable of playing the leading role in the new society. The agricultural schools experienced the most dramatic changes, with a sevenfold increase in enrollment and a plan to transform all the elementary agricultural schools into secondary schools by 1985. In 1980 there were some 14,000 students in the technical schools, 10,000 at the secondary level, 3,000 at the elementary level, and some 1,000 in the intermediate-level institutes. There were 43 courses offered at differing levels, including auto mechanics, civil construction, industrial electronics, accountancy, animal husbandry, and forestry. There were about 900 teachers. By 1981 21 percent of the secondary level students were female.

The plan for future growth was to maintain about 10,000 students in the secondary schools up until 1984, with only two new schools to be opened during this period—an agricultural school in Cabo Delgado and an industrial school linked to the coal mining industry in Tete. From 1985 on the schools would expand rapidly, increasing from 25,000 students to between 30,000 and 40,000 students by 1988/89.

The struggle to staff these schools was already a difficult one in the early years and would be more so if there were such dramatic growth. Up until 1976 there was no vocational teacher training in Mozambique. Those who had taught prior to independence had been trained in Portugal and were mainly army officers, engineers, and public servants who taught on the side. Most of these left at independence. The first effort to train technical teachers in Mozambique was made in 1976 when a number of intensive courses were offered. In 1977 a course was held in Beira and graduates from this course returned to the schools as workshop assistants. This training program was repeated in 1978 and 1979, using the facilities of the institutes, and many intermediate-level students took courses in pedagogy and psychology in preparation for teaching after completion of their studies.

In 1980 a ten-month course was held and 140 students were trained. Clearly they were not fully qualified after such a brief period, but nonetheless they assumed major responsibilities not only for teaching but for administration and for production programs. The dilemma was to find a way to contribute trained manpower directly and immediately to the workforce rather than simply to produce teachers for an expanding technical education system that would have an impact on production only in the distant future.

The principles of pedagogy that were adopted were based on the desire to establish programs that would enable a ninth-grade graduate to have enough skills to take his or her place immediately as a young worker and continue with night school or return at some future point for further studies. Despite adoption of the basic principle that practical training comprise 50 percent of the curriculum, in many schools the training still remained overly theoretical. For one thing, the schools themselves had virtually no equipment until the end of 1980 when massive shipments of laboratory and workshop materials began to arrive. If in 1977 and 1978 there was little thought given to establishing the material base for technical education, by 1979/80 there was full recognition of how long it takes to build or modify a school workshop, of how many specifications are needed to plan adequate equipment lists, of how long the purchase and transport of equipment from abroad takes, of how key the development of a capacity for installation and maintenance is to the whole endeavor. I spent many long hours working with the young secondary school graduates in the newly created

Technical Support Department of the Directorate of Technical Education to devise control sheets to keep track of equipment arrivals funded through international cooperation grants. At one point we were juggling arrival, customs clearance, warehousing, delivery, and installation schedules of equipment entering the country at three different ports and destined for forty different schools.

If some of the pedagogical problems were created by the scarcity of lab and workshop material and equipment, others arose from the inappropriate teaching methods inherited from the old system. In the practical classes, labs, and workshops, there was a tendency merely to lecture or demonstrate how to assemble a motor or file the parts without having the students themselves handle, disassemble, and reassemble the items. Some plans for providing genuine practical experience, on the other hand, were simply not realizable. The industrial institutes, for example, included in their new programs the submission of a course project after the final exam in the third year, but because of the lack of reading material for designing the projects and the lack of staff to supervise them, the projects could not be done.

Linking the schools to actual workplaces was another aim that was difficult to translate into practice. Experiences varied greatly. The Industrial-Commercial School in Nampula had functioned since the early 1960s. When I visited in 1980 it offered courses in mechanical welding, electricity, and accounting, and had 612 day students and a much smaller night school program, mainly because of the lack of teachers. It had developed regular contacts with factories and firms in the city, and students in their final year of secondary school worked one day a week in the Nampula branch of CFM, the national railway, or in the national electricity company. In Xai-Xai, the small provincial capital of Gaza, a largely agricultural province, the establishment of a mechanical welding workshop meant an important new capacity for repairs for the production sector. Even during a period when teacher staffing and machine maintenance impeded consolidation of the program, this workshop was able to repair parts for CAIL, the major agroindustrial complex in southern Mozambique, and even to do some urgent repairs on the town's electricity supply.

On the other hand, during a visit made to the CIFEL foundry by Canadian *cooperantes* a lively discussion with the young engineer in charge, a recent university graduate, brought forth this comment:

> I think the theoretical approach during my own training was all wrong and certainly did very little to prepare me for the work here in

the foundry. What did I know of how to cast these molds for the sugar industry when I came? I'm also a bit skeptical of the role we are playing for the technical students you met here today who are doing practical stints with us. They are here for such a short period of time and we haven't been able to integrate them genuinely enough into any particular task or process in the foundry's work. Despite a certain number of hours of general exposure, they are not really able to deal with any specific area of work.

The National Directorate of Technical Education was by no means oblivious to the problems of linking work and study. By 1980 it had issued directives on including a training component as a key aspect of all major projects for socioeconomic development; a technical school was to be part of important industrial or agricultural projects from the outset. The school would serve as a training center for youth during the day, specifically tailoring the courses to a particular sector of production and as a center for adults at night, providing both general education and professional upgrading courses. Such schools would imply direct responsibility on the part of the enterprise for training both its present and its future labor force. In fact, many sectors, such as the railways, the electricity board, and other large industries, had already embarked on programs of both general and professional education organized through their human resources departments. By 1980 there was lively debate about how to bring these two broad areas of activities together, the technical schools controlled by the Ministry of Education and Culture and the technical training programs in the economic sector.

As far as the agricultural schools were concerned, the original idea was that their restructuring should be closely linked to the development of a coherent policy for agricultural development in communal villages. To the degree that, until 1980, the whole policy in agriculture regarding the relationship between state farms, family farms, cooperatives, and communal villages was fraught with difficulties, there was little development of programs in the agricultural schools specifically geared toward communal villages and the mix of technologies appropriate to their development, the main stress being on large mechanized agricultural projects. Neither the agricultural schools nor the Faculty of Agronomy at Eduardo Mondlane University offered courses in running cooperatives. At best, the latter seemed to be viewed as mini-state farms; there was no real understanding of their internal dynamic, particularly their transforming role vis-à-vis family agriculture.

My several visits to the Namaacha Agricultural School confirmed this. In fact, the students seemed to be getting very poor practical training both in quantity and quality. The animal husbandry section, where pigs and chickens were raised, lurched from one crisis to another because of recurrent feed shortages, yet no way was found to break the total dependency on feed coming from outside the school complex. There were national directives at the time encouraging small animal production (rabbits, goats, ducks) and providing experience in this area in order to service small animal producers in the family sector and cooperatives might have been a more viable alternative, although here, too, feed supply was a problem.

Not only was the production sector precarious in terms of inputs, but it also did not adequately incorporate the students in its day-to-day activities. The paid staff of the school included agricultural laborers, and the students seemed very much on the fringes of actual decisions about seeds, planting techniques and timing, fertilizer application, and the like. They served more as an abundant workforce in peak periods—weeding, harvesting—but there was little in that experience that could serve as a basis for their later work. One sensed that the agricultural school, far from creating a capacity to resolve the problems typical of agriculture throughout the country, simply mirrored these problems in its own production program.

These inadequacies notwithstanding, the technical education sector became an important new subsystem, well established by 1980 as one of the most dynamic areas of work in the Ministry of Education and Culture. From a handful of dedicated cadres working in two small rooms as a Technical Education Commission in 1976, it had burgeoned into a strong national directorate systematically establishing a network of training institutions throughout the country.

The PPI, the ten-year socioeconomic development plan that set specific goals for the decade in all sectors, aimed to create some 1 million new jobs, about 200,000 of which would require professional training. The formal system of technical education, even with the rapid expansion envisioned, could only train between 30,000 and 40,000 people for these jobs. Thus there was a real need to link technical education with the Ministry of Labor's efforts to provide professional training and upgrading for workers, plus initiatives at the level of individual factories and enterprises to develop in-service training programs. These were items of intense study and debate in planning circles by 1980. One thing was clear: adult education had to play a major role in increasing the capacities of those already in the workforce, and much more attention had to be paid to short-term intensive professional upgrading activities, since the real impact of the efforts of the National Directorate of Technical Education would be felt only at the end of the decade.

What Comes Next?

> The National Education System is an essential element in the long-term plan for the decade, the decisive instrument in the battle to win economic independence.
>
> —Graça Machel, December 1981

The Ministry of Education and Culture took the decision to put a major effort into the development of a National Education System (NES) only a few years after its creation as a national ministry. The reasons were clear. In the education and training activities inherited at independence only the content and programs had been altered. The structures themselves had remained intact, each developing at its own pace with its own organization, methodology, control, and evaluation standards. The various components were never conceived of as a system, a set of interacting components with an overall internal logic, dynamic, and coherence and with an integral link to the socioeconomic development of the country.

The plan for a National Education System, which was presented to the National People's Assembly for approval in December 1981, was designed to achieve this. It proposed the creation of five interlocking subsystems—general education, adult education, technical and vocational education, teacher training, and higher education—in a four-tier structure of primary, secondary, intermediate, and higher education. The introduction of the NES was to be in phases, starting in 1983 with the first grade of general education and the first and second years of adult education.

General education is designed for children and young people, offering a seven-year program of basic primary education which eventually will become available to the entire population in a system of free compulsory education. Basic primary education will give no specific occupational or professional training and therefore does not have a terminal character, i.e., it will not equip its graduate to enter the workforce. It prepares young people for further study at secondary level, either in general or technical schools. It is also designed to have a polytechnic character, linking study with productive work and the school with the socioeconomic reality of the community. The general system includes day care and kindergartens, and over time will develop special schools for both the handicapped and gifted. After the seven years of primary schooling,

students may go on to secondary and intermediate or pre-
university training.

Adult education is for those aged fifteen and over and is designed to eradicate illiteracy in the first instance and then to provide basic primary education to enable adults to move into
technical/vocational schools, teacher training, and university programs. The literacy component is of two years' duration, taking
into account the special teaching and learning problems of literacy
in a second language. The third year of adult education is also
mass-based, with centers in workplace and community, and is designed to prevent reversion to illiteracy. With the fourth year, the
adult education program shifts to night schools, or to workplace-
based education programs separate from the general night school
program.

Technical and professional education is designed for both youth
and adults and is integrally linked to manpower planning and the
economic sector. It includes technical schools beginning at the secondary level (eighth grade in the new system) which will function as
day schools for youth and night schools for adult workers. This
subsystem also includes a coordinating role for the training and
professional upgrading programs run by the enterprises in the
economic sector. Unlike general education, technical/vocational
education offers training in particular professions and has a terminal character at each level. In fact, one of the potential dangers
of the new NES, which was pointed out by the Minister of Education and Culture in her presentation to the People's Assembly, is
the class differences that could emerge between the two subsystems, the one preparing youth for higher studies, general or technical, the other preparing them to assume an immediate role in the
labor force, their further study to be pursued at some future date
at night school only.

Teacher training takes on special importance in Mozambique
with its enormous need for both pre- and in-service teacher training. This subsystem is designed to sustain the other three, providing all the teachers for the general system, all the nontechnical
teachers in technical and professional education, as well as teachers
for the fourth and subsequent years in adult education. (The need
for the latter is particularly sharp in the rural areas, where no
voluntary teachers with the minimum qualifications of the sixth
grade exist.) The subsystem of teacher education is also responsible
for training pedagogical and administrative cadres.

Higher education is to give cadres a solid political foundation
and technical expertise, to equip them to do research and investiga-

tion and to apply their knowledge in solving the concrete problems of revolutionary transformation.

The underlying principles of the NES were, first, that it was to be a unified, internally coherent system with clear equivalencies between its component parts, rather than as assemblage of ad hoc programs. This was especially important with regard to rationalizing the professional training program for adults, which had proliferated in the immediate post-independence period. A second principle was that it would establish permanent relationships between the aims, content, and structures of education and the transformation of society, which would allow education to evolve in response to Mozambique's socioeconomic development. A third principle was that educational activities would be coordinated and integrated, eliminating duplication, bottlenecks, and irrational use of scarce human resources and equipment and creating better articulation between levels or programs in the same field.

In providing a coherent framework and a long-term perspective of how education was to develop, the NES represented a major achievement. The challenging question, of course, was whether it could be implemented, given the human and material resources available. Perhaps in the difficult years of transition to socialism in a backward country like Mozambique, there is never a "right" moment for instituting a large-scale plan for the future that demands maximum use of the very cadres who are most needed to carry out the day-to-day work in already existing programs and activities. One way or another, the NES emerged as a basis for organizing the education sector into a more coherent set of structures to carry out the major tasks of the decade, eradicating illiteracy, guaranteeing universal education, building up a skilled labor force, and developing scientific research.

Summing It All Up

> Each society organizes its system of education and instruction to pass on its experience and knowledge to new generations: to maintain and develop its economic and social structures, its values and its culture. . . . The way in which production is organized in a society, the relations of production which characterize it, determines its social consciousness. It is in this area of social consciousness that the education system is to be found. In turn, the manner in which a society educates and prepares its cadres

conditions its own social and economic development.

—"Education Systems in Mozambique,"
Ministry of Education and Culture, 1980

The transition from capitalism to socialism means not only a radical change in the economic and social structures of society but a profound change in the way people think about work, social relationships, and society in general. Clearly the changed consciousness is both a product of the existing economic and social conditions and simultaneously a shaper of new ones.

In a country like Mozambique, where socialism is being built on the soil of underdevelopment, the role of education as a shaper of the new consciousness is fundamental to furthering the revolution. The social consciousness forged during the decade-long national liberation struggle and during the first phase of the transition to socialism clashed sharply with the experiences, values, and knowledge characteristic of both traditional and colonial society. The question at hand is the degree to which changes in education have facilitated the carrying out of the central transforming task of each phase of the Mozambican revolution. Has education indeed been made revolutionary, a vital shaper of the new consciousness?

In the nationalist phase which grouped all patriotic Mozambicans in a broad front against Portuguese colonialism, we have seen that new forms of education did play a significant role. At the outset the colonized consciousness was widespread and debilitating, for the creature of colonialism

> is a man without a temporal dimension. He is a person unable to locate himself historically within his society and unable to locate his society historically. His point of reference is the colonial conquest. . . . The colonized man lacks the capacity to locate himself spatially. [He is] deprived of his own geography. His special point of reference is the metropole. . . . The colonized man is deprived of a third dimension. He is ignorant of the roots of his personality. He was educated to despise his own personality.[33]

Education during the armed struggle challenged this colonized mentality head-on. The education that was so vital a component in the political-military preparation of the freedom fighters situated Mozambique on the path of its own history once again. The schooling in the liberated areas celebrated the rediscovery of Mozambican history, geography, and culture, promoting a return from slavery to human dignity.

The class society of colonialism, with its need to legitimate existing forms of class domination, also attempted to prevent the

colonized from perceiving the real economic, political, and technological relationships governing society and production. The
worker in colonial Mozambique was profoundly ignorant of the
organization of industry and agriculture, of socioeconomic and
technical relationships. While there was a general consciousness of
being exploited, there was little understanding of the mechanisms
of exploitation and even less of alternative ways to organize a society.

When the anticolonial war advanced to a new phase through
FRELIMO's internal struggle in 1969–1970 to define the shape of
the new economy and society in the liberated areas, education was a
focal point in drawing out the central issues. Just as, in colonial
society, going to the *liceus* and thence to the university in Lourenço
Marques, South Africa, or Portugal signified grooming for a role in
the ruling class, so, in the minds of some, did going to the
FRELIMO secondary school and subsequent scholarships abroad
imply a role in the ruling class of post-independence Mozambique.
But was the FRELIMO education system set up to service the fortunate few who made their way from the primary schools in the
liberated areas to the secondary school in Dar es Salaam? Father
Gwenjere, agitating among the secondary school pupils, encouraged the view that the proposed return to serve the people in
the liberated areas before advancing to higher studies would be a
waste of time for them as future leaders in the new Mozambique.
This view became part of a broader antirevolutionary line which, if
it had been successful, would have seen a Mozambican petty
bourgeoisie assume the roles formerly played by the Portuguese,
while ordinary workers and peasants would have been confined to
their accustomed roles in production, exploited and politically
powerless.

As we have seen, the triumph of those committed to a genuine
social revolution meant the closing of the FRELIMO secondary
school for a two-year period. Instead of students being sent from
the primary schools in the liberated areas to higher studies, they
were sent back into those same schools to teach others or to use
their new knowledge to guarantee production, health care, and the
increasingly sophisticated weaponry and logistics of the war itself.
Education, then, was integrally linked to the central transforming
task of that phase of history, and the armed struggle for national
liberation was transformed into a process of radical social transformation.

Immediately after independence, as we have seen, FRELIMO
defined production as the transforming front. The key task was
that of actually taking control of the forces of production. There

was an all-out political and organizational offensive to mobilize workers as conscious actors in the struggle to harness Mozambique's abundant resources to create the necessary food, clothing, housing, transport, education, and health care for all Mozambican men, women, and children. To what degree did the education system in existence after 1975 succeed in relating directly to this transforming task? First, it became accessible to workers. The new stress on literacy and adult education, the many professional training and upgrading programs helped to empower workers, giving them the technical knowledge and political consciousness to play a new role as the leading force in directing their economy and society. Serious efforts were made to check the tendency to cream off the most able students and send them to the university. The placing of ninth-grade graduates in sectors needing cadres was one such check. The many worker-students at the university was another. The discrimination against technical schools was tackled and their educational inadequacies began to be overcome, albeit slowly and with many difficulties. Significant advances were made, then, with a dramatic broadening of the base of the education system. Even with all the problems of quality this brought in its wake, the expansion must be seen as a major accomplishment.

To what degree did schools really succeed in linking study with production, imbuing students with knowledge of, and respect for, workers and work? Here the results were more problematic. Indeed, to what degree did the schools succeed in organizing programs of production, thereby concretely linking themselves to the central struggle of this phase and lessening the burden of the state for education expenditures? Once again, the record is one of both significant successes and failures, but there was no wavering on the correctness of the principle.

Mozambicans talk boldly today of creating the "New Man"— men, women, and children with a new set of socialist values, a new view of the world and themselves, a new confidence in their capacity to create their own history. This is seen as a crucial battle in combatting the colonized mentality to which so many succumbed during the long years of Portuguese rule. Has the new education— with its focus at all levels on Mozambican history and geography, its strong emphasis on political education, on developing Mozambican personality so long despised by colonialism (and by Mozambicans themselves) succeeded in implanting such a consciousness?

There is no doubt that Mozambique has seriously addressed this need to create the new person out of the complex tangle of the old—feudal, colonial, bourgeois—and the new—independent, socialist, collective, and working class. Supernatural explanations have given way to scientific explanations. Efforts have been made to break the habit of blind obedience to authority and to encourage an activist and critical outlook. The relegation of women to secondary roles has also been seriously challenged, although far greater attention has been paid to structural changes than to attitudinal ones. The new values of respect for work, of the collective rather than the individual, of equality and participation are an integral part of all education activities. The harder question is to what extent the new education has succeeded in creating teaching-learning situations in which these new values can be explored and internalized by conscious choice rather than imposed as the new dogma.

"Let's make the entire country a school in which everybody learns and everybody teaches." In reality, perhaps, that kind of behest does not accord with having orderly, well-run schools and literacy centers with adequately trained teachers, sufficient supplies, and a teaching-learning process qualitatively advancing year after year. The genuine wish for learning by the people outpaces by far the capacity of the Ministry of Education to provide even the rudiments of a satisfactory response. Thus many situations of confusion, frustration, and demoralization cropped up during the broader march forward. In such a massification of the base, extraordinary strength and determination are required, be it among the untrained primary school teachers trying to deal with the eighty to one hundred first-graders packed into their tiny, inadequate classrooms or among the workers-turned-literacy-teachers (by virtue of a three-week training course) trying to help their unlettered colleagues master reading and writing in noisy factory classrooms, with inappropriate teaching materials, the students exhausted after eight hours of shift work.

I, like many others, found myself in constant debate over the difficulties I observed. Could they have been avoided with existing resources or were they an unavoidable part of the reality of that phase and resolvable only in the future, when the proportion of literate to illiterate, trained to untrained, had altered significantly? The reality of the phrase "shortage of trained people" has to be lived to be understood, but in a society where 85 percent of the population is unable to read and write, where a mere six years of not very solid basic education ensures one of innumerable job possibilities, where a ninth-grade education places one in the upper echelons of leadership in workplace and community—in such a society, clearly, there are very few people to carry out the many tasks of development, all urgent, all complex.

For me, and I think for many other *cooperantes* from the West, the years spent living and working in Mozambique have probably been the richest and toughest of our lives. The sense of richness comes from our respect for the integrity and commitment of the FRELIMO leadership, for their honesty and open self-criticism, and for their genuine efforts to create structures of people's power. It derives from the special moments at work or during community or national events when we have felt the great privilege of being part of a process in which ordinary workers and peasants really take control of their economy and society.

The years in Mozambique have also been the toughest I have ever known, perhaps in part because there is no respite from dealing with the "now," however problematic it may be. I no longer have the comfortable option, as I did in Canada, of dissociating myself from the system at will because, after all, it was "theirs" and not "ours," the comfort of imagining that when we gained power it would surely be different. In Mozambique, those who are fighting for people's power really do have the party and the state to use for that purpose—albeit a young and inexperienced party and a highly dependent state. And so one hurts for the failures and weaknesses, not only in one's work sector but in others, and one's own energies and emotions are engaged in the larger political process with an intensity that is difficult to sustain.

The years of work in Mozambique have had a complex texture of victories and defeats, advances, retreats, and holding patterns, raw edges and confusions. Yet they have also had recurrent moments of celebration, of experiencing new forms of collectivity, love, and solidarity. For those of us who came as internationalists, they have been years of learning—learning how difficult the path to socialist transformation really is and learning to despise even more the capitalist systems in our own countries which allow no time or space for a people to build its own road to socialism.

Notes

1. Samora M. Machel, *Let's Make the Entire Country a School Where Everybody Learns and Everybody Teaches* (Maputo: INLD, 1978). The text comes from a speech launching the first national literacy campaign, July 3, 1978.
2. Quoted in Eduardo de Sousa Ferreira, *Portuguese Colonialism in Africa: The End of an Era* (Paris: UNESCO, 1974), p. 58.
3. Quoted in David Hedges, "Education, Missions, and the Political Ideology of Assimilation, 1930–1960" (Maputo: Eduardo Mondlane University, 1982), p. 5.
4. Ferreira, *Portuguese Colonialism*, p. 43.
5. Allen Isaacman and B. Isaacman, *Mozambique: From Colonialism to Revolution* (Boulder, CO: Westview Press, 1983), p. 40.

6. Ferreira, *Portuguese Colonialism,* p. 71.
7. Ibid., p. 77.
8. Hedges, "Education," p. 10. *Xibalo* refers to the practice of forced *(chibalo)* labor through which the colonial administration imposed labor contracts at will on "idle" Africans, forcing them to work for periods of six months on tasks in either the state or private sectors.
9. Ibid., p. 11.
10. Eduardo Mondlane, *The Struggle for Mozambique* (Harmondsworth: Penguin, 1969).
11. Hedges, "Education," p. 6.
12. Quoted in "The Match That Lights the Flame: Education Policy in the People's Republic of Mozambique," an official document submitted to UNESCO (London: Mozambique, Angola, and Guiné Information Center, 1976), p. 3.
13. Samora M. Machel, "Education in the Revolution," *Mozambique Revolution* (Dar es Salaam) (October–December 1973): 21.
14. Interview with Mario Sive, Bagamoyo, Tanzania, 1970.
15. "The Match That Lights the Flame," p. 6.
16. Machel, "Education in the Revolution," p. 22.
17. "The Match That Lights the Flame," p. 7.
18. Machel, "Education in the Revolution," p. 22.
19. Graça Machel, "Opening Address to the Third National Meeting of the Ministry of Education and Culture," 1979, mimeo., p. 13 (my translation).
20. Samora Machel, "Let's Make the Entire Country a School in Which Everybody Learns and Everybody Teaches," p. 5 (my translation).
21. Graça Machel, "Opening Address to the Third National Meeting," p. 16 (my translation).
22. Interview with Andre Carvalho given to representatives of the Swedish International Development Authority, 1979.
23. For an excellent account of life in the schools in the immediate post-independence period, see Chris Searle, *We're Building the New School! Diary of a Teacher in Mozambique* (London: Zed Press, 1981).
24. For a more lengthy discussion see Richard Gray, "Khalai-Khalai: People's History in Mozambique," in *People's Power* (London: Mozambique, Angola, and Guiné Information Centre) Publication No. 18; [Summer 1981]: 3–17.
25. Speech by Graça Machel to tenth and eleventh grade students being mobilized to train as teachers as part of the response to the directives of the Third Congress.
26. Interview with Deolinda, a seventeen-year-old trainee at the Namaacha Primary Teacher Training Center, October 1981.
27. *A Formação do Professor Primário e a Sua Actuação no Meio Social* (Maputo: African Studies Center, Eduardo Mondlane University, 1984), mimeo.
28. Sérgio Vieira, "The New Man is a Process," address to the Third National Meeting of the Ministry of Education and Culture, 1979, mimeo., p. 22.

29. Interview with Deolinda, October 1981.
30. Interview with Eugénio Bahane, Maputo, October 1981. Bahane had graduated from the fourth grade at Chonguene Primary School in Gaza Province in 1942 and was a student in the fifth grade at Hulene Community Secondary School in Maputo Province in 1980.
31. Rui Fonseca, "Information on the Development of Literacy Programs in Mozambique," paper presented to an international symposium on Cooperating for Literacy, sponsored by the German Foundation for International Development, Berlin, October 1983, mimeo., p. 2.
32. Interview with Eugénio Bahane, Maputo, October 1981.
33. Vieira, "The New Man," pp. 3–6.

Helena Dolny

4. The Challenge
of Agriculture

The introductory chapters of this volume provide an essential context for the present chapter's focus upon Mozambique's attempts to advance the cooperativization of the peasant sector. There, for example, the agricultural sphere was situated more firmly in relation to the dynamics of the broader economy and, in particular, in relation to the urban/industrial sphere. In addition, a more detailed account of the interplay within the agricultural sphere between the state farm sector on the one hand and the peasant-cum-cooperative sector on the other was presented. Here it is the latter sector that is emphasized. Drawing on her own extensive first-hand experience, Helena Dolny is able to specify in a very concrete manner the many difficulties that have confronted the cooperativization program, as well as to highlight some of the positive lessons—for future reference—which have been learned by Mozambicans in the post-independence period.

Since Dolny finished the main body of her text in late 1982, the rural situation in Mozambique has, if anything, deteriorated (as we saw in Chapter 2), with continuing drought and the intensification of South Africa's war of aggression adding to existing difficulties in the areas of internal trade and agricultural organization. FRELIMO's Fourth Congress in 1983 strongly affirmed the need to give increased emphasis to transforming the peasant sector, but its NEP-style preoccupations led to its focussing as much or more on the development of "family" and "private" agriculture as a short-term means of increasing production as on advancing the cause of cooperativization. Nonetheless, the latter remains an important goal for FRELIMO. As its pursuit continues on the new and economically more vibrant terrain that FRELIMO hopes the end of the war will bring, the lessons Dolny draws from the earlier phases of attempted cooperativization should be of particular importance.

Mozambique has a population of over 12 million, more than 90 percent of whom live in the rural areas. During the period of colonial capitalist penetration, the peasantry was a major producer of surplus: it sold both its produce and its labor. But the standard of living always remained low and the daily diet consisted mainly of carbohydrates (maize, cassava, or millet), accompanied by a small quantity of beans or vegetables. Education was for the privileged few and the rate of illiteracy was 90 percent. When agricultural assistance was provided, it was devoid of educational content. Low wages and low prices for agricultural produce meant that the majority could afford to buy little beyond meager quantities of cloth, oil, soap, salt, paraffin, sugar, and new hand tools. Today housing remains basic: thatch, reeds, and clay. Access to running water is rare. Personal possessions are scanty: few people have bicycles, fewer have radios, and even fewer have sewing machines. Tools are minimal: some households have oxen and ploughs; most have *a* hoe, *an* axe, *a* hatchet.

These are the conditions in the countryside, the conditions that FRELIMO is working to transform through its policy of promoting agricultural producer cooperatives. This policy not only takes into account the experiences of the peasantry before independence, but is put in a class context. It is not a policy that aims to provide privileged conditions of credit, improved inputs, technical services, and the like to specially chosen groups of better, richer farmers but is an integral part of the strategy for "socializing the countryside." As Marcelino dos Santos put it:

> The demands of the revolution are great. The people wish to improve their lives, they want more food, more clothing, better housing. . . . With the gaining of independence they feel these things to be within their reach. . . . Inevitably we will make our way toward economic growth. But the revolution may fail to be carried through if we do not socialize the countryside. Some peasants will develop and transform themselves into proprietors and through this others will be exploited.[1]

The key plan for development in Mozambique has been the Prospective Indicative Plan (PPI), a ten-year program for the decade 1980–1990. Since the PPI's adoption, it has been repeatedly affirmed that socialization of the countryside is a priority and should embrace the majority of the peasantry. The plan hoped to have 5 million peasants engaged in cooperatives by the end of the decade. And subsequent government statements were to reiterate that unless "development"—i.e., material advancement—is linked to the creation of new relations of production, the Mozambican revolution will have failed to achieve its aims.

However, implementing the policy by spreading the cooperative experience of the liberated zones in the years since independence in 1975 has met with a number of problems. Figures produced at the People's Assembly meeting of October 1981 described a situation in which individual peasant farms took up 94 percent of the area cultivated and produced 80 percent of the gross value of agricultural production, while cooperatives controlled only 1 percent of the area and .3 percent of production. Delegates at the meeting described their experiences since independence. One deputy, Maponda, a peasant from the northern province of Niassa whose links to FRELIMO go back to the first days of the armed struggle, had this to say:

> Initially many people joined the cooperatives. In the beginning they were promised tractors and other things. But these promises were not carried out. There were failures and then some people went back to their individual farms. There they felt the results were better. We insisted that they stay. We managed to convince some, but not others. Even ourselves, the leaders, we too have difficulties.

Certain themes recurred at both the October 1981 meeting and also at Ministry of Agriculture meetings. These included:

—The role of the party and the state in building a cooperative movement.

—The methods of work of state technicians and the transformation of state-peasantry relations.

—The problems of reorganizing production processes and securing good economic results.

—The type of technical assistance, input, and training needed by the cooperatives.

The discussion that follows attempts to provide a framework in terms of which the above points can be considered. There are four sections. The first gives a general description of the Mozambican peasantry and its production experience during the period of colonial rule. This will be the base against which we can counterpose and assess "transformation" in this transition period. The second section sets out in more detail what happened in the countryside after independence: how new cooperatives were formed, where the land came from, and how the cooperatives were structured. In the third section, two case studies furnish specific details about concrete situations to which we can relate the abovementioned themes, which are so important in a transition to socialism. Finally, the fourth section focuses on more recent debates among Mozambicans as to how best to learn from their experiences and carry the struggle for rural cooperatization forward.

Colonial Capitalism and the Mozambican Peasantry

Traveling along dirt roads in the Mozambican countryside one sees the traditional "snapshot" image often shown on television: a poor, scantily dressed peasant toiling near his mud-and-thatch dwelling. A woman may be approaching, hoe in hand and bundle or clay pot on her head. The development literature often refers to these peasants as subsistence farmers, those who produce only enough to eat and reproduce. They are projected as self-contained "islands" with little or no connection to the market economy.

Yet consider the household of Solinjala N., who lives in the northern province of Tete. His home is built of baked earth bricks. The roof is well thatched and two of the rooms have glass windows, a sign of affluence in rural Mozambique. The house is used only for sleeping. Nearby there is a simple round hut that serves as a kitchen. At the edge of the living area a two-compartment bathroom has been built, one section containing a pit latrine, the other for bathing. Trees divide the house from that of Solinjala's neighbor, and along one side a reed fence protects the courtyard from the wind. Four large granaries woven from strips of bamboo have been erected on a platform of stones and rainproofed with thatch. One granary is full of groundnuts and beans, another contains millet, and the remaining two are full of maize.

Solinjala's wife, Siueta P., is busy preparing maize flour. The dry maize has been dehusked, milled, and washed. It is now sifted onto straw matting and will be left to dry thoroughly in the sun. As she works, Siueta listens to the radio, the family's one luxury. They are saving to buy sheets of roofing zinc and a fifty-liter water barrel to supplement the earthenware pots they now use. But the first priority is the education of the children. The three oldest attend secondary school, which means they have to live away from home. Schooling is free, but a contribution of $12.00 per month is needed for food and other necessities. The two youngest go out daily to the pasture lands, where they stay with the family's six cattle. When they are older and attend primary school, the family will have to find other children, perhaps nephews and nieces, to do this work.

As a picture of a low standard of living, the "snapshot" may be true. It fits well within a theory of "dualism," i.e., the conception of an economy made up of "modern" and "backward" sectors. Colonial agricultural statistics, for instance, are divided into two sections: "traditional" family farming and "enterprise" agriculture. But such a picture impedes an understanding of the extensive and varied forms of capital penetration in the peasant economy. It ignores, for instance, a southern region heavily affected by migrant labor employed in the South African gold mines, or a peasant agriculture subordinated to the labor needs of the plantation sector, especially in the central region of the country. Rural researchers in the post-independence period in Mozambique have so far failed to find any omnipresent subsistence peasantry.

Solinjala himself has spent more than eight years of his active working life as a wage worker. He completed two contracts in the South African mines, two six-month periods of forced labor on settler farms, two years as a railroad construction worker, and one year on the docks at the port of Beira. His family now works together on three hectares of arable land, as well as in their riverside vegetable garden. Using careful, labor-intensive cultivation techniques, substantial amounts of maize, beans, potatoes, and vegetables are produced, a considerable part of which are marketed. But Solinjala does not confine his activities to the family farm. He is a member of the agricultural producer cooperative, where he works three mornings a week. There his past experience of working in disciplined labor groups serves him well, as he and other members discuss the organization of the work groups and the setting of work norms.

Such diverse economic forms, which to some extent fall into regional patterns, means that there is not one homogeneous Mozambican peasantry but several, and that each peasant brings into the present a specific experience that affects his or her attitude toward, and his or her initial potential contribution to, the cooperative movement. Three forms of colonial economic exploitation are described in more detail in the following pages: the peasant/forced cash-cropper, the peasant/plantation worker, and the peasant/migrant worker. They have been selected because each represents a widespread experience and provides an important context for the transformation of peasant agriculture in the post-colonial state. An understanding of these categories will throw important light on the dynamics of the rural areas which are the starting point for the implementation of FRELIMO's strategy for socializing the countryside.

The peasant/forced cash-cropper

On coming to power in 1932 Portuguese Prime Minister Antonio Salazar clearly stated that the colonies had three functions to fulfill for the "mother country": to accommodate Portuguese settlers, to produce raw materials for Portugal's nascent industries, and to provide a market for the sale of Portuguese products.

One of the most sought-after raw materials was cotton. In 1955, 33 percent of Portugal's industrial workers were employed in textile factories. Ensuring supplies was of utmost importance and the colonial state wholeheartedly devoted itself to this end. Heavy demand for labor for the plantations and mines in the central and southern regions of Mozambique meant that the north became the major cotton-growing region.

Various companies were granted territorial monopolies for cotton buying and ginning on condition that they build the ginning factories. The colonial state in turn guaranteed to organize the cotton-cropping activities of the peasantry so as to secure the necessary level of supply for the factories. It was the colonial administrator who, in terms of practical organization, assumed this role. He was responsible for the functioning of the *capatazes, cipaios, regulos,* and *cabos.**

By 1944, 790,000 families, probably one-third of the entire Mozambican population, were involved in forced cotton production. Little effort was made to increase productivity through the use of inputs such as insecticides, fertilizers, or machinery. Increased production was achieved rather by involving a greater number of people and intensifying coercion to extend the labor-time spent working in the cotton fields. All this was happening during a postwar period in which other (non-Portuguese) colonies were moving toward political independence.

The peasants of Netia, a productive cotton-growing area of Nampula, had this to say about their experiences in colonial times:

> Almost all of us were forced to cultivate and to live by the roads [here used in the meaning of both dirt road and the adjoining farms]. There, each family had a strip of six hectares of ground, one alongside the other. Each year we had to cultivate three patches of one hectare each. The other three hectares we left fallow. They forced us to produce cotton, sorghum, and cassava, and they told us how to rotate the three crops.
>
> Along the road, we used to work from five in the morning to five at night, first on the cotton farm, then on the food crops. We worked under constant supervision of our captains, commanders and chiefs, cotton agents and foremen, native police and police from the Netia post. They gave us no respite and were always on the watch that we would not leave the field. But the one who gave orders throughout the fields was the administrator in Netia and the head of the cotton company in Namialo.
>
> When we did not put up with work in the field, we were denounced to the chief, arrested, bound, and handed over to the native police who took us by force to the administration post. There in Netia, they beat and tortured us with the *palmatoria.†* They could send us to forced labour in the sisal plantations. The only way to escape the punishments was to make "friends" with the native police. One had to bring them chickens, money and other things.[2]

Capatazes and *cipaios* were employees of the colonial administration; *regulos* and *cabos* were members of tribal structures who collaborated with the colonial authorities.

†*Palmatoria:* a wooden-pronged instrument used for beating the hands.

What the peasantry refer to as the *picadas* the Portuguese authorities called "cotton concentrations." These represent a brutal phase of colonial exploitation, equal to that in the period of forced sisal cutting and railroad construction earlier in the century. This manner of cotton production on the best lands enabled the colonialists to supervise production closely and to extend the working day. Violence and repression were the means used to resettle thousands of families on the better cotton producing areas:

> We received orders to abandon our lands and villages, to open new plots for us to cultivate cotton along the roads. Each family had to cut down the bush and remove trees by hand on the plot assigned to them.[3]

In the late 1950s and early 1960s Portugal was busy canvasing for international acceptance of its non-decolonization policy. It maintained that its colonies were provinces of Portugal, and that Mozambicans, Angolans, etc., were Portuguese citizens. During this campaign, Portugal requested admission to the International Labor Organization (ILO) and an offshoot of this request was the formal abolition of forced cropping, although the actual practice continued. The peasants in the key cotton areas are very clear that for them it was only FRELIMO's accession to power that signified the end of forced cropping, at first in the liberated zones and then on a national level (in 1975):

> Serving along the roads ended. Many peasants deserted the land allocated by the colonialists and returned to their land. They grew cotton where they wanted, or left off growing it.[4]

The peasant/plantation worker

The peasant/plantation worker can be found in all parts of Mozambique, be he a peasant from the most northern province of Cabo Delgado who goes off to work on a sisal plantation in Tanzania or someone from the south working on the sugarcane plantations of that region. The large plantations developed mainly in the central provinces, sugar, tea, sisal, and copra being the principal plantation crops. These plantations were characterized by monocropping, low levels of mechanization, and high seasonal labor needs. The creation of a permanent labor force was barely initiated.

When companies began to invest in plantations they needed land and a seasonal workforce to till the land. They met both needs by force. Land was taken and money taxes were introduced. When this failed to ensure a sufficient number of workers, a law was passed requiring all men involved in peasant farming to engage in paid employment for at least six months of the year. Each male received a *caderneta,* a document that registered tax payments and dates of employment.

After the 1930s the state assumed direct responsibility for labor recruitment:

> Men and women were caught for forced labor on the plantations of Sena Sugar Estates. The workers were chained and made to travel many kilometers on foot to the administrative post. Afterward they were sent to the plantations. The salaries were sent to the administration at the end of six months' work, whereupon the tax was immediately discounted. Later in Gurué they took people's land so as to open tea plantations. The people fled into the mountains to the north to escape land clearing, which was hard labor. Many men fled as the result of that work.[5]

Peasant agriculture in the central region was thus subordinated to the plantation economy. An annual six-month absence meant a serious decline in the amount of labor available to a family for its own farming needs. Where peasants were forced to move to poorer lands, their living standard dropped and a situation of utter dependence on the plantation economy developed. Income from plantation work became necessary for the basic reproduction of the family. There was no option of full-time employment, even though the money received by a plantation worker was not enough to sustain him and his family for the rest of the year.

Conditions on the plantations were hard. The use of the migrant laborer, who after six months would return home to recuperate, permitted the setting of daily tasks that sometimes took twelve hours to complete. The day's work was only registered on completion of an allotted task—a worker who failed to complete the set task was recorded as absent. Often the day's work was done without a rest period, and for decades Sena Sugar Estates, for instance, failed to comply with a labor regulation that stipulated a worker's right to a lunch interval.

One worker had the following to say about working conditions during this period:

> They checked if you had many absences marked on your card. If you did, they asked where you'd been. If you said you'd been sick, they asked if you'd been to a hospital. If you said that you'd been tired, they said, "A black gets tired?" You were then punished and sent to work on road construction, for which you received no payment.[6]

Resistance to this coercive labor system took a number of forms. Some evaded the six-month compulsory service by going on the run; many fled to preferred work in the Rhodesian mines. Those who did work on the plantations used various ruses to make it appear that a task had been completed. For example, workers would load the wagons so as to make them appear to be full; they would make shallow planting holes for the cane plants instead of the deeper ones technically required; they would be deliberately careless about stripping the foliage from the harvested cane, clogging the blunting and chopping machinery in the processing factory.

But in general it was difficult for the peasantry in this region to develop coordinated forms of resistance in the workplace. This is not surprising given the character of migrant labor. Workers come and go; if a man does return to the same plantation it is probably to work on a different block and with workers he has never seen before. It was thus only in the post-independence period that the population of the plantation region came to have its first real experience of mass political activity.

The peasant/migrant mine worker

As with peasant/plantation workers, peasants with mining experience can be found in all of the country's ten provinces, but intrastate labor-recruitment agreements meant that it is the south that has been most deeply affected, and a large number of men have spent the majority of their working lives in the South African mines. In 1938 the Sena Sugar Estate representative in Lourenço Marques wrote the following:

> The emigration to the Transvaal has depopulated the whole of the country south of the Save river. One only sees the old, the sick, and women and children. . . . The little agriculture that we have today makes no progress for lack of labor, and those farmers who do succeed in recruiting pay out higher wages than those defined by law, because of the high mining wages.[7]

As many as 125,000 Mozambican men have been to the South African mines in every year since the beginning of this century. In the 1940s an average of 85,000 men meant one-quarter of the active male population, although by the early 1970s the annual recruitment of 100,000 was only one-fifth of the active males (because of population growth). Nevertheless this was still substantial, with considerable economic effect.

Mine labor migration began toward the end of the last century. The gold mining industry on the Witwatersrand sought long-term arrangements for a flow of cheap labor, and intrastate treaties were entered into. Colonial Mozambique guaranteed a stipulated quota of able-bodied men and received income for this in various forms:

a capitation fee for each recruit, reimbursement of the taxes paid by miners while in South Africa, and foreign exchange in the form of gold accruing from deferred payments.[8] In turn, South Africa agreed to use Mozambican ports and railways for the routing of a fixed percentage of its goods.

Labor recruitment for the Rand mines was not, however (as in the case of plantation recruitment), the direct responsibility of the colonial state. This task was carried out—in fact monopolized—by the Witwatersrand Native Labor Association, whose tightly organized system of district managers, compound managers, and paymasters maintained close links with chiefs and *cabos* within the Portuguese administration system.

Such large-scale and long-term mine recruitment had a marked effect on agriculture and on the proletarianization of the peasantry. Established patterns of the division of labor changed and farming became almost exclusively women's work. The mine contracts were for a longer period (twelve to eighteen months) than those on the plantations (six months) and radically cut the labor available for family farming, causing reduced harvests:

> Joe Taola N., the son of a miner, is forty-one years old, married, with three children, and has two sisters living with him. Between 1953 and 1976 Jose completed ten contracts, all but one of eighteen months' duration. He usually spent six months at home between contracts.
>
> His work history shows him to be a miner with a rising range of skills permitting him to increase his earning power. Beginning as a "pickanin cheesa boy," he became a plumber's aide, a "feeder boy" and finally a "boss boy."*
>
> When there is rain his *machamba* [farm] produces enough food and in good years he sells up to fifteen sacks of groundnuts. His earnings from mine labor have enabled him to build up his agricultural base. But he says he has to keep returning to the mines not from choice but out of necessity.[9]

Income from mining became for many families a prerequisite for survival. This situation was accentuated with the increased appropriation of the most fertile land by settler farmers. New consumption patterns also developed, more than in the rest of the country because of the greater cash flow involved. Consumer durables, such as radios, bicycles, and sewing machines, became commonplace household items. The flow of cash also stimulated the

---

*"Pickanin cheesa boy," "feeder boy," "boss boy": as observed in *The Mozambican Miner* (see note 9 below), "The vocabulary used in the South African mining industry is a reflection, on the level of language, of the African miner's subordinate position. Africans are insultingly referred to as 'boys'." (p. 81)

emergence of specialized artisans who were paid out of the mine wage income for those tasks (housebuilding, carpentry, mat weaving) previously carried out by the family itself. In 1967 money income from the mines in the three southern provinces was nine times that resulting from crop sales (about $28 million and $3 million respectively). Most miners came from the poorer families and their wages were used primarily for maintaining the family. But there were some who were able to save. Oxen and ploughs were bought and this made it possible to cultivate the heavy fertile soils, which could not be worked with a hoe. As a result of this process a small group of richer peasants emerged, owning larger farms, tractors, carts, and water pumps. The differentiation among the peasantry in this region is thus greater than in the rest of Mozambique.

There existed other forms of colonial exploitation besides those described above. For instance, the widespread settler farming sector often used forced labor, known as *chibalo*. The country's road and rail system and its harbors were also built with *chibalo* labor.

In an interview Madelena Mandlazi, a resident of Nyampungwani Communal Village in Gaza province, spoke of her experience of forced labor:

> My husband was away in the mines in South Africa when the colonial police came to my house and arrested me. Together with other women I was taken away to open a new road. It was all thick bush that we were forced to clear and they did this simply because our husbands were away in the mines. This was very hard work and I worked there until my husband was able to send money with which to pay the hut tax. I worked two months on that road down there—building the Guija-Chibuto road.[10]

In addition, the peasants did more than supply labor to other sectors and produce cotton. In spite of the constraints on the development of peasant agriculture, the sum total of peasant marketed surplus was of major importance to the national economy. Statistics from 1967 (the most complete set of annual statistics available before independence) show the peasantry to be the source of one-third of all marketed crops, producing 100 percent of the cassava, 90 percent of the maize, 67 percent of the cashews, 67 percent of the cotton, 43 percent of the rice, 100 percent of the groundnuts, 21 percent of the copra, 20 percent of the tobacco, and so on. Rice, maize, and groundnuts were important to the internal food market, especially for the plantations and the cities. Cashews and cotton were—and remain—major export earners: the peasantry makes a substantial contribution to Mozambique's foreign exchange earning capacity.

Mozambique's present-day agricultural sector shows the marks of colonial capitalism. A transformation policy must take into consideration existing linkages. For instance, a labor stabilization policy for the plantations will affect peasant agriculture. Employment will no longer be available to some of those whose family reproduction system hinges on plantation work. For the majority it is not an option to retreat into subsistence farming; colonial capitalism put an end to that possibility. Whether through sale of labor or of commodities, the Mozambican peasant is firmly rooted in, and dependent on, a market economy. That is the ineluctable situation of one Mozambican miner whose workplace was a foreign country:

> I am a worker and I cannot do without a paid job. Everyone here has been to the mines—our grandfathers went. I do agriculture when at home because the wages are never sufficient for a decent life. But there is no security in agriculture because you cannot control the rains.[11]

The sharp drop in labor recruitment means that a huge workforce is now resident and unemployed in the countryside, men with considerable experience in industrial organization and work discipline who need to be encompassed within Mozambique's transformation strategy.

Agricultural Policy in the Liberated Zones and After Independence

FRELIMO's accession to power opened the way for a possible transformation of the entire countryside. Many colonized countries have inherited a similar situation—an economy that is the result of colonial capitalism—and the wish to develop, to obtain greater surpluses to invest in different economic sectors, is a common objective. What differs is the strategy chosen.

What would be an appropriate policy to transform a situation containing the following elements?

—Plantations.
—Settler farms.
—A southern region a large part of whose active male population was the workforce of a neighboring country.
—A peasant agriculture characterized by one of labor-intensive techniques and by low productivity, which in some areas is linked to declining soil fertility.
—A peasantry that was deprived not only of vocational training but also of general education and basic literacy and numeracy.

FRELIMO policy was the direct result of the political struggle between different class positions during the liberation war. FRELIMO's successes of the 1960s and its growing popular support led to a rapid increase in the land area falling under its control. Liberated zones were established in the rural areas of the northern provinces of Cabo Delgado, Niassa, and parts of Tete; these constituted over one-quarter of Mozambique's land area, with a population of about 1 million. What was to be the new political, social, and economic organization in these liberated zones? Should there be private ownership of land? Should the exploitation of labor continue? Different class positions within the FRELIMO leadership gave rise to sharply conflicting political positions. There were some who saw themselves as replacing the colonialists, taking command over resources and continuing to exploit the people. Others, who represented the aspirations of the working class and the poor peasantry, strongly opposed a position that implied continued exploitation and fought to ensure that the fruits of the struggle would not be usurped at the point of victory by a new class of exploiters.

The Second Party Congress in 1968 came out in support of this position, and it was decided to encourage collective production as the means of changing relations of production in the countryside. *"Abaixo a exploração do homen pelo homen"*—"Down with exploitation of man by man"—eventually became the main mobilizing slogan. The peasants in the liberated zones organized plots on which they worked collectively part of the time. The production of these plots helped the liberation army. This practical experience of working together to create a surplus for collective disposal provided the foundation for the more far-reaching policy formulated after independence.

Thousands of Portuguese settler producers abandoned their farms between 1974 and 1977. Some plantations were abandoned as well; others were nationalized after their owners refused to continue to invest in them. FRELIMO's policy was to "advance and transform"; abandoned land would not be distributed to individuals but would be gathered into state farms and cooperatives.

In February 1976, several months after independence, the rural transformation strategy was outlined at a major Central Committee meeting. The main emphasis was to be the creation of communal villages *(aldeias comunais)* as the "backbone" of development in the countryside. Peasants would no longer live in dispersed groups of houses. Production was to be predominantly collective and the surplus generated by the production units would provide the basis for village development. Social infrastructure, schools, stores, and health posts would be built. The rest of the surplus would be directly invested in the production base of the cooperative to increase output and productivity. Furthermore, the villages would be the new political and administrative units of the countryside, with party cells and elections to the People's Assembly being organized on a village basis. In short, the communal villages were to become the fulcrum of a new political and economic order in the countryside: they were to be the *dominant* productive enterprise, encompassing the majority of the peasantry. (However, a year later, in 1977, the Third Party Congress proclaimed that the *determinant* force in the countryside would be the state farms. These would act as a catalyst for further development; they would be influential in building the cooperative movement by giving technical support, training cooperative members, etc. They would create a skilled permanent proletariat.)

FRELIMO's strategy for the socialization of the countryside then addressed two fundamental issues: the advance of productive forces and the transformation of production relations. The colonial domination of the past meant that the state had to play a leading role in these two areas: the largely illiterate peasantry was dependent on the dissemination of such skills as accounting, registering information, and production planning to enable them to take control of decision-making in the cooperative. Furthermore, cooperatives were dependent on the state for the dissemination of scientific knowledge and for the tools, machines, and inputs which make greater productivity possible. The key role of state cadres in the transformation process had immediately to be considered, given the repressive role previously played by the state. The new ideology had to be conveyed through the working methods of its cadres, who had to put a radically different class line into practice. One much emphasized slogan was "Transform the state to serve the people."

By April 1976 an initial restructuring of the Ministry of Agriculture had taken place. The most significant change was the creation of a National Directorate for the Organization of Collective Production (DINOCPROC). This directorate was to be led by a "crack team" whose members were handpicked for their political background as well as their skills. It had two branches, one dealing with state farms, the other with cooperatives. The state farm team consisted of fourteen agricultural specialists or economists. In contrast, the cooperative team numbered only three, whose skills were mainly in the area of political organization and the preparation of propaganda material.

The state farm sector rapidly organized a skeletal infrastructure of cadres and technicians. Each of the ten provinces had a nucleus that gave planning, accounting, and technical support. On the farms themselves there was a joint directorate that included a political commissar and a cadre with a technical background. Coordination was good, and an overall plan dealing with the development of each of the farms was formulated. By August 1977 machinery and technical cadre requirements had been minutely detailed, and an active investment program begun. Hundreds of tractors, milking machines, pedigree bulls, etc., were imported. This investment and expansion demanded personnel, and the initial small group of cadres grew dramatically. Foreign technicians were recruited and Mozambican technicians transferred from other branches; newly qualified cadre were preferentially allocated to this sector.

No similar process took place in the cooperative sector. Here the focus was less on developing the productive base and more on the political process of changing production relations, a process, however, that proved to be unsustainable in the absence of an improved material base.

Thus during the early post-independence period the dynamics of the cooperative movement were not well connected with the state agricultural extension service. The organization of *grupos dinamizadores* (dynamizing groups, or GDs) has been described in other chapters in this book. In the countryside these groups became the core for mobilizing the new cooperatives. "Let's repeat the experiences of the liberated zones" was one mobilizing slogan. Literally thousands of "collective *machambas*"* started producing in the 1974/75 and 1975/76 agricultural seasons.

But this early phase was beset with difficulties. One peasant from the Nampula cotton-growing area described this period as follows:

> We no longer produce as much cotton as before. The *palmatoria* does not scare anyone any more. The chiefs and commanders, the captains and the native policeman no longer order anyone around. One had to rest a bit. And we had lots of meetings and all the support tasks for FRELIMO. At that time, the school teachers were secretaries of the dynamizing groups. They mobilized people to make collective farms. We teamed up with our neighbors, but when one dropped out, the others gave up likewise. So we produced almost nothing.[12]

The political and economic secretary in Namarroi district in central Zambezia had the following to say about these first collectives situated outside the liberated zones:

Machamba means farm, but whereas a state *machamba* implies an area of some size, a "collective *machamba*" implies a relatively small area.

Here there were several collective *machambas* of maize, beans, peanuts, and rice, organized on the level of the *celula** but without clear objectives, lacking minimal organization, and producing little.[13]

By 1977 the inadequate response to the numerous attempts to begin collective production led to much discussion about how to give better political and technical support. On the ground there was a shortage of advanced and experienced political cadres. Those with experience from the liberated zones were either working at the national level or were involved in the struggle against Rhodesian incursions. The only technical support available to the cooperatives was from the disintegrating district agricultural services. Many of the Portuguese technicians at the time of independence had signed a two-year contract and were preparing to leave. Many Mozambican technical cadres were either receiving additional training or being transferred to the state farm sector to help secure an optimal return on the large investments now being made.

In an attempt to improve the quality of support, the collective initiatives were evaluated and categorized in order to set priorities to achieve a more effective distribution of limited resources. The categories were collective *machamba*, pre-cooperative, and cooperative. The Ministry of Agriculture published a description of each. In essence, the collective *machamba* was to be a production initiative at the level of the *celula* or village. Participation was expected to be irregular, voluntary, and basically unplanned. The profits were not to be distributed but were to be reinvested in something of common benefit. In the pre-cooperative, production was to be organized by a definite number of participants who were to share the profits among themselves. However, in organizational terms it had no accounting system or adequate planning and its leadership was informal. The cooperative was to be a higher level cf organized production than a pre-cooperative in terms of planning, accounting, etc. It was to have an elected directorate and administrative bodies.

The 1981 Ministry of Agriculture statistics (which do not include collective *machambas*) showed that there were about 350 cooperatives and pre-cooperatives. The detailed case studies that follow are of two of these cooperatives.

First, however, I will outline some of the characteristics of the cooperative movement in general.

---

*A *celula* is the smallest unit of political representation and organization; the others, in ascending order, are the *circulo*, locality, district, and province.

Cooperative production that is the result of a reorganization of dispersed family fields is as yet unknown in Mozambique; instead, cooperatives have been organized on abandoned settler farms or on newly cleared land. Cooperative members continue production on their family farms, but have reorganized their cropping patterns to make a part of their labor-time available to the cooperative experiment (for example, three mornings a week is a common choice). I use the word "experiment" deliberately because many of the participants have taken a wait-and-see attitude; the continuing activities on the family farm permit a tentative commitment to the cooperative. Should the cooperative "fail," they can simply return to family farming.

Each year a technician from the district agricultural service comes to each cooperative to discuss crop planning for the next season. The planning usually concentrates on quantitative questions. How many hectares are available? How many people will work the land? What kind of crops can be produced and in what quantities? The planning does not extend to making a monthly schedule of necessary work days or to calculating the income that will accrue at different levels of production. The planning process is restricted to a calculation of such inputs as machine hours, seeds, and fertilizers. As will be illustrated in the case studies, cooperative members in the early post-independence years were not helped to increase their decision-making skills or their ability to control and administer the cooperatives.

Techniques of administration remain underdeveloped and diffusion of simplified record-keeping aids has been slow. Thus one better organized cooperative in its third year of production was found to have two suitcases, one for receipts, and one for unpaid bills. In general there is hardly any record keeping except for the register of days worked per person. This obviously affects a cooperative's ability to plan and control—it is unable, for instance, to evaluate the costs or labor days used in the production of various crops—although such an evaluation forms the cornerstone of any real planning.

On the other hand, credit is easily available, although in practice inherited bureaucratic procedures have sometimes been an obstacle to actually obtaining it. For example, one cooperative that wanted to buy oxen for ploughing found that the oxen had been sold to someone else by the time credit approval had come through.

The minimum organization consists of a president, a production leader, and a treasurer, all elected by the cooperative members. Some cooperatives have a more elaborate directing body, including a production leader, a secretary, a bookkeeper, a person responsible for supplies and marketing, another person responsible for social affairs, etc. The cooperative is usually divided into brigades, which then subdivide into teams. A common pattern is for each brigade to work three days a week, alternating the days with the other brigades.

Remuneration takes the form of a fixed sum of money for each day worked, the sum being determined by the overall productivity of the cooperative. There is no system of differential remuneration based on the quality of work. To implement such a system would require a level of organization and administrative capacity that does not yet exist. A few cooperatives have, however, made some distinctions regarding those members who do not participate fully the whole year or who miss work days in crucial periods, and who therefore receive a lower daily remuneration. "You can't come to plant and then not turn up to weed and expect to get the same as everybody else" is the logic employed. "When you don't come regularly at weeding time in the cooperative, you're endangering the work of all of us."

Despite the common characteristics noted above, there is no uniform cooperative experience throughout Mozambique. There are two particularly important areas of difference: the variation in the participation of men and women, and the distinction between those cooperatives based in communal villages and those that are not.

The extent to which men or women or both take part in the cooperative movement differs regionally, a direct result of colonial experience. In the south, membership is almost completely female because the men have always looked for nonfarming wage work. In the present situation, cooperatives with a regular monthly payout may make some headway in winning male members, but cooperatives with low levels of remuneration, shared out only once or twice a year, have not. Two or three months as a casual laborer on a state farm can provide as much income as a whole year on a cooperative. In the cash-cropping north, on the other hand, while both men and women have participated in the newly emerging cooperatives, there has been a tendency for the men to regard them as their domain. Thus in many cases the women have continued to work on the family farms while the men concentrate on the cooperative; women are called in for extra help with the weeding and harvesting.

As regards cooperatives and communal villages, it was intended that the first would provide the economic base for the development of the second. In practice, however, such harmonious links have not proved to be the norm, and figures presented to the People's

Assembly in October 1981 showed that while there were 1 million people in communal villages, there were only 70,000 in the cooperatives. It is thus clear that the inhabitants of most communal villages still only cultivate their family plots. One reason may be that many of the villages were formed as a response to natural calamities, such as floods and droughts. People were first grouped together in order to receive aid and then villages were established for those who had been displaced by the disasters. The discrepancy between village residence and cooperative membership thus reflects a willingness to live together when social services are provided but a hesitation to participate in a new production form whose economic results are uncertain.

Although the vast majority of the new villages are not engaged in any form of collective production, they still have great significance as structures in the new political order. The villages have party cells and choose representatives to the People's Assembly, people's tribunals, and youth and women's organizations. Thus they play an important political role in a countryside otherwise characterized by dispersed dwellings that are difficult to organize politically.

Case Studies

The case studies that follow provide a detailed description of two cooperatives that I came into contact with through my work in the ministry of agriculture. Their story helps to highlight many of the problems that are common to the cooperative movement across the country, particularly the following: (1) state-peasantry relationships, especially in terms of the planning process and the problems connected with technical assistance; (2) relevant forms of training for cooperative members and state and party cadres assigned to work in this sector; (3) the difficulties involved in establishing relationships between the cooperatives and communal villages; (4) the difficulties encountered in changing from the peasant family form of production to cooperative farming.

Eduardo Mondlane Communal Village and Cooperative,
Maputo Province

Eduardo Mondlane Village is forty kilometers from Maputo city center, about a half hour drive along a paved road. There are about a hundred families in the village, which has a cooperative farm. Not all the village members work on this farm; as in nearly all cooperatives in this southern region, the majority of its members are women. Many of them are effectively heads of households. The village men are absent doing wage work. Some are in the South

African mines, on state farms, or on the nearby sugar plantations; others have jobs in Maputo city as domestic workers, factory hands, bakery assistants, and the like, sleeping in the city during the week and coming back to the village only on weekends. So the weekday residents of the village are mainly women, older men, and children. As the case study shows, the cooperative does not yet provide an economic alternative to migration; men continue to leave the village to seek wage work.

However, all the village families, whatever their income from wage work, do some family farming. The main crops are maize, beans, pumpkins, and sweet potatoes. Most families have only hand tools, although others have saved enough from their wage work to be able to buy oxen and ploughs. Once they have these they can cultivate some of the very fertile *machongo* soils that are difficult to work with a hoe. It also means they can till more land—particularly since there is no land shortage. They can also hire out their oxen and ploughs to other families. If there isn't enough family labor to weed their own fields, the practice is to organize a work session of "friends" or relatives, at the end of which a meal and some drink is provided. This is what is often described as "mutual aid" or "traditional forms of cooperation," although once a process of class differentiation has begun such terminology often blurs the real employment aspect of these work sessions, which effectively offer employment to the poorer peasants.

Some of the present cooperative members were part of the first collective production initiatives that took place in the district in the 1974/75 season. As previously noted, during the transition period following the April 1974 coup in Portugal, FRELIMO encouraged the formation of GDs, which were to promote FRELIMO ideas and objectives. It was such a group in Marracuene District that first formed a *cooperativa de povo*—people's cooperative, in other places called a collective *machamba*.

In that first year the members of the Eduardo Mondlane Cooperative worked on land in a flood plain area called Ilha de Incamine. They used their own oxen and ploughs to till the land, and their first production results were encouraging.

During this transitional period many of the Portuguese settlers who had large farms along the banks of the Incomati, cultivating rice and fresh vegetables for Lourenço Marques, packed their bags and left. In Marracuene District there were several abandoned settler farms. Four large tracts were taken over by the state to form the basic agricultural blocks for a new state farm, but others were available for cooperative production. The many small *cooperativas de povo* were then encouraged to amalgamate. Those on the Ilha de

Incamine formed two cooperatives, one called "25th of June" (national independence day) and one "Samora Machel." Both were encouraged to take out bank loans to purchase one of the fairly new second-hand tractors left behind by the settler farmers. In February 1977 the growing crops and households situated in the Incomati River valley were washed away by the torrential rains that hit the southern provinces. The party encouraged people to start a communal village and rebuild their houses at the top of the escarpment five kilometers away. Clearly there would not be the same access to fertile land, but they would be safe from flooding— this was not the first time that their production had been destroyed by a flood and they agreed that a village with better housing and social infrastructure was worth moving for. The members named the embryonic new village Eduardo Mondlane Communal Village, and elected as president Jaime Na, a middle-aged man who had done several contracts in the South African mines and had an air of solidity and maturity; he had also been among the first to join one of the cooperatives on the Ilha.

Many of the new village members were from the 25th of June and Samora Machel cooperatives. They decided that now that they lived in the same village they would pool their resources and form a single cooperative on an abandoned farm that had an irrigation infrastructure. By the beginning of the 1978/79 agricultural season, however, the unified cooperative had expanded and included all the adults living in the village. This was the result of work carried out by the district party and agricultural cadres, who were part of the group that was encouraging the formation of communal villages in the area. Having studied the party documents, the village mobilizers reiterated the party's sentiments.[14] They held meetings and agreed that the cooperative should belong to, and be the responsibility of, all the village members.

There were many other tasks that had to be done to develop the new village, and these were already being done collectively: constructing wells, preparing tree poles for houses, cutting bamboo, collecting rabbit food (for the village unit), assigning militia duties, building a guest house, a meeting hall, a school. Agricultural production would become one more such task.

The 1978/79 agricultural season: confusion about the relationship of the cooperative to the village

Nevertheless, the 1978/79 agricultural season was characterized by confusion about the relationship between the cooperative and the village. The 25th of June and Samora Machel cooperatives had met with moderate economic successes, but their members found that the new orientation presented great difficulties. Those activities that produced a saleable surplus and would contribute toward building up a productive base to support the development of the village did not receive special priority when labor brigades were being organized. There was considerable confusion over the objectives of the cooperative and over whether—or how—the harvest should be shared out. As long as the cooperative had been separate from the village this question of remuneration had not caused any difficulties: the members had decided to sell their produce, to use part of the funds to finish paying for the tractors they had bought, to put a little aside to buy next year's inputs, and to share out the rest.

Once the cooperative was simply one more village activity, however, it no longer had a membership that could expect to receive individual remuneration. The villagers were divided into brigades, and a certain number of brigades allotted to each task; the brigades rotated at intervals. This created a number of problems. Many members were absent from the village doing wage work, so family contributions differed, leading to bad feeling. The output and quality of work of the brigades went down. The various construction projects could be completed slowly, but the diversion of the labor force from cooperative production was more immediately felt: a badly weeded field affects yields and a later intensive work session will not make up for lost potential.

Besides these internal factors, there were also external ones that created problems that the village members could not resolve for themselves. The tractors, for instance, were mechanically unreliable and technical assistance in maintaining them was inadequate; thus ploughing was often late or interrupted by breakdowns. Late planting, together with poor weeding, resulted in poor yields. Another problem was the lack of experience with irrigated farming. Training was needed but was not forthcoming. Further, nearly all the people working in the collective were women. If they had ever been employed on the settler farm, it was as casual labor during weeding and harvesting times; they knew little about pesticide application or regulation of the irrigation canals, let alone about labor organization and planning.

For all these reasons production was very low, while the decision as to what should be done with the little that was produced had not been resolved by the end of the season. Should there be an equal sharing out of the produce? Why should those families who had hardly participated receive any benefits? Should the produce instead be sold and the money contributed to the village as a whole? In the end some of the produce was shared out equally; the rest was sold and the money kept in a fund for a future consumer cooperative.

The 1979/80 agricultural season: problems of planning, technical assistance, and labor organization

The plan for the 1979/80 season's production still needed to be made. State technicians from the district and province came to assist in the planning process. They also had a special task: to persuade the cooperative to put most of its effort into rice cultivation. Maize and rice are considered strategic in meeting national planning goals. Province-by-province goals had been elaborated by the National Planning Commission, and the provincial and district cadres now had to discuss with the producers (those who fell under the central plan—state farms, cooperatives, private farmers) their per crop hectareage so that the goals could be met.

The state technicians encouraged the village to plan for eighty hectares of rice. They assured the village leadership that mechanics would come and repair the larger of the two irrigation pumps, which was presently out of order. In spite of the village's organizational problems, the leaders decided to accept this goal. Rice was in short supply. An increase in local production was needed. Their contribution, together with that of others, could help reduce foreign exchange expenditures on rice imports. Their decision demonstrates the widespread willingness among the peasantry to collaborate with the government in the new situation of national independence.

But all did not go according to plan. Tractor breakdowns meant that in the end only sixty-nine hectares were ploughed, harrowed, and seeded. In addition, the main pump was not repaired and the smaller one could only irrigate about thirty hectares. Participation in the cooperative, already weak, was reduced still further by this fact. People were demoralized. Ninety sacks of unhusked rice was harvested, or 115 kg/hectare. This was only enough to cover one-fifth of production costs. The village certainly could not repay what it had borrowed for inputs, let alone the loan it had taken out to buy its two tractors.

Faced with a serious crisis, the village leaders called a meeting to discuss the future of collective production. The participants decided that the cooperative needed a registered membership. Only people who were committed to trying out this new production form should join, and cooperative work should no longer be simply another collective task of every villager. The cooperative would be under the control of its members. It would have an elected leadership, conferring with—but separate from—the leadership of the village. The members would divide themselves into brigades, each of which would work three days a week. Labor days per person would be recorded throughout the season and remuneration would be related to this labor input. Furthermore, given the difficulties of maintaining the tractors in working order, there was discussion about returning to the use of oxen and ploughs—they may not have had skilled mechanics among them, but they certainly had skilled users of oxen and ploughs!

The 1980/81 agricultural season: another year of inadequate planning and estrangement between cooperative members and state technicians

The state agricultural technicians then returned to the district to help define the production plan for the next agricultural season. One participant described the meeting to which the leadership of the cooperative was summoned:

> We were called to a meeting. We didn't have any idea what it was going to be about. Then we were asked to present our plan for the next season. We hadn't yet discussed a plan with all the members of the cooperative and were reluctant to present anything, but in the end we suggested thirty hectares of rice, thirty hectares of maize, six hectares of sunflowers, one-half hectare of tomatoes, two of onions, and one of mixed vegetables.[15]

The planning technicians pushed for eighty hectares of rice, but the leaders explained their difficulties in taking on such a plan: the probability of late ploughing, the nonfunctioning main irrigation pump, and the huge number of labor days that would be needed at the weeding stage. They were assured that this year these difficulties would be resolved: the land would be ploughed on time—if the cooperatives' own tractors were not working, others from the district machinery hire station would be sent; and the irrigation pump would be repaired well in advance of its being needed.

The verbal interchange did not lead to a formal agreement, however, although the planning technicians left with an entry in their files putting the rice goal for this cooperative at eighty hectares. The cooperative leadership, on the other hand, went away firmly convinced that they would only aim for thirty hectares. They were confident that they could work this area with some success, in terms both of labor and of the irrigation capacity of the smaller pump.

January 1981: questioning the planning methodology and work relations

A few months after the meeting a team of planning technicians from the National Cooperative Department of the Ministry of Agriculture arrived in the village. They explained that their work methods and those of the provincial-level cadres had been much criticized during a national meeting attended by representatives of cooperatives from all ten provinces. The mathematical, limited planning methods of the past seasons had been discussed, judged, and rejected. A plan was needed that took the organization of the entire production process into account and was based on the experience of the cooperative members—their evaluations of past seasons, the labor norms operating in the cooperative, and so on.

The team was therefore to work with the cooperative to develop a planning framework and a teaching methodology that could be used in training courses for cadres and cooperative leaders. Given the low level of literacy and numeracy, special attention was to be given to finding methods of discussion that would be easily understood by cooperative members—for instance, the non-numerical representation of arithmetic calculations.

The poor relationship between the district level technicians and Eduardo Mondlane Cooperative members was highlighted during a discussion of the existing plan. The ministry team was first told by the cooperative leaders that in this season they would cultivate thirty hectares of rice. A little later the leaders felt they had made an error. After all, they knew that the district technicians had registered the cooperative as having committed itself to eighty hectares. The leaders' presentation of the plan thus suddenly changed; they stopped speaking about thirty hectares and began referring to eighty. The ministry team was confused and attempted to clarify the situation. A lively discussion of work methods ensued, resulting in various proposals as to how the team of technicians should use its time in the village. It was decided that during the mornings the team would integrate itself into the field work to learn the organization and functioning of the cooperative. The afternoons would be reserved for meetings about the planning process itself. Given the difficulty of getting all the cooperative members to join in the discussion, fifteen of them were elected to participate in the sessions.

During the next three days the team and the cooperative representatives worked out how much labor would be needed to carry out a series of alternative plans, including both the eighty- and the thirty-hectare proposals. The cooperative's reorganization, the formation of brigades, and work schedules were taken into account. A great deal of oral testimony was collected, which made it possible to discuss such things as the optimal number of hectares for rice cultivation, given cooperative weeding norms, and so on. The different possible income levels resulting from various crop mixes, yield levels, and hectareages were also discussed.

There was a great deal of participation in this particular part of the discussion. Never before had there been any debate over alternative production plans, or over the differing levels of income according to crop yields. Projections were made: if the land is ploughed, planted, irrigated, and weeded at the optimal times, a yield of x kg/hectare is probable, whereas late weeding will probably reduce the yield, and therefore income, by x amount. The use of such examples made the planning discussion concrete rather than abstract.

The ministry team knew little about the technicalities of production in this part of the country. What it attempted to do was to synthesize information from the cooperative members in a systematic, schematic manner in order to create a basis for discussion. The cooperative members agreed that the team's method permitted them to more clearly conceptualize the essentials of formulating a plan, and were pleased that it was they themselves who possessed much of the information that was needed.

Conclusion

The problems encountered by the Eduardo Mondlane Cooperative between 1978 and 1981 demonstrate the importance of good political and technical training of state and party cadres. The fact that the cooperative leadership withdrew from a real discussion of the 1980/81 plan indicates the alienation caused by poor work methods. The confusion created when the cooperative was treated as just one more village activity highlights the problems which develop when party policies are implemented without debate or discussion. And finally, a planning process that limits itself to a mathematical calculation of machine hours, seeds, and fertilizer, that fails to ascertain labor needs, and that does not include discussion with the cooperative members illustrates not only poor work methods but also the poor technical level of the state technicians trained during the colonial period.

The ministry team's subsequent work developing material for a training program for both state cadres and cooperative members was a positive step forward. If it is successful, it will contribute to changing state-peasantry relations and lead to more effective planning, control, and administration by cooperative members themselves.

Lussanhando Communal Village, Lichinga District, Niassa Province

One of the romantic notions that dies hard in every revolutionary movement is that getting people to produce collectively

will, in itself, generate greater surpluses. What happened in Mozambique shows the opposite to be true: in those cooperatives
where basic cultivation methods were the same as on the family
farm, the productivity per hectare generally fell. Given existing
levels of technology, the gains from a more complex division of
labor are offset by the difficulties of initiating collective work.
Building group confidence takes time, and such confidence is easily
destroyed. The new collective form of organization is also time-
consuming, involving many hours of discussion and debate. In the
light of such obstacles to higher productivity, it is clearly of tactical
importance to identify those technological inputs and forms of
organization that will permit the cooperatives to achieve greater
surpluses.

The Lussanhando example is chosen precisely because it illustrates the complexities that must be confronted when the change
from one production system—the family farm—to another—the
cooperative—is attempted.

The setting

Lussanhando is near the Niassa provincial capital. Large areas of
this northern province were liberated as the struggle for national
independence advanced, but the inhabitants of this particular village had been grouped together by the Portuguese in an *aldeamento,* or strategic hamlet. The *aldeamentos* were guarded.
People were watched over when they went to cultivate their nearby
fields; evening curfews were in force. Great efforts were made to
prevent any contact with FRELIMO and any activities that might
be supportive of the liberation army.

Before independence substantial areas of peasant land in the
Lichinga District had been appropriated and occupied by Portuguese settler farmers. As in Cabo Delgado, another northern province where FRELIMO was very active, the colonial government
offered special concessions and subsidies to settlers in an attempt to
create communities that would act as barriers to FRELIMO's advance southward. When independence came all but a handful of
the settler farmers left.

In 1976 two hundred families from the old *aldeamento* of Lussanhando moved their belongings and their animals to a new site
on one of the smaller of the abandoned farms. It had more than
two hundred hectares of cleared land suitable for tractor ploughing, several brick buildings, a house, a store, a piggery, etc. The
provincial housing directorate had drawn up a plan for the location
of the village's housing units, using a grid system that took into
consideration the future installation of piped water and electricity.

The families built temporary dwellings of mud and thatch at the rear of their allotted plots, leaving space at the front for the construction of more permanent brick structures.

The village members discussed the proposed cooperative, which was to make use of the resources of the abandoned farm. They evaluated their 1974–1976 experience of collective *machambas* in which everyone had participated on an ad hoc basis, without clear economic objectives—a participation undertaken as a manifestation of respect for the collective *machambas* of the liberated zones that had helped feed the FRELIMO army. The village members decided that the new cooperative should be an economic venture as well as one with political aims. Enrollment would require regular work from those members who had committed themselves; the others would continue to produce solely on the family fields. However, membership would not be closed—the cooperative wanted eventually to attract the remaining adults.

One hundred and thirty-three adults from the two hundred families enrolled. For most of them moving into collective production meant taking a step beyond anything encountered before. Some of the older men had worked on plantations, others had done forced labor, and four had worked on mining contracts abroad. But to plan work and to organize production for a large group (rather than be the recipient of harsh orders) was a new, strange, and awesome experience. They balked at the prospect of doing accounts—not even those who were literate felt confident enough to try, and teaching materials designed for such situations did not as yet exist. They overcame this problem by asking a young primary school teacher to help.

The organization of the cooperative was simple. The members divided themselves into three brigades of forty-five people each. Each brigade then subdivided into three teams. The leaders of the brigades and teams met daily to organize the distribution of tasks. Once a week there was a general meeting of all the cooperative members to tackle any big problems that might have arisen.

The main problem was fundamental: what type of farming to undertake. The members had to ask themselves how the settler farmer produced, how peasant farming was organized, and what path of change—what innovations—the cooperative should undertake.

The settler farmers' agricultural organization

The settler farmer in this hilly region had chosen to cultivate the flattest lands, where using tractors was easy. His farming was characterized by the monoculture of maize—the planting of the same crop every year in the same fields. The tractors from the machine-hire station would come twice, first (in September) to plough and then to harrow when the weeds came up after the first rains. The harrowing killed the weeds, and the crop was sown. Everything but land preparation was done by hand. Weeding, the largest task, had to be done twice within a short space of time to ensure good yields. The need for a large number of casual workers at weeding time might have posed a problem for the settler farmer, but he resolved it with the collaboration of the administrator, who "helped" recruit labor. The crop was harvested in May and June, and the lack of irrigation prevented the sowing of any further crops during the dry season. Planting only one crop also meant that increasing amounts of fertilizers and pesticides were required to maintain yields when soil fertility declined and pest infestations increased. But fertilizer costs were still relatively low and cheap labor was easily "mobilized" so that the settler farmer did make a profit.

The family farm

Family farms in this area all follow the same agricultural practices—it is as though generations of empirical observation have produced the optimal system given the limitations of a family's labor supply and of the hand tools in use. Although there is no land shortage, the land is intensively cultivated, for planting new land means grueling work clearing bush with an axe.

The families grow maize, two crops of beans (one to be eaten green, the other to be dried and stored), potatoes, cassava, and vegetables. The time and place for planting varies to make the best use of the geographical and climatic conditions for each crop. Since the rains fall only from November to March and the region is hilly, the low-lying areas with soils still moist from water filtration are used in the dry season. For example, maize is planted on the uplands when the rains begin in November and harvested four months later when the rains have stopped and the grain is dry and ready to store and make flour. Another planting of maize, to be eaten in cob form, takes place in the low-lying areas in August, when there is enough soil moisture for the early plant growth; when it comes time for the cobs to fatten the rainy season is already well under way.

But it is rare to see maize as the only crop in the field; intercropping is the common practice, with maize and beans the usual combination. The field is prepared with a hoe, leaving raised furrows. In the upland plantings, as already noted, maize is sown in November; a little later, when the seedlings are established, beans are sown. The following March, as the crops are harvested, the furrow is shifted and a new planting of beans takes place. After four years of continuous cultivation, the field is left fallow to give time for a more complete recuperation of soil fertility.

The system has several attractive features. The total land area and labor needed to prepare for planting are minimized. The combination of maize and beans contributes to maintaining soil fertility. The continuous cultivation gives good weed control. The use of furrows that follow the land contours is important in reducing the soil erosion that would otherwise be caused by the heavy rainfall and steep slopes. Furthermore, the use of furrows makes good use of soil moisture, which is important because of the irregularity and intensity of the rainfall. And finally, the production per field is the sum total of three separate harvests.

Of course, it is not being proposed that the cooperative should continue this pattern of peasant agriculture. Although it seems ecologically sound and self-sufficient in terms of the inputs needed (an advantage in a situation where resources bought with foreign exchange—machinery, fertilizers, pesticides—are scarce), the system is nevertheless rudimentary and limited, and incapable of generating sufficient surpluses to fund the development of the productive forces. Nor was the settler pattern, premised on monoculture, forced labor, and the like, entirely appropriate—although the cooperative members did not at first think through the full range of questions about technology and work organization and as a result carried over uncritically certain limited aspects of the settler's manner of organizing production. However, slowly but surely a new pattern—different from both family farm and settler farm— was being constructed.

The 1977/78 agricultural season

The cooperative planned to cultivate 150 hectares of various crops in the first season. Later they decided that they had overestimated their capacity and the area to be cultivated was reduced. They decided to plant other crops besides maize, partly because of prices and partly because of the advisability of spreading the demand for labor over a more diversified growing region. The decision was not, however, taken with the need for land rotation in mind. In the event, productivity per hectare was very low, showing no improvement over yields achieved on family farms. The members registered more than 13,000 labor days, a "labor day" representing, on average, a morning's work of three to four hours. The average member worked a total of 134 days (of a possible 156, at three days a week), which indicates a consistent participation on the

Table 1
Production Results 1977/78

Crop	Area planned (hectares)	Area cultivated (hectares)	Production (kg/ hectare)	Production total (kg)
Beans	50	25	180	4,500
Sunflower	70	50	108	5,400
Garlic	0.5	0.5	3,880	1,940
Maize	30	30	624	18,720
Hectareage totals	150.5	105.5		

part of most members. Average payment for this work, from money that remained after paying for the inputs (the cooperative received subsidies for tractor hire and transport), was the equivalent of U.S.$50. The daily remuneration was thus as low as $.37.

The 1978/79 agricultural season

The next season was a particularly difficult one. On the basis of initial enrollment the cooperative once again planned to cultivate 150 hectares. It was decided to use improved varieties of maize seeds and more fertilizer. A large amount of credit was requested for these inputs, but only half the amount granted was in fact used because the total cultivated area was subsequently reduced and because the top-dressing fertilizer never arrived. The cooperative members had become demoralized by the low remuneration of the previous season, and only forty-three people participated regularly throughout the year. Productivity was once again low, and only the maize crop produced a higher yield than did the family plots—but at a higher unit cost because of the expenditure on seeds, fertilizer, and tractor hire.

The financial outcome of the season's production was a negative balance of US$2,456. The season's output had been paid for with a bank loan, and receipts were not enough to repay it. Indeed, if receipts had been used solely to reduce the loan there would not have been any cash left for the forty-three members who had worked regularly throughout the year. In the circumstances, a partial moratorium on the loan was requested and granted. This enabled the collective to share out some of the income according to labor days recorded.

The 1979/80 agricultural season

The 1978/79 season's results created a crisis for the cooperative. A debate flared up in the village. Some villagers agreed that party

members who attended courses and meetings had said that the
cooperative was to be the economic base of the communal village,
and that the cooperative would be doing better if a more solid
effort was made by all village members. As a result of these discussions a total of 189 adults enrolled at the beginning of the 1979/80
season. That year's results are shown in Table 3.

The financial outcome of the season's production was a positive
balance of U.S.$1,411.

The provincial agricultural directorate had initially suggested
that 150 hectares be planted, but this was rejected by the cooperative members, who maintained that more labor on a smaller area
would raise productivity per hectare. Maize is the first crop to be
sown; beans and sunflower follow later. In practice the number of
people who worked on the cooperative throughout the year was
the same core of forty-three adults as in the previous year. The rest,
in spite of having enrolled, effectively opted for producing only on
the family farm. The hectareage for sunflower and beans was reduced, so that the group worked a total of 102 hectares, about 9

Table 2
Production Results 1978/79

Crop	Area planned (hectares)	Area cultivated (hectares)	Production (kg/ hectare)	Production total* (kgs)
Beans	50	40	165	6,600
Sunflower	50	40	152	6,080
Maize	50	30	888	26,640
Horticulture	3	1	?	?
Hectareage totals	153	111		

Expenses† (U.S.$)		Receipts (U.S.$)	
Machines	$1,800	Beans	$1,400
Seeds	2,990	Sunflower	1,500
Chemical products	3,386	Maize	1,900
Sacks	420	Horticulture	1,600
Interest on loan	260		
Total	$8,856		$6,400

*All production was sold, except for 12.8 kg of maize, which was distributed for the
members' household consumption.
†A per crop breakdown was not made by the cooperative.

Table 3
Production Results 1979/80

Crop	Area planned (hectares)	Area cultivated (hectares)	Production (kg/hectare, approx.)	Production total (kgs)
Beans	50	35	174	6,077
Sunflower	50	36	206	7,417
Maize	30	30	1,809	54,282
Horticulture	2	1	?	?
Hectareage totals	132	102		

Expenses (U.S.$)		Receipts (U.S.$)	
Machines	$1,400*	Beans	$1,714
Seeds	966*	Sunflower	2,135
Chemical products	9,090	Maize	8,920
Sacks	472	Horticulture	570
Total	$11,928		$13,339

*These figures imply subsidies.

less than in 1978/79. The yield per hectare did increase: for maize it was double the previous year. Total receipts more than covered the costs of inputs, not including labor. Yet the balance of U.S.$1,411, even if it were to have been shared out equally among the forty-three members only, would still have given a meager U.S.$33 each, leaving nothing for investment or social funds.

Thus after three years of effort and despite subsidies, including the moratorium on the bank loan, the members received very little. But is such an outcome unavoidable during the initial experimental and training period, and can rewards be expected later? Or was something radically wrong with the approach adopted by the cooperative toward the organizing of production on the ex-settler farm, on which the members seemed to apply none of the wisdom accumulated from their family farming experience?

There were reasons for the low production, of course. Settler farm monoculture had led to a serious decline in the soil fertility; the fact that fertilizer (lumped together with insecticides as "chemical products" in our table) constituted the cooperative's biggest outlay provides an accurate index of this problem. Furthermore, there was the problem of the late arrival (or nondelivery) of inputs.

One year the late arrival of tractors made it impossible to sow the maize at the right time, and as a result yields were reduced; moreover, the tractors came only once, ploughing and harrowing at the same time, which led to weeding problems for the cooperative. Another year the maize seeds were of inferior quality and germinated badly, and there was also a shortage of pesticide sprayers. Thus even though the chemical products were available, the work could not be done, again affecting the size of the yield. The Portuguese settler farmer presumably suffered less from such vagaries, and in addition the large increase in labor needed for weeding and harvesting was not a problem. The cooperatives, however, do not hire labor at peak periods; nor do the members work uninterruptedly since for the moment the family farm is their security and requires a good portion of their labor time. Thus although availability of labor is of crucial economic importance to the cooperative, the peasants are understandably reluctant to give it too much of their labor-time when the cooperative's ability to provide a higher—and consistent income—must still be demonstrated.

An evaluation meeting

At the end of the 1979/80 season the cooperative members called a special meeting to evaluate their past efforts and to discuss their future. The dismal production figures of the previous three years were analyzed. Was it worth continuing or should they give up before even more bank debts were accumulated? The committed group of forty-three were almost unanimously determined to continue. They recognized the political importance of solving the cooperative's problems. They realized, too, that family farming offers no long-term potential for raising the standard of living for the majority of the rural population.

Broadly speaking, the discussion at the meeting covered the following points.

1. The first priority was to sort out the problem of labor input. Cooperative members felt the need to plan on the basis of a secure labor commitment from those enrolled. They admitted to partial responsibility for the low production results, insofar as these were caused by their own delays in weeding, fertilizer application, and harvesting. (Late weeding affects yields; late fertilizer application affects plant uptake and response; late harvesting impairs crop quality.) They decided that during key periods cooperative members should work six mornings a week and that family plot production should be organized to allow for this. Land adjacent to the cooperative was earmarked for inclusion into family plots, so as to save some of the time spent walking to more distant fields.

2. They debated the economic viability of continued fertilizer

use, given its high cost in relation to production levels. They decided that more legume (nitrogen-fixing) crops should be planted in an effort to recoup fertility.
3. They decided to ask the provincial agricultural directorate to consider a higher maize price because, although the cooperative was losing money on the maize, the directorate continued to pressure the members to include maize production in their planning goals.
4. They debated who was responsible for repaying the loan. Was this the responsibility of the village as a whole, or only of the cooperative members? Part of the debt had been accumulated when there were more participants from the village. On two occasions the cooperative had planned for the larger number of people (who had enrolled), but they had then hardly participated in the work.
5. They debated whether they should buy some oxen and ploughs. They were reluctant to give up using tractors even though their late arrival from the hire station meant that they were not able to plough at the most opportune time. Furthermore, animal ploughing was not a current practice in the region; there were few cattle, although the area is free from the tse-tse fly, and before independence only the settler farmers possessed any. However, since the National Directorate of Cooperatives was offering animals and implements at reduced prices, as well as training courses, the cooperative decided to try ox ploughing. If successful, they would have a means of production under their control which they could use not only for preparing the land but also for weeding and transport.

The experiences of the first three years had enabled the cooperative members to evaluate the problems involved in changing from one agricultural system to another, from family to collective organization. Their discussion led them to resolve the internal problems, which were under their own control, and to seek alternative, economically viable production methods.

Throughout this period the villagers continued to build the new village and, in contrast to the cooperative, the village flourished. It developed its political organization, creating a party cell and electing representatives to the provincial People's Assembly. A health post and a consumer cooperative were established, and a school was built. Adult literacy classes were begun, and one village member attended a course for health workers. There was an unquestionable improvement in the quality of life, and the level of political participation was unknown to the peasantry before independence. But without the advancement of the material base of the village—

the cooperative—a high degree of political mobilization and motivation may weaken.

The Struggle Continues

The case studies were chosen to illustrate the various themes that require constant attention, such as the state-peasantry relationship, training, and the question of technology. In the early 1980s, for example, two national projects were launched by the Ministry of Agriculture which have attempted to respond to the latter two problem areas. A first project involved the establishment of regional centers to give courses to cooperative leaders in order to build their planning-related skills and deepen their political understanding of the role of the cooperatives. By December 1982 there were three modest centers, one each in the north, center, and south. The second project was to set up regional centers to experiment with, and disseminate, improved agricultural technology. This was closely related to the agricultural cycles, and it will be some time before they can hold training courses on the basis of knowledge acquired in the field.

The need for these projects illustrates the difficulties, under Mozambican conditions, of "counting on one's own forces," a phrase frequently used to express the need to solve problems based on self-reliance. Lack of education and colonial repression denied present cooperative members those skills that are crucial to the success of the cooperative movement. The transmission of these skills devolves largely upon the state, which is why the transformation of the state-peasantry relationship is so important. Samora Machel recognized this explicitly:

> To cooperatize . . . by the end of the decade requires the correct use of all our energies, the use of the best of our intelligence, of our creative and inventive spirit, in order to transform the immense potential of our peasantry into a creative, productive, and highly organized workforce.[16]

In consequence, at a meeting after the eighth People's Assembly during which the cooperativization plans for the decade were fully discussed, the Council of Ministers decided to expand the two projects referred to above, recognizing that the effective implementation of this decision would require a larger allocation of material resources and high-quality cadres than in the early postindependence years.

Of course, taken alone, improved training and educational efforts are not sufficient. As demonstrated by the case studies, the transformation of family farming into cooperative farming also means changing the state-peasantry relationship and reorganizing the process of production. How can these objectives be achieved? Class struggle continues. Not all technicians actively accept or put into practice a revolutionary line. They are not all "red and expert." How is the party fulfilling its role of mobilization and of ensuring that the party line is implemented by the state structures? This, too, was a subject of intense discussion as the new decade dawned. In August 1980, five years after independence, a national cooperative conference was held. More than a hundred cooperative members from all ten provinces attended. There were forty people connected with the Ministry of Agriculture—national-level administrators, technicians, and district field officers. There were also representatives from party headquarters, from the bank responsible for supplying credit to the cooperatives, from the women's organization, the university, and so on.

The conference focused on three principal areas: the methods of work of the state technicians, the role of the various agricultural services and of the state farms, and the creation of a union of cooperatives. Cooperative members were uninhibited in voicing their opinions about the methods and quality of the work of the state technicians. Planning methods came under much fire. It was alleged that while cooperative members were supposed to be in control of decision-making, in practice they were "informed" rather than consulted on what targets they were to achieve. Technical assistance was called inadequate. Work visits by members of state structures were described as similar to medical appointments because of their brevity. The routine described by cooperative members went something like this: the Land-Rover stops, formalities are exchanged; the fields are cursorily visited. Instructions are then given, comments passed: "This needs doing, why hasn't this been done yet?," etc. The technicians then drive away, having had no real discussion and having left nothing of educational value behind. The "instructor" role adopted by the state technicians inhibited the inherent creativity of the cooperative members themselves, and their paternalism undermined the cooperatives' sense of control. Likewise, state cadres carried out the money distribution calculations but did not impart their skills so as to make themselves expendable in this sphere. The buildup of such dependency relationships was a particularly sensitive issue given the peasantry's historical experience of subordination and compliance with orders issued by state technicians and administrators in colonial times.

The cooperative conference concluded its discussion on the work of state cadres by debating the question of leadership of the cooperative movement. It was decided that state support for a national cooperative movement could not be the sole responsibility of a small group of people in the Ministry of Agriculture: socialization of the countryside was the responsibility of the staff of all the government agricultural services; they should "put politics in command" and apply themselves to achieving the prime task in hand. This decision placed responsibility in the hands of national-level bodies in an attempt to make them dynamic and politically active. In this regard a special role continued to be assigned to the state farms, where a great part of the available human and material resources had been concentrated; as noted earlier, it had long been conceived that state farms would have a key role in dynamizing the cooperatives, disseminating information, and providing technical assistance and support services.

The discussion moved on to the question of the representation of the cooperative movement. While accepting that the state has a leading role to play in the development of cooperatives, it was felt that some form of organization among the cooperatives themselves was also required. In fact, most of the cooperatives were working in isolation and did not share their experiences with each other. The meeting decided that it was necessary to concentrate on training cooperative members and encouraging contact and sharing of skills among cooperatives. A union of cooperatives was to be encouraged and subsidized. Such a body would handle those tasks in which cooperation presents real advantages: accounting, marketing, purchasing supplies, contracting specialist technicians, and so on. It would also become part of a national network, having representation in ministry meetings and being an active proponent of the needs of the cooperative movement.

In practice the building of a union of cooperatives proved to be a slow process. Moreover, the attempt to give a dynamic role to the state apparatus and to state enterprises was largely unsuccessful, giving rise to a series of searching discussions on the part of the Central Committee and the People's Assembly regarding the party's ability to control policy implementation. There were clear instances where state enterprises failed to furnish support to the cooperatives and gave priority to private farmers in such matters as machine hire, purchase of agricultural implements, and so on. The Council of Ministers was to say, in April 1981, that "the direction, the support and the conjugation of efforts in relation to the movement of communal villages and agricultural cooperatives have not been secured by either the central or local organs."[17] To which Samora Machel added, later in the same year:

Socialization of the countryside is not a mechanical and bureaucratic process. It requires a huge effort in political mobilization and material stimulation. . . . Mobilization must start from concrete premises and with clear objectives. The results will always be the best kind of example to the peasant.

Socialization of the countryside constitutes the most important component of the PPI [Prospective Indicative Plan]. It is a political fight. It is the class struggle in the countryside that requires the complete involvement of us all.[18]

It was no accident that, several months earlier, two key party leaders, Minister of the Plan Marcelino dos Santos and Minister of Information Jorge Rebelo, were relieved of their ministerial duties to enable them to concentrate their energies full-time in strengthening the role of the party.

Moreover, the assumption by the party of a more active role in the development process began with a reflection on existing practices and the quality and methods of work of its cadres. Witness, for example, the self-critical remarks that came out of a July 1981 meeting of the party ideological committee of which Jorge Rebelo is full-time secretary:

[The] sector for the party's ideological work has closed in on itself. It is not directed toward the masses. It is isolated from the people. It is a sector where at present the central practice is not so much political mobilization and ideological education of the people but the holding of meetings and seminars. There are few meetings with the masses, especially in the rural areas, and those few meetings that are held are often meetings in which the party member arrives, talks, and then goes away. They are not meetings to hear from people about their problems. They are meetings in which people participate only as listeners, as observers.

Such statements illustrated an awareness of the party's relative weakness, especially in the rural areas, and demonstrated an encouraging readiness to challenge and change current practices when evaluation deems them to be negative.

Of course, the case studies have suggested that something more than mere pronouncement of good intentions from on high was required in order to realize positive results. This is equally true of such recommendations as that made by the party's Central Committee (in December 1981) to create "a new and distinct state body to stimulate the development of agricultural cooperatives." This notion was slow in being fleshed out; moreover, it was left unclear what the relationship of such a state body to the party might be and which Mozambicans with the necessary political qualities and experience could be released from their current posts to create an effective vanguard at the level of the state apparatus. It is also the case that the party cannot merely substitute itself, across the board, for the work of state technicians, a greater allocation of resources to the latter being equally crucial. In this regard, the history of the demobilization of many collective *machambas* and cooperatives in the early period because they could not secure productivity levels above those of the family farm shows how necessary a strong technical component to the struggle for cooperativization is.

In any case, as seen in Chapter 2, the issue of how to revitalize the struggle for cooperativization was still very much under debate by the time of the Fourth Congress in 1983—although the debate was by then qualified by a number of other considerations as to how best to stimulate production *in the short run* in a desperately crisis-ridden economy. Yet even in the difficult days of 1984 and the Nkomati Accord, cooperativization remained on the agenda, and it is on the long-term realization of that goal that the material presented in this chapter continues to have special bearing. To have written a triumphalist account of Mozambican agricultural cooperatives would have been a disservice to the real experiences, analyses, and debates that have taken place in the post-independence years. There have been setbacks, yet they have not led to lethargy or resignation. Each phase has led to renewed discussions and to the decision to tackle the problems once again, armed with the analysis of recent experience. Moreover, as the cooperative members of Lussanhando Village have shown, this analysis is not limited to higher party and state echelons: the members of the cooperative themselves have been able to make a vital contribution. Despite the complex tasks that await fulfillment in this important area of the Mozambican revolution, there is reason to have confidence in FRELIMO's ability to sustain the struggle to resolve the issues we have sought to identify in the present chapter.

Notes

1. Marcelino dos Santos, speech to the People's Assembly, Maputo, Mozambique, November 1981. (All translations from the Portuguese are by the author.)
2. Kurt Habermeier, "Cotton: From Concentration to Collective Production," *Mozambican Studies* 2 (Center of African Studies, Maputo; English edition 1983): 37.
3. Ibid., p. 38.
4. Ibid., p. 41.
5. Marco Texeira, "Namarroi—uma reserva de mao de obra," *Noticias* (Maputo) (17 February 1982):8.
6. Unpublished research material collected in Zambezia Province in 1976 by the Center of African Studies, Eduardo Mondlane University, Maputo, Mozambique.

7. Cited from an unpublished study by Judith Head of the Center of African Studies.
8. The miner received only part of his wages while in South Africa, the rest being paid to the Mozambican government in the form of gold. On returning home, the miner received the remainder of his wages in local currency.
9. Center of African Studies, *The Mozambican Miner* (Maputo: Eduardo Mondlane University, 1977), p. 81; a revised version of this text has been published as Ruth First *et al.*, *Black Gold* (Brighton: Harvester Press, 1983).
10. Quoted in Alpheus Manghezi, "O Mulher e o trabalho," *Estudos Mozambicanos* 3 (1981):50.
11. Center of African Studies, *The Mozambican Miner*, p. 66.
12. Habermeier, "Cotton," p. 41.
13. Texeira, "Namarroi."
14. Resolution on Communal Villages, eighth meeting of the Central Committee, February 1976.
15. Interview with the author, 1980.
16. Samora Machel, opening address to the People's Assembly, October 1981, reprinted in *Noticias*, 7 October 1981.
17. From the fifth session of the Council of Ministers, 17–20 April 1981.
18. Machel, opening address.

Peter Sketchley

5. The Struggle for New Social Relations of Production in Industry

Peter Sketchley gives us a sense, in this chapter, of the structure of Mozambique's industrial sector, in this way complementing material presented in the introductory chapters. But his main focus is on workplace organization and, in drawing on his own experience of working in a steel mill in the middle years of the post-independence decade, he provides insight into a little researched area of Mozambican life. His is first and foremost a dramatic case study of the cross-cutting, sometimes contradictory, forces of party, state, and working-class action that have defined the politics of transition in Mozambique's industrial sector.

Sketchley thus lends further concrete substance to other of the themes discussed in the introductory chapters. True, the extended period required to bring this book to publication has dated his account somewhat. As discussed earlier, the most recent of events—the formation of trade unions, the more open invitation to private capitalist activity in the industrial sphere—raise fresh questions about the organization of this sector, questions which it is too early to answer definitively. Nonetheless, the difficult situation in industry which Sketchley describes has continued to be characteristic as broader economic difficulties have plagued the country. And, as we have seen, the government has continued to wrestle with the problem of how best to combine efficiency and democracy, leadership and mass action, within the development process generally and within industry specifically. In consequence, Sketchley's exciting account remains of exemplary interest.

National Hero's Day in 1979 coincided with the tenth anniversary of the death of Eduardo Mondlane, the first president of FRELIMO. At CIFEL (Companhia Industrial de Fundição e Laminagem), a steel rolling-mill and foundry in Maputo, the workers agreed to commemorate the day with a fiesta, which was to be held on a Saturday afternoon after work. A committee was formed and it was decided to hold the festival in the heart of the factory, the main gallery of the foundry. There could not have been a more grimy or gloomy setting. The walls were thick with smoke from the furnaces and everywhere there was the fine black dust that comes from the molding sand. So the first task was to paint the walls white. The workers also painted pictures representing the new

Mozambique, such as peasants planting and harvesting crops, and slogans about the continuing sacrifices required for the war and the need for everyone to contribute to the national reconstruction program.

The opening speech was made by a young woman from the Ministry of Industry whom I recognized as the typist who used to prepare my paycheck. Here at the factory, surrounded by four hundred workingmen, her small frame dwarfed alongside the great, looming machines, she spoke with a confidence and force that commanded respect and attention. It was incredible to think that her mother had almost certainly been bought as a wife to work her husband's plot of land. And here stood the daughter, a leader, a dynamizer of the new revolution, a symbol of the new Mozambique.

Next followed the first performances of one of the new popular culture groups. We had all been looking forward to this. We had seen them practicing around the factory. But this was their first public performance.

Popular culture in Mozambique is a difficult problem. Many of the dances of the precolonial days had their origins in tribal initiation rites, practices related to tribal conflict, and the like—patterns inconsistent with the new Mozambique. So these dances, which maintained more or less the traditional forms, are now given new content.

First came a spectacular dance that featured a lot of "limbo"-style body stretching. In the next two dances, which were from the south, the performers lined up and executed a series of ritual steps. Out of the line emerged one figure who performed a sequence of stylized dance routines while uttering a chant that the audience obviously found hilariously funny. The administrator was being satirized, and the audience loved it, but no one would translate it for me from Shangaan, the local African language!

The second dance was led by Pedro, the leading furnace man. Extremely tall, he had a striking physical appearance but incredibly gentle eyes and a sensitive manner. His contribution, in Portuguese, was a story of the "Flame of revolution." The flame is in the hearts of the Mozambican people, he said. It is spreading across Zimbabwe, and it has turned up in Nicaragua too. He ended with a passionate statement about the liberation of all people from oppression. The gradually increasing rhythm of the dances and the passion and compassion expressed in the words made this a real piece of art.

The final dance was another acrobatic warrior dance that involved kicking up a lot of molding sand and dust, which seemed to bother no one.

Then the administrator rose to his feet to make a short speech. He looked very solemn as he said, "Well, before we come to the meal, I would like to remind you that FRELIMO is opposed to drunkenness and alcoholism. That is correct and we support that." There were anxious looks, and a kind of rumble went around the room. Suddenly he smiled, showing a line of white teeth. He said, "No one is going to be rigid about implementing that, of course. We're not here to impose dogmatic positions, we're here to grow to understand what these things mean."

He went on to make a very beautiful and passionate speech. Looking around at the silent machinery he said, "During the colonial period these machines dehumanized man. The avoidance of work was the only form of protest that the Mozambican people were able to make. Work was alienation. Now we have to defeat that, to understand that work is for the liberation of people—liberation from suffering, from poverty, from crippling ill health, from old forms of cultural deprivation." Then he turned to the audience and said quietly, "Our struggle is not just a struggle for production. It is a struggle to make ourselves more human, to create human relationships of a new kind." He continued, "Today we may drink a drop too much, but no one is going to worry about that. What is important is that we use this time to talk to each other, to say things that, because of the tensions created by day-to-day problems, we couldn't say. Perhaps we can use this time to get to know each other, to feel ourselves to be more human and caring." He then reminded us that this was the first fiesta that had ever been organized in the factory, that it was possible only because of the blood of Mozambicans who had given their lives in the sacrifice of the armed struggle. He said, "Let's celebrate with joy the new possibilities, because this is now our factory, and we're able to make it a factory fit for humans to work together in."

It was a beautiful speech, and for me it was a very moving experience to be in that room, decorated as it was, with those ordinary working people, themselves moved by the words and by the warmth of the sentiment. As the administrator sat down there was a great roar from the workers—not just applause but a *roar*. Some workers got to their feet and there was a spontaneous cry of "Viva FRELIMO!" This was not clenched fists going up in a mechanical way, in compliance with party directives, not brainwashing, not propaganda, not anything that fits Western stereotypes, but a true cry from the hearts of people who recognized something of what they had gained and what the future held for them.

This event was perhaps the high spot of a political experience that has turned many of my political ideas upside down. I spent two and one-half years working at CIFEL, and they were not all singing and dancing. The fiesta, and the new relationships it represented, did not fall from the sky. They were the result of a bitter and protracted struggle between those who represented—and continued to defend—the values of the colonial period and those who shared FRELIMO's vision of "people's power" and sought a transformation of the social relations of production within the factory into something more consistent with the aims of a government committed to a particularly Mozambican road to socialism.

From postrevolutionary Russia, Lenin has given us the theoretical tools to enable us to understand that the *confiscation* of the means of production (i.e., state expropriation of capitalist enterprises) is not to be confused with the *socialization* of the means of production. Socialization (i.e., society's ability to dispose effectively and efficiently of the means of production and their products) exists to the extent that there is a democratic, popularly based national system of regulation and control of the fruits of production.

But this does not mean that the transformation of the social relations of production is merely a "systems problem" that will be resolved "automatically" as state planning systems become more efficient. It is precisely this trap that has snared socialists around the world. The transformation of the social relations of production is not just a question of the "primacy of the development of the means of production" (i.e., the development of productive capacity); nor is it the automatic evolutionary result of a more sophisticated system of accounting and planning. In the last analysis the transformation of the social relations of production is essentially about the question of which class is controlling the decision-making process of the enterprise and of the different levels of the apparatus of the state, and in whose objective interests it is doing so.

The search for the answer to these big questions leads to the question of the role of the party and the working classes. Just as nationalization does not automatically result in a spontaneous transformation of social relations of production, so the seizure of state power does not automatically result in the spontaneous flow of revolutionary class consciousness. Rather, the development of class consciousness and class confidence is the result of a patient and consistent intervention on the part of a party deliberately constructing this consciousness and at the same time living a process of continual renewal and purification.

Class Formation and Class Consciousness

At last to Mozambique and our starting point: the nature of the industrial working class. In an excellent paper, David Wield has traced the development of industry in Mozambique,[1] and I shall draw heavily upon it as I paint with a broad brush the context of what follows.

As already seen in Chapter 1, Portugal was the weakest and most impoverished of all the colonial powers scrambling for control of southern Africa. Without capital, Portugal could only maintain its African territories by in effect leasing out Mozambique to anyone willing to invest in them, and two-thirds of the country—mainly the north and center—was leased out to non-national charter companies. Usually controlled by British capital, these could extract taxes, determine policy, sublet land, and force people to work.

Although this did generate a certain amount of revenue for the Portuguese state, it did not compare in importance to the sale of transport services to neighboring British colonies. The two ports of Lourenço Marques and Beira became the major outlets for South Africa and Rhodesia respectively. The ports themselves were built by British capital, sometimes with minority local participation, and Mozambican traffic never amounted to more than 10 percent of the total. The ports and railways were well established by the beginning of the century. All of the skilled jobs—vehicle maintenance, crane driving, points, and signal operation—were held by white Portuguese who maintained an aristocratic and racist separatism from the Mozambican workers. Further, the stevedores (as with stevedores the world over) faced the problems of casual day labor: they were, as an ex-transport minister said to me, a divided and marginalized lumpen force that would line up and "buy" a place on the day's allocation from the mafia ring that controlled it. Or, if they were unlucky, they would spend the day on the margins of society (and the fringes of the law) as part of the great mass of urban underemployed. Perhaps most significantly, this was a group of workers who had suffered crushing defeat on the two occasions (1936 and 1963) when they had rebelled against their colonial oppressors and they had been killed in the streets, their leaders jailed. (Despite that, a strike wave that spread like wildfire in 1974, engulfing nearly every major enterprise in the country in those first few months after the coup in Portugal, had its origins among the stevedores on the quaysides of Lourenço Marques.)

The largest single revenue raiser for the Portuguese state—even greater than the railways and docks—was the institutionalized sale of migrant labor, on six-month contracts, directly to the mine and farm recruiting agencies from neighboring states. This affected the vast majority of males in southern Mozambique. As the result of a longstanding agreement, the Portuguese were paid directly in gold at the South African market rate; it was resold on the international market at a huge profit.

It is difficult to know the impact of the migrant work experience on the Mozambicans who participated in it. Certainly, former migrant workers brought back tales of intertribal conflict in the compounds, and of the invidious role of the black "boss boys," who acted as the company's informers and controllers at the slightest hint of protest. Such an experience certainly disrupted the continuity of the peasant mentality, but it would be premature to talk of the "proletarianization" of consciousness as this term is usually understood. For our purposes, suffice it to say that the migrant workers were "proletarianized" only to the extent that they became dependent upon wage work as a means of supporting themselves and to the extent that they were able to realize some of their increased expectations. In a minority of cases, wages from migrant labor contracts were the basis for accumulating means of production for private use, and thus sometimes employing labor.

Industrial manufacturing in Mozambique developed slowly, primarily because of the weakness of Portuguese capital, but from the early 1960s through 1974, there was a period of relative boom. Portuguese finance capital, through the banks and credit organizations, together with some settler capital, participated with foreign capital (mainly British, channeled through South Africa and Rhodesia) in extensive construction projects, both high-rise private accommodation for the settler class and commercial enterprises. Maputo's wide boulevards were one result of this—and how favorably they compare with anything in Lisbon. The production of commodities for the settler class expanded. Most of the factories were modern and well organized, and the industrial sector was substantial—easily outstripping that of neighboring Tanzania, for instance. But "development" was mainly in end-of-the-line finishing operations rather than the exploitation of Mozambique's natural resources. Thus, the steel rolling-mill brought in rolled steel billets from South Africa and rolled them into reinforcing bars, even though Mozambique has its own iron ore. The oil refinery imported all of its crude oil. The railway wagon and truck factory actually had its buying department in Johannesburg, bringing in kits of materials for assembly. The tire factory (built before independence from bank-raised capital but only commissioned after independence) imported all its raw materials. The bicycle factory imported kits for assembly. The huge cement industry imported 50 percent of its raw materials. And so on down to Companhia Vinicola—the Mozambican wine company—which imported its grape concentrate, and to the corrugated galvanized roofing sheet company, which imported flat galvanized sheet. In addition, the amount of wine that could be produced and the amount of cotton that could be ginned and woven were regulated and controlled by the Portuguese to prevent production in the colonies from competing with big capital in the metropole. Contrast this with the current situation where local wine production and a huge planned extension of the textile industry, as well as projects geared to exploiting the reserves of iron, coal, natural gas, and other minerals, are seen as vital elements in a development plan designed to reduce the built-in dependency of the economy.

And what of the working class? Let us now look inside the steel rolling-mill to see what sort of an industrial proletariat was in formation.

Every worker I spoke to had his favorite story about PIDE, the Portuguese secret police. PIDE agents were either recruited from among the factory workers themselves or brought in (disguised as ordinary workers) from outside. A typical tactic was to wander about the factory complaining about the bosses, watching for reactions. If an agent or suspected agent came into the room, everyone would suddenly think of something they had to do elsewhere, and the room would empty out. But the effect was that no one could be absolutely sure that anything he or she said would not get back to the bosses. It was a climate of mistrust occasionally punctuated by brutal shows of force, when the factory would suddenly be invaded by police and army trucks, sirens wailing. All of the workers would be lined up in front of the building and the local garrison commander would proceed to give a fiery lecture on the need for discipline and for guarding against "FRELIMO terrorists." Two or three workers would then be dragged off in the trucks, never to be seen at the factory again.

Of course at this time there were no true trade unions, and I have yet to find evidence of even one successful strike up until the coup in Portugal. So-called trade unions, similar to those of Mussolini's Italy, were part of the state and had no right to strike or act for the workers in any way. They succeeded in heading off any demand for genuine worker organization and improved the international image of a regime that was still using forced labor.

The result was that there was no proletarian consciousness among urban black industrial workers. One reason was the relatively small size of this group. Wield estimated that in 1974, out of a population of just over 9 million, employment was as follows:

Total white wage workers employed	100,000
Black agricultural workers (90 percent on contract)	300,000
Black servants and hotel workers (temporary)	300,000

Black migrant workers abroad	200,000
Black industrial, construction, and transport workers	250,000
Total	1,150,000

Not only was the working class small, but it was also a very recent phenomenon, since most industrial production had only begun in the last fifteen years. For instance, the foundry (which preceded the rolling-mill) was only built in 1964 and yet was one of the oldest of the major industrial plants. All of the workers were first-generation urban dwellers from small peasant backgrounds, and this was typical of every industry.

A second reason for the lack of proletarian consciousness was the widespread illiteracy (estimated at over 90 percent in 1974). Of the 500 workers at the steel mill, 85 percent were completely illiterate, with only a handful having even a lower secondary school education. In June 1978 the first 350 started first level literacy courses. Combined with basic illiteracy (and of course innumeracy) was what we could call "technical illiteracy," caused by the systematic exclusion of Mozambicans from any understanding of the technology with which they worked.

Yet the ability of workers to assume control of the means of production is central to any notion of the transformation of the social relations or production. Here the example of the production crisis at CIFEL is appropriate since it demonstrates the problems faced by workers dealing with a technology they had been denied knowledge of for so long.[2]

In the foundry, castings are made by constructing a wooden model and compressing it in a steel box filled with sand. The model is then removed and the space in the sand filled with molten steel. The sand itself is prepared with additives, some that bind it together and others that keep it from burning. During one absolutely disastrous month, the quality of the ploughshares plummeted and most of them had to be scrapped. An investigation revealed that the section preparing the sand had run out of one of the additives and had simply doubled the quantity of the other. As a result, when the steel was poured the sand collapsed.

When confronted by the Workers' Council and surrounded by a mountain of scrap metal, one of the workers turned to us and said, "Don't be angry, comrades. Remember in the colonial days the fascists never explained to us what these were for. As far as I am concerned, they are just two powders." The next step was to identify the missing powder, find its English name and the companies in South Africa that supplied it, calculate the amount used per month, write a telex in English (which no one spoke or wrote), get approval from the Ministry of Industry, and get a letter of credit from the bank (where it would sit in a mountain of requests for toilet paper, chickenfeed, penicillin, and spare parts, waiting for nonexistent foreign exchange). This process could, and often did, take months, during which time production was halted or switched to something else.

Innumerable examples of such problems could be cited. Here is just one more. Once when we were conducting a review of procedures in order to improve quality control we found that samples were taken at regular intervals every day to measure the moisture content of the sand (fundamental to surface quality), but that all of this measuring was wasted because no one knew what the moisture content should be! As with the additive, the workers had no idea why they were performing this function and were unable to take corrective action when a problem arose.

The third factor that severely handicapped the development of class consciousness in the colonial period was the lack of any independent workers' organization. It is through the experience of union branch meetings and shop stewards' committee meetings that workers learn the elements of organization and delegation of authority. Mozambican workers did not have this rich experience of setting agendas, collecting and recording union dues, and the like, which the working class in Europe and North America takes for granted. Instead, they had only models of fascist authoritarianism and mindless bureaucratic procedures.

We should not draw unduly pessimistic conclusions from all of this, however. One advantage for the development of consciousness is that Mozambican workers do not have the social democratic illusions that still exist in the British labor movement, or the Cold War anticommunism that can be found among North American workers. Moreover, experience at CIFEL suggests that manual workers in Mozambique are willing to discuss issues together and then accept any decision as binding on all. This is often referred to as a passivity handed down from colonialism, but it is just as easy to underestimate black manual workers as it is to idealize them. (The opposite, however, is true of the few "assimilated Mozambicans" who had some secondary education. These workers were much more like the youth of the colonial class, disaffected, self-interested, and therefore antagonistic to the developing systems of collective discipline.)

What, then, were my first impressions arriving at the steel rolling-mill in 1977, just eighteen months after independence? How was the Mozambican working class in this factory taking to its first taste of power?

As discussed in Chapter 2, at an October 1976 meeting of workers from all the major enterprises, Samora Machel had proposed the formation of Production Councils. Their task was to mobilize the workers in order to increase production and productivity, combat sabotage, fight against labor indiscipline, and generally promote the health, safety, and well-being of the workers. They were to be a means of enabling the working class to play a more active role in the planning and control of production (although, significantly, their precise relationship to the state-appointed administrator was left unclear).

Six months after its formation, the twenty-seven man Production Council at CIFEL had de facto control of the factory. But "control" is the last word to use for a situation in which electric motors were burning out daily because of lack of routine maintenance: where stock records had fallen into disuse and storerooms became disorganized dumping grounds; where production had plummeted from 44,000 tons of steel bars in 1974 to just 6,000 tons in 1977; and where, even worse, the scrap rate (the percentage of spoiled and wasted raw material) had risen from 10 percent to over 30 percent. This last point meant that the raw material—steel billets—was being imported from South Africa in 10,000-ton lots, at US$250 per ton, and nearly a third of it converted into virtually worthless scrap metal after consuming huge amounts of imported energy. And this at a time when Mozambique did not have enough foreign currency to import food and medical supplies! The same production graph, like the profile of a Swedish fjord, could be found in virtually every factory, in some places steeper, and deeper, than in others. Moreover, after 1977–1978, there was a gradual, but steady, increase at CIFEL until production leveled off at a new level (this in turn reflecting either the prevailing level of demand or the level of production possible given the scarcity of foreign exchange for imported raw materials).

How moving it was to sit in on "board meetings" in the executive conference room, with its cocktail cabinet in the corner (still with a half bottle of scotch, which no one had had the audacity—or "indiscipline," as they would say—to expropriate). Twenty-two tense faces; eighteen pairs of bare feet and meticulously mended and re-mended work clothes; a room full of people shuffling papers that most of them could not read. What did they make of the almost daily exhortations from people like me, calling on them to assume their historic role in the revolution? Exhortations were the last thing they needed. What was needed was patient consciousness-raising to begin to undo the inferiority complex that four hundred years of colonization had drummed into the very center of their souls. What was needed were courses in basic literacy, new and readily accessible ways of presenting data, skills of organization and delegation, the clear definition of goals and objectives at all levels, and a reintroduction and simplification of control and reporting procedures. All of these were needed, but certainly not exhortations.

It was during those meetings that my naive preconceptions about slogans to the effect that the "spontaneous flowering of revolutionary consciousness releasing at a stroke all the creative potential of the class which produces all wealth" were finally smashed. What I learned was that class consciousness—and, equally important, class confidence—is the product of a slow and tortuous process led patiently by the vanguard party. It is this aspect of political leadership that I shall turn to now—although it bears emphasizing that, despite all the problems and inadequacies, the workers at CIFEL had kept that factory open and producing during the difficult period of the initial transition to independence. Had it closed and the workers dispersed into the bush, it might never have opened again. Given the circumstances, that was a truly historic victory, even if something more was needed for the long haul.

Political Leadership: The Role of the Party

FRELIMO was a liberation movement, drawing most of its support from the peasantry in the liberated zones of the north. Although it had a clandestine presence in Lourenço Marques (witness the decisive way it was able to step into the preindependence power vacuum), it did not have an organized mass base in the factories or neighborhoods. Further, until February 1977 (two weeks before my arrival in Mozambique), FRELIMO existed as an anti-imperialist front. Only then, at the Third Congress, did it make the decision to redefine and restructure itself as a Marxist vanguard party.

How FRELIMO coped with the post-1974 crisis by rapidly organizing *grupos dinamizadores* in urban neighborhoods, rural districts, factories, hospitals, schools, and so on is already well documented, both in this volume and elsewhere. In general the GDs were hurriedly formed, in consultation with the local population, by inexperienced and overworked FRELIMO supporters. They were therefore inevitably unequal in their ability to achieve their objectives. They organized around three watchwords, *unity, vigilance,* and *work: unity* of all democrats regardless of race, class, or sex; *vigilance* against all attempts by the colonial bourgeoisie, the

petty bourgeoisie, and opportunistic criminal elements to sabotage
independence and the economy; and *work* to be done collectively in
order to maintain production and distribution during the deepening crisis created by the settlers' leaving.

The GD at CIFEL was formed in 1974 and led by a black
Mozambican laboratory technician. Sengo, as he was called, was
about twenty and was the best-educated Mozambican in the factory.
He spoke excellent Portuguese and was very much of the up-and-
coming urban petty bourgeoisie. As leader of the GD he liked to
refer to himself as the "president."

Sengo's rule became increasingly tyrannical, and his own sense of
self-importance inflated to the bursting point. He would stand up
in front of the weekly factory meetings (when the party area coordinator wasn't there) and harangue everyone in sight: "You," he
would say, "stand up. What does 'socialist emulation' mean? . . . You
don't know, eh? Not interested, eh? Don't you support FRELIMO?
Then I will tell you because I have studied these things and *I* know.
It means: produce more in less time. Now . . ." and on he would go
about discipline and being on time. Yet everyone in the room knew
that most of the members of the GD were in the top twenty worst
offenders when it came to absenteeism and lateness!

One day I gave Sengo a lift home and, as he smiled and waved to
the workers, he turned to me and said, "You should get a hole cut
in the roof of the car so that all of the workers can see their president better." Clearly, he was riding for a fall, and it came in January
1978, when the brigade from FRELIMO provincial headquarters
arrived during the campaign to restructure the party. Soon young
comrades spread through the factory, carrying clipboards and
sharp pencils, canvassing opinions, collecting ideas for lists of likely
candidates, and listening to complaints. Within a week the dissolu-
tion of the GD as a "corrupt and spent force having no confidence
or respect among the workforce" was announced. Sengo left a
subsequent meeting with party leaders from provincial headquarters with red eyes and head down. He was the first casualty of a
campaign to clear opportunists out of the political leadership.

GDs were now dropped, and a party cell was incorporated at the
factory. A list of twelve candidates for party membership was
drawn up. Each one had to stand up before a meeting of the
section in which she or he worked and face a rigorous and often
painful examination of their lifestyle and attitudes. This was repeated at the departmental level and then again in front of the
whole factory. It was not until this process was completed—even
the party structure in the *bairro* where the workers lived was con-
tacted for information about the candidates—that party member-

ship was conferred. The Minister of Industry officiated at the ceremony. In a speech widely covered in the newspapers and on the radio, he described how the GDs had filled a vacuum during the transitional period, combatting sabotage and counterrevolutionary movements, and how they had been a "school of democracy" for the Mozambican people. This phase was now over, however, for what was needed was an offensive that would mobilize the people to meet the new demands of the revolution. In a moving appeal to the workers, he stressed the need to reincorporate the members of the disbanded GD fully into the life of the factory. He reminded them that there were only two roads in Mozambique: one was with FRELIMO and the revolution; the other was with the enemy and the forces of counterrevolution. In a booming voice, he reminded us that the *only* privilege a party member has is to serve the people. It is the responsibility of each of us, and of the entire workforce working together, to control the conduct of each party member; they must be exemplary workers in every respect.

Sengo's bubble had burst, and now his lateness and general attitude came under the watchful eye of the very workers he had abused. I wish that I could report that his story had a happy ending, and that he was finally won back to the revolution. But that was not to be: he applied to leave the foundry to work in a nearby private factory where he could earn more money but was refused because his contribution was needed in the foundry, which was of strategic national importance. He then fell further by the wayside, regressing into sporadic fits of temper and petulance that often reduced the women he worked with to tears.

Sengo's story highlights a serious problem that the revolution faced. Desperately short of skilled cadres, Mozambique has been—and remains—dependent on an assimilated petty bourgeoisie cast in a mold more appropriate for a neocolonialist future. Sengo's experience reflects the agonies of this petty bourgeoisie, which find an outlet in ultra-leftism, cynicism, or, as with Sengo, demagogic opportunism. All the more to FRELIMO's credit, then, that the Sengos have continued to be an issue in the various offensives that have been launched since the revolution. "Politics in command" means nothing if good policies are merely passed on to such people for their implementation. It is not unduly melodramatic to say that all of Mozambique is one huge battleground in which nothing less than the control of every aspect of the state is the prize: during my stay I found both dedicated young comrades who worked and studied all hours of the day and night and Sengos by the dozen, people whose enthusiasm extended only to what they could gain from the system for themselves.

The Social Relations of Production at the Factory Level and the Production Council's Management Problems

During the same period that the GD was having problems, the factory administration was also undergoing a crisis. In August 1977, after a period of confusion and disorganization, the Ministry of Industry appointed an administrator with executive powers. He had been a member of the city council of Lourenço Marques and still owned two small factories. He immediately set about forming a capitalist-style management structure: a pyramid with himself at the apex and the remaining six Portuguese technicians as "heads of departments" at the base. (The head of the wire drawing and galvanizing department was not Portuguese, but rather than invite the Mozambican head, the administrator asked the rolling-mill technician to represent that section as well!)

The administrator told the Production Council to concentrate on "first things first"—meaning labor discipline—and let him control other matters. That is not to say that labor discipline was not a problem: during the colonial period one of the few forms of protest open to workers was to avoid work, and serious problems of lack of discipline, absenteeism, lateness, and drunkenness remained in a situation where self-discipline had not as yet developed. The factory was tense and tempers occasionally flared. It was a bad time to work at CIFEL, and confirmed my belief that workers' control and state-appointed management were antagonistic concepts.

An alliance existed between the administrator and Sengo, who was still chairman of the Production Council at that time. The administrator even persuaded Sengo to visit his other factories to give his workers a lecture on the need for "revolutionary discipline and self-sacrifice"—something normally only done by a representative from provincial headquarters.

Despite the tension, production improved remarkably. A phone call to the bank released a long-awaited letter of credit, billets came in, and the much-needed steel rolled out. I felt very frustrated. I couldn't go along with what the administrator was trying to do, yet as a foreigner I could not be too morally pure about it when the steel was desperately needed.

Gradually, the small gains in confidence and organization on the part of the Production Council began to slip away, to be replaced by passivity—and maybe even some relief. Whenever I read statements, in some socialist literature, regarding the supposed "supremacy of the development of the productive forces over the development of new social relations of production," I think of this period in Mozambique. Productive forces (or, more accurately, the level of production) were expanding, yet at great social cost. What did this mean for the future of the Mozambican revolution? Isn't it just what I had seen with nationalized industries in England?

This era in CIFEL's history ended when Sengo's did, and for the same reason.

Toward the end of the exhaustive round of meetings held by the brigade to restructure the party to select and screen candidates for the party cell, a mass meeting was held to air all of the problems, "big or small," in the factory. It was led by a senior cadre from provincial headquarters, a likeable man with a witty if somewhat theatrical way of conducting a meeting. He won the workers' confidence from the start. All of the old chestnuts came up— irregularities in the supply of the daily loaf of bread allowed each worker, the lack of boots and safety equipment, the lack of spare parts, and so on. This went on for two hours, and nothing came up that I had not heard before. Then, as the meeting was drawing to a close, the party cadre repeated his appeal: "No issue is too big or too small to raise."

Suddenly a worker from the back of the room came forward. I recognized him as an unskilled worker who sorted scrap in the foundry yard. He stood for a moment staring at the floor, shuffling his bare feet and fingering his heavily patched workshirt. Then he cleared his throat and in a voice croaking with emotion declared, "Imperialism is still here at CIFEL!" He went on to denounce the administrator as being just like the colonialists. He spoke for about a minute and sat down to a roar from every throat in the room. Suddenly everyone wanted to speak. The same stories were repeated again and again, and some of the Portuguese technicians also came in for criticism. It was as though this ordinary worker had pulled the cork and all of the frustration and anger in the factory flooded out. Serious now, the party cadre took everything down in his notebook and promised that the matter would be raised at the highest levels, first in the party and then in the Ministry of Industry.

Within a month the administrator had been removed and replaced by two young Mozambicans, both party members attached to the Ministry of Industry. Thus ended a very significant period in the factory's history. But before turning to the sweeping changes that followed, it is important to reflect on the reason it had happened, and why it changed. The administrator had been appointed in 1977 by the Ministry of Industry. At that time this was a new and weak ministry, due once again to the lack of Mozambican cadres and to the fact that the economy was falling apart and was riddled with acts of sabotage. The administrator had been appointed because he had some organizational experience and had declared himself a supporter of the revolutionary process. Had FRELIMO decided to appoint only those it knew well and could trust, it would have meant closing down all but a handful of enterprises. The administrator had to be given a chance to prove his class allegiance in practice. Had the workers had the technical capacity to assume control of CIFEL, then the appointment would have been unnecessary. Nevertheless, it is clear that the "socialism" that would have developed had this situation continued and expanded would have had little relation to the vision of "people's power" in FRELIMO documents. But to see the problem is not necessarily to see the solution. Every revolution surrounded by hostile imperialist forces and with a local bourgeoisie (and/or petty bourgeoisie) in potential revolt has to find a solution to this problem, one which will not sow the seeds of its ultimate destruction.

Let us turn to ways in which the negative situation at CIFEL was reversed. From one point of view, it was an organizational reshuffle within the Ministry of Industry, with the vanguard party acting to guide the process. But perhaps it is more useful to see what happened as being the result of a conscious revolt by the working class, taking the initiative and using the party to effect the changes it demanded. For it was far more this than merely being the case of a small weak working class having its historical role taken over by the "vanguard" party.

From this point onward the situation at CIFEL was transformed. The heavy demagogic style used at meetings was dropped, and the new administrators and the party cell visited each section in turn on a regular basis, listening to problems and calling for criticism and self-criticism to help solve them. When one section criticized another, a joint meeting would be held, like one heated one between the rolling-mill workers and the electricians. After letting the shouting and recriminations run their course, the administrator would quietly draw everyone together and suggest new procedures and guidelines. After an agreement was reached, everyone would sing a FRELIMO song. Meetings were also held to report on the results of the regular Friday afternoon section meetings, which were led by the Production Council. These were important, both to focus the conclusions and to create a more smoothly functioning organization: instead of Production Council and factory meetings being merely "talking shops," conclusions could now be coordinated and implemented. A factory is a complex system which must be coordinated to achieve its goals. The electricians, for instance, cannot decide which job they think they should do today without reference to factory priorities; the rolling-mill workers cannot decide to buy electrical equipment without reference to established standards or similar equipment elsewhere in the factory. In such situations the administrator can act as a coordinator and stimulate workers to realize their creative potential. The issue is thus not whether the idea of an administrator is in contradiction to the idea of workers' control, but rather one of the class relations which exist between the administrator on the one hand and the Production Council on the other. Nor, as the following anecdote shows, is this simply a question of being "red" or being "expert."

It was during the first few months of this new situation that CIFEL had to cast its biggest piece ever, a twelve-ton cast-iron sugarcane crusher. All the Portuguese technicians laughed at the idea when the minister rushed to the factory to tell us that there was no money to import sugarcane crushers, that if we could not produce sugar we could not export it, and that if that were the case, the situation would worsen for everybody. He made it clear that he was not asking *if* it could be done but, with that infuriating FRELIMO optimism, wanted to know the date when the first crusher would be ready.

Teams were formed to study the problem. The furnacemen designed a new ladle to carry the molten metal, and a re-usable molding box was made in a nearby shop. At every stage of the project meetings were held with the foundry workers and with workers in each section. The scrap rate fell from the devastating 30 percent to a rate better than the Portuguese had been able to achieve. The cane crusher was cast on the promised day and was perfect. The minister was delighted and wanted to know how soon they could have three hundred and fifty!

That is not to say that enthusiasm and democratic practices can solve every technical problem, but the social implications of this sort of victory compared with the "flash-in-the-pan" increases in productivity brought about by coercion were profound.

In the summer of 1980 I visited several factories in order to find out how typical the experience at CIFEL was. I found that TEX-LOM, the giant ultramodern textile factory just outside Maputo, had been through an experience very similar to that at CIFEL. One of the original directors stayed on after nearly all of the Portuguese had abandoned the factory. There had been tensions from the beginning between him and the Production Council and GD. A confrontation over what the GD called "racist practices" in the canteen resulted in a militant strike. The administrator took a hard-line position and turned to the Ministry of Industry and the party for support, which was not forthcoming. Both backed the workers' demands. As a result the administrator left and a Mozambican was appointed. When I visited, I was met at the gate by the party cell and the Production Council; they clearly felt themselves to be an important part of the management of the factory.

On the other hand, at a small foundry in Beira I found a Portuguese technician in charge, complaining that the workers were lazy and not interested in their work. The workers had another story: they said that he had forbidden them to hold Production Council meetings, telling them that "we are here to work, not talk," and that he only allowed two workers to attend meetings at a neighboring factory with which they were to merge while forbidding them from reporting back to meetings in the foundry. The workers had only irregular contact with party provincial structures, and these structures, it turned out when I questioned them, were unaware of any problems.

The General Tire factory in Maputo was another interesting case. It was founded before independence by banking capital under an agreement in which General Tire benefited from the sale of equipment, technical services, and a license fee for each tire produced. It is a beautiful factory, spotlessly clean, the powdered raw material being transported from automatically controlled silos along sealed conveyor belts. The factory was commissioned after independence in a contract signed by the government and General Tire. It was a far better organized factory than any in which I have ever worked, and claims higher productivity than factories with identical machines in the United States.

Yet on my visit in 1980 the party cell had still not been formed and the Production Council had only a token presence—a number of people commented that there was no role for it. Worker training was taken care of through various agreements to "Mozambicanize" all positions in the factory. Job descriptions had been issued for every worker, everyone knew what she or he should do, and it was the administration's job to see that it was done. This seemed a major failure, not to organize this important factory and learn from it how to adapt worker organization to a very different technological environment.

I also visited a huge sugar plantation and cane factory originally privately owned by Sena Sugar Estates (a British company) on the banks of the Zambezi. It had been one of the most flagrant examples of Portuguese colonialism. Management (mainly British) ruled with an iron rod. Arbitrary fines, beatings, and imprisonment for petty offenses, bestial living conditions and poverty wages for seasonal workers went side-by-side with luxury bungalows and four racially segregated clubs for the non-African employees, from the technician grades on up.

When the GD and Production Councils were formed at Sena,

they were quickly domesticated by management—even given a small office and a salary increase. It was very convenient for management that when, during the post-coup strike wave in 1974, it was forced to concede a pay rise (for the first time in its history), the council appealed to the workers to discipline themselves and make sacrifices on management's behalf! This situation remained until 1978, when Sena was nationalized, its management accused of economic sabotage, negligence, and illegally transferring huge sums of money out of the country.

Of course, the class orientation of the leaders of workers' organizations always reflects the class forces acting upon them. Where localized pockets of class resistance exist, as at Sena, there will be these kinds of distortion until the revolutionary forces assume effective control.

The problem of the relationship between the administration, the Production Council, and the party came to a head following the launching of the "Presidential Offensive" against corruption and inefficiency in 1979. At the launching speech in Beira, Samora Machel commented that many enterprises were paralyzed, with constant disputes between the administration and the other organizational structures. He declared that it was the administrator's function to manage the factory and that they should get on with that task. Many administrators took this as a signal of a change in direction and quickly called in the Production Councils and party members, announcing that the President had said that they were in charge and that Production Councils were a thing of the past.

This continued until August 1980, when a special conference of party cells in industry was convened and appeals were made to end the confusion that was paralyzing the production councils and placing impossible restrictions on party cells. During this same period (as seen in Chapter 2) highly self-critical resolutions regarding the need to strengthen these latter institutions were being adopted in other forums as well (not least in FRELIMO's Central Committee); such resolutions signalled the attempt to retain a creative approach (political rather than merely administrative) to resolving the various tensions discussed above.

The Revolutionary Transformation of the Apparatus of the State

The transformation of the social relations of production is not merely concerned with workers' control and organization within the enterprise at the micro-level. After all, these relationships reflect the social relationships that are reproduced in society as a whole, and the class struggle being waged throughout society. I want, therefore, to deal briefly with the transformation of the structure of Mozambican industry as a whole during the transition to a centrally planned socialist economy, and on the difficulties that this has involved. For instance, during the "Presidential Offensive" it became clear that the huge stocks of materials piling up in warehouses were not only the result of widespread corruption and inefficiency, but were the result of the lack of any mechanism for getting the material into circulation. Material had been ordered by the relevant ministry on a letter of credit from a bank, but the paperwork necessary to release it when it arrived was not being done. This was a serious and widespread problem. Another problem was the infamous system for requesting foreign currency using a document called a "BRI." Dating back to the colonial period, this was a recording and import-licensing document that was used to allocate foreign currency. Any request for a letter of credit to import anything, from toilet paper to penicillin or spare parts or steel billets, ended up in the Bank of Mozambique. Priorities were not allocated; credit worthiness and urgency were not assessed; and when the goods finally came in, there was no way of covering the payment or ascertaining which enterprise owned the goods or had the authority to remove them from the warehouse. It was not until mid-1980 that this sorry state of affairs was analyzed: the conclusion was that rather than transforming the apparatus of the state, FRELIMO had tried to simply adapt colonial institutions and procedures. The BRI, passing from the ministries to the banks to the enterprises and ending up in the Ministry of Finance, was never overseen by any single organization. Everyone knew that it did not work, but it was part of the "system." Yet at a time when foreign currency was scarce and sabotage and currency fraud so prevalent, the need to "smash the apparatus of the bourgeois state" was no empty slogan.

During this period the process of vertically and horizontally integrating industry was begun. In the building supplies industry, for example, some two hundred warehouses and small production units were merged into one large state corporation. This resulted in horrendous organizational problems, but it was felt that the concentration of such scarce resource as clerks and organizers, and equally scarce trucks and maintenance depots, would justify the disruption. More important, it meant that the few building materials available would go to those projects given a priority in a plan, not to building houses for the petty bourgeoisie. The building industry supply enterprise receives a list of building projects approved by the Ministry of Construction. Each of these projects is broken down into a materials requirement list. Then the steel needs are collated and set against the foreign currency allocated to CIFEL to buy steel. At the beginning of each year CIFEL is given a precise tonnage quota and a range of sizes and shipment dates, which is written up as a "contract"; the bank then allocates credit and foreign currency reserves. In this way the anarchy of the marketplace is gradually being replaced by a rational system of allocation according to priorities. The only missing element is the democratic participation of the masses in the process of planning. Yet this too was begun in this period. Again, I shall take CIFEL as an example.

The first planning process I participated in was for the first plan, in December 1977. The Ministry of Industry called for a planning committee to oversee the planning procedure at the factory. I was the secretary, and there was also an East German economist, a young Portuguese factory worker, the administrator (the one who also had two factories of his own), four members of the GD (selected by Sengo), and four members of the Production Council.

Although the workers had a formal majority on the committee, in practice their participation was minimal; they preferred, they said, to get on with the specific tasks they had agreed to do. Thus active worker participation was almost nil. Nor was there that much debate or discussion on the shop floor: what tended to happen was that the workers were read a list of proposals for their "approval." Planning was thus very much a technocratic activity. Nevertheless, a plan was produced with a set of production goals and a series of technical proposals to improve production and productivity.

At the end of this process it was suggested that we call a mass meeting to approve the plan. The East German opposed this: "What if the workers don't accept *our* plan," he said—a clear indication of his conception of socialist planning. The meeting took place, however, although it cannot be called a great success. Sengo was at his most obnoxious and demogogic. He read the plan through, and then, in patronizing language, tried to explain it. He belittled everyone who spoke and harangued those who didn't.

After all this, it is perhaps surprising to report that the CIFEL plan was one of the best (if not *the* best) submitted to the ministry! This despite the fact that it was characterized by the complete inexperience on the part of everyone involved, a total lack of data about what had happened at the factory, and a technocratic approach—a belief that all that was necessary was to go through the motions of getting the approval of the workers, a process which ended up making the plan very distant from the workers' experience.

The second plan, completed at the end of 1978, was successful in a much broader way. We held our first meeting in September, to give us more time. The new administrators, the new party cell, the Production Council, and I carefully reviewed what had gone wrong the last time and identified the things we wanted to change in order genuinely to involve the workers. We then formed a planning nucleus of twenty-four workers who had already shown themselves capable of making a contribution. We analyzed every point in the last plan, examining why various proposed targets had either not been achieved or had been achieved very late.

Next we held a series of meetings to discuss papers that I had written and the administration had edited. The first was called "Socialist Planning—What Is the Difference Between Socialist Planning and Capitalist Planning?" It discussed the differences between how capitalist corporations prepare annual budgets and the popular power perspective that people like Marcelino dos Santos, then Minister of Planning, had for the planning process. At the end of each meeting I wrote up minutes of the points discussed and the measures proposed. This made up an embryonic planning document.

When it was time to start the planning process proper, each section had a meeting with several members of the planning nucleus, one of whom took notes. Rather than ask a general question about what the problems were, we produced a checklist of questions about raw materials, machines that needed maintenance, and so on. We read this list out a week before the meeting, to give everyone a chance to think it over beforehand. This time the contributions came in thick and fast and the minute-takers were pushed to keep up with the flow of suggestions, criticisms, and ideas.

The minutes of these meetings were then read over at department meetings, where problems common to the sections were identified and further suggestions made. Then each department's plan was presented to a meeting of the whole factory. The final document was very rich indeed, and it allowed us to revise upward some of our provisional production targets as well as to further reduce the scrap rate.

One of the first ideas to be implemented was that a planning department be formed to give a permanent nature to the process. We had decided that planning had always been seen as an "event" or a "document" that would be drawn up and then filed away. We wanted planning to become a part of the day-to-day life of the factory. We therefore drew together three manual workers, two clerical workers, and two students, and for three months I had the very enjoyable task of training these enthusiastic young comrades. We began with basics. We drew a graph of six hens that lay eggs, but not every day, and, representing each egg by a big square, we plotted "production" for twenty days. We sweated over this for over three days. But by the end of the course we were producing a production-reporting graph that divided total production into twelve monthly blocks, each a different color and presented in a vertical column. Alongside that we showed, in contrasting colors, the actual production for that month, so that we could show ordinary workers how actual production compared to the plan. This was a very successful graph. We also made weekly graphs that showed scrap production and time lost on each machine, which became a valuable focus for our discussion at the Friday meetings. We began to calculate the theoretical capacity of each machine and the factors that limited that production.

There is much more that could be said about the planning process at CIFEL, including some of the anomalies that came to light during these discussions. But the key point is that in the second case, politics were at the helm and both administrator and party were able to encourage the workers to draw upon the richness of their experience.

Of course, participation in planning cannot be limited to the level of the factory. The masses must participate in setting planning goals for the economy as a whole, and the process must be enriched by participation at the ministerial level, where the different sectors are coordinated. The process of drawing up the 1978 plan gave some glimpses of how this might work in the future. The Ministry of Industry called together a group of workers selected by the provincial headquarters of the Production Councils to participate in the planning process. The workers were a bit diffident at first, but they soon became actively involved in the discussion, feeling they had a "practical" contribution to make. Interestingly, on a number of occasions it was this group that would suggest that, if everyone was prepared to work a bit late, a point could be completed.

In addition, and important for the future, the Production Councils are now being drawn together into industry-based organizations that will form the "unions" of the future. Thus textile workers are to have one union, metalworkers, hotel and catering workers, and so on will have others. Each union will include clerical workers, technicians, and manual workers—Mozambique has rejected as "divisive" separate unions for typists, electricians, etc. These "unions" may have the potential for discussing proposals for an entire sector, which will then be incorporated into the plan. The day when construction workers propose resolutions about the advantages of self-help schemes over prefabricated construction will be the day when we will be able to say that Mozambique is much further on the way to mass participation in the planning process.

This is still not on the agenda, for planning at the highest level remains in the hands of a few people, and certainly socialist relations of production are not generalized throughout Mozambican industry. Not that this could have been expected to happen overnight, given the distortions I have described in the small, young (though dynamic and rapidly evolving) urban proletariat. Still, the question remains: if the workers do not control industry unequivocally, who does? The answer must again be qualified. The administrators as a managerial "class" range from the best of the revolutionary left (such as the second administrator at CIFEL) through to the unrequited capitalists (like the first administrator, who still owned his two factories). Moreover, many Mozambicans laughed at my disparaging remarks about the first administrator, saying "What do you mean? He is one of the better ones. . . . Now you should see the worst!"

Obviously a real tension remains. It would be a gross idealization, bordering on "workerism," to pretend that an unprepared class can assume power in any very immediate or straightforward manner—although this was a way of thinking I myself tended to fall into when I first arrived in Mozambique. On the other hand, as Marcelino dos Santos (then Minister of Planning) once said during a visit to a factory: "You learn to swim by jumping into the water and trying it. Not by reading books about swimming." If that holds for planning, it holds equally for the exercise of popular power, for the way in which working people take control of their lives and assume responsibility for meeting real needs with the fruits of their labor while also finding new and more caring ways of relating to their fellow workers. As described above, while working in Mozambique I saw the tension between state-appointed factory managers—who had a necessary function to fulfill under the circumstances—and the revolutionary forces within the factory played out in a series of struggles. And tensions surfaced within the party too, as the balance of power shifted between the various forces involved. It seems clear that such tensions will continue to exist, perhaps for many generations, and there will be fresh victories and defeats on the terrain of planning and production, a series of more and less positive resolutions of existing contradictions. Nonetheless, what I saw at CIFEL specifically, and in Mozambique more generally, in the early post-independence years left me

with a certain guarded optimism: that FRELIMO and the Mozambican people together are up to coping with these tensions and to
meeting the challenges inherent in an attempted transition to
socialism.

Notes

1. See David Wield, "Mozambique—Late Colonialism and Early Problems of Transition," in Gordon White et al., eds., *Revolutionary Socialist
   Development in the Third World* (Brighton: Harvester Press, 1983).
2. See also Peter Sketchley and Frances Moore Lappé, *Casting New Molds:
   First Steps Toward Worker Control in a Mozambique Steel Factory* (San Fran-
   cisco: 1980).

Barry Pinsky

6. Territorial Dilemmas: Changing Urban Life

The tensions of urban development in Mozambique—these tensions having been reinforced dramatically by the country's deepening and primarily externally imposed military and economic crisis—were underscored by the mounting of "Operation Production" in 1983. As noted in Chapter 2, this was a forceful administrative and police action designed to remove the unemployed from the cities and put them to work on state farms, sometimes in distant provinces. A year later the scheme was abandoned with much public self-criticism. The impact on the urban poor, especially single mothers, was severe, the numbers relocated were less than natural urban population growth, and the new arrivals in the countryside were often merely an added burden on the peasantry—not surprisingly, since the evidence Barry Pinsky puts forward in the present chapter suggests strongly that no quick administrative fix can replace the broad-gauged development program that is required to reduce the dramatic disparities between rural and urban life in Mozambique.

At their best, as Barry Pinsky shows, Mozambican decision-makers have been alert to this reality. But the pressure has been severe and now military and economic crises have also produced the Nkomati Accord with South Africa, a significant development which is discussed at greater length in the concluding chapter of this book. However, as we shall see, many observers worry about the development implications of the accord and of other related initiatives. Isn't the renewed reliance on foreign investment, transit, tourism, and private farming which they imply uncomfortably close to the colonial model which produced uneven territorial development in the first place? There are also fears that "Operação Produção" may have had political costs, thus jeopardizing the efforts of the GDs to mobilize shantytown residents to assert their needs and overcome possible bureaucratic intransigence. Still, it is possible that the instances of Mozambican state support for modest local initiatives which Pinsky discusses in this chapter will return to the fore as compelling examples of how urban living conditions can improve without draining limited national resources. They are, after all, perfectly in line with FRELIMO's own most cherished traditions and practices. As is the case for many other sectors discussed in this book, much will depend on the relationship of forces—class forces, political and ideological forces, economic forces, both international and local—as it stabilizes in Mozambique in the post-Nkomati period.

On independence in 1975 FRELIMO inherited a national territory whose physical development reflected graphically the colonial economy on which it was based. Transportation and communication infrastructure was concentrated in the two short east-west corridors that link South Africa and Zimbabwe (then Rhodesia) to the sea. Profound disparities existed between urban and rural access to education, health care, and necessary goods and services. Within the urban areas, unserviced and densely populated shantytowns sprawled precariously on the edges of the modern settler cities.

Such a heritage is not uncommon in newly independent third world states. What distinguishes Mozambique, however, and makes the study of its recent experience worthwhile, is the already apparent depth of its commitment to the transformation of the spatial configuration of physical development. The essential components of this project include a reduction in the disparities in living conditions between urban and rural areas, as a first step to easing rural migration and creating the basis for the gradual amelioration of the urban situation. It can be argued that this program can only succeed as part of a socialist development project that can enforce such minimum necessary conditions as the nationalization of land and state control of the spatial allocation of investment. The extent to which Mozambique has succeeded in this effort thus reveals something of its progress toward its general socialist ambition.

The resources with which FRELIMO has been able to take on these formidable objectives were, and remain, minimal. The precipitous and destructive exodus of most of the Portuguese settler population around the time of independence, in combination with colonial policies that restricted access to education, left Mozambique desperately short of the technical, administrative, and productive capacity vital to the broad project of improving living conditions. The one resource FRELIMO could bring to bear on its post-independence reconstruction projects was the ability, developed during the arduous years of the liberation struggle, to mobilize and organize popular participation and popular forces in order to generate self-reliant solutions to problems.

Although this chapter focuses specifically on the urban situation, the inherent connection between urban and rural is also addressed, as is Mozambique's own emphasis on rural development—aimed at redressing the imbalance of the colonial pattern and reflecting the rural situation of most Mozambicans. A vital question for urban planning and housing in post-independence Mozambique has indeed been about this balance: given the country's severely restricted technical and economic capacities, how can living conditions in the urban centers be improved while preserving scarce resources for rural development? The mobilization of popular energies, complemented by supportive political, administrative, and technical organization and policies, is seen as an essential ingredient of this process. The chapter examines, in historical perspective, the range of urban realities and issues encountered by Mozambican policymakers and traces the development of the policies and strategies adopted in the critical years following independence. In the process, the major constraints upon ensuring state and party responsiveness to popular energies are also discussed. The tendency toward an increasing centralization and bureaucratization of political and administrative structures may well be a reflection of sharpening class lines and growing class struggle.

Urbanization in Mozambique

The pattern of territorial development that was in place at independence started as early as the eighth century, when Arab traders began to establish small coastal trading posts at Sofala, Angoche, and Ilha de Moçambique. The Portuguese first arrived in Ilha in 1496, eventually displacing the Arab traders. Unable to penetrate the interior very successfully, they continued to open up trading and military posts along the coast, moving south to Quelimane, Sofala, and eventually Delagoa Bay, the future site of Lourenço Marques. With only a tenuous hold on the coast, they skirmished with the French, the Dutch, and with tribal rulers for almost three centuries while developing and exploiting trade in gold, ivory, and, particularly in the first half of the eighteenth century, slaves.

It was not until after the Berlin Congress in 1885 that the few small trading posts began to grow larger. As the boundaries with Southern Rhodesia and the Union of South Africa were consolidated following a series of military escapades between colonial powers, the Portuguese were able to turn their military forces against strong tribal resistance. In the south, the Gaza state of Gungunhana was so powerful that before its defeat in 1895, it almost took Lourenço Marques.

In the same year, as military battles were superseded by the development of commercial relations, the Anglo American Company completed the first railway from the Transvaal to Lourenço Marques. The growth of this small settlement, whose administrative status had been raised from village to town only in 1887, was assured in a series of treaties that guaranteed that 50 percent of all transport from the Rand area would run through its port. In exchange, the Portuguese granted the South African miners the exclusive right to recruit labor south of the 22nd parallel, or over one-third of the country. The development of southern Mozambique thus became highly dependent upon relations with South Africa, and, as might be expected, this had an almost disastrous effect on the local economy, as well as on that of the city of Lourenço Marques itself.[1]

In a similar way, the history of the port and city of Beira, now the second largest urban center, was tied to the process of colonization and exploitation of the vast central regions of Southern Africa. Beira was founded in 1887 because it had the nearest navigable port to Southern Rhodesia. Between 1892 and 1942 political control and responsibility for the overall development of the town and the surrounding territory—compromising one-fifth of the area of Mozambique—was ceded to a huge concessionary company controlled by British, French, and Belgian capital. A railway link to Umtali was open by 1900, although the development of permanent port facilities lagged until 1929; from then until 1949 both the railways and port were controlled by the London-based Trans-Zambezi Railway. With the completion of links to Nyasaland in 1922 and the coal mines of Moatize in 1949, the importance of the city and its dependence on the transit trade were assured.[2]

The establishment of the smaller towns was also tied to foreign concessionary companies, which realized their profits more from slavery and forced labor than from capital investment. The countryside, however, remained severely underdeveloped. Thus the city of Tete grew up around rich coal deposits and Quelimane's port complemented the sisal and cocoa plantations of the Zambezi Company. These and other small towns, such as Nampula, also played a role as regional economic and administrative centers.

These developments were reinforced in the post-World War II period when the concessionary companies—even though they had lost their political jurisdiction under Salazar's policies of economic nationalism—continued their economic activities, with some participation from Portuguese capital.

With the entire country in Portuguese hands, the immigration of impoverished peasants from Portugal was encouraged, mostly in the form of *colonato* (agricultural settlement) schemes in the south. Institutionalized forced labor and mandatory cultivation of cash crops among the Mozambican rural population supported these initiatives, which in turn provoked a minor expansion of local transformation industries and civilian construction, mostly in Lourenço Marques.

The period following the founding of FRELIMO and the start of the armed struggle against Portuguese colonization in 1964 witnessed the consolidation of the spatial pattern of development that would be inherited at independence. Portugal, faced with a shortage of capital as military expenditures increased, was again forced to open up Mozambique to foreign investment. Much of this went into speculative urban development in Lourenço Marques and Beira, necessary to accommodate an expanding wartime administrative apparatus, to provide facilities for the growing transport and tourist trade, and for expanding commercial and industrial activity. The completion of a new pipeline from Beira to Umtali in 1965 and the increased U.S. demand for Rhodesian chromium (to build up the Vietnam war machine) resulted in an expansion of Beira's port facilities.[3] The shantytowns surrounding the two main cities grew with the need for a reserve of cheap labor for the war-led "boom," particularly in the service, transport, industrial, and construction sectors. Although on a smaller scale, a similar process took place in the smaller provincial capitals, especially Nampula, the principal staging point for the Portuguese war effort in the north. Lichinga, Tete, and Pemba all assumed strategic importance and grew as infrastructure was built to facilitate the war effort.

The countryside, where over 90 percent of Mozambicans lived, produced raw materials for the benefit of the towns and the Portuguese metropole. It underwent important changes during the period before independence. More than 1 million people, or 50 percent of the population of the three northern provinces (Niassa, Cabo Delgado, and Tete), were herded into *aldeamentos* (strategic resettlements) as part of what proved to be an ineffective counterinsurgency campaign. Various other schemes were also attempted, with limited results, to settle both new Portuguese immigrants and ex-soldiers in areas where they could serve as a bulwark against advancing FRELIMO forces.[4] Most important, the experience of collective life and active participatory politics in the liberated and semi-liberated zones of the north had a profound effect on the future direction of FRELIMO's strategy for resolving urban problems.

With the signing of the Lusaka Accords in September 1974, the structural weaknesses of the pattern of territorial development and dependency were exacerbated by the precipitous exodus of most of the 250,000 settlers. By early 1976 a serious unemployment crisis was developing in the cities, as industries closed down because they lacked technically skilled workers, raw materials, and/or spare parts (often compounded by South African maneuvers to delay needed goods). The nationalization of all rental housing in February 1976 only confirmed the crisis in civilian construction, which was virtually paralyzed. Many jobs disappeared in the service sector as the proprietors of hotels, bars, and restaurants and the employers of domestic servants left the country. FRELIMO's decision to honor

UN trade sanctions against Rhodesia closed down much of the activity at the port of Beira, putting thousands more out of work.

At the same time, rural unemployment was increasing as well, especially in the south, after South Africa decreased mine recruitment by 70 percent. The jobs lost on the farms of departing settlers were only partially offset by those on the new state farms, and the breakdown of the rural commercial network severely affected peasant producers in all areas.[5] When colonial pass laws were relaxed in the transition year, many more migrants joined the flood of people moving to the towns. They included the family members of earlier job-seeking migrants, youths seeking secondary school education not available in rural areas, and people dislocated by the war of liberation and the subsequent Rhodesian attacks. One result was serious food supply problems in the towns, particularly since many of the immigrants had been food producers. The pattern of rapid and difficult-to-control urbanization, a virtual corollary of independence in most developing countries, emerged in Mozambique as well.

Urbanization is not, of course, necessarily bad. It has always been true that as productivity increases, people are freed from agricultural work to move into the industrial and service sectors. In capitalist—and, by extension, neocolonial—societies, this process is primarily motivated by the demands of private capital accumulation, often without particular regard for its social or ecological consequences. A planned society, at least in theory, ought to be able to apply socially determined criteria to control the degree and rate at which it industrializes and urbanizes. This presupposes a well-coordinated national economy and the ability to implement rural development programs that will stem out-migration, thus creating the breathing space to develop other options, including amelioration of the urban situation. In practice, however, Mozambique was desperately short of the means to implement such a comprehensive strategy. With limited natural resources, and having rejected dependent forms of industrial development, the country was counting on agriculture for economic growth. A shortage of hard currency, due to the loss of mine jobs, the severe drop in agricultural exports, and military spending to support the Zimbabwe war made the task that much more imposing.

Inside the Cities and Towns

The inequities between town and country had their counterpart within the cities and towns, and these too provided dramatic evidence of the impact of Portugal's racist and colonial-capitalist policies. The four largest cities—Maputo (estimated total population in 1980 of 800,000), Beira (250,000), Nampula (150,000), and Quelimane (50,000)—and to a lesser extent the smaller towns, all have modern core areas of office buildings, hotels, and apartment blocks, along with expansive residential areas that were once reserved for the settler population. The rapid growth of these so-called cement cities in the 1960s and early 1970s produced enormous speculative profits for the landowners (or their corporate heirs), the largest of whom had acquired their holdings when the land around the cities was ceded for agricultural purposes.[6] The owners cashed in as the city expanded and the land was converted to urban use; some even sold it back to the municipal government, as when land was acquired for the airport and a second railway station in Lourenço Marques. Despite laws to the contrary, city officials were often financially involved in these deals and the direction of growth was undoubtedly determined in part by personal interest.[7]

Expanding urban development added to the misery of the 75 to 80 percent of the population that lived precariously in the shantytowns surrounding the cement cities. Since Mozambicans were not permitted to own land, many families were forced to occupy illegally land unsuitable for building or public and private land slated for future development. Some rented tiny plots from the landowners, and many were subject to periodic flooding or were bulldozed out of their homes at the whim of speculators and government bureaucrats.

At independence most of the shantytown areas lacked water, sanitation, and community services, despite the start in the early 1970s of a "psychosocial" program, a last-gasp attempt to culturally integrate the urban population, and not so coincidentally to develop a more skilled and loyal workforce. But the program's schools and bath houses were too few to convince the population of Portuguese concern for their welfare, and the newly paved roads were mostly used for police surveillance. Speaking in Maputo in March 1980, Samora Machel dramatically recalled what it felt like to live in the racially divided city of Lourenço Marques:

> Lourenço Marques, city of cement, built high to mark the difference between us and the colonists. . . .
> Lourenço Marques, city of reeds and tin, relegated to the flood plains, storehouse of human labor and suffering used to create luxury for the colonists. . . .
> On the one side, cement, opulence, the brilliantly clean streets; on the other side, the insecurity of social injustice, the discrimination, the poverty, and the gloom of misery.[8]

The enormous problem of improving living conditions in the growing shantytowns was made even more difficult by the collapse of local government as the professional and administrative staff abandoned the country. Originally created to serve only the cement city, the *camaras municipais* (city councils) combined inefficiency and corruption with an inability to finance the enormous infrastructural works that were needed to match the level of building activity.[9] The colonial division of local government responsibility further confused the situation. Not considered part of the city, most of the shantytown areas were under a separate administration, usually the rural district administration. In the case of Maputo, there was even a special "second administration"—the name itself is telling.[10] The unfortunate sites for some cities, such as those chosen for their harbors, added to the problem. Beira and Quelimane are barely above sea level in the dry season and large parts of Maputo are regularly inundated by flood waters from the rivers flowing into Maputo Bay. All three cities require massive drainage systems, and the limited areas of land suitable for building added to its price and increased the landowners' profits.

Services declined dramatically even as attempts were made to extend them to the shantytowns. Garbage collection, the emptying of septic tanks, and the maintenance of the drainage, sewage, water, and electricity systems all suffered from the lack of materials and spare parts, or even the know-how to order and install them. Competing private municipal service companies complicated the issue. The few public buses began to fall apart from overuse and increasing numbers of people had to get up very early to walk to work. Movement from the urban fringe to shantytowns closer to the center of the cities meant increased housing densities, and the space that remained available for parks and green areas diminished as sanitary conditions worsened.

A number of forces put additional stress on the "informal" commercial and economic life of the towns. These included the closing of the borders to tourism, the decline in shipping activity in the ports, and a deliberate policy to end the significant—although normally unaccounted for—sources of income, however degrading, from begging, prostitution, and a lively drug trade. Dwindling supplies of materials further affected the many small artisans working in the shantytowns, who were already facing a shrinking settler market for their furniture and other household goods. An early and very sensible FRELIMO prohibition against building permanent houses in the shantytowns, intended to avoid unnecessary demolition when re-planning these areas, resulted in the loss of opportunities for unemployed construction workers. In any case, building materials, particularly cement, were scarce. Long lines for food and other basic necessities, exacerbated by rural migration and black marketeering, were a very visible sign of the difficulties. Higher salaries and quick promotions for often underqualified Mozambicans which had been part of a settler strategy to encourage a reaction against FRELIMO and create a small anti-FRELIMO petty bourgeoisie among those already affected by the settlers' "Joe Cool" urban culture, particularly in Maputo and Beira, created problems as personal opportunism, lack of administrative skills, and routine imitation of colonial bureaucratic procedures combined to produce unsympathetic and unresponsive state and parastatal agencies. In short, the 1974–1976 period was one of increasing crisis in the cities and towns. Migration, unemployment, food shortages, lines of people, street fights, and assassinations added to the existing misery of cement city and shantytown inequities. The situation demanded a forceful political and organizational response. Fortunately, and not surprisingly for those familiar with the liberation struggle, this was FRELIMO's strength.

First Steps: GDs, Nationalizations, and the Third Congress

As a guerrilla movement, poorly equipped compared to the NATO-reinforced Portuguese forces, FRELIMO relied on the active support of the rural population during the struggle for independence. In the liberated rural areas, committees of FRELIMO militants organized collective agricultural production, as well as people's stores, schools, and health posts, all under the banner of "counting on our own forces." Numerous meetings helped people become involved in solving their everyday problems, and the practice of "people's power" gradually developed.

A similar strategy was attempted in the urban areas. FRELIMO members and FPLM forces moved quickly into the cities and towns after September 1974, helping to organize the selection of *grupos dinamizadores* ("dynamizing groups," or GDs) in neighborhoods, factories, institutions, and sections of the bureaucracy. GD members were sometimes militants known to FRELIMO from underground activities, but more often they were active individuals with some sense of organization and engagement; all were then confirmed in their posts at public meetings. Paralleling the committees in the liberated areas, the GDs undertook the massive task of mobilizing and organizing the transition to independence in hundreds of urban areas, as well as combating the occasional acts of sabotage by departing colonialists. The stories of two neighborhood GDs, the first in the cement city of Maputo, the second in the shantytowns of Beira, vividly illustrate their efforts and dedication.[11]

In 1974 Alto Maé was an almost all-white working-class neighborhood of 20,000 functionaries, commercial and bank employees, policemen, and their families living in two- or three-story apartment blocks, with a sprinkling of higher buildings. The newly "officialized" GD, including some sympathetic whites, first met in November and decided to launch information sessions in the schools, streets, and parks, and to distribute thousands of pamphlets explaining the Lusaka Accords and the FRELIMO program. As this effort increased, so did the reaction to it. Bombs were placed in garbage pails during community clean-up campaigns and GD members were physically threatened and photographed as a form of intimidation. In response, the GD set up a vigilance section which helped dismantle a ring of foreign exchange dealers. It also met with workers in the factories in Alto Maé and launched a public campaign to unmask acts of economic sabotage by the owners. It started a campaign to limit drinking hours in the bars, which were centers of prostitution and petty crime; worked with runaway children who lived by begging and stealing, and organized many dramatic reunions with families who had long since given up hope of seeing their children again; and instituted literacy and adult education classes.

At about this time a major crisis occurred within the GD. A national FRELIMO seminar decided that the activities of every GD should be analyzed: former secret police agents and other collaborators had infiltrated some GDs in order to take what they could for themselves while creating mistrust in the GDs, and, by inference, FRELIMO. During a long neighborhood meeting in Alto Maé several such people were discovered to have been obstructing the work of the GD. They were dismissed and it was decided to begin political courses for GD members and to assign specific tasks that could be monitored. The Mozambican idea of everyone being a "responsible" took on increased significance.

With the nationalization of rental housing in 1976, Alto Maé became over 95 percent Mozambican as people were relocated from flooded shantytown areas into housing left empty by departing Portuguese residents. The GD initiated many more projects among the new residents, including a consumer cooperative and a health post and cultural center, and also organized women's and youth organizations.

In contrast to Alto Maé's relative prosperity, Munhava is a very poor shantytown on the edge of Beira. Its 20,000 people come from all parts of Mozambique and live in rickety wood and mud-plaster houses perched on high ground, little islands surrounded by water in the rainy season. Before independence the people were lorded over by Portuguese administrators and *regulos*, "chiefs" who collaborated with the Portuguese and did the local landowners' dirty business. The landowner, a lawyer, had acquired a vast tract of land years earlier for the small price of the tax stamps on his formal petition and charged rent to those who built houses or planted small fields; those who could not pay had their houses demolished or their rice crops confiscated.

After the April 1974 coup in Portugal, the colonial government, trying to curry popular favor, suddenly permitted people in Munhava to make beer, despite laws to the contrary. Beer was sold and sometimes even given away. Drunkenness, banditry, and violent battles between brewers increased, as did problems for the GD, many of whose members had emerged from clandestine FRELIMO work, which had been supported by a Protestant church in the area. In the beginning it was dangerous to be a GD member and help from the FPLM was necessary to bring the situation under control.

Rumor campaigns started by the departing settlers were an additional challenge to the GD's political ability. Parents were reluctant to send their children to school after hearing that "FRELIMO will nationalize all children." There was a lot of resentment among the men over FRELIMO's policy for the emancipation of women, who began to attend literacy and adult education classes organized by the GD. An abortive settler coup late in 1975 created more "noise" in the neighborhood. But the GD remained firm, the crises passed, and the groundwork was gradually put in place. Children were able to go to school, women began to get involved in the neighborhood, people's lives and livelihoods were no longer threatened, and the GD embarked on an ambitious program of working with the residents to tackle the difficult problems facing the *bairro*.

The experiences of these two GDs were repeated in many urban neighborhoods. They were to become a valuable base for organizing self-help activities to improve the conditions in the shantytowns. But before popular energies could be fully mobilized, two other steps were necessary: the nationalization of·land and housing, and the definition of a strategy for rural development.

The constitution adopted at independence nationalized all land. According to Article 8, "The land and the natural resources in the soil and subsoil . . . are property of the State" acting in the name of the Mozambican people, who thus became collective owners of their own territory. At one stroke speculation in urban land ceased, since it could no longer be bought and sold. Every Mozambican family was instead guaranteed the right to own a house and to use land for this purpose. Family agricultural rights were recognized, and rights of use were transmissable to heirs, although the state has the right to expropriate land for development purposes—in which case the owner or heirs must be compensated for any improvements they have made.[12]

The revolutionary impact of this measure is perhaps difficult to gauge from a North American or Western European perspective, where the concept of private land ownership is so firmly entrenched and mystified. Some examples of the way in which the new constitution could lead to the reversal of spatial inequalities may make this clearer. First, allocation of investment in infrastructure and urban development could now be planned on the basis of political and social goals rather than market and racial mechanisms. The housing situation of shantytown dwellers, no longer "squatters" on private land, could be legalized and improved. New jobs, commercial facilities, and community services could be relocated away from the cement cities, minimizing transportation time and costs. Pollution could be reduced and foreign exchange otherwise needed for imported petroleum and vehicles saved. Finally, with market pressures eased, more green space could be allocated for recreation and production in and around the towns. As we shall see, many of these measures are now in the process of being implemented.

The accompanying nationalization of rental housing was motivated in part by the need to organize the use of housing abandoned by the Portuguese. Philosophically, however, it represented a commitment to ending the speculative rents that had stopped Mozambicans from living in the apartments that they had constructed. Rents were set according to income and type of accommodation, and a state agency, APIE, was established to administer apartment units. With over 25,000 in Maputo alone, this was a formidable undertaking.[13]

The nationalization measure proved to be an extremely timely one, particularly in the capital, where thousands of families were relocated from the shantytowns to the newly nationalized apartments following severe flooding in early 1976. Nevertheless, with over 80 percent of all urban dwellers still living in the shantytowns, tremendous problems remained, and the various city authorities made an effort to resolve them. In Maputo, for instance, six hundred plots were laid out for the flood victims and a self-help housing scheme was begun, the houses constructed collectively by groups of families assisted by trained construction workers. In other areas, town councils opened up new shops, markets, and consumer cooperatives in the shantytowns, and ministries began to plan for schools, health posts, and other facilities. There was no concerted attempt to reorganize the municipal councils, however, for although it was recognized that they were a problem, the very difficult job of redefining national- and provincial-level state structures took precedence.

The nationalization of land complemented rural development measures. Abandoned settler farms were converted into state farms to ensure food supplies for the cities, to provide rural employment, and to maintain exports. A communal village program was launched in order to bring services to the rural population while collective agricultural production was being developed. Capitalizing on FRELIMO's mobilizing capacity and making the best of a disastrous situation, over one thousand communal villages were established, half based on the old "strategic settlements" in the north and many of the rest formed after the Limpopo and Zambezi rivers flooded, in 1976 and 1978 respectively. A commitment to build at least one textile plant in each province, greatly expanded coal-mining activity in the remote province of Tete, and the start of road work to complete north-south links were further evidence of an intention to redress the imbalanced colonial development pattern.

The Third Congress in February 1977 clarified political and planning strategies. Its primary achievement was to constitute FRELIMO as a political party with a very explicit commitment to popular democracy and the transition to a socialist society. Party members were to work in constant contact with the population, and rural, town, provincial, and national assemblies were to be democratically elected to ensure popular control over the state apparatus at each level. Particular emphasis was to be given to the rural assemblies as a political counterweight to the relatively privileged cities.

The Congress also adopted a series of economic and social objectives, which in effect constituted the first national plan. Heavy emphasis was given to the state sector and a national planning commission was established to prepare annual and long-range production targets and to control the allocation of resources. The socialization and mechanization of agriculture was to be matched with industrial development "to create a balanced and harmonious development of all parts of the national territory." Town/country differences were to be reduced by bringing industry, health, education, and other services to the communal villages.[14]

State control over credit and over the construction sector completed the process started by the nationalizations and laid the basis for the elimination of the racist character of the cities, where life was now to be organized in "communal neighborhoods." Initially, the state assumed responsibility for constructing infrastructure (roads, water, electricity, sanitation) and social facilities, but any improvement in housing conditions was to come primarily from people's own efforts because of the severe shortages of materials and technical capacity. The civilian construction sector was to finish those apartment and office buildings, schools, and hospitals under construction at independence, and establish a distribution network for building materials.[15]

The Third Congress's policy commitments gave additional credibility to FRELIMO's earlier stated concern about rural development and the urban-rural balance. Although the remainder of this chapter focuses on measures to improve conditions in the urban areas—some of which were specifically designed to reduce the drain on the rural areas by discouraging migration and encouraging urban self-sufficiency—it must nevertheless be remembered that if "villagization," rural industrialization, and rural health and education programs fell short of the Congress's hopes, solving urban problems would become a Sisyphus-like task because the urban population would continue to increase uncontrollably.

The National Housing Directorate

The Third Congress recommended the formation of a state agency to define guidelines and strategies for planning urban centers and developing housing programs. Two months later the old urban planning and housing department for Lourenço Marques became the National Housing Directorate (DNH). Despite its imposing name, by the end of the year DNH had a professional staff of only twelve, ten of whom were expatriates (from five different countries). Even with assistance from the United Nations Development Program (UNDP), DNH was short of equipment, supplies, and transport. The budget was still passing through recently initiated national budgeting procedures, and even the most basic planning information was unavailable. No one really knew whether there were 10, 12, or 14 million Mozambicans, much less where they lived or how they earned a living. Nevertheless, as the only government body with any physical planning capabilities, DNH tasks quickly expanded to include communal village planning and localization, detailed land-use mapping, rural and regional planning, and investment siting. All of this had to be accomplished in the absence of any clearly defined land-use planning philosophy or strategy. The general problem facing the directorate was to determine how the political direction set by the Congress could be translated into specific policies and activities. This was accompanied by a host of subsidiary concerns that had enormous policy implications:

—Did self-reliance imply building factories to prefabricate concrete houses and/or finding ways to improve the use of locally available materials and encouraging self-help schemes?

—Alternatively, should efforts be focused on neighborhood planning, infrastructure, and community services before even considering individual housing?

—In any case, how could the use of limited resources be maximized without unduly benefitting the towns at the expense of the countryside, while still demonstrating a commitment to solving urban problems?

—Given a concern for ecological balance, achieving an appropriate relationship between neighborhood and workplace, reducing spatial segregation, and creating communal neighborhoods, what would the new Mozambican city look like?

—Finally, how could the experience of participation in the liberated areas be integrated into both the day-to-day practice of the directorate and the development of national planning procedures and standards?

Faced with so many questions that had no immediate answers and burdened with unusable colonial city plans, it was decided to move in a number of directions in order to discover both the problems and the possibilities for overcoming them. Recognizing that Mozambique would have to rely on expatriate architects, planners, and engineers for many years, DNH initiated a program to train planning assistants who could assist the professionals. After an initial six-week course early in 1978, the first group of planning "monitors" staffed the new provincial housing services, which began to provide a regionally based physical planning presence. In the meantime, projects already under way in the smaller towns of Pemba and Angoche were continued, with varying degrees of success, but resources were concentrated in Maputo in order to test out policy options quickly. The area set aside for relocating flood victims was expanded, efforts were made to improve the output of two small prefabricated housing factories, planning studies of Maputo were begun, and the directorate responded to urgent requests for small planning and housing schemes, usually in conjunction with economic development projects.

The major new initiative, however, was to develop a strategy for the gradual rehabilitation of shantytown areas based on a pilot project in the *bairro* of Maxaquene.[16] The project was to look for ways to spread resources more widely than had the 1976 self-help housing program, which was having difficulty servicing only two hundred families. It was also becoming obvious that people were building permanent homes despite the government prohibition against it.

To multiply DNH's capacities, active community participation was essential. This meshed with the need to find ways of working that would encourage the process of political organization already under way in the neighborhoods. The 45,000 residents of Maxaquene had been divided into 17 cells, each with its own GD which worked in conjunction with the GD of the whole *bairro.* Four cells, housing 10,000 people, were chosen for the first project. Each cell selected members for a planning commission which met regularly with the DNH project team and established the following priorities for action:

—With only one water tap for every two thousand people, women and children spent hours every day fetching and carrying water to their homes. Many more public standpipes were needed.

—A road network was necessary to open the way for ambulances, buses, fire engines, and garbage collection.

—Schools and teachers were in short supply and classes were held in three shifts, often outdoors. Childcare centers, parks, clinics, and other community facilities were all almost nonexistent and were badly needed.

—Finally, people wanted to build permanent homes of cement block or brick. Eighty percent of their houses were made of wood and reed walls, with corrugated metal roofs. Others were entirely corrugated metal, noisy in the rain, ovens in the heat, and damply chilling in the cool season. About 10 percent of the population had already built permanent structures despite government prohibitions.

At a long afternoon meeting, seven hundred Maxaquene residents endorsed the project. It was agreed that neighbors would help one another move those houses that were in the path of new roads or in areas to be reserved for schools and other community facilities. DNH then drew up a new plan for Maxaquene. It was organized around service corridors, each of which was to include a 6-meter paved road with space alongside for water mains, electric lines, streetlights, sewers, and footpaths. Blocks housing between sixty and eighty families and defined by a series of pedestrian paths were laid out on both sides of the corridors. The position of the paths was to be flexible in order to accommodate existing housing clusters and minimize the necessity of relocation and the loss of trees. Each block was to have at its center a small square with one standpipe, four taps, and a streetlamp to provide light for evening activities. Finally, space was set aside for future use, including a small industry zone to encourage the growth of neighborhood production cooperatives.

The plan was discussed and accepted in principle by the local planning commission, which then assisted in staking out the scheme on the ground, using simple instruments and procedures. Efforts by the DNH team to bend or move the smaller paths in order to save houses were unexpectedly rejected: those who had waited for the area to be laid out before starting construction felt little sympathy for those who had built permanent homes. Planning commission members were (unjustly) accused of accepting bribes so that they would influence the DNH staff, a situation that was firmly resolved when some of them were required to move their homes.

The residents also wanted straight streets with the houses parallel to them—this pattern, adopted from the grid-iron cement city, was thought to indicate "good organization." The DNH team reluctantly agreed, mostly because of its commitment to community participation. In any case, there were few complaints, and they were resolved by the GDs at public meetings. Many of those affected were helped to move and rebuild their homes.

Then a bulldozer, a menacing sight during colonial days, was brought in to open up the service corridors and the new streets. Once the boundaries of each block had been roughed out on the ground, the planning commission decided to bring more people into the rehabilitation process by forming block committees. These were selected at block meetings with assistance from the GDs, which insisted that women make up half of each committee to secure their still reluctant participation in neighborhood activities.

The first task facing the block committees was to respond to the growing demand to parcel each block into individual plots. The DNH team initially resisted this move because there were not enough land surveyors to do the job. Nevertheless, after one of the block committees, with minimal assistance, redivided its block into plots of approximately equal size, simple ground rules were established by the DNH team and the planning commission, an illustrated guide was prepared, and a model was used to show how the process worked. More expert block committees assisted those less geometrically inclined and the directorate was only called upon in cases where the existing arrangements were very complicated.

Once they were running smoothly, the block committees began to organize other activities. Working with the DNH staff, the residents of one block planted fruit and shade trees and built a small play area in their public square. Once again, this idea spread quickly and many blocks decorated their squares and began to use them for meetings and other community events.

The initial success of the pilot project led to a decision to extend it to a total of 10 cells and 36,000 people. By June 1979 an urban plan had been implemented in both the original project area and its extensions. Over 100 block committees were functioning and about 90 percent of them had undertaken plot division. Unfortunately, infrastructural work proceeded at a slower pace, although this was more because of the serious problems facing Mozambique than a lack of local initiative. Trenches were dug and standpipes constructed with assistance from the block committees, but the installation of main pipes was delayed due to the difficulty of obtaining materials from the plant in Beira. By the end of 1979 water was available in the 29 blocks of the original 4 cells, but its distribution to the extension area had to wait on the drilling of deep wells because the municipal water system, originally built for the cement city only, had reached its limit.

Despite efforts by the newly nationalized power company, the electricity project was held up by delays in importing materials. Eventually, however, streetlights were installed in the public squares of the original project area and along the main access routes. One new road was paved so that a bus route could be extended into the *bairro*. Blocks were 'numbered and names for streets chosen by the residents. The installation of public telephones increased the integration of the *bairro* into the city. Construction of community facilities proceeded slowly since priority was given to rural areas. Even so, two houses were converted into a small childcare center and space was set aside for other facilities. Despite the many tasks that remain, the Maxaquene project succeeded in demonstrating how a relatively modest state contribution could be multiplied by local involvement to make a substantial improvement in people's living conditions.

Unfortunately, despite strong neighborhood and international endorsement of the upgrading approach, the project was less well received by officials in the Ministry of Public Works and Housing (other than in the DNH itself). Unable to see beyond their own technically and class-biased perspectives, many were scornful of the work with *palhotas* ("huts," not houses—the choice of this word was itself indicative), and were not open to appreciating the increasing evidence of the initiative being taken by the people to build new houses and improve their plots. DNH could not convince the ministry to continue financial, technical, and material support for this work and further momentum was lost when it was decided that all project implementation should be taken over by the still disorganized city councils. The final stage of assistance to house builders never went into effect, although a very successful sanitation program went forward with overseas funds channelled through DNH. A second project in a higher density area with poorer drainage conditions faltered when it did not get the same level of local political support. In summary, then, the evidence of the pilot project suggests both some of the very real possibilities for creative innovation that exist in urban Mozambique and some of the difficulties that continue to stand in the way of such innovation.

Urban Government and Resolutions for the Future of the Towns

Even though national and provincial government structures were not yet well defined, the administrative void created by the rapid degeneration of the old colonial *camaras municipais* meant that some new form of urban government had to be initiated. But rather than simply fill a gap, a model of democratic urban government was needed, one that would help improve living conditions, largely through the mobilization of popular energies. It could support neighborhood initiatives by giving them high priority in the allocation of scarce resources, and by resolving conflicts between neighborhoods and between neighborhood and citywide planning objectives.

Following the instructions of the Third Congress, new city assemblies were elected in the ten largest urban centers, the first elections ever to be held in Mozambique on the basis of universal adult suffrage. The assemblies were to establish and monitor social and economic programs, which would then be carried out by the administrative arm of local government, the City Executive Council—(CEC), which had been created in April 1978, following the formal dismantling of the *camaras municipais*.[17] The CECs were to have a much broader mandate than had the *camaras municipais*, which before independence were run by a small business and professional group that was primarily concerned with smoothing the way for development in the cement city.

The CEC executive was usually made up of the CEC president and the heads of various city departments. This did not necessarily mean increased efficiencies, however. The number of departments and their responsibilities varied considerably and department heads often had very little practical or political experience. This made it difficult for the CECs to nurture the development of the city assemblies or bring important issues to their attention. They were also hampered by limited personnel, equipment, and budgets. Political direction, which was supposed to come from the newly formalized FRELIMO city committees—whose first secretary was also (at least until recently) the president of the CEC—was weak. Nevertheless, the city assemblies began to meet, with varying degrees of regularity and efficiency, to establish priorities and act on pressing problems.

Recognizing that problems remained, FRELIMO convened the First National Meeting of Cities and Neighborhoods in February 1979. Taking their cue from an address by Samora Machel to the National Assembly a few months earlier, the two hundred delegates examined ways in which the city assemblies and executive councils could help organize life in the cities and help solve existing problems.[18] During the first two days, hard-hitting reports highlighted political problems. In particular, the unresponsiveness of state structures to local initiatives was interpreted by the delegates as a sign of "sharpening class struggle," and the need to organize the population so that they would put forward their own needs was emphasized.

Despite reports of successes in *bairros* such as Alto Maé and Maxaquene, the meeting recognized that the lack of wider political organization meant that no systematic means had as yet been developed that would reverse the worst features of the colonial urban heritage—people continued to move to the cities and under- and unemployment increased, irregularities and speculation in basic goods continued, as did lack of water, electricity, public transport, and community facilities, and the "cement city" housing stock was falling into desrepair. Inadequate municipal finances added to the problem. These difficulties were analyzed by working groups and resolutions were presented to the plenary session at the end of the week-long gathering. Not surprisingly, the major thrust of these resolutions was political and organizational, advocating a return to the basic principles of self-reliance and popular democratic control.

The meeting also attempted to clear up the confusion that had developed about the future role of the GDs. It was resolved that the GDs had to be strengthened so that they could become the mass organization in the *bairros*, selected by and responsible to neighborhood assemblies. Party members would provide political direction and leadership, stepping in to support developing (or faltering) neighborhood efforts. The GDs were charged with the creation of "communal neighborhoods":

In communal *bairros*, people are to organize themselves in collective forms of life and work. The population will have a collective social and economic base made up of cultural and recreation centers, production and consumer cooperatives. The inhabitants of communal *bairros*, organized by the *grupo dinamizador*, will teach and learn to read and write, . . . develop popular culture and sports . . . organize for collective production of food and raising small animals, and organize artisans, carpenters, shoemakers, clothesmakers, and others . . . tasks are to be realized by residents organized into committees led by the GD. In summary, new social relations are to be established in the communal *bairros* based on voluntary and collective work; a new life is to be forged in the cities.[19]

Many additional resolutions reinforced the idea of "counting on our own forces." The GDs, together with the organizations of women and youth, were to be responsible for recycling garbage, setting up school/community committees, and starting neighborhood cultural, sports, and recreation activities. They were also to work with the CECs on other fronts, including production cooperatives, adult education and literacy campaigns, self-help housing schemes using local materials, shantytown improvements (following the Maxaquene model), improving public transport, and preventive health programs.

Concern that some neighborhoods, especially in Maputo and Beira, were too large to function as communities led to the proposal that *bairro* limits be redrawn to include 12,500 people at most, divided in turn into "communal units" of about 2,000 (equivalent to the former "cells"). Profiting from the Maxaquene experience, blocks of fifty families were to be the basic element of neighborhood organization.

Greater definition of the structure and role of neighborhood administrative and participatory structures was proposed to match the similar clarification of the role of the CECs. The GD was to include a secretary, an assistant secretary, and each member was to be responsible for a particular area of concern, working with a committee of interested residents. Whereas previously there had been considerable confusion as to how to channel local initiative, each committee was now to relate to its corresponding city department. For example, if the neighborhood committee for housing needed help constructing improved latrines at a local market, this request would be carried to the city housing department, which could supply materials, having already been instructed to do so by a policy decision made by the city's assembly.

The delegates took special care to specify that the CECs proceed rapidly to set up new city departments. Functions and priorities for each department were outlined and the need to train urgently needed personnel was emphasized. The most critical task was to support the new assemblies, which were urged to create committees of their delegates to work on specific issues. The delegates were also directed to be more conscious of their role in controlling the city administration and to remain in close contact with the urban population.

Schedules, deadlines, and responsibilities for organizational tasks were proposed, and these were tied to specific projects, including a bold new initiative, the development of "green zones" around each city. These are intended to help solve food supply problems, to make the cities more self-sufficient, and to create jobs for the urban unemployed. Recreation areas and natural preserves are also to be developed, taking such ecological factors as soil fertility, water supply, wind, and the possibility of using organic compost produced by the city into account.

Other major proposals included organizing for the census, which was to be held in 1980, preparing a financial plan for each city, launching a justice system rooted in neighborhood tribunals, establishing a pilot communal *bairro* in each city, and reviewing the serious problem of corruption and mismanagement confronting the state housing agency.

All the resolutions together constituted a blueprint for developing a socialist urban society based on local initiative and increasing urban self-reliance. Coming less than four years after independence, the National Meeting marked a clear break with colonial conceptions of urban reality. At the same time, however, a potential contradiction in the role of the GDs remained to be solved in practice. On the one hand, they were to be a forceful and critical representative of popular concerns; on the other hand, however, they were directed into a role as, in effect, the lowest tier of the state structure. The question was what would happen if they were required to represent unpopular initiatives and/or to cover for the lack of state responsiveness to neighborhood—and particularly shantytown—issues. If the GDs could not maintain their integrity as mass organizations, would they retreat into self-protective bureaucratization, or simply disintegrate? Although a complete study of this issue remains to be undertaken (and may in fact be premature), some indications of the direction taken are explored below.

Results and Directions, 1979–1983

Events in the four years following the National Meeting dramatically revealed both new possibilities and, once again, the limitations imposed by Mozambique's regional context. A brief recounting of the latter will situate the detailed discussion that follows on development of the GDs, urban government, and urban planning and housing policies during this same period.

The months leading up to Zimbabwe's independence in April 1980 were marked by an increase in the intensity of the terrorist activity that had been paralyzing development efforts in the central region of Mozambique. However, in cooperation with the Zimbabwean forces the FPLM quickly rounded up many of the outlaws and a period of peace seemed assured. Experienced FRELIMO military cadre were available for new tasks. These included General Hama Thai, who became president of the Maputo CEC.

Attention now focused on economic matters and a regional transportation and communications commission based in Maputo was created to explore, among other things, how Mozambique's ports and railways could best serve the region's development efforts. This represented a major break with the colonial configuration and, not incidentally, threatened South Africa's regional economic hegemony. National planning procedures had by then advanced to the extent that a development plan for the 1981–1990 decade was adopted, although it still suffered from a lack of hard data and from a limited consideration of its physical planning implications. One- and three-year plans were more realistic, however, and by the end of 1980 there was reason for optimism that a take-off point had been reached.

Over the next year, however, the South African regime succeeded in reorganizing its destabilization campaign, which had been based in Rhodesia. This began to have a serious detrimental effect on rural development efforts, whose impact had already been reduced by a continuing overemphasis on state farms at the expense of communal villages, cooperatives, and family producers. Military raids and sabotage made it increasingly difficult to maintain a rural commercial network, and cash crop production dropped, making it that much harder to import and/or manufacture the goods that provide the incentive for agricultural producers. These factors, combined with increased physical danger in the rural areas and the onset of a serious drought in southern Mozambique, provoked a major new wave of migration to the towns. As a result, urban unemployment, black marketeering, and social marginalization once again increased, especially in Maputo. As the military situation worsened, military cadre were once again redeployed and General Hama Thai was posted to the military command in Inhambane Province.

The limitations of the inherited territorial situation thus reasserted themselves in the 1979–1983 period. Attacks on infrastructure, such as railway lines, undercut both the attempt to decrease the dependency on South Africa and to reduce urban/rural disparities. In addition, current projections suggest that by the early 1990s Mozambique's population will reach 16 million, perhaps 20 percent of whom will live in cities and towns—2 million more than at present.[20]

Although the realization of Mozambique's plans for the urban areas will ultimately depend on the resolution of the regional situation, the successes and failures of this period nevertheless provide major lessons for the future. Once again, examining one case in detail will illuminate the larger situation.

The experience of a neighborhood in Nampula that was selected as a pilot *bairro* along the lines suggested by the National Meeting demonstrates some of the difficulties in implementing the meeting's mandate. By 1980 the community had collected enough money to buy concrete blocks and had started to construct two one-room schools, had cut trees and gathered branches in the countryside to build several new literacy centers, had opened a cooperative bakery at the back of an abandoned warehouse (which made 1500 small loaves a day), had built a modest market out of local materials, and had launched various other self-help projects. But then what happened?

The schools were never finished because the Ministry of Public Works could not supply the needed materials. The bakery closed because the Ministry of Education took over the warehouse. During a visit to the *bairro*, the provincial governor suggested that the market be doubled in size and that it be built of blocks, steel, and asbestos roofing. Four families were promptly relocated for this purpose, but again the materials did not arrive and the small bazaar was abandoned. Similarly, a government architect visiting the literacy centers was critical: they should have been built with more windows for ventilation. He had somehow missed the remarkable fact that the centers were being used by young volunteers from the *bairro* to teach neighborhood women to read. Many others seemed to miss the point as well. Fundamental FRELIMO precepts of "counting on our own forces" and "building a people's state to serve the people" were not being supported. It seemed that the relative privilege of the cement-city-based bureaucrats and even of party officials was leading them to respond to problems with increasingly technocratic solutions which could also falter badly if they proved to be too dependent on the expenditure of limited hard currency reserves.

This possibility did not go unnoticed, however, and in 1980 Samora Machel launched a political offensive against bureaucratization in both the state and the party. One campaign focused on reorganizing the Beira and Maputo ports in anticipation of the independence of Zimbabwe, but there were also two campaigns that reemphasized popular participation: new elections were called for the local and city assemblies, and a countrywide population census was ordered.

The election process opened up a discussion of ways to increase democratic control of state structures, and was accompanied by a critical analysis of the successes and failures of the first assemblies.[21] Both the collective work of each assembly and the individual contribution of each delegate were considered, first in the assemblies themselves and then in public meetings held in neighborhoods and factories. The consensus was that although the assemblies had taken some important first steps, such as defining green zones around the cities, assisting consumer cooperatives, and tackling social problems, better organization and mobilization of state resources was needed if community concerns were to be responded to successfully.

The idea of direct accountability to the people was reinforced by the meticulous examination of new candidates for the assemblies. Although the number of people participating in the elections dropped slightly, they had a better understanding of the process and were more critical in their participation.[22]

The first nationwide population census in August 1980 was especially difficult because of the need to overcome the fear associated with the colonial census, which had been geared to the payment of taxes and the maintenance of the forced labor system. After being briefed by census officials, the newly elected delegates, who played a major role in this effort, patiently explained to countless community meetings how the census was essential for national economic planning. They related it to the decade of struggle against underdevelopment, which had been announced by the president earlier in the year. At the same time, an attempt was made to link the delegates, who had been elected on a citywide basis, to specific neighborhoods and factories. The entire experience improved their skills at community mobilization.

The enthusiasm with which people participated in the census attested to the success of the delegates' efforts. Census workers in rural areas walked hundreds of kilometers to get needed census forms while neighborhood volunteers raised funds and prepared food for student census takers. Although it was several months before the initial data were released (there were 12.2 million Mozambicans in 1980), the census resulted in significant political and organizational achievements. In particular, the city assemblies, in collaboration with the GDs and following the Maxaquene model, used the opportunity to organize block committees of fifty families in every neighborhood in the country. The committees were to serve as another vital link between the population, the GDs, and the assembly delegates.

Efforts were also being made to reinforce the GDs by implementing the new organizational structure recommended by the National Meeting. In Maputo, brigades of assembly delegates and party workers helped reorganize the GDs, and permanent neighborhood staff were trained as well. The results of these efforts were mixed. City departments still rarely met directly with their neighborhood counterparts (e.g., the housing department and the neighborhood housing committee). The best of the paid *bairro* staff were those with previous experience in a GD; others, some of whom were not even neighborhood residents, were less responsive and tended to cover for their inexperience with ineffective paper shuffling.

Some of the large *bairros* took a long time to reorganize, particularly since they had been somewhat arbitrarily divided by the CECs into units of 12,500 people. Nevertheless, contact with the population did improve. The block committees continued to operate in many shantytown *bairros* and the effort to select and train a *mobilizadore* (organizer) for each group of ten families was reasonably successful. The proposed communal units of two thousand people were not encouraged, however, even though they had proved to be a useful level of organization for neighborhood improvement work.

After a long delay while FRELIMO party cells were being organized in the workplace, activists in many neighborhoods were integrated into *bairro* party cells. Neighborhood residents were encouraged to participate in the selection process: the party used the opportunity to reinforce local concerns and help solve immediate problems by confronting lackadaisical state agencies. The party cells are intended to help encourage GD activities, such as the 1982 campaign to increase the participation of the women's and youth organizations in *bairro* life.

There was, however, considerable overlap in the membership of the party cells and the GDs, which led to a blurring of the still unclear distinction between administrative/organizational and political tasks in the *bairros.* This left open the question as to whether it might not have been simpler and more effective to re-politicize the GDs directly, so that they would work with the block, women's, and youth organizations, instead of creating new and separate political structures. It also remains to be seen whether party directives will interfere with or promote local initiatives that are brought forward to the GDs.

The campaigns to control mounting urban crime and to alleviate serious food supply problems in Maputo—both linked to the increase in rural migration brought on by drought and war—have shown the contradictory position in which the GDs may find themselves. With the help of the block committees, the GDs have been enforcing a system of residency cards for employed city residents. These cards are needed for participation in a food rationing system that has been successful in distributing basic necessities. As a result, the program has enjoyed popular support and the hand of the GDs has been strengthened. However, if alternative opportunities cannot be provided for the unemployed rural migrants, attempts to control their movement may turn out to be a formalistic exercise that will result in a loss of political good will and respect at the *bairro* level. It will be hard for the GDs to distance themselves from such a failure.

In any case, regardless of the difficulties imposed by the continuing rural crisis, it is still possible to take advantage of the presence and credibility of the neighborhood organizations. Both the GDs and the more sensitive CEC directors remain strongly convinced that because popular interest in improving housing is intense, even the most moribund GDs and the residents of shantytown *bairros* can be motivated to participate. Such activity can then be used to reinforce the GDs' position as a mass organization.

The potential for mobilization in the "cement city" is much smaller, however. Despite the introduction of reasonable rents, the poorest inhabitants have had difficulty remaining and a tendency toward spatial segregation (based more on class than on race, however) has been reinforced by some continuing corruption and mismanagement at the state rental agency. The new residents are not very interested in neighborhood politics or collective work, despite decreasing standards of building maintenance and public works. Nevertheless, a strong concern about food supply problems has provided an entry point for re-engaging community action.

In the context of a new round of urban social problems, it is particularly important that the neighborhood GDs have state support in order to mobilize the population to maintain social order. Working together is essential if concrete concerns are to be responded to. What then of the development of local government?

Since 1979 the City Executive Councils have slowly increased their capacities. Ten of the twelve major cities and towns now have various department heads in addition to the chief administrative officer, first appointed soon after the CECs were created. All have defined new city and *bairro* limits, five have offices supporting family and cooperative production in green zones, and other projects have been initiated, including plot layout and distribution, markets, health posts, GD offices, and schools. The Department of Construction and Urbanization in Maputo—the only one with a professional staff—has started an ambitious program to open up housing sites and provide technical and material assistance to new residents. A pilot project to improve basic sanitation through mass mobilization and the formation of latrine production cooperatives has also been very successful.

While the scope of these efforts is remarkable considering when the CECs were established, the results are limited in relation to the scale of the problem. The difficulties are of two types. First, there is a continuing lack of the capacity to get things done. In the ten cities that responded to a DNH survey, there were only thirty-five draftsmen, surveyors, and other middle-level technicians (in addition to the four expatriate professionals in the capital). Eight cities reported a total of thirty out of forty vehicles and six out of twenty heavy machines to be in working order. Only five cities had any kind of budget or action plan for any year from 1975 to 1981. A long-standing confusion about who is responsible for assisting in these areas has recently been resolved, and national and provincial agencies have been designated to train new CEC personnel, as well as to help define plans and budgets.

Second, difficulties remain in assuring the responsiveness of the CECs to neighborhood concerns. This is particularly true in the older and denser shantytowns, where, in the absence of a strategy and resources for improvements, little is being done. But it is even the case in Maxaquene, where assistance is not always forthcoming. Residents have been waiting for three years for the CEC to establish construction permit procedures. In the interim, a limited black market in construction materials has allowed families to build permanent houses "illegally" on plots that they consider were defined during the upgrading period. One of these is the *bairro* secretary's neighbor, and the secretary is in danger of losing respect, whether his response is to support an unpopular prohibition against construction or to allow the construction to proceed.

The city assemblies have lost a lot of the initiative evident in the year following their re-election, and as a result they have not been filling the gap between neighborhood concerns and CEC actions. This has occurred in part because meetings of the assemblies have become increasingly irregular as the delegates, CEC presidents, and party committee members have been drawn into special campaigns. For example, there were almost no city assembly meetings in the year leading up to the Fourth Congress, and new elections scheduled for late 1982 were eventually put off to 1985. Other factors have contributed to this lack of urgency. As already noted, the delegates are elected on a citywide basis and continue to suffer from the lack of clear neighborhood or sectoral identities and responsibilities which could compel them to action. The combination of inexperience in civic political life and the tendency for the more articulate petty-bourgeois cement-city delegates to dominate the assemblies reinforces the bureaucratic underemphasis on shantytown problems and neighborhood-based responses to them.

On the other hand, regular meetings between the party committee for Maputo, all of the neighborhood secretaries, and representatives of the women's and youth organizations have been more successful. Local concerns have been raised very forcefully in these sessions, which have been reported in the press, and the CEC has been forced to respond to the meetings' resolutions. A more obviously delegated form of assembly might have the same effect.

Within the CECs, the lack of coordination between departments and empire-building on the part of some members have helped to perpetuate a personalized administrative style. The heads of public works departments seem to be particularly unresponsive to shantytown needs while using much of the limited municipal equipment and budget to take care of the cement city. Not surprisingly, in the absence of politically defined and monitored priorities resources are assigned in response to pressures from individuals or from particular GDs, with results that are often contrary to what might be considered good planning practices. The creation of administratively decentralized zones in Maputo may only reinforce this tendency, as more actors try to manipulate the same limited resources.

Despite these problems, the basic strategy of encouraging neighborhood residents and workers to organize themselves and to use the assemblies to keep their interests at the fore was reinforced in the debate leading up to the Fourth Congress. The lack of successful examples of this type of tactical collaboration suggests both that this is difficult political terrain and that the question of class struggle raised by the National Meeting will remain on the agenda for some time. There are no easy prescriptions for politicizing bureaucrats and technicians, although one suggestion—that they get out of their offices and spend more time working with their constituents—remains a powerful one.

In the past four years, DNH has consciously progressed from pilot projects and "fire-fighting" efforts to the establishment of a system of physical planning offices and procedures.[24] DNH has more clearly defined strategies and organization, and the results of its training programs have been impressive. By the end of 1982, there were 82 locality-level planning assistants and 102 district-level monitors who worked with the small expatriate professional staff, some of whom were based in the ten provincial planning services. A university level course is scheduled to begin in 1985, and by 1990 the first post-independence Mozambican architect/ planners will have been trained.

Urban planning and housing strategies are being considered in terms of their ability to contribute to local participation and self-reliance, and to strengthen the weak linkages between neighborhoods, assemblies, and the CECs. This effort includes the following:

Urban planning. Plans that will guide the growth of the major cities and towns over the next ten to twenty years are being prepared. These are based on an analysis of the towns and their regional context. Economic and population growth has been projected and the expansion areas for industry, housing, and so on have been located. The pressure of renewed rural migration has in turn led to the development of broader regional strategies, which are intended to limit the growth of the larger urban areas by encouraging the development of smaller centers.

If resources are to be allocated to regional programs, there must be renewed popular mobilization in existing and new urban areas. To some extent this has been taken into account. Green zones for food production are increasingly important, and improved access to jobs, clearer definition of neighborhoods, and better distribution of community facilities are also in evidence. It may, however, be necessary to pay more attention to *bairro*-based economic development and to the so-called informal sector. Even though all land has been nationalized and the restraints of the marketplace have been removed, it has not been possible to consider every long-range planning option. For example, the densities of the new housing areas are quite low, which may prove to be expensive when water and electricity lines are installed. Nevertheless, appropriate planning guidelines are slowly evolving.

In the short run, the implementation of planning objectives has been hampered by a limited understanding of the intended results of proposed interventions. Time and experience will lend force to efforts such as those of the Maputo city planners, who are trying to encourage the public transportation authority to redirect some of its very few bus routes so that settlement on new sites in outlying areas will be encouraged, while service to those *bairros* within reasonable walking distance of the city center will be reduced.

Local support for the plans will be enhanced as open and democratic planning procedures are adopted. In the absence of any detailed planning regulations, Xai-Xai, the capital of Gaza Province, was used as a pilot project to test ways of adopting and publicizing a new plan. A day-long session, attended by the city assembly and all the *bairro* secretaries, and presided over by the provincial governor (with help from DNH), studied and approved the plan in principle. A set of priorities that could be monitored by the assembly was adopted. At a later stage the plan will be reviewed by the *bairros* and detailed neighborhood plans will be prepared. Although many of the details remain to be worked out, the process should better link neighborhood and city needs, planning, and implementation—eventually leading to better living conditions. For this to happen, however, the GDs, assemblies, and CEC departments will have to work closely together.

Shantytown improvement. An estimated 1 million people are still living in unplanned and poorly serviced shantytowns, many of which are becoming increasingly dense and permanent as the GDs' capacity to halt permanent construction and new settlement is strained to its limit. The upgrading of existing shantytowns has not been resumed, at least in part because scarce resources are being used to develop new housing sites. At the same time, one pilot project was started in Quelimane and a second one is planned for Nampula, both intended to define a new strategy for upgrading, one that may more appropriately be called "improvement," rather than the Maxaquene "re-planning." The idea is that existing plot configurations will be maintained, with some space being redistributed, so that dislocations will be minimized, while basic infrastructure and community services will still be introduced. This should require less input from the state, particularly from professional staff, and much of the work can then be accomplished by the people in the community.

Housing. In accordance with resolutions from the Third Congress, the construction of houses in urban areas has been given relatively low priority. Most of the estimated four thousand new units have been constructed by state enterprises as part of large development projects. Much of this has been prefabricated housing, although there is evidence that this is expensive in terms of construction capacity and the use of cement, and that efforts may be better spent on improving site organization and training skilled workers. At the same time, there is a place for limited state support to the tens of thousands of eager self-help builders.

Aside from administrative barriers, the main constraint on urban house builders is the lack of material. Even natural materials, such as poles, reed, and thatch, are becoming ever more expensive in both local and foreign currencies as transportation costs increase for materials that are further and further away from the expanding towns. Cement is still in short supply and although distribution is partially controlled, a black market has developed. To alleviate this situation, various experiments are underway to make bricks and soil-cement blocks locally, as well as to use lime cements, plasters, and paints. Attempts are also being made to increase the usefulness and durability of local materials.

A complementary approach has been to rationalize and control the use of both local and conventional materials. Houses that can be built in phases and simple buildings that minimize the use of materials have been developed. The capacity to assist self-help builders is also being increased by developing workshops to produce building components and by licensing block makers and encouraging them to locate in planned areas. Appropriate building standards that can be administered in the *bairros* are being considered. In addition, some work is being done on housing cooperatives, but until the priority for this is clarified—in relation to material, transportation, and financial constraints—it is very preliminary. Most importantly, there is a strong desire to avoid the experience of many other countries, where the poorest are increasingly unable to participate in deciding and implementing their own housing needs. Finally, there is increased awareness of the very serious maintenance problems in the state-owned rental units, which still constitute the bulk of the conventional housing stock. Conditions have been deteriorating despite several management shake-ups and recent attempts at administrative decentralization. Rents remain uncollected, there are many empty units, and maintenance crews are generally unavailable.

South African-backed terror and destruction, drought, and the initial poor choice of a rural development strategy have all combined to put renewed stress on Mozambique's territorial situation. As a result, many of the attempts to improve rural conditions have collapsed and rural migration has once again increased dramatically. These are the least favorable conditions for improving life in the urban areas—it might even be argued that any attempt to relieve them is as likely to produce frustration as achievement. Nevertheless, resources continue to be made available to the cities and towns and the present conditions argue most forcefully for popular and self-reliant approaches to their use. This will continue to be the case even if pressures are reduced; recovery will be a lengthy process, and other areas of difficulty remain. These are of three types.

First, there are those limitations that can still be considered to be the legacy of the colonial past. It is obviously difficult to reverse entrenched and distorted territorial development patterns, regardless of the political will to do so, especially where resources are scarce. Even if ideas are clear and people can carry them out themselves, using local resources, it will still take many years to build up a new social, commercial, industrial, and transportation infrastructure. In the same way, it will only be possible to staff the new city administrations fully when the number of skilled personnel increases.

Second, there are the problems that have arisen since independence. These include many of the concerns debated during the initial period of the 1980 political offensive, such as the problem of insufficient talent and resources being directed to the rural areas and the overcentralized nature of state and party intervention. To some extent these have been overshadowed by events, but essential questions of class conflict remain. It remains to be seen whether it will be possible to consolidate an emphasis on neighborhood participation and democratic control of urban government. This is vital both to multiply the use of state resources and to ensure that class-biased priorities do not continue to disadvantage the shantytowns.

Finally, there are other imponderables to add to the geographic and political ones. There are no simple formulae for achieving an appropriate balance between urban and rural development, just as there is no clear choice of a technology to resolve housing problems. Solutions to these and similar questions will continue to depend on the interaction of considered policy and practical experience.

In the face of so many obstacles it would be difficult to be optimistic about the future if, in the years since independence, FRELIMO had not shown, on so many occasions, a remarkable capacity to respond to popular concerns and return to the successful methods of mobilization developed over the long years of armed struggle. Even though the specifics for a program that will reverse the territorial dilemmas inherited from the colonial past are not clear, the methods and directions are. With the development of a political process based on local initiative, self-reliance, and a politicized and popular use of state resources, the process of creating a new urban life in Mozambique can continue to move forward.

Notes

This chapter draws upon a previously published working paper, "The Urban Problematic in Mozambique: Initial Post-Independence Responses, 1975–80," Center for Urban and Community Studies, University of Toronto, 1982. The author worked on the Maxaquene upgrading project described in the chapter from 1977 to 1979. He subsequently returned to Mozambique to study the development of local government in 1980, and to work on guidelines for urban planning administration in 1983. The chapter and earlier paper are largely based on his research and experience.

1. Argument based on Center of African Studies, *Mozambican Miners in South Africa* (Maputo: Eduardo Mondlane University, 1979), pp. 2–3.
2. Information on the history of the port of Beira from Luis David, "Porto da Beira: O PASSADO," *Tempo* 496 (13 April 1980): 42–51. *Tempo* is a weekly newsmagazine published in Maputo.
3. Data on the value of building construction published by the Banco Nacional Ultramarino in a 1974 report, *Economic Information of Moçambique,* is indicative:

Year	Value of construction—buildings
1963	378,000 contos (1 conto = $37. Cdn.)
1964	344,000
1965	288,000
1966	371,000 [Start of war-related "boom"]
1967	438,000
1968	465,000
1969	584,000
1970	760,000
1971	886,000
1972	839,000

4. B.F. Jundanian, "Resettlement Programs: Counterinsurgency in Mozambique," *Comparative Politics* 614 (1974): 519–40.
5. Center of African Studies, *Relatório provisório sobre o desemprego no Maputo* (Maputo: Eduardo Mondlane University, n.d.), pp. 25, 39–41.
6. According to handwritten notes left by a departing engineer who worked for the city of Beira, it was said in 1893 that because of the quick methods of conceding land, the petitioner could get title in twenty-four hours while it took over one year in the rest of the province. Unfortunately, this resulted in a lot of confusion in later years when the city tried to determine the precise limits of each owner's property. As a result, some of the owners sued the city for huge indemnity payments despite having paid only pennies for land in the first instance.
7. For the history of Hulene neighborhood in Maputo see Albino Magnia, "Passado e presente do bairro do Hulene," *Tempo* (July 1979): 31–33.
8. Samora Machel, *Desalojamos o inimigo interno do nosso aparelho de estado* (Maputo, April 1980), p. 18.

9. There is some evidence that very low municipal taxation may, at least in part, have contributed to this situation. Sr. Valades of the new executive council of the city of Beira is studying this. Interview 17 July 1980.

10. The shantytown administrations were also closing down in the 1975–77 period and considerable effort was later required to transfer and reorganize responsibilities when the new municipal administrations were defined.

11. Information on Alto Maé from *Relatorio sobre o desenvolvimento da organização do bairro do Alto Maé*, RNC/Doc. 14/79, and from interview with neighborhood secretary 9 August 1980. Munhava story from interview with several neighborhood leaders, 27 July 1980.

12. Details from dispositions of the *Lei de Terras* (Law of Lands), which was passed in 1979. The law further provides for the transfer or sale of improvements on the land to parties other than heirs. All such sales must be approved by the state. In theory, this provides a measure for controlling speculation and "under the table" payments when houses are sold in more desirable areas (effectively reintroducing a land market.) In practice it has been very difficult to control this in other African countries. The strength and presence of the GDs might be put to advantage here if pressure on land increases should other programs, especially rural development, not succeed.

13. Under the terms of nationalization, owners were to be compensated. In practice there was very little compensation as most owners simply left the country. The nationalization also included rental units built out of "temporary" materials in shantytown areas. Following considerable confusion, these are now being turned over to residents in exchange for accumulated rental payments. Unlike the situation in surrounding countries, there were very few rooms for rent except in the shantytowns near Beira. The 1979 rental law permits roomers if the Ministry of Public Works is informed and the rent is set. This was done to encourage fuller use of "cement city" units but it may also become an incentive for future self-help builders. The GDs could play an active role in controlling speculation.

14. FRELIMO, *3rd Congress Program*, Doc. Inf. No. 10, CEDIMO, Serie E, 1978-06-23.

15. *Central Committeee Report to the Third Congress of FRELIMO*, Doc. Inf. No. 7, Serie E, CEDIMO, 1978-06-06, p. 56.
It is interesting to note that the first priority in civilian construction was in fact given to agriculture (e.g., irrigation works) and the next priority to improving transportation and communications, both in an effort to expand the productive base before investing heavily in the third priority area of housing and general improvements in living conditions. The supply of cement for all three was also severely limited by export commitments that totalled 50 percent of plant capacity and that were necessary to at least balance the imported inputs into production, which were running at 60 to 70 percent of capacity.

16. Barry Pinsky, "'Counting on Our Own Forces': The Maxaquene Up-

grading Project, Mozambique," *Habitat News* 3, no. 2 (November 1980). An educational slide/tape presentation is also available from TCLSAC, 427 Bloor Street West, Toronto, Ontario, Canada.

17. National Assembly Resolution no. 15/77, 23 December 1977, "Resolution on the General Bases for Organization of the People's Democratic State in Light of the Program of the Party," led to Laws 6/78 and 7/78, both dated 22 April 1978.

18. Samora Machel, "Opening Speech to the Third Session, National Assembly," CEDIMO, Doc. Inf. No. 18, Serie A, 1978-09-01, p. 5.

19. Renunião Nacional Sobre Cidades e Bairros Comunais, *Resolução sobre a organização dos grupos dinamizadores e bairros comunais* (Maputo: Imprensa Nacional, 1979), pp. 8–9.

20. Direcção Nacional de Habitação, *Approach to a Physical Planning Institution in a Socialist African Country* (Maputo, 1981).

21. According to the constitution, elections to village, locality, district, and city assemblies are to take place every two and one-half years and elections to the provincial and national assemblies every five years. The elections were not called specifically for purposes of the offensive.

22. In addition to the ten provincial capitals, the new city assemblies were chosen in Nacala, the third largest port, and Chokwé, an important agricultural center in Gaza province.

23. Interview by the author with the Maxaquene *bairro* secretary, December 1982.

24. Following the Fourth Congress, in May 1983, the DNH was renamed the National Institute of Physical Planning and moved from the Ministry of Construction and Water to the National Planning Commission, which is the central economic planning agency. Its director was elevated to the status of Secretary of State. These changes were much more than cosmetic. The DNH had long sought recognition of the necessity for more closely linking economic and land use planning in order to more successfully redress territorial disparities through the allocation of state resources.

Carol Barker

7. Bringing Health Care to the People

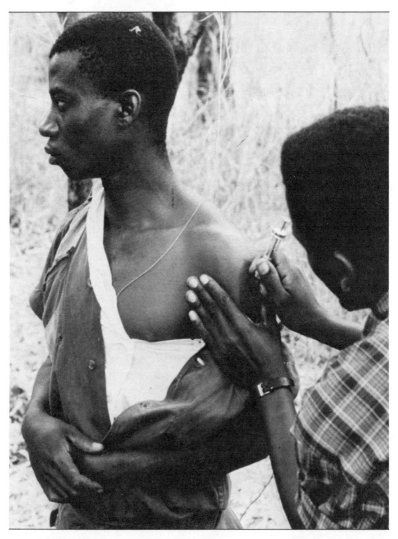

In the following chapter Carol Barker draws on her own firsthand experience of the Mozambican health sector—she was a cooperante *in the Ministry of Health with special responsibility for planning pharmaceutical policy—in the first half of the post-independence decade. She is thus able to underscore the considerable progress that the FRELIMO government has been able to make in this sphere, especially in comparison with the colonial situation. (This picture is fleshed out in even greater detail in a recent book,* Mozambique: Toward a People's Health Service, *edited by Gillian Walt and Angela Melamed [London: Zed Press, 1983].)*

Barker also identifies some of the key problem areas in the health sector, although some would argue that the temptations which she sees to revert to an urban-centered, curative, and high-technology medicine have more of the weight of the class interest of an emergent and newly privileged petty bourgeoisie behind them than she suggests. Her qualifications to any such reading of the situation are strong ones, however (even if her concluding concern regarding the ongoing need to democratize the health sector further does carry us back to an important and contested issue raised in the introductory chapters of this volume). We also know that difficulties linked to the war, to drought, and to economic crisis have more profoundly challenged, with each passing year, the ability of Mozambique to realize many of its high expectations in this sector—as they have in many other sectors as well.

> We have inherited a situation in which the vast majority of medical personnel and equipment is concentrated in towns to serve the majority who can pay, and what is more, this takes the form of intense racial and social discrimination in hospitals.
>
> —Samora Machel[1]

Health workers and medical structures were destined almost exclusively for the use of the colonial bourgeoisie and were concentrated in the major urban centers. The rural population and the people in the outlying town zones, the

working masses, found themselves practically
without medical aid.

—*Central Committee Report to the
Third Congress of FRELIMO*[2]

Health care is shaped by the nature of the society that provides it,
and the heritage bequeathed the health sector in Mozambique at
independence was scant indeed. The provision of health care had
been entirely determined by the needs of the colonial society, as the
records show.

Such curative health services as existed were largely set up for
the Portuguese settlers. They had come in the early twentieth century from a country that was backward in terms of health care, one
where infectious diseases were still prevalent.[3] They were afraid of
such local diseases as malaria and the plague. Malaria in particular
increased. A 1904 report analyzed the reasons:

This [increase] has its origins not only in the increase in Portuguese
emigration to this province and especially to Lourenço Marques, but
also in the economic crisis and consequently in the labor crisis which
has placed so tenacious a burden over this city. The majority of emi-
grants come as adventurers in the belief that one can just come since
the work is plentiful; but the days pass, the desired position is difficult
to find, and on arrival [the emigrant's] earnings are so paltry that at
times they barely cover food. In a short time he becomes the victim of
malarial poisoning, which disfigures [both] him and his small wage,
absorbing it, which absorption is facilitated by further attacks of this
illness.[4]

As the twentieth century progressed, the Portuguese continued
to receive most of the available hospital care. Disease patterns in
Portugal followed those of other European countries, with infectious diseases becoming less and less important, and the same was
true for the Portuguese in Mozambique. The preoccupation in the
hospitals was increasingly with coronary disease, cancer, obesity, old
age, and war casualties (among Portuguese troops), and the health
services became even more irrelevant to the majority of the population. "Tropical medicine" was only one specialty among many. Most
doctors graduating from Lourenço Marques University did not
have the first idea about how people lived outside of the European
quarters in the cities, let alone how to treat their ailments.

Not surprisingly, there was great preoccupation with preventing
the transmission of disease from Africans to Europeans, and with
the threat of infection, which was associated entirely with the African population. Mortality among those Africans who were hospi-
talized was much higher than among whites (white mortality due to
infectious diseases was actually very low).[5] This led to discriminatory treatment of Africans: natives who were suffering from

dangerous infections, or who were suspected to be, were in general treated as a threat to be controlled. Thus, for example, when precautions were needed to prevent the spread of an epidemic of plague from the Transvaal, all blacks entering Mozambique from South Africa were put in quarantine for ten days. Whites, on the other hand, had to agree to medical supervision for a twelve-day period, but were not detained.[6] And the 1908 annual report on health discusses the problems of organizing special suburbs for the black population—to "liberate the city of them"—as a public health measure of great importance.[7]

One intellectual legacy handed on to independent Mozambique thus included a set of ideas about the treatment of infectious disease that was antiquated, irrational, and even cruel, with an emphasis on isolation rather than prevention.

In the final decades of the colonial period, however, another set of concerns began to contribute to Portuguese attitudes to infectious disease. Portugal was conscious that its persistent hold on its colonies was anachronistic in world terms, and wished to be seen as a humanitarian benefactor of the indigenous inhabitants. The development of tropical medicine was one response to this concern for its image.[8] However, there were few real changes in health care. By 1959, a few vertical programs, such as the "Struggle Against Leprosy," had been launched, and the government had decided on a program to "allow preventive medicine to be practiced on a grand scale"[9]—allocating a grand total of five doctors and seven other health professionals.

Portugal also wanted to maintain a good relationship with South Africa. Since the economy of southern Mozambique was entirely bound up with that of South Africa, it was a matter of extreme practical importance that the Portuguese be seen by the South African authorities as scrupulous about any health considerations regarding the movement of people across the border. As a result, health control at the border was strict, and those who were turned back, or who were repatriated from South Africa, had to be catered for. Thus, for example, the 1927 annual health report refers to two services for repatriated natives, a leprosy hospital and a mental hospital.[10]

Civilizing and Assimilating the Natives

The 1927 health report refers to the Native Health Services as "our civilizing action."[11] It discusses the problem of the mentally ill, who are believed to have evil spirits and are therefore left to die, and it concludes that to permit things to continue in this fashion "cannot be allowed, since the prejudices of a race backward in civilization awake our humanitarian sentiments." The report also claims that curative health services in the interior will provide "a center of attraction to the rebellious native, obstinately holding to his traditional beliefs, to become attached to our scientific techniques." By the 1960s the Portuguese had devised "psychosocial brigades," consisting of a literacy worker, an agricultural advisor, and a nurse, who were sent to the rural areas with the twin tasks of curing bodies and winning hearts and minds.[12]

Until quite late in the colonial period, there seems to have been an explicit and close connection between health care, the military, and the police.[13] An important component of the health services was the "health company," which was staffed by health workers with military rank. This was not surprising, since the largest single group receiving medical attention was the military,[14] but it also provided the only medical care available to civilians in certain areas. This was not without problems, as we learn from a letter, written in 1911, from the director of the military and civilian hospital in Chibuto that suggests that many natives went without treatment rather than enter military quarters and have to undergo military formalities before seeing a doctor.[15] Similarly, the links between the Native Health Services and the police were explicit, about half the staff in rural health posts being indigenous policemen.[16] Presumably their function was to control the spread of infectious diseases.

Maintenance of a Skilled Workforce

Throughout the colonial period much health care was of an occupational nature, in that it was paid for, in part or in whole, by the employer. The 1908 annual health report gives a breakdown of fees received for treatment in Lourenço Marques in that year, and shows that half of all receipts were paid by military bodies, one-quarter by private patients, and one-quarter by employers, such as the railway, customs, police, port, etc.[17] The statistics on who received treatment show that blacks had a negligible chance of receiving medical care if they were not backed by an employer.[18]

Many workplaces, including big factories, plantations, and, in the latter decades of the colonial period, the railways and port, provided their own health services.[19] In the state health services, government employees received preferential treatment, as well as reduced fees or loans; how preferential the treatment was depended upon the employee's position in the hierarchy.

Fees were very difficult to come by for those not given the right to health services by virtue of their employment. For instance, at the end of the colonial period a hernia operation would have cost a third-class patient about 2,000 escudos, on top of which there would have been a "hotel" fee of about 50 escudos a day, plus charges for drugs, X rays, laboratory fees, etc. The total bill would thus have been several times the monthly income of a manual worker.

Doctors, by contrast, were the richest professionals in colonial Mozambique. Most spent a great deal of time in private practice, and for each separate duty performed within the state medical service there was a separate fee or "gratuity." It is perhaps noteworthy that some traditional (African) medical practitioners, especially in the urban areas, were also extremely well off, their consultation fees being very high.

FRELIMO's Health Program During the Armed Struggle

FRELIMO's health program began at the very start of the armed struggle, in 1964. The purpose of the first medical unit was to treat fighters wounded in the war, but it became immediately apparent that the most serious health problems were among the civilian population, including those wounded in enemy bombardments, and so the medical units began to concentrate on these. The number of available health workers was small however, and a crash training program for health aides was begun, followed by courses for medical assistants.

By 1965 a smallpox epidemic was raging, and FRELIMO launched a massive vaccination campaign. With the establishment of the first liberated areas in 1966, the need to provide medical aid to civilians increased dramatically. Sanitary education was begun. Smallpox vaccination continued, and vaccination against cholera was also begun. By 1968, 100,000 people had been vaccinated, far more than under any similar project under the Portuguese. FRELIMO also made its attitude toward the patient clear:

> An important part of our health system is that sick people are not inactive when they are in the hospital. If his physical condition and course of treatment permit, the patient is engaged in productive work, or follows a course in hygiene which enables him to become an agent of hygiene information when he returns to his locality.[20]

A network of health care facilities was gradually established, first by creating district health posts in the liberated areas, followed by central hospitals at the provincial and regional level, as well as mobile and semimobile units that could reach a larger number of people. Thus by 1972 the liberated areas in Cabo Delgado had 1 provincial hospital, 17 district medical posts, and 60 first aid posts, the latter staffed by 340 people trained to recognize common diseases and undertake minor surgery.[21]

Training programs for nurses and other health workers, however, declined between 1968 and 1971. This was a period of internal struggle. In the field of health, there were two opposing points of view about health care, described later by Samora Machel in broadly sketched images as the "capitalist hospital" approach and the "FRELIMO hospital" approach. The capitalist hospital was a center of exploitation, where a sick person could not enter and be treated in accord with his or her needs:

> Eminent doctors and university professors are brought in to treat the capitalist's cold, to cure the judge's constipation, while nearby children are dying, people are dying, because they do not have the money to call a doctor. . . . In the enemy zone, the rich man's dog gets more in the way of vaccinations, medicine, and medical care than do the workers upon whom the rich man's wealth is built.

FRELIMO hospitals, on the other hand, belong to the people:

> They are the fruit of the revolution. Our hospitals are far more than centers for dispensing medicines and cures. A FRELIMO hospital is a center where our political line—that of serving the masses—is put into practice. It is a center where our principle that the revolution frees the people becomes a reality.

The FRELIMO hospital is not a technical institution serving a narrow medical purpose, but a center for the education of patients, a center for production, with staff and patients together producing food; it is "one of our fighting detachments, a front line." Furthermore,

> whereas the capitalist hospitals have links with the exploiters, the settlers, because that is whom they serve, our hospitals have links with the people because they are there to serve them. Thus our hospital is a center of national unity, a center of class unity, a center of clarification of ideas, a center of revolutionary and organizational propaganda, a combat unit. Medical staff, students, orderlies, patients, and society as a whole are all closely united.[22]

In the liberated areas, FRELIMO was weaving a new fabric of society, eliminating not only colonial structures, but also local African class structures that had coexisted with colonialism. FRELIMO's ideas on health were an important part of the practical task of creating a health sector that worked, and this was a necessary component of the fight against reactionary aspects of the old order. As Machel put it,

> We conceived of the struggle in the field of health as a mass struggle, a struggle in which it is necessary to win the people to correct ideas and practices. . . . The principle task . . . is to provide the masses with indispensable scientific knowledge so that they can understand the

fight against the causes of illness. Health workers should be, above all, those who mobilize, organize, and orient the people.[23]

The First Conference of the Health Services, held in early 1973, laid out the broad outlines of *FRELIMO*'s health policy.[24] First and foremost, the conference insisted that politics must be in command: "In the relationship between politics and technique, politics comes first." The conference also insisted that health services, along with education, are of prime importance because for the majority of the population they are the most visible arm of the state, and the state will be judged by their success. Thus the aim of the health services should be "to cultivate love for the masses with whom they are in direct contact and among whom they represent our movement and political line." This approach leads to an emphasis on preventive medicine as a "way of serving the broad masses more effectively," not simply because it will cost less in the long run, but as a *political* necessity.[25]

The Period of Transition

In mid-1974 there were about six hundred doctors in Mozambique. Three hundred and fifty of these were in Lourenço Marques, two hundred at the University Hospital (to be renamed Maputo Central Hospital), and one hundred at Miguel Bombarda Hospital (although their prevailing work pattern was to spend mornings doing somewhat cursory rounds at the hospital, and to devote afternoons to private practice); the remaining fifty were in exclusively private practice. There were about fifty doctors in Beira; another twenty were in the north, either treating soldiers or in psychosocial programs. The rural population and the working masses in the outlying urban areas were thus virtually without medical care.

The Lusaka Accords, ending Portuguese rule and setting a date for independence, were signed in September 1974. In the months that followed, the transitional government gave some hints as to the direction of future health policy when it passed legislation prohibiting private medical practice by government-employed health workers. Trained health workers of all types were soon packing their bags and leaving for Portugal. When independence day dawned, Mozambique was left with only thirty trained doctors for the entire population of 12 million.

Health Care in Independent Mozambique

The following section will offer a general overview of FRELIMO's health policy from independence to the present, and will then examine in more detail the achievements in selected sectors. First, however, it is useful to review the major reforms and events in the health sector in the immediate post-independence years, as a background for discussing more recent developments.[26]

June 1975: Independence

July 1975: Nationalization of all health institutions and the abolition of private medicine.

October 1975: First National Health Seminar launches the National Campaign for Environmental Sanitation, mobilizing people to construct latrines under the slogan "Promotion of the Health of the Community by the Community." The number of pharmaceutical products allowed to be imported is reduced from 13,000 to 2,600.

June 1976: National Vaccination Campaign begun.

October 1976: Major speech by Samora Machel to the workers of Maputo Central Hospital, initiating the process of democratization and collective administration through ward councils.

January 1977: Publication of a new National Formulary, reducing the number of pharmaceutical products for use in the health services from 1,100 to 640.[27] Regulations are enacted making prescription of drugs by generic name mandatory.

February 1977: Third Congress of *FRELIMO* confirms the policy of giving priority to preventive medicine, and of extending coverage to the rural areas and to those communities already organized on a collective basis. First session of the National Health Coordinating Council, the overall planning and coordinating organ, henceforth to meet twice a year. Clarification of the strategies to be used in the struggle against the principal diseases endemic in the country (malaria, parasitic diseases, tuberculosis, leprosy, and sleeping sickness).

August 1977: Formation of two state enterprises, one for the importation of pharmaceutical products, the other for their internal distribution and sale. Although private commerce in, and importation of, medication continues, it is now a limited activity controlled by the state.

September 1977: First training course begins for *agentes polivalentes elementares,* village health workers for the communal villages. Publication in limited numbers of the National Formulary, defining the drugs that various types of paramedical workers are allowed to prescribe, according to their training and level of competence.

November 1977: Socialization of Medicine Law promulgated, providing for primary health care.

1979: Health portion of the total budget is 11 percent, or about US$3.80 per capita—about three times the size of the health budget at independence.

Early 1979: The state enterprise is given the exclusive right to import pharmaceutical products.

May 1980: Publication of a new edition of the National Formulary, listing only 355 medications.

Major Policy Directions in the Post-Independence Period

As described above, FRELIMO's general approach to health was defined during the period of armed struggle, and the policies laid down in that period have been retained since independence. What is of interest, then, is how those policies have been implemented and elaborated.

The nationalization of the health services in July 1975 was one of the first acts carried out by the newly independent government, and was seen as being of prime importance if health care was to be democratized and put at the service of the masses, and if the illness of some was no longer to be the basis of the livelihood of others.[28] Given the wholesale emigration of doctors and other health workers during the transition period, nationalization was an act of some bravado. There was not nearly enough staff to run the existing health services, much less to cope with the increased demand that was expected to result from nationalization.

On the other hand, making this one of its first acts may have been an extremely astute move on the part of the new government. With its line clear from the start, there was no time for the buildup of a movement in favor of leaving a small private health care sector. Those doctors who remained knew that they were relinquishing any hope of an income on the pre-independence scale, and no doctor stayed on for pecuniary reasons. On the contrary, those who stayed felt that they were engaged in an endeavor of utmost importance—literally holding the country's health services together. Medical students, largely from white upper- and middle-class backgrounds, had to decide whether to go with their families to Portugal, where they could pursue the kind of life they had always expected, or whether to break away from their families and stay and contribute to Mozambique's health services. (It was hoped that few would stay to finish their training at Mozambique's expense and then leave for Portugal, although this did in fact happen.) Nationalization also meant that the few people available for work in the health sector were automatically at the disposal of the state. Most important, early nationalization made it clear to the general public that FRELIMO was serious in its concern for health care.

Mozambican doctors refer to those early days with the air of those remembering a dream they cannot believe was true: the hectic days, the doubling-up on night duty to cover emergency admissions. Although the situation improved with the arrival of foreign medical personnel and with the graduation of the remaining medical students, in the meantime existing staff had to cope as best they could. The President paid his first visit to Maputo Central Hospital in August 1975,[29] a morale-building act, and underscored the necessity of effectively integrating those who had previously been in the private sector.

Two other important steps were taken in the first year after independence. In the field of preventive medicine, national sanitation and vaccination campaigns were initiated, and a new policy was instituted in the area of pharmaceuticals. Drugs and medical supplies are the interface, or link, between effective health care and the giant multinational corporations. FRELIMO was aware that the corporations wanted to sell Mozambique the most expensive—and therefore most profitable—drugs, and that this ran counter to the need of the health services for the most cost-effective remedies in order to be able to treat the maximum number of people. The effort to reduce the number of drugs available and to mandate prescription only of generics was an important part of FRELIMO's program. And with the enormous increase in the demand for health care since independence, this policy has continued to be of crucial importance.

By October 1976, however, it was recognized that while nationalization had been a gain for the Mozambican people, enormous problems remained; it was time to mount a new political offensive in the health care field. Machel chose Maputo Central Hospital as the site for a major policy speech, not only because it was a good place to assemble a large number of health workers but because it was (and is) a very visible symbol of health care in Mozambique. Machel noted that "If medicine is not politicized, it will be transformed into a dangerous instrument against the people and will undermine our political line."[30] He went on to describe the hospital as dirty and disorganized. He pointed out that this left abundant room for the enemy to create a center of rumor and intrigue, a center of demobilization of the people and of slander against foreign comrades. All this, he said, would lead to the idea that nationalization is bad and private medicine good, would demoralize the masses and create discontent, and would promote hostility against nationalization in general and FRELIMO and the government in particular.

While making it clear that he considered it likely that the hospital was a center of organized reaction, Machel also stressed that discontent among ordinary workers was the fertile ground on which such activity could grow. And discontent was rife because nothing had been done to dismantle the organizational structures—"the structures that keep us slaves"—that maintained the colonial face of the hospital.

The response had to be a revolutionary action that would smash the old structures and put collective and democratic ones in their place. If the hospitals could be transformed into a new, socialist model, other health institutions could be similarly organized. The first step, therefore, would be to create a structure of collective leadership among the workers in each ward and in each department: a ward council, laundry council, laboratory council, and so on.

In creating these new councils, not only would the colonial structures be dismantled, but so would the GDs, which had become moribund, with few workers attending their meetings—not a surprising development, since the meetings did not have a clear purpose. From now on there would be a hospital committee, whose composition would be determined by the political leadership of FRELIMO. It would give political direction to the hospital, aid in setting up the new collective structures, and ensure that foreign comrades were involved in what was going on and that patients were engaged in such activities as productive work and political and health education during their stay in the hospital. In addition, each ward council was to meet with the patients at least once every two weeks so that the latter could present their criticisms and suggestions.

At its Third Congress, held in February 1977, FRELIMO reevaluated policy in all areas. In the health sector, its report reaffirmed its general policy aim—"to preserve and continually improve the immense revolutionary capital constituted by the health of the masses."[31] More specifically, it underlined the political nature of health work: "Our policy . . . directs us to develop intense political work in the hospitals, engaging all health personnel and the patients in the struggle to eradicate divisionism, elitism, racism, and opportunism."[32] It also emphasized the origins of the party's views on health, which came not from intellectual abstraction but from "our practice, born in the liberated areas"; in fact, the latter was to be a continuing touchstone for health policy, even if identifying the precise implications of precedent established there for the far more complex post-independence situation was not easily done.

The Congress's directives laid down detailed goals for preventive medicine, defined target areas for the vaccination campaign, and stressed the need for effective maternal and child care and for family planning programs; it also announced the target of 1.25 beds per 1,000 population by 1980. The need to discover and use the country's heritage in the field of traditional medicine was stressed. And the importance given to the pharmaceuticals policy was underlined by the announcement that a pharmaceuticals industry would be set up within Mozambique itself.

It was during this same month that the first session of the National Health Coordinating Council was held. This overall body for planning health policy was to take the form of a meeting of provincial health cadres two times a year. It would draw up provincial health programs, which would then be sent back to the provinces and districts. After local health officials discussed the feasibility of each program, their conclusions would be fed back into the planning process at the national level.

Once policies were enunciated and a planning and consultative framework was in place, the next step in structuring the health care system was to establish a suitable legal framework. This was provided by the 1977 Socialization of Medicine Law.[33] This statute embodied the right of all citizens to health care and the obligation of the state to provide it; created a legislative framework for a primary health care system, with the local health center as the basic unit, and a structured referral process; set up uniform criteria for payment; and created a simple system for both referrals and payments, eliminating the colonial bureaucracy.

These measures were badly needed, as the health services had been stumbling along, relying on what remained of the old colonial structure. For instance, the lack of a structured referral process had meant that patients went straight to the large hospitals, even for minor ailments, increasing the waiting lines and diverting the attention of senior medical personnel away from difficult cases. In addition, the new law eliminated the system by which separate fees were charged for consultation, laboratory tests, and treatment, and in which the patient had to engage in a humiliating struggle to prove himself or herself poor enough to qualify for an exemption. Furthermore, the new system reflected the importance attached to preventive medicine. All prophylaxis and "basic" medicines—i.e., those for the treatment of the major communicable diseases—were now provided free of charge. Diagnostic tests and in-patient treatment also became free. Medical consultations cost a minimal US $.19 and even this charge could be waived or paid in kind in appropriate cases: the law states that inability to pay will never constitute a reason for withholding medical help. Clearly, this legislation has laid the groundwork for making health care truly accessible to a much larger proportion of the population.

In May 1978, the first plenary session of the *conselhos de base* (ward councils) met to make the initial review of the progress achieved in the restructuring of Maputo Central Hospital. Workers came forward to present the difficulties they had encountered; among these was the problem of understanding, and using, the links between the various political and administrative structures that now existed in the hospital, and also the problem of integrating expatriate *cooperantes* into the work.[34] The hospital director, who was also president of the restructuring committee, stated that "Although it still has negative aspects, our hospital is today more accepted by the community, which participates in our work and collaborates in all our programs."[35]

When Samora Machel returned to the hospital in October 1978, two years after the visit that had initiated the restructuring process, he agreed with these sentiments, noting that the hospital was "an example for the other health structures in the country to follow." But he also warned that the continuing "persistence of the old structures objectively sabotages the action of the councils, suffocates the initiative of the workers, and impedes revolutionary transformation."[36] On the whole, the ward councils were judged to have been useful in improving relationships between different levels of health worker and between worker and patient, and it was resolved to extend the idea to other parts of the country.

One more year of experience led to a further evaluation, and in December 1979 the President made a second major speech to health workers in which negative criticisms by far outweighed approval. He vigorously attacked "leftism" and "petty-bourgeois radicalism with a revolutionary facade."[37] He noted the lack of respect accorded to doctors, and asked that they be addressed as *Senhor Doctor;* he also said that people should wear neat uniforms to work. This emphasis gave the impression of a concern for appearances and order over and above political direction, and may have been interpreted by many as a shift to the right. At the same time, however, Machel confirmed that the ward councils would continue to be a forum for democratic discussion of issues among the staff, and that every individual would be responsible to them with respect to certain tasks. However, the chief of each council (normally the most qualified professional in the department whose council it was) would nonetheless take an active leadership role in the council while being sensitive to the views of all its members. He then pointed out that in many parts of the country the councils were weak or had never really got off the ground and many had no clear leadership because the dispersal of power had led to a dilution of responsibility. He saw the roots of this problem to lie in the social origins of those supposed to be in positions of leadership. *Cooperante* doctors often felt uncertain about exerting authority

330   A Difficult Road

over Mozambican staff, while Mozambican doctors, who were generally of European or Asian origin and from petty-bourgeois social backgrounds, were afraid to be seen giving orders. This "false modesty" was in fact "petty-bourgeois radicalism"—the inability of those who were called upon to give leadership to put politics before a preoccupation with their own class origins.

The political line was therefore not a new one, for ever since the days of the armed struggle the party had recognized the importance of giving power to organized groups of workers and at the same time maintaining strong leadership. In fact, Machel's speech was part of a broader political offensive, and one month later—in January 1980—a more general attack was launched in order to "dislodge indiscipline, negligence, and incompetence."[38] In another major address, Machel stressed these same problems: the use of populism and paternalism to promote incompetence and the use of ultraleftism to undermine authority. These, he said, were the tactics of the internal enemy, which had concentrated its activities in those state structures most closely linked to economic development and the satisfaction of the needs of the people, such as housing, health, and the productive sectors. A few days later, the Council of Ministers met "to study the implementation of the decisions announced by the President in the offensive and verify responsibility for errors and irregularities detected at the level of the state apparatus."[39]

At the Enlarged Consultative Council of the Ministry of Health, held in Maputo the following month, important policy statements were announced.[40] The first was the decision that all doctors and paramedical workers doing administrative work in the ministry must also do some clinical work each week. This move was to make better use of labor power, and to keep the administrators in direct contact with the hospitals, and with the patients and their illnesses, rather than seeing everything from the perspective of the office.

In a second policy area, the Council decided that the balance between curative and preventive medicine was wrong, because, as one participant put it,

> When anyone goes to the hospital and is poorly attended, he reacts much worse than if he went to a government office and was not attended at his own convenience. When someone goes to hospital, it is to be cured and not merely to take note of what preventive measures should have been taken if he had not fallen ill. Such an attitude has, politically, a very negative impact.

On the other hand, the council noted that advances in preventive medicine were unique and an example for all Africa. Therefore it was not that the party's priorities should be redefined, but that the efficacy and quality of care should be increased.

Third, in the area of training the national director noted that "We have been preoccupied with quantity rather than quality." It was decided to reduce the number of paramedical training centers and increase entry qualifications for trainees. It was also decided that after some years of postgraduate experience, doctors should have the right to specialized training in order to create a "core of national specialists and a national body of teachers capable of training doctors suited to the country."

Taken together, these three directives show a shift in emphasis toward curative medicine, and toward specialist, hospital-based care. Even the first—sending doctor-administrators back to the hospital—was more likely to increase their allegiance to "disease palaces" than to enlarge their views of the health service. When resource constraints are as great as they are in present-day Mozambique, "to plan," as Julius Nyerere once put it, "is to choose," and there is room for some concern about the choices that seem to have been made. On the other hand, it is important to underscore the point that in crucial areas, like the primary health care sector discussed in the following section, important progress continues to be made in improving the health of the masses.

The Primary Health Care Approach

> Primary health care is essential health care based on practical, scientifically sound, and socially acceptable methods and technology, made universally available to individuals and families in the community through their full participation and at a cost that the community and country can afford to maintain at every stage of its development in the spirit of self-reliance and self-determination.[41]

This primary health care (PHC) approach, first advocated formally by the World Health Organization and UNICEF at a conference held in Alma-Ata in 1978, advocates first-contact services and basic medical care within the framework of an integrated health service that embodies five key principles: (1) an equitable distribution of care; (2) community participation; (3) a focus on preventive and educational services; (4) the use of appropriate technology in the pharmaceuticals sector; and (5) a multisectoral approach. The slogan for the program—"Health for all by the year 2000"—was agreed upon by the conference participants.

The Mozambican delegation was extremely active at the Alma-Ata conference, producing a book that set out in detail the Mozambican approach to primary health care at the time.[42] Both this document and a 1982 Ministry of Health report support the WHO definition of PHC given above, and outline the same basic principles.[43] Both documents stress that these principles were being adhered to in Mozambique even during the liberation struggle—long before they were defined by WHO. Given Mozambique's socialist approach to health care, the PHC approach was indeed the most rational strategy. It would be simplistic, however, to assume that an approach adopted in the liberated areas, and under conditions of struggle, could be easily continued after independence. As we have seen, the colonial health service was structured toward entirely different ends: it was a class-biased, mainly curative, service, available at a price to the upper and middle classes, and providing health coverage for only 7 percent of the population.

This meant that independent Mozambique had a legacy of buildings and staff geared toward this kind of service, along with a public starved for health care—many of whom were now expecting to receive it. Those medical personnel who remained were clearly committed to altering the system, but they had received a colonial education and were caught between a political line they believed to be correct and roles that they found easier, and felt better equipped, to fulfill. The task of implementing the PHC approach in this context was therefore different both in scale and kind from that of developing basic health services in the liberated areas, where there had been no services before and where people were united by the war effort. How successful, then, have the new strategies been in achieving the goal of health for all?

Health Service for All

For a start, since independence the structure of the health services has been both simplified and rationalized. Certain outdated units—leper hospitals, anti-leprosy posts, and specialized health posts dealing only with children's diseases or tuberculosis—have been abandoned in favor of a more integrated approach. Health care at the primary level is now centered on health posts and health centers. The health post is the smallest unit, and the village health worker operates from it. Three-quarters of the posts planned for the 1980s will be built in communal villages using local labor and materials. The health center, by contrast, serves a group of villages or urban area with a population of between 30,000 and 35,000 people. It is the linchpin of the system, providing an integrated preventive and curative service, including maternity care. Health centers are staffed where possible by a team, including medical assistants, a preventive medical worker, a midwife, a nurse, and a technician.

The second level of care is the hospital—rural hospitals in the countryside and general hospitals in urban areas. These are usually in the main town or population center of each district. It is hoped that they will offer a certain level of specialization in internal medicine, surgery, pediatrics, and obstetrics/gynecology, although by 1982 78 out of the 109 districts still lacked a hospital.

The third level of care is represented by the seven provincial hospitals, and the fourth level by the three central hospitals, in Maputo, Beira, and Nampula. The entire structure is shown in Table 1.

Table 1
The Structure of the Mozambican Health Service[44]

Type of unit	No. of units	No. of beds	No. of new units 1977–1981
Health posts	629	5,710	333
Health centers	285		28
Rural general hospitals	26	2,308	1
Provincial hospitals	7	1,489	—
Central hospitals	3	2,564	—
Psychiatric hospitals	4	1,109	—

It is thus clear that both the intensity and the amount of health care have increased since independence, and the proportion of the national budget allocated to health has also increased, from 3.7 percent in 1974 to 10 percent in 1979. In 1959, expenditure on health care amounted to only about US$.50 per capita;[45] by 1979, per capita expenditure was US$3.80, and by 1981 it was US$5.40. In 1974, only 7 percent of the population had access to health services; by 1980, 30 percent had access to curative and preventive facilities at the primary level, and certain preventive activities, such as vaccination campaigns, reached an even greater number of people. The population served by each primary health care unit decreased from an average of 16,200 in 1977 to 11,600 in 1981. And between 1975 and 1983, 3,250 new health workers were trained.

Increasing the Equity of Distribution of Health Care

Yet despite the fact that basic health services exist in many parts of Mozambique where there were previously none at all, and despite a major effort to improve facilities and service at the primary

Table 2
Distribution of Health Resources in 1979[46]

	Maputo	All provincial capitals	All other districts
Percent of total population	5.9	17.5	82.5
Percent of doctors	52.5	89.8	10.2
Percent of all health workers	32.1	66.1	33.9
Average population per doctor	4,450	7,750	257,500
Average population per health worker (all kinds)	180	290	2,670
Average population per primary care unit	12,416	13,095	13,600
Annual per-capita out-patient consultations	1.4	1.1	0.4
Annual per capita expenditure for personnal (US$)	15.00	9.30	0.85

level of care, major inequalities in the distribution of resources still exist. Table 2 gives some idea of their extent, and is the governments' own attempt to analyze the extent of the inequality—not surprisingly, no such attempt was made in colonial times.

It is clear from these figures that while primary care is available on a reasonably equal basis, the provincial capitals and cities remain far better off than the rural areas. Yet even these discrepancies represent an advance over the colonial situation, in which providing health care for all was not a significant concern.

Moreover, one further sign of the increasing equity of resource distribution can be gleaned by comparing allocations for different kinds of health units. Table 3 shows a real shift in the proportion of resources going to quaternary (central hospital) care in favor of lower levels, both in real terms—a feat that health planners elsewhere regarded as politically impossible—and as a percentage.

Detailed evaluation of progress toward the PHC approach is always bedeviled by the need for appropriate statistical data over a period of time. A number of indicators have now been developed for this purpose, including measures for assessing health policy as well as health care, prevention as well as cure, and requiring the collection of socioeconomic data to put the health data in perspective.[48] It will take several years, however, before accurate results can be obtained from the new evaluation process. In the meantime, impressions back up that data which is available. In what follows, I will examine a few key areas that both the government and the proponents of the PHC approach agree are of central importance: village health workers, traditional medicine, appropriate technology for the pharmaceuticals sector, and community participation in health care.

Village Health Workers

As is the case with an increasing number of countries, Mozambique has opted to train village health workers *(agentes polivalentes elementares)* to operate at the lowest level of the health care pyramid and provide the link between the community and the health professional. Village health workers do not work full-time at the job, but are volunteers selected by their own village or cooperative and given six months training in the basics of environmental health, preventive medicine, and the recognition of the most common local medical conditions; they are taught to treat a few ailments and refer the rest to a health center. Communities that send volunteers for training are expected to support them on their return so that they can do the job. And in fact, although volunteer health workers are supposed to work only part-time, leaving some hours for production and household activities, they do spend a larger part of the week on health activities than is the case in many other countries.[49]

Under the regular supervision of the staff of the nearest health center, volunteer health workers are expected to play an important role in community mobilization on health issues, organizing such activities as vaccination campaigns and the construction of latrines,

Table 3
Allocation from the Health Units Budget[47]

	1978		1980	
	US$ millions	*Percentage*	*US$ millions*	*Percentage*
Total	4.18	100	5.01	100
Central hospitals	2.34	56	2.10	42
Provincial hospitals	0.59	14	0.85	17
Remaining health units	1.25	30	2.05	41

promoting the hygienic treatment and storage of water, encouraging preventive malaria treatment, treating a restricted number of common complaints, giving first aid, and keeping records of their activities.

Up to 1980, 664 volunteer health workers had been trained, and 6,000 more are to be trained by 1990, despite acknowledged difficulties such as a high drop-out rate—15 percent of the first 664 dropped out—and the inability, or unwillingness, of the villages to support their volunteers on their return from training.[50] (Sometimes production does not yield enough surplus to pay the volunteer in cash or kind; sometimes there are organizational problems.) In 1980 the National Health Coordinating Council resolved to take two actions to help reduce the drop-out rate: the first was to offer the program only to those villages considered to have adequate levels of production and organization, and the second was to give the volunteers greater curative medical skills, thus enabling them to better meet the villagers' expectations and reducing the volunteers' own frustration at not being able to meet those expectations. Recently, annual one-month refresher courses have also been instituted.

One problem with the volunteer health worker program—a problem common to all countries where such programs exist—is that the need to train huge numbers of volunteers in a cost-effective way runs counter to the desire to involve the communities in designing the volunteer's work and choosing the criteria for his or her selection, which might be expected to lead to greater commitment. But the village is simply asked to choose a person with a minimum of four years of school, who may well be one of the richer and more powerful members of the village, for these are the people who have, until now, been able to afford schooling. In such cases, social barriers may make it difficult for the volunteer to communicate with the poorer village members. In addition, those with formal education are likely to be the younger members of the village, and so less likely either to command respect in general or to be taken seriously on matters of family health—particularly if the volunteer is not married or has no children. The villagers may also feel reluctant to tell their health problems to a young unmarried volunteer. Finally, a young volunteer is much more likely to regard his or her training as the first rung on a career ladder, and thus may leave the community when opportunity offers, leading to the high dropout rate.

On the other hand, older people with families may be less willing to leave home for the six-month training period. This problem could be solved by shortening the time—it is considerably shorter in other countries—or by sharing the training among two or three village members, perhaps one to learn about maternal and child care and another to act as health promoter, and so on. There are also infrastructural problems that must be tackled if the program is to flourish. In terms of his or her tasks, the volunteer health worker leads an isolated existence and badly needs the support of the health services, but supervision is acknowledged to have been irregular and/or ineffective. Transport problems make it difficult for volunteers to meet together at the local health centers and the delivery of medical supplies is often irregular, leaving the volunteer without the tools needed to demonstrate credibility.

Traditional Practitioners and Their Medicine

In international health circles there is a trend toward incorporating traditional practitioners and their remedies into the primary health care system. In part this reflects a growing feeling that scientific medicine is overmechanistic, and that something can be gained from more holistic traditional approaches. In part it comes from an increased awareness that traditional structures and values cannot simply be ignored or uprooted. At the same time, many governments, while wishing to demonstrate their ability to provide primary health care, lack the resources—or are unwilling to redistribute the resources they have—to do so. The idea of involving traditional practitioners in modern health care is therefore both attractive and convenient.

Mozambique has not attempted to cover the gaps in the National Health Service in this way, but has instead begun to analyze the activities of the traditional practitioner. As in other parts of Africa, traditional medicine in Mozambique has been passed on orally, and most peasants are able to describe several simple herbal remedies. But for outside help, they would go to the *curandeiro,* or medicine man, who is much more than a herbalist and treats other than physical ailments. The *curandeiro* is at once doctor, psychologist, marriage counselor, insurance agent, weather forecaster, and even priest. There are also different kinds of *curandeiro:* some rely almost entirely on magic; others use various combinations of ritual and herbalism. For instance, many *curandeiros* use bones as a diagnostic tool, throwing them on the ground and reading the resulting pattern. Herbal remedies are prescribed if a physical ailment is diagnosed. *Curandeiros* pass on their knowledge to a family member, although there is a belief that only those can be trained who have, in the course of recovering from a serious illness, been bidden by the spirits to learn how to cure others. Nowadays *curandeiros* may take apprentices who can afford to pay for their training. Many *curandeiros* became wealthy during the colonial period, when the government health services were weak. Although the traditional payment was a gift in kind—a chicken, for instance—*curandeiros*, like other peasants, were forced into the money economy by the need to pay taxes to the colonial authorities, and so began to sell their services for cash. Some were very successful, their reputations spreading far, and people traveled long distances for consultations—not only Africans, but Europeans as well. Given the wide-ranging role they played in society, many *curandeiros* came to have extensive political influence. The result was that by the time of independence there were many different kinds of *curandeiro*, including rich practitioners in urban settings and some rural areas, fetishists, and herbalists.

The distinctive feature of Mozambican policy toward traditional medicine is that this diversity is recognized. It is not assumed (as it often is among academic "experts") that if practitioners are "traditional," they are therefore "of the people." Academics often see rural societies as classless, and the *curandeiro* as a kind of people's doctor, ready to become the village health worker and acceptable to all. The Mozambican government recognizes, however, that while some *curandeiros* will be accepted in their communities, others will not, and so it has not singled them out to play a special part in the primary health care system. Village health workers are selected by the villagers, and if a village happens to choose a *curandeiro,* that is its decision. But if it selects a candidate with no traditional medical knowledge, it is assumed that there is a good reason for this. Following this reasoning, associations of *curandeiros* are officially disregarded, and traditional practitioners who wish to make their views known must use the political structures of the party, the People's Assembly, and the democratic mass organizations, just like anyone else. *Curandeiros* are not forbidden to practice, but they are given no special recognition; further, since health care is free, *curandeiros* are not allowed to charge fees. (However, it is left to the vigilance of local people and community organizations to enforce this ruling, and they are not always able to do so.)

But at the same time that the *curandeiros* themselves are given no special place in the health care system, traditional practices are taken seriously. FRELIMO's position was made clear in the *Report of the Central Committee to the Third Congress* in 1977: "In the field of traditional medicine we will instigate research, eliminate obscurantist practices, and scientifically evaluate the positive aspects."

The aim is to make those herbal remedies that are of genuine therapeutic value available for use in the state medical sector as one means of restoring their heritage to the people. The result has been that the *curandeiros*, who were at first fearful that their practice would be outlawed altogether, have been extremely cooperative, helping the Ministry of Health to investigate their herbal remedies. Three hundred and fifty *curandeiros* have been trained to collect and preserve proper botanical specimens of the plants in their pharmacopia and to provide detailed descriptions of how they are prepared and used.

This single element—herbal remedies—cannot be abstracted from the integrated system of traditional medicine, with its concepts about the nature of health and illness. A more holistic approach would provide useful knowledge about the way people think about physical illness, how taboos affect behavior, how villagers related to health workers, and so on. It is a pity that only the medicinal plants have been investigated, because research that integrated botanical and sociological studies would have been far more valuable. On the other hand, the pharmacological and biochemical investigation of herbal remedies may itself provide enormous benefits. The first fruits of such research will be to show how traditional remedies work; this will be followed by the commercial development of some of these remedies, for as the petrochemical base for pharmaceuticals manufacture diminishes, there will be a growing need for medicinal plants as a source of drugs, not only in Mozambique but worldwide. Any achievements in this area will thus be of far more than local interest. Although on a world scale, studies of the drug content of plant species abounds, such research is being carried out under government sponsorship in relatively few developing countries. Most work in this field is done by the multinationals, which are only interested in new (and therefore profitable) drugs and are unlikely to be enthusiastic about the discovery of a herbal source for an existing drug. Mozambique, on the other hand, could exploit such a discovery by setting up local production, freeing itself somewhat from the present total dependence on imports.

Appropriate Technology

Too often in a third world context the term "appropriate technology" is interpreted to mean the provision of low-level, cheap technology for those who cannot afford anything better—while continuing to provide high technology for those who can. Applied to medicine, this means that while the most desirable forms of health care involve expensive drugs and highly complex equipment, basic health services at the primary level should be able to make do with almost nothing. Two examples from the Mozambican experience show the obvious fallacies of this assumption. The first concerns the equipment found in the major hospitals after independence. Some doctors, knowing they would be gone by the time their actions were discovered, had either succumbed to salesman's bribes or set out to waste money as an act of sabotage, and at independence expensive new equipment was found lying around, in some cases not even unpacked. Given the lack of skilled labor, however, much of it was too complex to run or maintain and had to be abandoned, a sheer waste of resources.

The second example concerns the equipping of the small health center laboratories that are an important part of the diagnostic technology now available at the primary care level. The cheapest and simplest supplies for such labs—the lowest level of technology—would have been bottles of chemicals from which to make up the test reagents. The decision, however, was to purchase already made-up reagent kits. The laboratory worker merely had to add the patient's sample to a drop of the reagent or dip an impregnated piece of paper into the sample and watch for a color change. Although such kits are more expensive, they are well worth it in a situation where laboratory technicians have little training or basic education and work unsupervised. In other words, "appropriate technology" is technology that will be effective in a given circumstance, taking into account not only the available resources but potential use and maintenance, the availability of manpower and its level of skill, and so on. The appropriate technology must be carefully chosen for each level of a health service, or the high technology often needed in the hospital will swallow up resources desperately needed at the primary level.

Pharmaceuticals are the point at which the world of technology most forcibly impinges on the health sector. In most underdeveloped countries, drugs take up one-third of the national health budget (29 percent in Mozambique in 1979). At the health center level, however, drugs can take up an even larger part of the budget, since the share going to personnel is small. A rational pharmaceuticals policy is therefore an essential part of a rational primary health care strategy, and it is an area that, as we have seen, has received maximum attention in Mozambique.

Prior to independence drug costs were borne by patients, self-medication was frequent, and, despite official regulations regarding pharmaceutical imports, there was only minimal control of what came into the country and onto the market. The price structure within the pharmaceuticals industry encouraged the import of those products with the highest profit margins, and the tendency was for doctors to prescribe—and pharmacists to encourage the sale of—extremely expensive products.

Conscious of the need for financial stringency, the Mozambique government has attempted to structure drug expenditures to meet the needs of the mass of the people. The main premises on which this policy is based can be summarized as follows:[51]

(1) Between 80 and 90 percent of ailments can be cured using a very few inexpensive drugs.

(2) New drugs are disproportionately expensive and their efficacy and safety are often unknown, while older drugs that have been tried and tested tend to be cheaper.

(3) Prescribing medications by generic name allows the bulk purchase of drugs at a low price.

(4) Furthermore, a name brand is not necessarily a guarantee of quality.

(5) The prescribing powers of less educated health workers should be limited.

(6) The promulgation of therapeutic rules and guidelines, along with the education of health workers, can lead to increased cost effectiveness in drug-prescribing habits.[52]

The acquisition of medications has been improved enormously by careful planning, particularly in bulk purchasing and in the institution of an international bidding system. The National Formulary is now a slim volume containing only 355 carefully chosen therapeutic substances. Some drugs are now being obtained for up to 100 percent less than they were in 1975! In real terms, of course, total drug expenditures have risen because health care has become more widely available. Further, distribution has improved in favor of the lower levels of health care. For instance, while in 1975 the Maputo Central Hospital received 48 percent of the drug budget, in 1979 it received only 10 percent. A great effort has been made to assure equitable distribution among the provinces, although much remains to be done. Better distributioin waits in part upon an improved transportation network, for the rail links and roads inherited from the Portuguese were constructed to facilitate exports, not to service the economy as a whole or to bring supplies to the mass of the people. Certain changes have helped alleviate this problem, however: for instance, the use of ministry vehicles has been rationalized, and air transport is employed in certain circumstances. But until resources permit a vastly expanded road and rail system, the basic problem of distribution cannot be solved.

Community Participation

The active participation of local communities in identifying health problems and finding appropriate solutions is recognized as a crucial aspect of the primary health care approach. During the independence struggle, the creation of the most basic health infrastructure in the liberated zones depended almost entirely on the efforts of the people themselves. As a result, the Third Congress explicitly endorsed the continuation of such participation: "We must mobilize and organize the people so as to enable them to participate actively in the struggle against disease, implementing the slogan that everyone is to be transformed into a health agent to promote sound hygiene, guard the health of the community, and keep the people in good health in order to carry on the struggle."

While community participation is often taken to refer only to the village level, clearly the efficacy of the concept depends on an overall decentralized planning structure, with meaningful interaction up and down the structure in terms of both making and implementing policy. At this point, some flow from national to local levels has been achieved; proposals issued from the central and provincial levels are discussed by workers at the district and even lower levels. Problems arise when proposals are too detailed and the main issues submerged, and when workers lack the experience to challenge inappropriate programs or unrealistic targets and provide good alternatives. Coordinating structures exist at the district and health center levels, and these attempt to secure the cooperation of the party, the ministries, the mass organizations, the women's organization (OMM), and local committees. Nevertheless, it is also true that, in practice, active participation in the planning process at the local level has not been sufficiently stressed; instead, communities have been encouraged to focus more narrowly on implementing established policies and on organizing health activities based on local resources, such as environmental sanitation, immunization campaigns, and construction of health facilities. Among mass organizations enlisting local involvement in implementation, the OMM has been particularly active, organizing its members to monitor infant mortality rates and take part in maternal and child health programs and training them as nutrition teachers. But mobilization from above, even when successful and directed toward filling real needs, is no substitute for a decentralized planning structure that permits real policy debates and decision-making at the local level and that promotes initiatives from below, including the village level.

Rather surprisingly, the documents of the Fourth Congress tell us little about future strategies in the health sector; the directives on health consist of technical objectives and targets for the training of health workers, increasing health units, decreasing morbidity due to particular diseases, and the like.[53] In other words, the directives deal primarily with health services and health professionals. Yet it is clear that an exclusive preoccupation with delivery of health services will not lead to "Health for All by the Year 2000"; as past party pronouncements have made clear, a strictly technical approach to health would in fact be a reactionary one. There is, of course, every reason why those in the health sector should be concerned with increasing that sector's tangible resources, and under the fearful pressures of the present—war, drought, and economic crisis—this is all-the-more tempting a preoccupation. In this as in other sectors, however, it will be important to see whether important intangibles—the active involvement and commitment of the people in health promotion, the ability to see health first and foremost as a political issue—can be brought back to the forefront of strategy for the future.

Notes

Most of the information used in this chapter was collected during the period from 1976 to 1979, when I was employed as a *cooperante* in the Ministry of Health. I would like to thank the vice-minister of health, the national directors of the various sections of the central ministry, the director of the faculty of medicine, and the director and staff of the health services for Maputo for their cooperation when I paid a return visit to update my information. I am also extremely grateful to the director and staff of the Archivo Historico de Mocambique.

1. Samora Machel, "FRELIMO's Tasks in the Struggle Ahead," *Mozambique Revolution* 60 (July–September 1974): 20.
2. *Central Committee Report to the Third Congress of FRELIMO* (London, 1977).
3. Discussion of the health situation in the annual reports of the health services shows a preoccupation with "tropical" diseases, with very little attention being given to certain other diseases even though they appear to have been fairly prevalent—e.g., tuberculosis, syphilis, influenza (the latter found almost entirely among African patients). Presumably such diseases caused less apparent concern because the Portuguese did not regard them as unusual.
4. Archivo Historico de Mocambique (AHM), Secretario Geral do Governo da Provincia de Mocambique, Reparticao de Saude, *Relatorio do servico de saude da Provincia de Mocambique e estatistica hospitalar, ano de 1904* (Lourenço Marques: Imprensa Nacional, 1905), p. 9.
5. This point is made in AHM, Colonia de Mocambique, Direccao dos

Servicos de Saude e Higiene, *Relatorio e estatistica dos servicos de saude, Ano de 1927,* (Lourenço Marques: Imprensa Nacional, 1929), p. vi and introduction; and also in the 1908 report (see n. 7), pp. 43–45.

6. See AHM, *Relatorio do servico . . . 1904,* section on public health.
7. AHM, Provincia de Mocambique, Reparticao de Saude, *Relatorio de servico de saude 1908* (Lourenço Marques: Imprensa Nacional, 1909), chap. 1.
8. See for example, J. Fraga de Azevedo and J. Pedro de Faria, *Quatre siecles au service de la sante humaine* (Lisbon: Agencia Geral do Ultramar, 1952), which argues that the Portuguese were the first from the Western world to discover the tropics, describe tropical diseases, and pioneer the discipline of tropical medicine.
9. AHM, Portugal, Provincia de Mocambique, Direccao dos Servicos de Saude e Higiene, *Relatorio e estatistica, Relatorio Annual* (Lourenço Marques: Imprensa Nacional, 1959).
10. See AHM, *Relatorio e estatistica,* pp. xx, xxviii. The mental hospital was to be for indigenous cases only; mentally sick Europeans were sent to the hospital in Pretoria.
11. Ibid., pp. xvii, xxvii.
12. D. M. Abshire and M. A. Samuels, eds., *Portuguese Africa: A Handbook* (London: Praeger Publishers, 1969), p. 194.
13. According to the 1959 health report, it was in 1945 that the Military Medical Services became the Civil Medical Services.
14. In the 1908 health report (p. 47), one-third of the hospital cases treated in Lourenço Marques were military. The same report lists only 35 civilian staff employed by the health services, whereas as of December 1, 1908, the "health company" had 139 men (p. 161). Many of the medical auxiliaries were indigenous Mozambicans, and desertion from the company is mentioned as a problem (p. 162).
15. AHM, Cx 595, H-3148, Register of correspondence to the authorities from the director of the military and civil hospital of Chibuto; letter to the director of health services, 12 January 1911.
16. AHM, Colonia do Mocambique, Direccao dos Servicos de Saude, *Relatorios e estatistica dos servicos de saude, ano de 1937* (Lourenço Marques: Imprensa Nacional, 1941).
17. AHM, *Relatorio do servico de saude 1908,* p. 175.
18. Ibid., pp. 46–47. Ninety percent of patients treated were male, and 95 percent were of working age.
19. The 1927 health report (p. xix) gives details of the types of arrangements that were made between private firms and the state. Firms in the urban areas wishing the state to provide basic health care for their workers paid fixed amounts to the government health services. Other firms, such as the Companhia de Zambesia, which had a large number of employees out of reach of existing services, came to an arrangement whereby the hospitals constructed by them were substantially subsidized by the state.
20. FRELIMO, quoted in *Daily News* (Tanzania), 29 June 1972.
21. David Martin, in *Daily Telegraph* (London), 12 July 1972.

22. Samora Machel, "Our Hospitals' Role in the Revolution," *Mozambique Revolution* 58 (1974): 12–17.
23. *Central Committee Report to the Third Congress of FRELIMO*, pp. 14–15.
24. "The Struggle to Build a Healthy Mozambique," *Mozambique Revolution* 55 (1973): 17–18.
25. Eighth Meeting of the Central Committee, "Resolution on Health," *Tempo* 293 (16 May 1976): 44.
26. This chronology is the Ministry of Health's own view of the most important landmarks, summarized and translated from RPM, Ministerio de Saude, *Cuidados de saude primarios em Mocambique* (Maputo, 1978).
27. The 640 products included surgical dressings and diagnostic reagents. The total number of different therapeutic substances was 408.
28. *Principal legislaçao promulgada pelo Governo do Transicao, vol. II* (Maputo: Imprensa Nacional, 1975), Decreto-Lei 45/75.
29. At independence the old Hospital da Universidade and Hospital Miguel Bombardo, on adjacent sites, were combined to form the Hospital Central de Maputo.
30. Samora Machel, "Transform the Central Hospital into a Hospital of the People," speech, 6 October 1976, published by the Department of Information and Propaganda (Maputo, 1976).
31. *Tempo* 333 (20 February 1977): 26.
32. Ibid., p. 54.
33. The complete text of the law is to be found in *Tempo* 365 (2 October 1977).
34. *Tempo* 399 (28 May 1978): 10.
35. Ibid.
36. *Tempo* 419 (6 October 1978): 21.
37. Samora Machel, "Organizar a batalha a frente da saude," reprinted in *Tempo* 479 (16 December 1979): 24.
38. Samora Machel, speech of 18 March 1980, reprinted in *Tempo* 493 (23 March 1980): 20.
39. Ibid., p. 61.
40. *Tempo* 500 (11 May 1980): 14.
41. Director-General of the World Health Organisation and the Executive Director of the United Nations Children's Fund, *Primary Health Care,* a joint report, International Conference on Primary Health Care, Alma-Ata, USSR, 6–12 September 1978 (Geneva and New York: WHO, 1978), p. 24.
42. Republica Popular de Mocambique, Ministerio de Saude, *Guidados de saude primarios em Mocambique* (1978).
43. Ministry of Health, *Report of the People's Republic of Mozambique"* WHO/UNICEF Primary Health Care Workshop, Nazareth, Ethiopia, 8–18 February 1982 (mimeo).
44. Ibid. The figures for new construction are from FRELIMO, *Relatario do Comite Central ao IV Congresso* (Maputo, 1983).
45. AHM, *Relatorio Estatistica.* Actually, of the 129 million escudo health budget in 1959, only 15 million escudos were allocated for the "native

health services"—intended for the bulk of the estimated 5.7 million inhabitants. About 85 percent of the money went on health care for the 117,000 *civilisados.*

46. Ministry of Health, *Report of the People's Republic of Mozambique.*
47. Ibid.
48. Ibid.
49. UNICEF/WHO, *National Decision-Making for Primary Health Care,* study by the UNICEF/WHO Joint Committee on Health Policy (Geneva: WHO, 1981).
50. Ministry of Health, *Report of the People's Republic of Mozambique; Tempo* 519 (29 September 1980); *Tempo* 500 (11 May 1980): 14.
51. A more detailed account is given in Carol Barker, "Are 300 Drugs Enough?" in G. Walt and A. Melamed, eds., *Mozambique: Towards a People's Health Service* (London: Zed Press, 1983).
52. On this point, see C. Barker, C. Marzagao, and M. Segall, "Economy in Drug Prescribing in Mozambique," *Tropical Doctor* 10 (1980): 42–45.
53. Fourth Congress, "Directivos economicas e sociais—saude," *Tempo* 665 (10 July 1983): 35–37.

Stephanie Urdang

8. The Last Transition?
Women and Development

The following chapter reflects the ongoing situation of women in Mozambique and the continuing commitment to their liberation.

The problems and obstacles that have undermined the process of transformation in Mozambique in general have had particular impact on women. In particular, the failure of the policies of agricultural development, for the reasons outlined elsewhere in this book, have had specific implications for women as they are almost exclusively responsible for family production. Hence the inability of women to fulfill this critical task and to gain the level of participation in development and in the society as a whole has undermined the process toward their liberation. One of the recent events to have far-reaching implications for women's role in development was the decision at the Fourth Party Congress in April 1983 to focus primarily on family farming, rather than cooperatives, as a solution to the critical problems of agricultural development. In light of the extremely urgent situation confronting Mozambique at this stage—one of the worst aspects being widespread drought and hunger—the refocussing on family agriculture is sound policy: feeding the nation is the immediate priority. But as this refocus does not encompass the transformation of women's roles within family farming, it seems to be in contradiction to the revolution's goal of liberating women.

The impact of the lack of such transformation can be seen clearly at this stage. Stephanie Urdang, who has visited Mozambique several times since 1980, discerned, on her most recent visit at the end of 1983, a noticeable demobilization around women's issues at all levels. It is connected to the fact that women's workload has, if anything, increased. Political mobilization, without the necessary accompanying transformation, is insufficient to bring about the deepseated changes needed to move the peasant woman away from her status as—in the words of an official statement—"the most oppressed and exploited woman in Mozambique."

A second recent event highlighted this. Political mobilization was key to the preparations for the special conference sponsored by both FRELIMO and the Organization of Mozambican Women (OMM), focussing on social problems concerning women. The eight themes included polygamy, lobolo (bride price), initiation rites, prostitution, etc. Preparation for the conference, which was held in November 1984, included the organization of brigades to lead discussions on these themes at all levels throughout the country. The debate at those meetings in the rural areas was enthusiastic and heated. Many concrete suggestions came out of these meetings, which were then reflected in the reports to the conference. The conference itself tended to be dominated by the party, which limited the contributions that women participants could make. However, a debate had been generated, one that OMM could push forward. But as long as this remains in the realm of political mobilization the advances will be limited.

In looking back over the first decade of Mozambique's independence, it is possible, with the luxury of hindsight, to raise some "if only's." What if women themselves had been consulted for their views of the priorities for the development of their country and the improvement of their daily lives? It is highly likely that they would have insisted on strong state support for family agriculture rather than the available agricultural resources being pumped into state farms, as discussed elsewhere in this book. Such consultations are not something new for FRELIMO: they were in fact the core component of mass participation during the war; they were the basis of the third and fourth party congresses; and they could be found in the work of the brigades in preparation for the recent women's conference.

These are some of the problems worth bearing in mind in reading the pages that follow. How they can be resolved, given Mozambique's crisis, is at this point far from obvious.

The small, rather worn hall is crammed from one end to the other with women. They occupy every available chair and are seated, straight-backed and straight-legged, on the floor. They have come from the *bairros* of Xai-Xai, capital of the province of Gaza, to greet me, a journalist visiting their country. They sing their welcome in rich-voiced harmony and shout their *vivas* with strength. The atmosphere in the hall is quite electric.

When a cultural group comes forward to express in dance the change in the lives of women, some are dressed in men's trousers and ties. "We are dressed like men," one dancer explains, "to show that women can now also express their own ideas about life, make their own decisions, and do the work of men. We were not able to before."

Many women want the opportunity to speak, some fighting shyness, others more confident. One of the first to stand up is an old woman, her face creased with decades of hard work in the fields under the sun. "I am old. All my life I never believed such things could be possible. Now I can even write my own name! I still will do many more things, even though I am old."

A younger woman gets to her feet. "I stand up to continue to show our appreciation. If I could jump, I would jump so high to show how happy I am. I have witnessed many, many changes for women. We put on trousers and work like men. We work as brick-layers, we construct our own villages, we do all the work we were not free to do before. We are feeling liberated because we can be absent from our homes for one or two weeks and our husbands don't mind. Before they could have beaten us. I am not saying that women aren't beaten anymore, some are. But most of our husbands are supporting us and making sacrifices to allow us to do the work of the OMM."

Two hours pass, filled with accounts of the hardships suffered during the colonial period. Each with her own story, the women piece together a patchwork that portrays the horrors that they bore for so many years. Listening, it is easy to appreciate how deeply felt is their gratitude to FRELIMO and how thankful these women are for an opportunity to forge a better life.

When the district *responsavel* for OMM brings the meeting to a close, she adds her own words from the platform, picking up the theme raised by the younger women:

"We have talked a lot. We have related many stories. But I must talk about something we seem to have forgotten. We have forgotten to say that women had no voice. Where matters were being discussed, there were no women. Men said women could not think. But after we got our independence, this changed. FRELIMO says that all of us, women and men, can develop our minds, all of us can work. FRELIMO knows that women can think very well, that women are as capable of making decisions. A woman can be somebody. In the past days we never had a chance to have a hall full of women talking about our lives. But today we can be together from morning to night discussing our problems."

Although women speak of being "free," about "feeling liberated," there is still much difficult terrain to traverse before this potential can move toward a reality. However, the implication of these sentiments—that the liberation of women is a goal to be strived for—has not arisen accidentally; nor is it peripheral. Such a perspective results from the clear acknowledgment by FRELIMO and by the government that such a goal must be integral to the total revolutionary process that is under way in Mozambique. This chapter will attempt to assess how this is manifested in practice—how it affects the day-to-day lives of Mozambican women.

"Why bother with the emancipation of women?" To answer this rhetorical question posed in his opening speech to the founding conference of the Organization of Mozambican Women in 1973, Samora Machel had the following to say:

> The emancipation of women is not an act of charity, the result of a humanitarian or compassionate attitude. The liberation of women is a

fundamental necessity for the revolution, the guarantee of its continuity and the precondition for its victory. The main objective of the revolution is to destroy the system of exploitation and build a new society which releases the potential of human beings, reconciling them with labor and with nature. This is the context within which the question of women's emancipation arises.[1]

The recognition of the interplay between the total revolutionary process and the liberation of women is a basic principle in the ideology of FRELIMO, one that dates back to early in the armed struggle. It was a factor in the political mobilization of people during the war and was put into action in a major way through the establishment of a women's detachment. The founding of the OMM a few years later provided the occasion for a statement giving FRELIMO's analysis of the situation of women in Mozambique and the importance of the liberation of women to the revolution.

"Generally speaking, women are the most oppressed, humiliated, and exploited beings in society," Machel continues, giving weight to a fact that is often acknowledged only begrudgingly— if at all—in other countries of Africa. This condition, he states, arose from the time when early humans began to produce more than they could consume. "Material foundations were laid for the emergence of a stratum in society which would appropriate the fruits of the majority's labor. This appropriation . . . is the crux of the antagonistic contradiction which has divided society for centuries."

With the unleashing of this exploitation, women along with men were subjected to the domination of the privileged stratum. But while women are also producers and workers, there is a special dimension to the nature of their oppression: "To possess women is to possess workers, unpaid workers, workers whose entire labor power can be appropriated without resistance by the husband who is the lord and master." Hence in agrarian economy, polygamy ensures the accumulation of a great deal of wealth, and husbands "are assured of free labor which neither complains nor rebels against exploitation." In this way the woman offers her owner benefits beyond that of a slave. "She is a source of pleasure and above all, she produces other workers, [and thus] new sources of wealth."

Machel points out further that in order to sustain the oppression of women, an exploitative society requires the "establishment of a corresponding ideology and culture, together with an education system to pass them on." It is a process that evolves over thousands of years, and deliberately keeps women in "ignorance, obscurantism, and superstition with a view to making them resigned to

352 A Difficult Road

their position, of instilling in them an attitude of passivity and servility." Because of this, women have not been involved in the planning and decision-making processes in society.

The antagonism does not lie between women and men "but between women and the social order, between all exploited people, both women and men, and the social order." This is emphasized as a fundamental point: "Men and women are products and victims of the exploitative society which has created and formed them. It is essentially against this society that men and women should fight united."

This position—that socialist transformation is the only basis for the liberation of women—is the main theme of Machel's speech. It is the system that oppresses, and it is the system that has to be changed. Thus the emancipation of women can only come about within the total revolutionary process. Machel identifies four criteria to be met in order to achieve this:

1. A political line of action must be established. For women to emancipate themselves, conscious political commitment to the revolution is essential. This will then translate into concrete action, leading them to take part in making decisions affecting the country's future.

2. Women must be engaged in production. This will release productive forces and launch a process of economic development essential to a deeper ideological understanding and sound knowledge of the world around them.

3. Women must be able to benefit from a scientific and cultural education in order to achieve a correct understanding of their relationship with nature and society, thereby destroying the myths that oppress them psychologically and deprive them of initiative. This will foster women's participation at all levels of leadership and work.

4. There is a need for a new revolutionary concept of the couple and the home. The relationship between man and wife has until now been based on man's superiority over woman, aimed at satisfying the male ego. The new Mozambican family should be founded exclusively on revolutionary love between two equal people.

In attempting to assess the changes that have occurred for Mozambican women since independence, I will be looking at these four areas to help gauge the achievements, the problems, and the setbacks encountered on the road to the liberation of women.

Political Commitment

• Virginia José Chambissé is the president of the agricultural cooperative of the 25th of June Communal Village in Gaza. It is a position that embodies considerable and varied responsibility. Although women workers outnumber men in many such cooperatives in Gaza, 25th of June is one of the few to have an elected woman president.

• Amelia Saia is the vice-president of the agricultural cooperative of Eduardo Mondlane Village, not far from 25th of June. Her confident manner contrasts with that of the shy younger women members. To observe her interact with the cooperative's president and visitors confirms an impression of unusual self-possession. When her cooperative's president describes their work to the visitors, the English words "two hours" pop out of his careful explanation in Shangaan. Amelia Saia bursts into laughter and with a huge, teasing grin, she interjects: "He's just showing off! He wants you to know he speaks English." He is proud of the few words of English he has learned working in the South African mines and is unperturbed by the fact that a woman has chided him in this manner. Besides being vice-president, Saia is active in other areas of political life in the village—a member of the People's Assembly, the head of the justice tribunal that represents three neighboring villages, and a member of FRELIMO. Her husband, on the other hand, who was a Portuguese-appointed chief during the colonial period, is barred from party membership and from holding positions of authority.

• Arminda Jaime Hombé is the OMM secretary for the district of Chibuto, Gaza, as well as the party *responsavel* for ideological work in the district. Chibuto has a large number of communal villages and Arminda knows each one well. Her visits are frequent as she goes about her OMM work, setting up projects, helping with problems, mobilizing the women politically, and generally keeping in touch. She is young and dedicated, with an easy-going manner that stems from an obvious ability to do the job well. Although she began her work as a teacher, a myriad of other tasks slowly took over. She now combines her already full day with caring for her four young children, her youngest just a year old.

• The elected members of the OMM secretariat for the four sections of the Mavalane *bairro* in Maputo handle a wide range of problems that undermine women's lives in the sprawling slum area. They are involved with such tasks as organizing meetings to discuss OMM work, encouraging women to join evening literacy classes, mobilizing volunteers for collective work projects, urging women to attend political meetings. Those responsible for "social affairs" find themselves embroiled in family problems exacerbated by the overcrowding and sordid physical conditions that plague the 16,000 residents of the *bairro*. Inherited from Portuguese colonialism, these problems typify the urban areas. Employment has to be found for an illiterate woman whose husband has taken a young lover and abandoned her and her five children; a payment schedule for child support has to be arranged for a deserted wife who returned to her parents' home in Inhambane; intervention is needed to try to reconcile a young married couple locked into constant quarrels over finances; money has to be collected for the funeral expenses of a recently widowed woman who has been left destitute. This intensive work by the OMM secretariat means that the women of Mavalane have somewhere to turn when their conditions become too hard to bear, or when they simply need advice. The support the women get from OMM and FRELIMO, along with the new services such as water pumps, schools, clinics, are beginning to ease the burden of their overpressured urban lives. The OMM leadership is kept on the go trying to initiate and entrench a variety of such changes.

A common denominator running through these anecdotes is political commitment. It results from a political consciousness that grows out of active mobilization by FRELIMO and mass organizations such as OMM. It is the fuel which drives the revolutionary process, but one whose energy can only be sustained if concrete improvement in the conditions of life are seen to result.

The political mobilization that was undertaken during the liberation struggle was in many ways an easier process. Every oppressed Mozambican knew to the core of his or her being what it meant to live under the brutality of Portuguese colonialism. Mobilizing people to take up arms to rid the country of an external enemy needed skill but got visible results. Even those standing skeptically on the sidelines, certain that the strength of the oppressors was too powerful to break, found themselves swayed by the successes FRELIMO began to achieve in liberating portions of their land, and were impressed by the first schools, the first health care services, the first democratically elected political councils that the rural people had ever known. Women, it was found, became particularly adept political mobilizers and it was a role that they gravitated to in increasing numbers. Then came what seemed the ultimate victory: independence and control over their own country at last. But FRELIMO and the new government understood that the roughest battle was ahead. The problem was profound: how to continue to mobilize people under even more difficult circumstances when expectations had been raised—often unrealistically—in the course of the independence struggle itself. Continued mobilization required that the people understand that independence does not bring with it instant relief from poverty and underdevelopment. Without a visible enemy and without dramatic victories in guerrilla warfare to act as a spur, it is a huge task to develop a political awareness that this phase of the revolution continues to require great sacrifice and hard work.

With independence, the commitment to the emancipation of women at the governmental and party level remained in place and, along with the revolution itself, moved into that new phase. OMM was charged with the responsibility of continuing the mobilization of women. Many women had resisted mobilization for a number of reasons—the heritage of feeling inferior, of lack of practice in speaking out in public and in making decisions, of less exposure to the world outside their homes, of being more firmly embedded in tradition and less open to change. A critical shortage of women cadres compounded the problem. But once women begin to move, many quickly develop commitment and leadership qualities that often outstrip those of their male colleagues, often because of the added impetus of women's knowledge of their own double oppression. They have more to fight but more to gain.

One way of assessing progress since independence is to look at the level of women's political participation. There is a long and uneven route to be traveled before increased political commitment can be effectively translated into equality in political participation. Despite the Amelia Saias, the Arminda Hombés, the Virginia Chambissés, the numerical evidence is sobering.

Early efforts to involve women in political life came with the establishment of *grupos dinamizadores* in residential areas and at workplaces. These provided women with one way of gaining leadership experience, and their involvement was assured because one of the seven members of each group had to be the OMM representative for the area. But one out of seven is not a lot, and only rarely were women chosen for other positions of significance. Men were loath to relinquish their monopoly over decision-making, and with women's participation secured in this way, there was little incentive for them to change their ways. It became, for the most part, an exercise in tokenism, with issues relating to women put to the side. In general the *grupos* took the position that they were responsible for all decisions except those affecting women, which were considered the exclusive preserve of OMM. Thus it was widely accepted that only women could convince other women to get involved in collective production to raise funds for crêches or to engage in other work seen as being within the parameter of "women's affairs." For some women, though, even this circumscribed involvement provided the first opportunity to develop politically, and the leadership potential of many active women militants was first released in this way.

The *grupos* arose somewhat spontaneously, with fairly limited initial direction from FRELIMO, and with a differing understanding from one to the next of the concept of the liberation of women. But by the time FRELIMO began a campaign (in 1978) to create party cells throughout the country there was a conscious recognition of the need to integrate women more broadly into political affairs, in part the results of the concern felt over the unequal representation of women at all levels. Of the 249 provincial delegates elected to FRELIMO's Third Congress in 1977, 48 (19.2 percent) were women. Their representation on the Central Committee was only 5 out of 67 (7.5 percent), while all ten members of the Standing Political Committee of the Party were men. Graça Machel, Minister of Education and Culture, was (and is) the only woman minister. The poor representation of women at the local level was criticized by the leadership and discussed at the Congress, and the different levels of the party structure were instructed to redouble their efforts to mobilize, organize, and integrate women. As part of this campaign, it was stipulated that at least one representative of OMM join the brigades that went out to explain the work of the party and the importance of party membership, and to generally increase political consciousness. In addition, OMM members were included in the national and provincial planning groups set up to coordinate the campaign.[2]

Figures are not available, so it is difficult to assess the success of such measures in increasing the number of women party members. However, the proportion of women at the 1983 Fourth Party Congress had *dropped*. Of the 677 delegates, 105 (15.5 percent) were women. A 1979 survey of a few villages in Gaza and Nampula indicated wide regional discrepancies. In Gaza, with its high percentage of women and their active role in the political life of the communal villages, over 50 percent of the candidates for party membership were women. In Três de Fevereiro, for example, thirty-two of the fifty-four members were women (59.3 percent), possibly the highest percentage in the province. In five other villages, the figure was over 50 percent, although precise data were not available. In contrast, in five villages from four different districts in Nampula, the only women party members were the local OMM leaders, and of the five Nampula villages surveyed, the highest percentage of women was 28.6, the lowest 8.7.[3]

As the figures in Table 1 illustrate, the proportion of women party members fluctuates from one factory to the next, according to no apparent pattern. At some it is higher than the proportion of women in the workforce; at others it is much less. These figures would be affected by a variety of factors, most particularly the level

Table 1
Party Participation of Women in Selected Production Units

Factory	Sector	Province	% Women workers	No. Women workers	% women party members	No. women leaders
Belita	clothing	Sofala	26.8	72	18.1	1
Favezal	clothing	Zambezia	8.6	4	0.0	0
Emma	Textile	Manica	16.1	77	19.5	0
Facobol	Shoes	Maputo	31.6	28	35.7	1
Soc. Ulta. Tobac	Tobacco	Maputo	8.3	20	5.0	1
Caju de Mocambique						
Chamanculo	Cashew	Maputo	82.5	130	86.2	5
Machava 1	Cashew	Maputo	67.1	44	36.4	?
Machava 2	Cashew	Maputo	62.6	68	45.6	0
Manjacaze	Cashew	Gaza	52.9	63	17.5	?

Source: Ministry of Industry and Energy questionnaires, July 1979.[4]

of political mobilization at the factory itself, as well as the activities of OMM at the workplace and the support it gets from the district's OMM committee.

To become a party member, an individual is expected to exhibit traits consistent with the ideals of a revolutionary. This was articulated in a speech by the OMM Secretary General in 1978:

> One of the prerequisites to being a member of our vanguard Party is recognition of and respect for the dignity of women. From that stems the dialectical relationship between the Party structuring campaign and the advance of the struggle for the emancipation of women.

One of the stated characteristics of a party militant, male or female, is to be a "defender and promoter of the emancipation of women." In turn, among the reasons often cited for the ousting of a male party member is his attitude toward women; there have even been a few examples of this in high levels of leadership.

While the role of the party is to guide the ideology and political perspective of the nation, the People's Assemblies provide a foundation for the exercise of democracy. The first elections took place in 1977 for assemblies at the national, provincial, district, and local levels. As Table 2 shows, women's representation generally decreased with the move from local to national levels, the latter comprising a small number of women.

Três de Fevereiro is an interesting example of one of the few villages that fall outside this trend. The People's Assembly has twenty-three women among its thirty-three members. In addition, two of the five members of the Executive Council are women.

These two women described to me how the selection process had taken place. First there had been a list of candidates presented by representatives of the provincial structures of the party. These had been chosen initially from village residents who had shown leadership qualities and commitment to the village during its formation and construction. Then a meeting of all the villagers was called, the names presented, and one by one the candidates had to give their background and face up to questions as well as to criticisms of past behavior from the assembly. Those considered unfit for leadership were struck off the list. By the end of the day thirty-three names remained, constituting the first People's Assembly. Then came the election of the Executive Council. Despite the two-thirds majority of women, the residents proceded to choose five men for the council. "No," intervened party representatives, "you must have women on the Executive Council as well." So two names were withdrawn, and two women elected instead. It was clearly difficult for the villagers to voluntarily choose women among the top leadership of their village, even though the majority of those attending the meeting were women.

Três de Fevereiro is not, unfortunately, reflective of a generally high participation of women in People's Assemblies. Rather it is an indication of what is possible for the future. The record in other regions and provinces is far less favorable to women, with some villages unable to muster up even one woman member.

Local justice tribunals provide another measure of changing political roles. Already widespread, the goal is to have such tribunals set up throughout the country—in urban neighborhoods, communal villages, and localities. The tribunals are responsible for handling problems relating to the family and between families, as well as petty offenses, and they have the power to impose small fines and other appropriate, but limited, punishments. In precolonial times this role was played by chiefs or councils of elders, who were exclusively male. While there is no official policy stipulating

Table 2
People's Assembly Deputies

Level	No. of assemblies	No. of deputies	Men		Women	
			No.	Percent	No.	Percent
National	1	226	198	87.6	28	12.4
Provincial	10	734	628	85.3	108	14.7
District	112	3,390	2,583	76.2	807	23.8
City	10	460	364	79.1	96	20.9
Locality	894	22,230	15,939	71.7	6,291	28.3

Source: Anexo ao Relatorio da Comissão Nacional de Eleicoes a Assembleia Popular, Boletim da Republica, no. 150, 1°. Serie, 24 December 1977, Suplemento.[5]

that women be included on these tribunals, in fact most have at least one woman member, and a few have more than one. In the villages I visited, all the tribunals had women members. In fact, Amelia Saia was one of two women members of the tribunal in her village and its judge-president. On a later occasion when I attended a hearing of a Maputo *bairro* tribunal, I found the judge-president to be an extremely capable woman. This tribunal, too, had two women among its five members and two alternates.

OMM and party structures are often a critical factor in ensuring women's participation on tribunals. The lack of visibility of the OMM committee in Mecufi District, Cabo Delgado, for example, was felt. When the all-male composition of the tribunal was queried in one village, the visitors were told that it had not occurred to the village or to the tribunal members that a woman should be included. If it had been requested by the "structure" they would have complied, tribunal members said.[6]

A woman member of a FRELIMO cell in a communal village . . . a woman member of the People's Assembly, perhaps even on its Executive Council . . . a woman on the council of the agricultural cooperative . . . an active OMM secretary who plays an energetic leadership role in the village . . . a woman in a special four-month leadership and literacy training course: when presented as statistics, these indicate wide involvement of women in political activities. But what a flat statistic masks is the frequency with which six positions such as these are held by the *same* woman. It is a pattern regularly repeated at the district or provincial level, an overlap that seldom occurs for men, and if it does, not for as many tasks. The reason is not always want of encouragement, but the want of women coming forward to run as candidates or to give the kind of political commitment that such time-consuming tasks demand. The causes for this are diverse.

The emphasis placed on political mobilization at a national level is carried out at the local level in an uneven way. Much is dependent on the effectiveness of the OMM structures at the provincial and regional levels. The fact that the number of women cadres continues to be small is an exacerbating factor. Not infrequently, if a woman militant demonstrates capabilities as a cadre, she will be transferred to work for the party. This siphoning off to FRELIMO has made it difficult for OMM to hold on to its own trained mobilizers.

The actions and support (or lack of it) of the normally all-male FRELIMO district and provincial structures can also affect the mobilization of women. If these *responsavels* appreciate the importance of the emancipation of women and integrate the goal into the political education they undertake, the work of OMM in the general area gains strength. This is an important way in which FRELIMO can have a positive influence on reluctant men.

Traditional attitudes of both women and men toward what is considered the only legitimate position of women in the society continue to curtail women's aspirations and ability to strengthen their own political commitment. Because women did not in the past play an overt political role, they have to take a bold leap into the present in order to assert themselves as militants. Often this has to be done against strong pressure from antagonistic husbands. It is not uncommon for husbands who feel threatened by politically active wives to prevent them from attending OMM meetings and refuse to allow them to join the organization. "If you love OMM so much," is a frequent comment, "let OMM buy your *capulano*" (the length of cloth wound around the waist, worn as skirt). Other men have resorted to physical restraint, locking their wives in the house to prevent them from attending meetings. Some women have been thrown out of their homes by their husbands for persisting, and OMM reports an increase in the incidence of wife beating for the same reasons. (However, the latter might well reflect an increase in the reporting of such cases because women now have somewhere to go with their complaints.)

In addition there is the practical reality of women's role within the household. The continuing burden of the sexual division of labor in this sector and women's total responsibility for reproduction leave them little time for outside activities. It is not surprising that when women do participate in political processes, it is most often on a local level (as Table 2 on People's Assemblies shows) so that they do not have to travel far from home to attend meetings, etc. Government and party encouragement and ongoing political education are not enough. Women's work drains the energies and resources of even the most committed women. As long as this continues to be largely ignored as an urgent problem needing practical solutions, a substantial constraint remains upon the quest for the emancipation of women, as will be discussed more fully in the next section. It is only those women most dedicated to the Mozambican revolution or those receiving support from their husbands and families who can carry out all the required functions.

Although progress has been slow, its rate is less discouraging when considered within two contexts. Firstly, if compared with the absence of participation by women in political affairs prior to independence, the advances made are far from negligible and one can only be impressed by the number of committed women at all levels, local to national.

Secondly, the advances made in Mozambique in the years since independence can be favorably compared to the rate for Africa as a whole. Countries that have been independent for well over a decade longer than Mozambique show a fairly dismal record on the question. The mid-decade conference of the United Nations Decade for Women held in 1980 pointed out in its evaluation of progress of women's political participation (based on answers to a questionnaire from under fifty percent of the continent's nations) that "the median participation in 1978 for all [African] countries responding to the questionnaire was 12 per cent at the local level and 6 per cent at the national level."[7] For the same period, as we have seen above, the participation of women in Mozambique was 28.3 percent at the local level and 12.4 percent at the national level. No report from individual countries showed figures even close to these. Kenya, for instance, reported that women constitute 20 percent of the local officials and 8 percent of the national.[8]

With few exceptions, most countries in Africa pay little more than lip service to the idea of emancipating women. The extent of Mozambique's commitment in terms of both political mobilization and programming stands out as unique.

Engaging in Production

Of the four criteria that form the basis for women's liberation, women's role in production receives the most weight in independent Mozambique. Its importance was emphasized in Samora Machel's speech to the second OMM conference in 1976:

> The decisive factor for the emancipation of woman is her involvement in the principal task—the task of transforming the society. In the previous stage of the Mozambican experience, this was the national liberation struggle. The principal task in the current stage of the revolution . . . [has been defined by FRELIMO as] building the material and ideological base for the construction of a socialist society. In other words, in the application of this strategy for struggle . . . *the principal task is production.*[9] (Emphasis mine)

The emphasis in this speech moves from the static formulation of the problem (women need to engage in production) to stress on a more far-reaching need of the revolutionary process: the need for women to be more fully integrated into the process of *transforming* production.

It is a significant distinction. To engage in production is relatively straightforward. It requires little beyond work, although it can lead to changes in other spheres of the worker's life. Participating in the actual process of transforming production, however, affects many aspects of the lives of those involved. It leads to contributions to new directions, to participation in decision-making, ultimately to control over the worker's role in the labor process as well as to a stake in the distribution of the resources that are the fruits of one's labor. It goes beyond transforming the worker's role in production to transforming his or her role in social life. For women, who have not been expected to play this kind of role in society, it burrows deep into many facets of their activities and profoundly influences the process of their liberation. In a word, it means revolution.

The mechanisms for ensuring this kind of integration differ, depending on whether the setting is rural or urban, peasant agricultural production or wage-labor industrial production. In Mozambique, the population is overwhelmingly rural (some 90 percent) and therefore what happens in this sector is crucial to the total revolutionary process.

Agriculture is the key to the future of Mozambique. The most critical problem confronting the country is the need to produce enough both to feed the population and to help generate urgently needed foreign exchange. Therefore, agriculture has been targeted as the main focus of development.

In 1981, FRELIMO expressed its goal for the decade: the collectivization of all agricultural production. The thrust toward this as a solution to agricultural development was stressed soon after independence at the Third Party Congress in 1977:

> The Revolution demands that we extend the experience of the liberated areas to the entire country. The organization of peasants into rural communities is essential for the development of collective life in the countryside and for the creation of necessary conditions for socialized agriculture. . . . It is in these, through collective production, that the workers' ideological battle grows stronger. The villages permit a rapid growth in revolutionary clan consciousness and the consequent freeing of the workers' immense creative capacity. The organization of the people into Communal Villages makes it possible for us to achieve self-sufficiency in food relatively quickly, and also enables us to satisfy health, educational and cultural needs.[10]

How will these new programs of communalization and collectivization affect women?

There have been a few significant statements of policy that reflect an understanding of women's role in the rural sector, and of the oppression of women that emanates from this. One of the most detailed appeared in a text prepared for the 1976 conference:

The woman peasant is the most oppressed and exploited woman in Mozambique. Reduced to an object of pleasure, a reproducer of children, a producer of food for the family's subsistence, an unsalaried worker in the service of the "head of the family," the woman peasant at the same time has a very great revolutionary potential from which the Mozambican Revolution cannot be cut off. This observation is based on the objective reality that our principal activity is agriculture and that most agriculture is for subsistence and is done by women; the revolution must aim at transforming this agriculture into organized, planned, collective agriculture. Mozambican women not only cannot remain outside this process, but they must be its principal agents and beneficiaries. The Mozambican peasant woman has to be assured equal opportunities to learn new techniques, to have access to the use of machines, to the acquisition of theoretical knowledge and above all to participation in the political organs, in the direction and management to the same extent as her participation in the work.[11]

A discussion of agricultural cooperatives is to be found elsewhere in this book, and points to the difficulty of implementing these ideals in practice. But while the general process is under way there is little or no discussion of precisely how such changes will affect women. Their role in agriculture certainly differs from that of men, given their heavy involvement in family agriculture. What will collectivization of this form of agriculture mean to them? Thus far, these questions are considered as part of the overall problem and are not articulated with specific reference to women.

The fact is that such transformation can only be achieved if women participate fully in this process—an obvious fact which is all too often forgotten. Although it has been acknowledged in Mozambican policy statements such as the one quoted above, no concrete plans have been proffered detailing how women's participation can be realized. The gap between theory and practice is seen most clearly in the absence of such proposals in the plans of action worked out each year by OMM. The question has not, thus far, been seriously taken up by OMM or viewed as central to its work.

Furthermore, some apparently contradictory elements are evident in the overall ideological perspective. While emphasis is placed on the fundamental need to fully integrate women into the process of transforming production, insufficient cognizance is taken of a basic fact about women's labor in Mozambique. Women are already heavily engaged in production. In agricultural production. While the text quoted above points out that women in the rural areas are oppressed by the burden of their many-sided labor, it does not bring out the fact that women are already so intensively engaged in the production process that they cannot heed a call to "engage in production." In order to resolve this situation, agriculture in its present form must be transformed—as the above quote points out—and women's role within this must be fundamental—a fact acknowledged at this juncture mainly on the level of theory.

Collective work—be it in agricultural cooperatives or in urban factories (discussed later in this section)—does provide an arena for women to begin to struggle for their liberation. In the first place, it provides them with crucial economic independence. But while the socializaton of production provides a *material* basis for equality, this in itself is not sufficient. In order to forge more fundamental changes in the role of women, political leadership and participation in political processes are necessary. Collectivization enables them to play an equal political role with their co-workers. This point is critical; changing their social relations of production can lead to true equality. However, the leap that women must make from participating in the transformation of social production to actually wielding equal political power with men appears to involve far more than can be accomplished by the collectivization of family agriculture or by the participation of women in cooperatives, as wage-laborers on state farms, or as members of an industrial wage-labor force. The bridge that is needed to link these two elements is essentially political. And political mobilization is key.

During the armed struggle, when the immediate priority was to oust the Portuguese colonialists, fighting the war was not seen as an end in itself; the goal was not simply to replace the Portuguese administrators with Mozambicans. It was to totally transform the society into a nonexploitative one, based on government by the people. So even in the midst of war, political mobilization was energetically undertaken to make this long-term goal a reality. Similarly now, after independence, when the major thrust has become development, development in itself is not a sufficient goal. Development has taken place in many of Mozambique's neocolonial neighbors but has benefitted a favored few and has not resulted in a new society. Choosing a socialist path to development has meant many hardships for the people of Mozambique but assures a future that will benefit the whole population and not simply a governing and bourgeois elite. Hence the raising of political consciousness goes hand in hand with the process of economic transformation.

But although FRELIMO has stressed the importance of mobilization through the phases of its revolutionary struggle, it seems to be curiously absent from the strategy proposed for the emancipation of women. Discussion of the need to mobilize women politically centers rather on mobilization to join the general tasks of the current phase of the revolution. But political mobilization expressly to fight for their rights as women, and against the attitudes and customs that perpetuate women's subordination within both the home and the larger society, is treated for the most part as secondary. It is interesting to note in this context that the OMM plan of action for 1981, setting the direction for the decade, focuses on mobilizing women to contribute to the fulfillment of the plan for the country as a whole. No section of OMM's plan relates to women per se. There is a presumption that the problems that confront women as women (such as polygamy or bride-price, which were so energetically attacked at the 1976 OMM conference) will be taken care of if brought under the aegis of the development plans for the year or the decade. This entrenches the view that the emancipation of women can only be achieved as an integral part of the current phase of the struggle. While this is certainly a critical aspect, it is not the whole picture. It fails to confront some crucial obstacles to women's emancipation.

There appear to be two interconnected problems with FRELIMO's overall approach to the question. The first has to do with the sexual division of labor and women's role within the household. The second relates to the fact that the scale of both industrialization and agricultural cooperativization is still limited, meaning that the capacity to employ numbers of women is itself extremely limited.

Over the past five or six years, Marxist feminist writers have grappled with the question of social reproduction as being fundamental to the subordination of women. This work has made significant contributions to our understanding of women's oppression and the struggle to overcome it. The concept of reproduction is used here in its broadest sense, and refers both to biological reproduction and the daily maintenance of the labor force, and to social reproduction, or the perpetuation of entire social systems. An integral part of this is the notion of the sexual division of labor.[12]

This sexual division of labor allocates to women certain specific social tasks. As described above, such tasks place an excruciatingly heavy burden on women's daily lives. There are therefore two interlinked elements that are crucial to any effort to change the sexual division of labor (and by implication begin the process of releasing women from their subordinate role in society): (1) the need to ensure the full participation of women in production outside the home as well as their equal access to and the appropriation of society's resources resulting from such production; and (2) the need for both men and women to share domestic labor and responsibilities within the household, so that women *can* participate in outside production.

It is precisely here that a contradiction arises out of the theory—

as presented by Machel and FRELIMO—and the practice found in Mozambique. As we have seen, the first need is addressed as fundamental. But because of the lack of emphasis on the interconnection of production and reproduction as far as women are concerned, the second need is not given necessary emphasis in the conceptualization and implementation of practice.

This is not to say that it is ignored. Women's workload is recognized as an unfair burden, but because the sexual division of labor is not confronted as a structural problem, it is not dealt with strategically. For instance, in his first OMM speech, where Machel delineated the theoretical underpinnings for the emancipation of women, he identified two obstacles that arise in training women as cadres to lead the struggle for production: (1) obscurantism, superstition, and tradition, to be overcome by scientific study and participation in the practical tasks relating to production; and (2) an absence of consciousness on the part of women of their own double exploitation, the principal weapon to overcome this obstacle being a combination of political study, exchange of experience of sufferings, and collective discussion. While these mental obstacles need to be confronted in order to liberate women, the picture is not complete: the cause of such attitudes is not discussed, and the double workload of women is not identified as an obstacle.

Once the oppressive nature of women's work is recognized, how is it to be challenged? One way is to take some of women's work out of the household and collectivize it. As we have seen from the text prepared for the second OMM conference quoted earlier, collectivization of family agriculture has been expressed as an official goal, although, at this stage, there is no concrete policy for its implementation in the plans for transforming agriculture in the coming decade.

The projected collectivization of family agriculture, for instance, will go far to improve the conditions of life for the rural woman and to release her from the all-consuming nature of reproductive labor. Child care centers are also seen as critical to help women workers, and these have already been established by a number of factories, agricultural cooperatives, state farms, communal villages, and government departments. Yet while child care contributes to women's ability to leave the home for many hours a day, it does not relieve them of the daily grind of cooking, housecleaning, evening child care, and so on that continues to be their responsibility.

While political mobilization remains vital in encouraging women to take on men's roles, the mobilization of men to do "women's work" is absent. In fact, the demand that men take on household chores equally with their wives is labeled as "mechanistic" and described as something prevalent in the West where, as Machel states in his first OMM speech, "the aim is to transform the contradiction with men into an antagonistic one." Further in the speech he says:

> There is a profusion of erroneous ideas about the emancipation of women. There are those who see emancipation as mechanical equality between men and women. This vulgar concept is often seen among us. Here emancipation means that women and men do exactly the same tasks, mechanically dividing their household duties. If I wash the dishes today you must wash them tomorrow, whether or not you are busy or have the time. If there are still no women truck drivers or tractor drivers in FRELIMO, we must have some right away regardless of the objective and subjective conditions. As we can see from the example of capitalist countries, this mechanically conceived emancipation leads to complaints and attitudes which utterly distort the meaning of women's emancipation.

When I raised the question about the intensive nature of women's double workload with OMM leaders and other women, they seldom viewed it as a problem that needed to be confronted through political mobilization of men, although many women felt it was unfair and the basis for continued inequality. Rather they believed that over time it would be dealt with in various ways, e.g., by the provision of services that released women from certain tasks and/or by men offering to help their wives as part of the process of becoming revolutionaries. Equal responsibility, as opposed to "help," was seldom expressed as a goal for family life. Women are discouraged from confronting their husbands in frustrated anger. At meetings, OMM urges women to "speak with kind words" to their husbands so as not to raise the ire of men who already find OMM threatening. Rather, they are encouraged to demonstrate their ability to do what men can do, in addition to their household work, by getting up earlier and going to bed later.

The conflict between women's role in reproduction and their increasing role in nonhousehold production is evident as one travels through the country talking with women in factories, in communal villages, on state farms, in government ministries. But it is a contradiction that could in the end give rise to its own solution through the demands of women unable to cope with the pressures placed on them by their work and by the expectations of their revolutionary commitment to the development of their country.

The emphasis on women's increased role in production is strong and has gone far to give many women opportunities in diverse kinds of work. Hence, positive advances are being made for women in this area and energy is being invested in encouraging them to take part in development in a way that surpasses the goals and achievements of most third world countries.

But this thrust is undermined by external factors, which brings us to the second problem raised earlier—that of underdevelopment.

The call to enter paid productive labor is mounted against a backdrop of severe underdevelopment: lack of industrialization, coupled with lack of jobs in factories, the still limited number of state farms to provide paid employment, and the fact that agricultural cooperatives in communal villages are in the early stages of development. This is exacerbated in the southern provinces by the fact that one major source of wage-labor for males—the South African mines—has been substantially reduced. In many neocolonial situations, this would be considered more than sufficient reason to discourage, even prevent, women from entering the wage-labor force. Men must be given priority, is the repeated argument, until such time as the country is fully industrialized and has enough jobs for women as well.

While a much lower proportion of women than of men is employed in factories and on state farms, and in skilled positions in the urban areas and small towns (within government ministries, for example), the official policy is to denounce this as unacceptable and to encourage a reversing trend. Further, there is genuine commitment not only to providing jobs for women, but to ensuring equality at all levels of production in order—as Machel stated in his 1973 speech—to "lead to deeper ideological understanding and a sounder knowledge of reality, of society and nature."

This was reflected at the 1976 OMM conference when the foundation was laid for enhancing women's role in production. The conference resolved that women "must participate actively on an equal footing with men in all tasks of production, organization, and planning . . . learning tasks that were traditionally reserved for men."

In keeping with such declarations, women are to be found in a variety of workplaces: stoking trains, driving trains, as miners, in the army (there is compulsory military service for both men and women although women have more grounds for exemption), as auto mechanics, as police, as carpenters, as tractor drivers.

Entry into skilled positions is still sorely hampered by lack of technical education and specific skills, as well as by a basic lack of literacy. Attempts are being made by government ministries to alleviate this by providing technical training courses that are explicitly open to both men and women who have the qualifications.

It is not only the lack of such qualifications that has kept women's participation low. Many women either were unaware that the courses existed, lacked the self-confidence to apply, or faced problems at home with discouraging husbands or lack of child care. The situation has improved a little as a result of OMM taking on the task of publicizing the courses and mobilizing the women to attend.

More successful is a training program organized by OMM to involve women in positions that they never held before, and which takes into account the very low level of literacy among women. It is a crash apprenticeship program designed to circumvent years normally spent at a technical training school so that women can learn skills and earn simultaneously.

These latter approaches toward lessening the deleterious effects of underdevelopment are more relevant to women in the urban areas, whose situation, as can be anticipated, differs widely from that of peasant women. It is worth looking at the contrast to build a broader picture of women's lives.

• The row upon row of cashew nut sorters at Mocita Cashew Factory in Xai-Xai, capital of Gaza, are mostly male. In two rows, however, near the center, pale-blue-scarfed heads of women are dotted among the men's, representing almost a quarter of the total workforce. The relatively small number of women comes as a surprise when one reflects that the workforce of nearly every other cashew factory in Mozambique is overwhelmingly female. However, this factory is more mechanized than most. At Mocita, the presence of women doing the same work as men and earning the same salary is a sign of victory. For two years, the provincial structure of OMM and active OMM members in the town waged a campaign against the administration of the—at the time—privately owned factory, against the male workers and the husbands and fathers of potential women workers, to permit women to apply for jobs that up until then had been open only to men. Now there is an OMM committee at the plant which, after exerting further pressure, was given permission and space to organize a child care center for the women.

• Four heavy tractors, dwarfing their drivers, maintain a steady pace as they traverse the vast open fields of Moamba State Farm, preparing the ground for the sowing of corn. The leader of the team wears a dust-impregnated floppy hat and perky yellow sneakers. Only when the tractors reach the edge of the field does the *capulano* wound around her waist come into view. When the third driver makes a U turn, it becomes clear that this tractor, too, is driven by a woman. Five of the sixteen tractor drivers for "Block

One" are women, and similar ratios can be found in the other four units. Before this farm was taken over by the government after its owner fled the country, no women were employed. The number is, however, still small, but a decided change. Again the OMM structure, this time at the district level, got into the act. As a result, a period of a few weeks was set aside during which only women applicants were accepted for jobs in the fields. The male workers did not like it at all. Women wouldn't be able to do such heavy work, they complained, and yet they would get the same salary. But the women, used to no less strenuous work on their family plots, proved they could, and the men ceased to grumble. Resentment resurfaced sharply, though, when women were selected from among the agricultural workers to train as tractor drivers and thereby increase their salaries substantially. But the administration chastised the men and went ahead with the training of women.

• Among the thousands of tea pickers in the north of Zambezia Province, only a few are women. Perhaps the lack of effective OMM organization in Gurué—a fact bemoaned by the FRELIMO district cadre responsible for ideological work—may have something to do with the almost total absence of women workers in the district's many state and privately owned tea complexes. Only a small number of women are to be found working in the factory as tea packers. My questions to management-level employees—male—elicited stereotypical responses: Women can't carry the large tea baskets while picking tea because they carry babies on their backs. There is a higher absentee rate among women; they are not committed to work (implication: it's only for pocket money). Women can't work on the factory floor because they can't handle the heavy bags of tea. All of this was roundly denied by the OMM secretary in the largest of the tea complexes, under the state-owned Emocha. She spoke bitterly about the difficulties they were experiencing in hiring women. "Women come and apply for work in rags. They need the money as much as the men, and still they are seldom hired."

And yet next to the Emocha factory building is a large garage which repairs the tractors, buses, and cars belonging to the complex. Among the twenty auto mechanics are four women apprentices, while another woman is employed to keep track of the tools. Two more women apprentices had just been hired.

Thus, while many women are taking on new and diverse roles, they still represent only a small proportion of the wage-labor workforce. In many cases, their presence is the exception. And the majority of the women that are employed, particularly in factories, entered the labor force well before independence.

Visits to three Maputo factories and interviews with women workers helped me develop a general profile of the female workforce. The three factories differed from one another in the skills demanded of the workers. At Investro, a clothing factory, where workers use sewing machines and do piecework such as turning collars, trimming seams, etc., a certain level of skill and training is required. Many had at least grade-four education and their salaries, equal to those of their male counterparts, rank them among the highest-paid factory workers in general. Many of the women I interviewed had begun to work because of pressing economic need—desertion by a husband, the need to support an ailing parent, or simply no other means of support and no relationship to the land. They were essentially urban dwellers. Most women spoke of being in stable relationships and their husbands (*de facto* or legal) seemed content that their wives continue working. Most could tell me what their husbands—often themselves factory workers at different plants—earned, although one commented spiritedly: "He *says* his salary is six *contos* (6,000 *meticais*), but how can we trust men?" The fact, however, that the women had some idea of their husbands' income is significant. I was told by different people that men seldom tell their wives what they earn. In any event, men contributed to household expenses, though seldom to household labor.

But more typical of the female workforce were those women I interviewed at a biscuit factory and a cashew factory. Because these plants rely on unskilled labor they are the largest employers of women. In the latter, almost the entire labor force was female. In fact, the cashew factories provide virtually the only opportunity for large-scale employment of women. The Mocita plant in Xai-Xai notwithstanding, almost without exception the women employed in these factories were single mothers. A number of the women I interviewed in the cashew factory in Maputo and a few in the biscuit factory were driven by a desire to repay their *lobolo* (brideprice) as the only way of being released from an unhappy marriage—in some cases after they had been abandoned by their husbands in the first place. Many others were forced to work to support children fathered by *companheiros,* men that they considered partners, even though they had other wives. The few fathers that provided child support did so only after the mothers had taken their cases to the local justice tribunals.

Given the extensive poverty among urban dwellers, it may seem surprising that more married women are not seeking employment to supplement family income. A number of factors influence this. Husbands continue to view women's working as being solely within the home and either they prevent their wives from applying for work outside or the question simply never arises. In the rural areas where women are needed for family agriculture, this attitude is particularly pronounced. Many women do continue to have their own plot of land which they cultivate during the agricultural season to produce food for the rest of the year. This is an important supplement to the husband's wages.

For those women who work in factories, new programs are being established which ease their day. At the factories I visited, as well as many others, crêches have been established. Women are chosen from the factory floor to train as day care workers and run the crêches, receiving the same pay. However, most women workers still prefer to have their children cared for by relatives or older daughters.

At a growing number of workplaces, dining facilities and company stores are being established. The company stores are particularly helpful to working women, enabling them to avoid the long lines at other stores for basic provisions. However, at some workplaces, such as the Limpopo Valley Complex, the workforce is so large that I found women—either workers or wives and daughters of workers—lining up for many hours to make purchases.

Whether single or not, one of the major problems associated with women workers is a high rate of absenteeism. Most of the absenteeism is a result of difficulties relating to their children. After the creation of production councils in the factories, the absentee rate dropped noticeably. But women who are consistently absent are fired and some factories—even state-owned factories—use this as a reason why they prefer to hire male workers (e.g. Emocha in Gurué).

And so the principal motive for seeking work is economic hardship, in most cases a lack of any other means to support their children. This predates, by many years, Mozambican independence and FRELIMO's policies regarding the integration of women into wage-labor production. The continued scarcity of jobs means that the female workforce has not increased, either numerically or proportionally. What has changed are the salaries and working conditions, as well as the political role that women are able to play as members of the production councils, workplace party cells, and OMM structures. This in turn has had a visible impact on the relationships between men and women workers. When I asked women why they worked, many included in their replies the satisfaction they derived from knowing that their work contributed directly to the development of their country. Working at meager wages for the profit of colonialists certainly offered no such gratification. A number of women said that this in itself was enough reason to continue working even if, hypothetically, they found themselves in a financially secure situation. This is one indication of a raised political consciousness among women workers resulting in and reflecting raised political commitment.

Despite the difficulties and inevitably uneven progress in trying to integrate women more fully into wage-labor production, the Mozambican government and party have made a serious commitment to this task, even when a dire scarcity of jobs for the population as a whole persists. The official policy has continued to emphasize that—as written into the constitution—"work is the right and duty of every citizen of either sex."

If this continues as positively—and every indication is that it will—the contradiction between women's work in reproductive labor and their work in the productive sector will be heightened. As the country develops, more jobs will become available to women and the problem will intensify. Because this goes hand in hand with political mobilization and the raising of consciousness among men and women about women's oppression, it is conceivable that women themselves will make the kind of demands needed to have an impact on government and party policy and lead men into sharing domestic labor. Hopefully, this issue will then be picked up more forcefully by the women's organizaton.

Scientific and Cultural Education

The end-of-the-year exams for literacy were in progress at Coca Massava Communal Village in the Chibuto District of Gaza. The class was assembled under a tree in a jagged semicircle around their young literacy monitor. With question papers on their laps, the students sat on the ground or on horizontal tree trunks— generally the women on the ground, the men on the trunks. Infants suckled at their mother's breast, toddlers grabbed at pencils or persistently tried to secure the attention of their mother or a classmate. But the children were ignored as the class sat in silence, each student deep in concentration. All their energies were directed toward the problem at hand. On a worn and chipped blackboard propped up against a tree was written the arithmetical problem: 378 minus 49.

Those attending the exam had persevered against great odds. Hands that for years had wielded hoes and machetes and pestles, hands stiff and calloused from heavy manual labor, were now hold-ing pencils, having been coaxed to perform the delicate task of forming letters and numerals. The progress is slow for many rea-sons. Literacy is taught in Portuguese, but for most of the rural population, Portuguese is a foreign tongue. Lessons are held after many hours in the fields, and students arrive tired and hot, with little other time outside of class to do homework. This being Gaza, there are more women in the class than men, but while the women spend two hours in class a day, there must be someone to attend to their chores at home. One explanation of the smaller number of men was suggested by a monitor at another Gaza village, and would, one presumes, apply generally: men do not relish the idea of displaying their ignorance in front of the women, particularly their own wives. Another reason, though, is the fact that illiteracy among women in the communal villages is close to 100 percent, while men have sometimes had the opportunity to acquire a little bit of education—perhaps in the mines, perhaps at a Roman Catholic mission school. Once in class, many older people discover they cannot read the blackboard because their sight is failing. As a result the older women and men often drop out. It is not surprising that few villages are able to meet the goals set by the literacy cam-paign for the number of residents completing each level each year. But for those who stick with it, a new world begins to open.

A fifty-year-old market woman, Adelina Penicela, enrolled in OMM's first intensive literacy course in Maputo, described this new achievement:

> I began to learn to speak Portuguese with FRELIMO, with the OMM in its first literacy course. The course at first astonished me. We women in our 50's who knew no Portuguese, when they called us to come eat, we couldn't understand. We had to speak with gestures because we spoke only our maternal tongues. But after a month, we began to understand our first words. We came with our eyes closed, but little by little our eyes and our ears began to open and we began to understand. We learned many things—about our provinces, the largest river, the mountains. Before, we found each other strange, we didn't mingle. But there at the centre we learned that we are all equal. We participated in cultural activities and sports, we saw many films, some about women in other countries. Many of us didn't even know that women also worked alongside men in factories.[13]

Such literacy classes are part of an effort to increase women's access to scientific and cultural education as an essential element in fostering women's participation at all levels of leadership and work. As was stressed by Samora Machel in his two OMM conference speeches quoted earlier, the lack of access to such education undermines women's advancement. In the past, Machel noted in the 1973 address, an informal education system had acted to pass on an ideology and culture that evolved in order to maintain the economic exploitation of women.

> Obscurantism is the beginning of the process. The general principle is to keep women in ignorance or give them only an essential minimum of education. Everywhere we find that illiteracy is higher among women . . . even though they are the majority of the population.
>
> Science has always been kept as man's monopoly, their exclusive domain, in the developed civilizations of the past as in capitalist society of today. To keep women away from science is to prevent them from discovering that society is created as a function of certain specific interests and that it is therefore possible to change society. Obscurantism and ignorance go hand in hand with superstition and give rise to passivity. . . .
>
> It must be recognized that the centuries-old subjugation of women has to a great extent reduced them to a passive state, which prevents them from even understanding their condition.

Referring in particular to women in the urban areas, Machel stated in his 1976 speech:

> A great number of women in the cities exist effectively as domestics in their own homes. Depending on which predominates—the feudal ideas or the bourgeois conception of the home—their life resembles that of the peasant women or the colonial capitalist model of the women in the home. But in one way or another, the woman at home is also marginalized and on the periphery of the essential problems of social life. The very nature of the work of the housewife determines her individualist conception of the world. Reduced to an existence of futility and unimportance, without opinions and without initiative, she often becomes guardian to feudal or bourgeois prejudices, the principal vehicle for the transmission of tradition or religious obscurantism.

Education for women—both formal and within society in general—will free women from the web of ignorant beliefs and repressive values that binds them to their subordinate position and will lead them on a path to struggle and participation in social transformation. The resultant new set of values and scientific knowledge that is internalized will be transmitted from mothers—regarded as the first educators—to the next generation.

The emphasis on the need for women to be educated in the broadest sense of the word in no measure suggests that the majority of males were able to read and write. FRELIMO estimates that close to 98 percent of the population were illiterate at the beginning of the liberation war in 1964. At present a generous estimate of those potentially able to read a daily newspaper would be 10 percent, the literacy rate now closer to 90 percent as a result of FRELIMO's education programs already begun before independence in the liberated zones, and continued in the mass literacy programs launched annually since 1978. However, the percentage of illiterate women is much higher.

While the constitution guarantees the right to education for all Mozambican citizens, there are still insufficient resources to establish schools for the whole population. Schooling is therefore not compulsory. As a result, the reasons that lead, in Africa as a whole, to a smaller proportion of girls than boys in school, also pertain in Mozambique: the economic reality, given the sexual division of labor, means that mothers cannot afford to lose their daughters' labor by sending them to school during the day; the belief that girls, as potential wives, do not need education, since they will be able to depend on their husbands; the fact that many girls drop out of school in order to get married at a young age.

Hence one finds the enrollment figures for girls decreasing at each level. In 1979, for instance, the percentage of girls in primary school was 42.6; in secondary general, 29.1 percent.

In an attempt to compensate for the lack of basic education, and their low representation in secondary technical schools, women are being encouraged to enroll in special short-term training programs organized by some government ministries. As a result, women are to be found training as technicians in courses previously reserved for men and as such providing important models for other women. One example is an eleven-month course for low-tension electricians sponsored by the Ministry of Labor. Of a group of fifteen graduates in 1978, four were women, three of whom were among the best five students in the class.[14]

The 20 percent participation of women in secondary technical schools is not discouraging when one considers society's attitudes to women taking up such positions, the lack of the prerequisite general education, and the fact that genuine efforts are being made to right the balance.

In the work of OMM, priority has been given to the literacy campaign in order to increase women's involvement. (For details of the literacy campaign, see the chapter on education.) This takes the form of mobilizing women in the towns as well as establishing literacy centers in the rural areas. First access to these centers goes to the OMM secretaries in the communal villages, who spend either three or six months in an intensive course away from their homes. Although some of the villages have their own literacy and adult education classes, the heavy workload of the OMM secretaries makes it nigh impossible for them to attend classes on a regular basis in their home villages and they quickly fall behind. This could be seen in Três de Fevereiro, for example, where the days of OMM secretary Leia Manhique were crammed with myriad tasks and problems, so that although she managed to finish the second course at the village adult education school, she dropped out of the third one. She was scheduled to attend a six-month literacy course in early 1982 at a communal village in a neighboring district. But Leia Manhique was not the only woman in Três de Fevereiro who dropped out. The monitor for literacy told me that the 1981 enrollment goal of 160 for this village had initially been surpassed, with a total of 164 students coming at the beginning of the term. But, he lamented, by the end of the year, at the time of my second visit to the village, the exams had been cancelled. No one was attending classes. On the other hand, a special class established for members of the village's structures such as the People's Assembly, the OMM secretariat, and the youth organization had twenty members (the majority women) and seemed to be going well.

Not all the literacy centers or courses in the villages functioned without problems. The lack of adequately trained monitors is chronic. At a center I visited for OMM secretaries in Cabo Delgado, the class was sitting in front of the blackboard learning by rote. The literacy monitor had chalked the sentence *A Luta do Povo é Justica* (the struggle of the people is just) on the blackboard. The students repeated the words as she pointed to each one with a long rod. No one noticed that *Povo* was spelled *Pvo*.

Just how extensive the problems relating to literacy are was conveyed to me during my visit, at the end of 1980, to an OMM "experimental center" near Nampula, the capital of Nampula Province. The center had been functioning for almost a year. The class was made up of more than twenty women chosen by their villages in each of the five northern provinces. The course was designed to educate them about nutrition and hygiene: the nutritional value of breast-feeding, how to get the best out of the limited food available, how to build latrines, basics of hygiene and preventive medicine, the importance of bathing their children regularly, of keeping the households free of garbage to lessen mosquitos, and so forth. On completion they would return to their villages and pass on what they had learned to women there. It was a course designed for students with third- or fourth-grade education, entailing note-taking and the use of booklets handed out as reference once back in the villages. But in both of the two cycles of the course held thus far, none of the women who came were able to read and write. Clearly if they could, they would already have been absorbed in other work, and not free to give up four months for such a course. To compound the problem, these students spoke some seven different languages, none of which was spoken by the instructors, who were from the south. And so the prospectus for the course was put aside and replaced by a three-month literacy course, with the hope of concentrating much of the nutrition and hygiene training in the last month. My visit coincided with the end of the course, and in fact basic literacy was continuing. I asked to interview some of the students, and was able to meet with a group of young women (the rest did not speak Portuguese). As an aside, two of the young women asserted in a very definite, almost defiant, tone of voice that when they returned home they intended to pass on the information they had learned to men as well as women. They did not see nutrition and hygiene as work that should be carried out by women only. It turned out that this was the last course held. The center has since been closed for reassessment and redesign. Meanwhile a similar center built with the aid of UNICEF funds and benefitting from the experience of the first was set up in Gaza, scheduled to open in 1982.

The problems affecting women at Coca Massava and other communal villages referred to earlier are to be found to a greater or lesser extent throughout the country, in rural and urban areas alike. Additional obstacles prevail: The husbands who simply forbid their wives to attend classes. The women who feel too old to begin something so new. The husbands who argue energetically that their wives do not have time because they must work in the home, but who really fear that their wives will become "smarter" than they and "get out of hand." The husbands who fear that, given this freedom, their wives will meet other men and begin having extramarital relationships. If the woman complains to OMM, members of the secretariat will try to speak to the husband and urge him to change his mind. But this may well have no effect. Just as often, the wife will say nothing either to her husband or to OMM. Despite the host of problems, both attitudinal and relating to lack of resources (teachers, equipment, etc.), OMM feels that significant inroads have been made and that overall participation in literacy classes has exceeded expectations.

And so for many women, this focus on education has made dramatic changes in their lives. Take the OMM secretary in Inhambane, responsible for social affairs. She found it difficult to carry out her work, as she could not read the messages left for her, or the written instructions. She could take no notes about the problems she was trying to solve. When she was offered the opportunity to attend a three-month intensive course, she jumped at it. She was lucky: her husband agreed to take responsibility for their eight children. The many friends who chided her about being too old were proved wrong. Having taken this first step in education, she returned home and continued her studies there.

The New Concept of the Family

The family as it existed in Mozambique in precolonial and colonial times and persists in much of the country today is considered by FRELIMO to be a major obstacle to the achievement of equality between men and women. Practices such as polygamy, *lobolo* (brideprice), child marriage, forced marriage, lack of divorce for women are all intrinsically bound up with the structure of family life and are considered detrimental customs that in time must be brought to an end. Needed to replace the old view of the family, says the party, is a new concept of revolutionary love, based on FRELIMO's political line. This concept was first expressed in Machel's address to the 1973 OMM conference:

> We must state here—and this is something new in society—that the family relationship, the man-woman relationship, should be founded exclusively on love. We do not mean the banal, romantic concept of love which amounts to little more than emotional excitement and an idealized view of life. For us, love can only exist between free and equal people who have the same ideals and commitment in serving the masses and the revolution. This is the basis upon which the moral and emotional affinity which constitutes love is built. We need to discover this new dimension, hitherto unknown in our country.

In the process of discovering the new, the old has to be relegated to the past. It is anything but a straightforward challenge. Transforming attitudes, though a decided element in the process, is only a portion of the battle. It is necessary to change the family structure, reaching deep into the foundations of the family and out to the local rural economy.

Polygamy, for example, has an economic base. For the husband it means more workers to till the fields and an ability to feed his family. It means security as well as the possibility of accumulating wealth. Equally important, it means the reproduction of future workers.

The main thrust of the campaign to bring an end to the practice has been ideological—through political education conducted by OMM and FRELIMO. To back this up, certain restrictions have been placed on "new" polygamists, denying them and their later wives positions of responsibility in dynamizing groups, mass organizations, and party and government structures and disallowing their candidacy for representative assemblies and councils at all levels.

In explaining FRELIMO's analysis of polygamy, the OMM second conference report states:

> In our patriarchal society, the man is the owner of all material goods produced within the family. Polygamy is a system whereby the man possesses a number of wives. As head and proprietor of the family, he acquires more wives to augment the labor force at this service.

The campaign has produced the best results in communal villages, and in fact, this reorganized form of economic and social life is seen as the most effective arena in which to end the practice. In villages I visited in Gaza, for instance, women were emphatic in stating that no new polygamous marriages had taken place in their village since inception. Those that had wanted to be party to such a union had been talked out of it. My experience, though, was that the practice continued, but at a reduced level.

OMM's early involvement in this process of change in Gaza was described in a 1977 interview with a member of the provincial secretariat of OMM, Sarifa Amati:

> We should try to educate women at meetings as well as confront those wanting to engage in polygamy. We point out that it is not a just relationship, but is perpetuated by men to facilitate the exploitation of women. One man who has two or three wives is unable to provide the emotional support and affection which is the basis of a healthy marriage. OMM emphasizes that it is the women themselves who must take the lead in combatting polygamy. Women are beginning to understand this and the level of polygamy seems to be declining.[15]

If a woman agrees to become a second or third wife, Amati explained, she is criticized heavily and told to attend re-education classes held by OMM. Sometimes they are sent for re-education outside the locality as a way of preventing them from entering polygamous marriages. However, even in communal villages new polygamy could still be found. It may have decreased, but it certainly has not ended. Take the case of Juliana Caetano, who lives in a village in Namacurra District, Zambezia Province.

Juliana Caetano married her present husband—her second— over twenty-two years ago. During that time they had one child, a daughter, who is now married to a FRELIMO district *responsavel* and lives in the same village, Mutanga. Juliana Caetano's family was one of the first to move to the village in 1977, which by 1980 had increased to 236 families and is still growing. A new life opened to her when she moved, she said. No longer is her house isolated from neighbors by miles. No longer does she have to walk over a mile to get water. No longer is she lonely. Now she works together with other women, and with men, to build the village. She has close neighbors and feels their support, particularly the women. She has been active since she arrived, is a member of the People's Assembly, and will be the secretary of OMM, which she is helping to organize. Her pride in her village can be seen in her enthusiasm when speaking about the changes. She is proud of the new health center that is being finished, the first cement structure in the village. She is proud of the consumer cooperative where necessities can be purchased, eliminating long journeys to the store. And there are the water pumps, driven by a manually operated wheel, the schools for the children, the literacy classes for the adults.

But although proud, she is personally unhappy. The fulfillment of impossible dreams has been painfully marred. Her husband has taken a second wife. When she speaks of it, her face hardens with anger.

At first, when the discussion with her and five other women from the village turned to polygamy, she sat closed-mouthed. The other women were equally unresponsive. Occasionally they smiled sideways at each other, looked a bit uncomfortable, made comments under their breath, sometimes grinned, but voiced no opinion. Juliana Caetano's son-in-law, who was translating from the local language into Portuguese, tried to coax them to speak of their feelings about polygamy. They would not. As he lived in the village, he was very aware of the women's feelings. "They know very well what they think about polygamy." he said. "They don't like it at all. But they are afraid to say this to visitors, as their husbands will hear and get very angry with them." Of the five women present, four were in polygamous marriages.

When the questions were phrased less personally, they began to respond. Yes, polygamy was still practiced in the village, particularly by the younger men, they said. When the OMM talks to the men to try to discourage this practice, they will not listen. "This has nothing to do with you," the man typically retorts, "it is I who arrange for the second wife and I who support her, not you."

An old man who was listening offered his opinion. He is a Catholic and has one wife. "Sometimes a man takes another wife because his first does not bear him any children. But even when a man has many children he wants another wife. As long as he sees pretty faces, he wants more wives."

Throughout the discussion, Juliana Caetano had said little. Her face still looked grim, but it also looked very hurt. Suddenly, she

382   A Difficult Road

broke into an impassioned speech, propelled by her antagonism toward her husband and his new young wife and the sense of abandonment she felt.

"Polygamy is bad. Very bad. Why do men want more wives? I am a woman, just like the new wife is a woman. Why does he want more than me? Sometimes when the first wife won't accept this, she quarrels with her husband. And he leaves and starts a new life with the second wife. It is hard on the first wife. A woman has to organize the house. Life is difficult and there is not enough—not enough food, clothes, other necessities. He can't even support the one wife, how will he support two? But when a man has decided, the woman can do nothing. When a man takes two wives, each has her own house. But the first wife is left alone, alone. Her husband no longer takes good care of her, or even thinks about her."

Her husband had been married to his second wife for three months. This woman, with whom he now spends a lot of time, is very much younger than he. "He thinks he is young, although he is old. Otherwise he wouldn't marry someone so young. I love him because he is my husband. He can go out whenever he wants. When he comes home, I am always there. I love him, but he is ceasing to love me. Why am I not allowed to love my own husband?"

Other customs that contribute to women's unequal status within the family—*lobolo*, forced marriage, child marriage—have, like polygamy, been the target of intense political campaigns, with equally varied success. *Lobolo*, like polygamy, has an economic base. As pointed out in the second OMM conference, "This practice exists throughout the country. Its rationale is that it is compensation for the transfer of labor power from one family to another. This puts women in a situation of total dependence on men, who because they have paid for them, can use and disown them like mere objects."

Again, the most effective inroads against this custom have been made in communal villages. However, OMM now finds that it is often up against a new practice that is emerging to replace it. The bridegroom's parents are passing on "gratification gifts" to the family of their future daughter-in-law to express "gratitude" for its having reared her as an appropriate wife for their son. As this is supposedly spontaneous, it is harder to bring to an end, but is often as expected by the bride's parents as *lobolo*.

Two young men, recently married, whom I interviewed in Três de Fevereiro, told me that the parents of their future wives had told them what to bring as "gratification." The gifts were to include cloth, a watch, a gold ring, and other consumer items which appear to equal the value of the *lobolo* customarily paid in that area of the country. According to the perceptions of the men, this was not another form of bride-price, as the latter implied the establishment of an unequal relationship within the family. They criticized the *lobolo* custom for the way in which it gave men power over their wives, reflecting what women told me: that husbands often hold the bride-price over their wive's heads at times of strife. "I gave your parents *lobolo* for you," men would state in anger, "now you have to obey me." "Gratification," these young men insisted, could not play the same detrimental role, and neither would it be returned in the event that the marriage broke down. There were, however, reports of conflict between families because the wife's family refused to return the gratification gift when the marriage failed.

Although such customs continue, they do seem to have declined since independence, markedly so in certain areas. Mutanga notwithstanding, the sharpest decrease has been in communal villages, particularly the areas where political mobilization and commitment are more developed. A man's need for more workers in the form of wives and children in rural Mozambique means that people will not readily relinquish the customs that guarantee these. It is more likely to happen when an alternative way of life is offered which can provide answers to the problems that gave rise to such social devices in the first place. Once the required economic reorganization has taken place, it might well be easier to change the attitudes that have acted to hold such customary practices in place. However, until now, efforts for change have been mainly ideological and hence rather top-heavy. There is insufficient understanding at the base about the oppressive aspects of such customs which are unquestioningly accepted as the only way, as well as with insufficient understanding at the leadership level of just how deep-rooted such customs are. However, preparations for the special conference on social problems affecting women to be held in 1984, as earlier mentioned, have taken this into account. They have been accompanied by self-criticism among the leadership for a tendency to approach the need for change in a mechanical way. *Abaixo* ("down with") slogans are not the answer in themselves.

At the end of 1981, a new family law was in its final stages of revision. It has not yet been adopted. One of the provisions expected to have particular impact is the recognition of common-law marriages as legally binding after a simple registration. In conjunction with this is an insistence that a man recognize and be responsible for all children he has fathered, whether he lives with the mother or not. Already it is possible for women to take their cases to the children's court or to the justice tribunal of their *bairro* to demand child support from the father. Child support may then be held back from his salary and given directly to the woman each month, or sent to the tribunal to be handed on to the woman; in this way there is a check on whether he is meeting his responsibility or not. However, it is still the minority of women who resort to such a remedy or see it as their right. It is hoped that the education campaign planned to accompany the implementation of the new law will publicize this measure and thereby increase women's requests for child support.

My visit to the three factories in Maputo showed just how widespread this phenomenon of children abandoned by their fathers is in the city. It was not uncommon to interview a woman with seven or eight children, fathered by two or three different men, who each in turn had abandoned the mother. At one factory, the assistant secretary of the party cell said she urged women to take such cases to the courts, as only then would men begin to think twice about the way they used and abused women. If faced with deductions from their salaries for all the children they casually brought into the world, they would have to reassess their behavior, she emphasized.

Although common-law marriages are to be recognized, the law intends this not as approval but as an acknowledgment of a past and current reality in order to protect both women and children. The clear goal is that registered marriages should take place with a conscious commitment between the couple to each other and to the joint rearing of children.

While the concept of equal rights and duties is stressed as a crucial principle for the new "revolutionary family," the law offers no guidance as to how this equalization should occur. Neither does it provide any constraints on negative conduct by men within the family or the possibility of redress when spouses violate the spirit of the law. In this regard the law lacks bite, and the political education generally outlined by OMM cadres at all levels offers few practical interpretations of the concept of equality.

As pointed out above, the sexual division of labor within the household is seldom addressed as a problem to be solved by means of greater participation and responsibility on the part of men. OMM cadres stress that women must encourage change with "kind words," patient encouragement, and education of men; it is incorrect to speak in anger. Arminda Hombé, the OMM secretary for Chibuto District, Gaza, explained this to me:

> Perhaps a young wife has three children and is breast-feeding the youngest one in the evening. The two older ones are playing at her feet. Her husband, just home from work, sits in a chair and reads the

paper. The wife tries to attend to all three children at once. Then the toddler messes on the floor. The husband does not notice or ignores the exasperation of his wife. She then turns to him and says, "Dear, our second child has dirtied the floor. As you see, I am feeding our youngest. Nutrition is extremely important for his growth, so it would be wrong to stop feeding to attend to the other's needs. Would you mind cleaning it up?" If she says this politely, the husband will respond, and next time he will notice on his own accord and attend to it without being asked. This is how we explain to women at meetings the way to change men's behavior within the family.

OMM leaders emphasize that the woman must set an example within the family. For only then, they believe, can the man appreciate the heavy workload of the woman and try to help her with it. This method of change-by-example often means that the woman must get up an hour earlier and go to bed an hour later in order to complete her work. This is true not only for women engaged in wage-labor, but for women militants who work within OMM or party structures and in other volunteer work as an essential contribution to social reconstruction. Those of us from societies where any change that has come about in the sexual division of household labor has generally been the result of "political education" involving frequent direct challenges of male behavior and assumptions, often accompanied by expressions of deep anger, will find it difficult to believe that tolerant "kind words" are all that is required.

Another important role assigned to the Mozambican woman is that of educator within the family. The family is often referred to as the "first cell of the party" and is seen as having a critical function in developing the next generation of revolutionaries. It is the mother who is the "dynamizer" of this cell, the one responsible for nurturing good relations within it. Much emphasis is placed on how she fulfills this role. This is not insignificant. In African society women have in fact been the educators of young children and the communicators of the values of society, teaching the young how to behave and work not only within the family but in the community as a whole. It is a role of genuine importance and responsibility, but it has been largely considered immaterial because it is tied to "women's work." So this new emphasis is extremely relevant to the recognition of women's work and status in the process of transforming attitudes. In order for women to carry out this role, their liberation is essential. Machel points to this in his speech to the first OMM conference:

> If we . . . consider the basic need for the revolution to be continued by the new generation, how can we ensure the revolutionary education of the generation which will carry on our work if mothers, the

386 A Difficult Road

first educators, are marginal to the revolutionary process? How can one turn the homes of the exploited and the oppressed into cells of revolutionary struggle, centres for the diffusion of our line, encouraging the involvement of the family, if women remain apathetic to this process, indifferent to the society which is being built and deaf to the call of the people?

The question that arises is whether the revaluing of the mother's role as educator in the family is a step toward equalizing responsibility for the household between husband and wife, or whether it reentrenches her particular role within the family, as an immutable fact. At this stage, emphasis tends to be placed on the latter.

For a young woman coming to puberty in a communal village, for instance, the changes to her role in respect to family life have thus far been profound. She no longer has to enter a marriage to a man—likely to be many years her senior—chosen by her parents. She can expect to be the only wife. She knows that OMM will help her at times of conflict and that should she be maltreated by her husband, she has recourse to divorce. Although, if she is militant, she will be stretching her energies to the limit to engage in all aspects of productive, political, and reproductive work, she can look forward to the introduction of services and technological advances to help lighten the load. She can demand the respect due to her as an equal member of the society and refuse to play the role of an inferior, dependent wife. This, along with her participation outside the home in income-producing labor (in agricultural or other cooperatives), provides crucial ground for her development into a self-confident and emancipated woman.

Crucial, but not quite sufficient. A major obstacle endures: the sexual division of labor within the household. Only the most militant of women would be able to rise above the constraints perpetuated by the lack of concrete measures to transform this unequal division. But the seeds of its destruction are encased in the groundwork already established. The transformation that has occurred or is possible may itself be the impetus needed to give women the resolve to struggle for a transformation that is total. Without that putting into practice the concept of "revolutionary" and "militant" love appears an illusory hope.

The very nature of revolutionary process dictates that steady upward and onward progress is impossible. The process always breeds its own contradictions, which, once recognized, can in turn be dealt with. Revolution is a slow process, often seeming to embody the familiar image of two steps forward, "one-and-a-half" steps backward. The emancipation of women is especially complex, touching as it does all facets of the revolutionary struggle, relying on advances in all fields for its own victories, and falling victim to the failures that occur in other sectors. In evaluating progress along the obstacle course to the emancipation of women, it would therefore have been naive to have expected great leaps forward. Revolutionary change is not achieved by miracles.

What is clear is that strides have been made, and that the impact of FRELIMO's policy toward the liberation of women has been felt by women throughout Mozambique. Without the backing of FRELIMO and OMM this would have been impossible. The credibility given to OMM's work by the party has meant that men, however reluctant, have had to reassess the role of women in the social, economic, and political affairs of their immediate environment.

The emancipation of women is a goal voiced at all levels of the government and party structures, and echoed in a variety of ways by women and men workers, peasants, and students throughout Mozambique. The contradictions that emerge in the process, as I have described in the preceding pages, have potentially within them the seeds of their own destruction. If in fact there is continued encouragement of women to enter men's fields of work, to take on political leadership, to become more educated, to broaden their vision of the world, to take a more active role in transforming production as wage-laborers, as well as to revalue their fundamental role in family agricultural production, then it may be possible for women to make more unequivocal demands for further changes. In no small measure women shoulder the country's most fundamental task: the provision of food for the majority of its people. They are a force to contend with. While definite progress is being made, only time will tell where the first early steps that are now being taken will lead.

Notes

Research for this chapter was made possible by a grant from The Ford Foundation and a supplemental grant from Carol Bernstein Ferry and W. H. Ferry. I wish to thank Barbara Isaacman for generously sharing the material and perspectives derived from her extensive research in Mozambique on women.

1. Samora Machel, "The Liberation of Women Is a Fundamental Necessity for the Revolution," in *Mozambique: Sowing the Seeds of Revolution* (London, 1974), p. 24.
2. Barbara Isaacman and June Stephen, *Mozambique: Women, the Law, and Agrarian Reform* (United Nations Economic Commission for Africa, 1980), p. 30.

3. Ibid., p. 32.
4. Cited in ibid., p. 33.
5. Cited in ibid., p. 35.
6. Ibid., p. 37.
7. World Conference for the United Nations Decade for Women, "Review and Evaluation of Progress Achieved in the Implementation of the World Plan of Action: Political Participation, International Cooperation and Strengthening of International Peace." Copenhagen, July 1980.
8. Ibid.
9. Samora Machel, Address to the Second Conference of Mozambican Women, 1976. (Author's translation.)
10. Documents of the Third Congress of FRELIMO, Maputo, 1977, cited in Isaacman and Stephen, *Mozambique,* p. 68.
11. *Tempo* (Maputo), no. 318 (7 November 1976): 55.
12. See Lourdes Beneria, "Reproduction, Production, and the Sexual Division of Labor," International Labour Office, Rural Employment Program, Research Working Paper (Geneva, July 1978).
13. OMM Archives, interview with Adelina Penicela, Maputo, cited in Isaacman and Stephen, *Mozambique,* pp. 101–102.
14. *Tempo,* no. 385 (19 February 1979): 11.
15. Interview by Allen F. Isaacman, August 1977.

PART III

Afterword

John S. Saul

9. Nkomati and After

A difficult road? We have already seen the many positive achievements recorded in preceding chapters to be shadowed by the grim realities of the setting that frames them. However, the Nkomati Accord struck with South Africa in March 1984 has underscored such realities in a particularly dramatic fashion. It has been difficult for even the most sympathetic external observor of the Mozambican revolution to view this as anything but a retreat, while some would go further and see it as marking the final winding down of any transition to socialism which once may have been in train. It bears noting that the Mozambican leadership itself has chosen to present the Accord quite differently: not as a defeat, not even as a retreat, but as a victory. We will want to explore its reasons for doing so later in this chapter, along with other matters, including the explanation for the Accord on the one hand and its possible implications, both nationally and regionally, on the other. Of course, we have had something to say about these matters, particularly the former, in our introductory chapters. Here we shall merely attempt to refocus some of that material around the moment of the Accord, using it as a kind of litmus paper by which to gauge the current state of the Mozambican project.

But first, what is the actual content of the Accord? Formally it is defined as an "Agreement on Non-Aggression and Good Neighborliness," one which reaffirms "the principle of noninterference in the internal affairs of other states." For Mozambique the crucial clauses are surely the following:

> II. 1. Both the high contracting parties shall resolve the differences and disputes which arise between them and which could endanger mutual or regional peace and security, through negotiations, mediation, conciliation, arbitration and other peaceful means, and undertake not to resort individually or collectively to the use of force against the sovereignty, territorial integrity, and political independence of each other.

> III. 1. The high contracting parties shall not allow their respective territories, territorial waters, or airspace to be used as a base, transit

392

point, or in any other way by another state, government, foreign military force, organizations, or individuals planning or preparing to carry out acts of violence, terrorism, or aggression against the territorial integrity or political independence of the other, or which could threaten the security of its inhabitants.[1]

From the time of a meeting held with the South Africans in December 1982, Mozambique had been engaged in efforts to bring South Africa to admit openly its responsibility for MNR activities and to force it to bring its counterrevolutionary puppets to heel. South Africa seemed now to be acknowledging the former fact and promising the latter result. Needless to say, there were quid pro quos for South Africa, not least that Mozambique was to scale down its own support for the African National Congress of South Africa. And there were economic dimensions to the negotiations between South Africa and Mozambique as well. Here discussion came to focus on the possibility of some kind of revitalization of the structural links between the two countries which, as we have seen, had been disrupted (more or less unilaterally by South Africa) and rapidly run down in the years after 1975—especially in the sphere of migrant labor, payments for it, and in the use of the Maputo port by the South African rail authorities. Indeed, in principle, economic linkages were also to be extended into new spheres. In the event, concrete results have been slow to come, but the joint meetings on security from which the Accord emerged were paralleled by a further series of meetings between the two parties whose agenda "comprised questions relating to matters affecting transport, migrant labor, agriculture, fisheries, industry and commerce, finance, tourism and energy," these seeking "to catalogue areas of common interest and determine concrete procedures to ensure the viability of relations in the various commercial and economic fields."*[2] As we saw in Chapter 2, this opening up to South Africa formed part of a more broad-gauged tactical turn by Mozambique toward international capital, but it will be evident that including a freshly expanded role for South Africa in the line-up of Mozambican economic partners has quite special implications, both bilaterally and regionally.

---

*Of particular prominence were special meetings on tourism; these involved such figures as the head of the South African Tourist Board and the president of the South African Federation of Hotel Owners, among others, and "covered a wide range of subjects, including the existing potential of across-border tourism flows, short- and long-term projects, the up-grading of the tourist infrastructure in Mozambique, the ready availability of visa and immigration procedures, means of transportation, the possibility of the introduction of package tours, and the feasibility of a limited marketing campaign within South Africa."

Is there a "winner" here? Certainly, Mozambicans are quick to argue that South Africa is by no means omnipotent, that it cannot be seen as having simply dictated terms. The land of apartheid is also beset with contradictions, including a profound economic crisis of its own. Indeed, the ongoing recession there has been described by Finance Minister Owen Horwood as being much the worst since the years of the Great Depression. There are arguments against the further financing of foreign wars which spring from this fact alone. Moreover, it could be argued that the crisis-ridden South African economy needs economic links—markets, investment outlets—at least as much as Mozambique needs the economic inputs themselves.

In more strictly military terms there have also been risks involved—though some South African decision-makers apparently feel this more forcefully than others—in overextending the country's military machine, formidable though it may be in comparison with that of any of its neighbors. Finally, Mozambicans argue that there have been diplomatic constraints brought to bear on South Africa by its Western allies. Indeed, it seems likely that a major motive of Samora Machel's European visit in 1983—and perhaps an additional motive behind Mozambique's strongly expressed and widely publicized interest in receiving Western investment—was quite precisely to mobilize such pressure. In its desire to break out of diplomatic isolation and present a reformist image South Africa may have been prepared to make concessions to Mozambique it might not otherwise have contemplated. Indeed, in the wake of the Accord one Mozambican minister went so far as to claim that Machel's diplomatic offensive, taken together with Mozambique's "regional strategy" and its continuing military campaign against the MNR, had provoked a "profound crisis in the South African regime."[3]

Of course, most of these arguments could be quite readily turned inside out and seen as evidence of South Africa's relative strength. The "total strategy" which has emerged in South African ruling circles in response to crisis has all along had both political and military dimensions. It may well have seemed to cooler heads there that, having applied the stick with sufficient force to bludgeon Mozambique into economic prostration, it was now time to proffer some economic carrots instead. A further deepening of Mozambique's economic links to South Africa might then serve to tame and control an otherwise hostile neighbor. And these links could serve as an important step in reconsolidating the southern African regional economy as South Africa's hinterland and market as well. Just as SADCC had been the indirect target of much of the MNR's sabotage activity throughout the war, so now the peace might be used to break the SADCC front and weaken the attempt to construct a new regional grid outside the orbit of South African economic power.* And what of the international implications? P. W. Botha was quick to use whatever legitimacy had been conferred upon him by Nkomati to stage a European tour of his own in the late spring of 1984. Though the results of the tour were mixed—and many of the gains from it were, in any case, negated when South Africa's internal contradictions boiled over once again later in the year—it did represent a diplomatic advance for the apartheid regime. Here was a result that could hardly have been displeasing to such Western allies of South Africa as the United States, which could now present the Nkomati "success" as some vindication of its notorious policy of "constructive engagement."

We shall return to a discussion of South African strategy shortly; it is germane to any evaluation of Mozambique's decision to present the Nkomati Accord as a victory. In whatever way we may choose to interpret South Africa's strengths and weaknesses, however, it is clear that, in comparison with South Africa, Mozambique had come to the bargaining table in a far less powerful position than its apartheid counterpart. We have examined the severe economic crisis in which Mozambique has found itself. The National Planning Commission report of January 1984, which was cited in Chapter 2, presents a veritable litany of economic distemper and its tone was echoed in April's People's Assembly, when President Machel described the country as being in its "worst economic crisis ever."[4] On the same occasion, Finance Minister Rui Baltazar "painted a grim picture of the current state of the Mozambican economy," citing such facts as the 40 percent decline of Mozambican exports in comparison with an already low 1982 figure and "the shortage of imported fuels, raw materials and spare parts which had caused a drop of production in many industries."[5] We have also hinted at some of the political demoralization which has begun to accompany this crisis.

Opinions will differ as to the precise balance of causes of the crisis: the abysmal inheritance from the Portuguese colonial system and the subsequent crisis of that system, natural disasters, class contradictions within the transition process itself, as well as failures

---

*The alternative long-term South African goal for the region is, in opposition to SADCC, the construction of a "Constellation of States" under South Africa's own economic hegemony; on this and other aspects of South Africa's regional strategy see Robert Davies and Dan O'Meara, "Total Strategy on Southern Africa: An Analysis of South African Regional Policy Since 1979" (unpublished paper, 1984).

of omission and commission by the leadership. Perhaps our introductory chapters will have equipped readers to make some judgment on this question for themselves. Nonetheless, there do seem strong grounds for agreeing with Samora Machel that the single most important cause of Mozambique's current economic problem "lies in the situation in Southern Africa and in the wars that have been forced upon us."[6] Nor has the economic impact of South Africa's war against Mozambique been a mere accidental by-product of aggression. On the contrary, the war has been directed quite cunningly at producing a desired effect: the targets that have been hit are those whose destruction weakens the infrastructure of economic life. The intent: slowly but surely to bleed Mozambican socialism to death. A comparative perspective may help. Certainly Mozambican realities were to seem even clearer to me after I had visited Nicaragua in September 1984. While there I was struck by the forceful parallels between South Africa's strategy of economic warfare on the one hand and American strategy vis-à-vis the Nicaraguan revolution on the other. A Jesuit priest, now working in Nicaragua's agrarian reform sector but also active in Chile before the coup, put the point to me with scalding simplicity. "In Chile," he said, "The Americans made a mistake. They cut off the revolution too abruptly. They killed the revolution but, as we can see from recent developments there, they didn't kill the dream. In Nicaragua they're trying to kill the dream." So, too, in Mozambique.

In Nicaragua, one could begin to see the draining effect that this was having on the populace, despite the many exciting programs in train there, and I left that country with a rather sobering sense of *déja vu*. Nicaragua had too much the feel for me of Mozambique a few years earlier, on the way to Nkomati. One moment, in particular, stuck in my mind. I was in Nicaragua for a reason. Some fifteen or twenty of us had been invited to participate in a workshop on "Problems of the Transition to Socialism in Small Peripheral Economies," and we worked hard at it for six days. Finally, toward the end of the workshop, we received a visit from Jaime Wheelock, one of the nine *comandantes* who lead the Nicaraguan revolution. The minister of agrarian reform, he was now spending most of his time back in military harness, organizing the defense against the *contras* in the Sixth Region. His face was gray with fatigue, tired not merely from a few nights without sleep, but much more deeply, his face mirroring those of Mozambique's leaders as they lived the South African seige. It was a bad time, a Friday evening after a hard week's work, and Wheelock was in an almost elegaic mood. Perhaps he was poking fun at us, the intellectual observers of the passing scene, just a little bit when he said, "Transition to socialism? There's no transition to socialism here. We're surviving, that's all. We're living from Friday to Friday."[7] Poking fun at us. And perhaps, too, a certain self-dramatization to achieve an effect. None of the *comandantes*—least of all Wheelock—and few other Nicaraguans whom I met operated on such a premise. But there was a certain chilling realism in what he was saying. For me it also underscored what must be the bottom line of any serious discussion of the Nkomati Accord. At one important level Mozambique has had no choice but to sue for peace with South Africa; there can be no escaping the hard fact that Mozambique has been literally bludgeoned into "compromise." To the extent that this is the case, the fundamental question becomes one of whether, under such testing circumstances, Mozambique has made the best of the limited room for maneuver it has been able to find—and whether it has been left with enough such room to revitalize its socialist project.

Mozambicans have sometimes come close to echoing this tone, tacitly acknowledging the overdetermining impact of the destructiveness of South Africa's war upon their policy options. In this connection there has also been some bitterness over the inability of critics to grasp sympathetically the hard realities of the terrain upon which Mozambique finds itself. For example, in debate at a meeting of the People's Assembly held a month after the signing of the Nkomati Accord, Joaquim Chissano, Mozambique's Foreign Minister

> criticized the "ultra-left myopic revolutionaries" who objected to the agreement. "They don't hesitate in asking us to die so that they can applaud us as heroes," he remarked caustically.
> Mozambique did not mind this when the sacrifice was useful, as it had been during the independence war, "but we ought to tell them that our people don't just die to win applause. They don't die so that statues can be built to them."
> Mr. Chissano warned that, in itself, the agreement "will not bring us happiness. It is not the Nkomati Accord that will eliminate hunger, or provide us with clothing." What the accord did was "create conditions for our efforts in production to give better results."[8]

Not that the public mood has been elegiac, however. In an important speech at a special post-Nkomati ceremony in Maputo, Samora Machel stated forcefully that "the Nkomati Accord defends the first workers and peasants state in the region, one that is constructing socialism on the basis of Marxism-Leninism."[9] And Sergio Vieira, the chairman of the Mozambique side of the joint security commission set up to implement the Nkomati Accord, invoked the historical precedent of the Treaty of Brest-Litovsk and argued that "to be a revolutionary in the Africa of 1984 demands the defense and consolidation of Africa's socialist revolution. The touchstone of internationalism today is the concrete attitude taken toward the first liberated zone on the continent."[10]

In Machel's and Vieira's formulations we also begin to see emerging the premises for Mozambique's presentation of the Nkomati Accord as a *victory*. For Machel, South Africa's

> objective was to overthrow the socialist and progressive systems of the region. In relation to our country, the objective was also to destroy our people's revolutionary state. The objective was to destroy the alternative civilization which Mozambique represents. . . . [But] the policy of regional destabilization did not have the desired effect. South Africa did not achieve the political objectives for which it launched the war. . . . [I]t has failed to achieve armed victory. . . . With _ the signing of the Accord of Nkomati, the main project, the destruction of our state, failed. In signing the Accord of Nkomati we guaranteed the objective of our fight—peace.[11]

Similarly, for Sergio Vieira "the agreement was a defeat for those in South Africa who had staked all on racism and expansionism, and who had made their anti-communism into 'a pathological obsession'":

> Against those who claimed for themselves the right to intervene in any state south of the equator, the Accord imposes strict respect for sovereignty and territorial integrity. . . . Against those who used to boast that they could destroy any African state between breakfast and lunch, the accord obliges coexistence with our anti-racist state.

And he concluded, "The strategy of the struggle for peace in Southern Africa consists 'in obliging the anti-communists to coexist with socialist states.' "[12]

Certain aspects of these formulations are debatable, of course. We have already hinted at several reasons for questioning whether the dominant actors in South Africa have ever contemplated the kind of total military defeat of FRELIMO that Machel and Vieira feel themselves to have preempted. As one South African academic with close connections to the defense establishment there has argued, in presenting an alternative scenario (in 1982):

> Assuming [sic] that South Africa is either engaged in destabilizing Mozambique or contemplating it, several objectives are readily discernible. First and foremost, South Africa would want FRELIMO to abandon its active support for ANC, which means denying it sanctuary. A more ambitious objective would be to influence Mozambique to loosen, if not cut, its close ties—particularly in the military field—

with Communist powers. South Africa would also welcome Mozambique toning down its revolutionary fervor and moderating its condemnation of the republic. What Pretoria essentially desires is a friendly cooperative neighbor instead of a Marxist state threatening its security. To achieve these objectives, support for the MNR and severe manipulation of economic ties are the two obvious means to apply. To talk of the MNR overthrowing FRELIMO or even forcing it into a compromise seems highly premature and indeed highly unrealistic. South Africa would therefore have to confine its objectives to changing political behavior, not political structures.[13]

As the same writer put a related point two years later, at the time of Nkomati, South Africa's "hawkish strategy toward its neighbors had the intended effect of producing or aggravating domestic instability in target states. But SA does not have a master plan for removing regimes in power in neighboring states, nor has it the resources to dislodge several governments and sustain perhaps unpopular puppet successor regimes in the face of determined resistance."[14]

Certainly MNR strategy has seldom seemed one crafted to really win the war. It has done relatively little to present a "counter-hegemonic" project by means of ideological mobilization of the populace—despite a context of economic crisis and some political weakness on the part of FRELIMO. Instead, brutal intimidation and maximum economic destructiveness have remained its predominant style. No doubt this testifies to the MNR's reading of the level of FRELIMO's continuing legitimacy in Mozambique. But it may equally well reflect the war aims of its paymaster. Small wonder that even Mozambique's Minister of Information could suggest in mid-1983 that "South Africa probably prefers to destabilize FRELIMO rather than try to install a puppet regime. That would be too costly for them."[15] Yet if this were the case, one might equally argue that, by early 1984, South African strategists (and their allies in Western capitals) had merely reached the point where they felt they had Mozambique on the ropes, a point at which, to return to an earlier metaphor, carrots rather than the stick could be used to consolidate the complete reintegration of Mozambique into the international-cum-South African capitalist network. Of course, it does not necessarily follow that such a calculation on the part of Mozambique's enemies would necessarily be an accurate one. But putting the matter in such terms does suggest that any too pronounced a spirit of triumphalism on Mozambique's part may lead to a serious underestimation of the dangers of the new terrain on which the country now finds itself. It also returns us to a by now familiar question: has FRELIMO the realistic prospect of control-

ling the compromises it has made and of keeping something more
than mere survival—socialism, for example—on the agenda?
We must be cautious here. There is surely room for differences
of opinion regarding the correct reading of South Africa's war
aims. And who could begrudge Mozambicans their enthusiastic
embracing of the prospect of peace after twenty long years of war?
Perhaps only by excerpting an extended passage from the President's speech, cited above, can we expect the reader to grasp the
full import of this fact:

> If it is true that Nkomati crowned our socialist policy of peace with
> success, it is also true that we came out of this fight with severe
> wounds. Only future generations will show the precise extent of the
> social trauma caused by the horrors and barbarity of the armed
> gangs. The children who witnessed atrocities and repugnant acts of
> violence and destruction will grow up with the nightmare of their
> tragic memories. Men and women have been permanently mutilated
> and maimed, both physically and psychologically. They will be the
> living evidence of the cruelty of this war waged against us.
>
> Our people had their property looted, their houses destroyed, their
> granaries raided, their crops pillaged and flattened, their cattle stolen
> and killed, their tools burned and destroyed. The communal villages
> and cooperatives, the schools and clinics, the wells and dams built by
> the people with so much effort and sacrifice became targets for the
> enemy's criminal fury. The systematic destruction of economic infra-
> structure, bridges and roads, shops and warehouses, sawmills, planta-
> tions, agricultural and industrial machinery, electricity supply lines,
> fuel tanks, lorries and buses, locomotives and carriages has prevented
> the implementation of economic development projects of the utmost
> importance for the well being of the Mozambican people.
>
> Eight hundred and forty schools have been destroyed or closed,
> affecting more than 150,000 schoolchildren. Twelve health centers,
> 24 maternity clinics, 174 health posts, and 2 centers for the physically
> handicapped have been sacked and destroyed. Nine hundred shops
> have been destroyed, thus hampering marketing and supplies for
> about 4.5 million citizens.
>
> The bandits have murdered and kidnapped peasants and members
> of cooperatives, parliamentary deputies and party militants, teachers
> and students, nurses, lorry drivers, engine drivers, agricultural, con-
> struction, and commercial workers, technicians in various sectors,
> nuns, priests, private shopkeepers, journalists, and civil servants. . . .
>
> This is the enemy's cruel nature—kill everything, steal everything,
> burn everything. All this is part of a long process of twenty years of
> our history, throughout which the Mozambican people have been
> subjected to systematic and persistent aggression.[16]

It has also been argued—in part in light of the facts catalogued
above—that it makes good sense to have presented the peace as a
victory to the Mozambican people; in this way the latter have been

offered a glimpse of the light at the end of a very dark tunnel. Not that this is an entirely risk-free approach. As we shall see, the Accord's promise of peace is by no means guaranteed; no more is the economic payoff said to be attendant upon it. Failing an early and discernible amelioration of the situation any overselling of the original pact might come to backfire in terms of popular attitudes. There are those who would argue, in consequence, that presentation of the Accord as a tactical retreat rather than a victory might not only have been more accurate but also wiser in terms of political tactics.

An open question, but alongside this there must also be placed a second tactical consideration, one that may have been even more important in encouraging FRELIMO to set in motion the extraordinary hoopla which accompanied the signing of the Accord. One suspects that all the fanfare, including as it did the lavish and public embracing of P. W. Botha and Co. by the Mozambicans, must have made many FRELIMO members cringe. Yet it was hoped that the sheer extravaganza of the victory celebration, garnering as it did so much international coverage, would attach the South Africans to the Accord in a particularly public manner. Having thus admitted before the world its responsibility for the MNR, South Africa would have great difficulty in future in backing away—should it wish to do so—from its obligation to bring its puppet under control.

To be sure, the powerful symbolism of the event also carried its fair share of costs, costs which some argue Mozambique has underestimated. We have already noted South Africa's attempt to use Nkomati to legitimate itself further internationally, and we have mentioned the reinforcement which Reagan's Africa team could take from this kind of example of a "peaceful solution" in southern Africa. Just as striking was the shockwave the Accord sent throughout the region. To be sure, Machel's speech at the Nkomati signing ceremony reaffirmed Mozambique's "total fidelity" to the development of the SADCC economic network and to the refusal by the SADCC countries of "economic dependence on South Africa, as on any other country."[17] A Mozambique Information Agency editorial of the period (on "The Nkomati Accord and SADCC") went further, arguing that the Accord would, in fact, make a positive contribution to SADCC's development.[18] In particular, as the war wound down transportation and other linkages through Mozambique, which are so crucial to SADCC's proposed new economic grid, could be reopened and developed with confidence. This was also a point made in favor of the Accord by land-locked Zimbabwe's President Robert Mugabe.

Yet Machel may have been protesting just a little too much when he asserted in that same Nkomati speech that "SADCC was not created against South Africa." One need not overstate the importance of SADCC's accomplishments to date—it remains a diffuse, relatively modest, and only slowly expanding set of sectoral attempts at regional cooperation—to have misgivings about this formulation. Certainly it is difficult to square with the tone of numerous previous pronouncements which linked the development of a nondependent regional economy to the struggle to overthrow the apartheid system. Mozambique's enforced decision to deal so fulsomely with South Africa must be seen as a setback for that kind of SADCC spirit. Small wonder that the front-line states' meeting in Arusha shortly after the Mozambique–South Africa *rapprochement* were in no mood to have the Nkomati Accord defined as any kind of "good thing"—although their public pronouncements evidenced sympathy and understanding for the difficult, even contradictory, position in which Mozambique found itself. Machel himself said boldly to the South Africans at Nkomati that "the differences between our political, economic, and social concepts are great, and even antagonistic." Yet Mozambique had been forced, at least temporarily, to come to conciliatory terms with the hard fact of South African economic and military power.

It is difficult to show grace under the kind of pressure South Africa has brought to bear upon Mozambique. A small item in the Mozambique news shows the lighter side of the contradictions involved:

> A group of forty-three South African anglers arrived in Maputo on 9 June en route for Inhaca Island at the mouth of Maputo Bay, for a week-long fishing contest that would count in the South African championships. A government spokesman told AIM that the contest was being held in Mozambique at the request of the South African angling authorities. Mozambique had agreed to the request in order to publicize the country's tourist attractions, but Mozambican anglers were forbidden to participate in the contest to prevent any violation of the sports boycott against South Africa.[19]

However, the nature of Mozambique's relationship to the African National Congress of South Africa in the context of Nkomati reveals such contradictions in a much more somber light. To be sure, Mozambique has argued that in the horse-trading leading up to the Nkomati Accord it had conceded far less to South Africa than the latter was demanding. In negotiations with Pretoria, Machel was to tell the People's Assembly, "we firmly condemned the apartheid system and its bantustan policies," rather than agreeing to accept any part of them. Moreover, "we restated our political, moral, and diplomatic support for the ANC, which is fighting for democracy against racial discrimination, and for equality amongst all races in South Africa."[20] The ANC, he told representatives of the Socialist International meeting in Arusha, is "the legitimate representative of the . . . South African people."[21]

Yet there is more to the story than this. For the fact is that whoever may be said to have won at Nkomati, it was definitely the ANC that lost, suffering at least a "temporary setback" (in the phrase of its president, Oliver Tambo).[22] By the very nature of the case it is impossible for an external observer to gauge with precision the scope of such a setback. Certainly the ANC does not conform to the image of it projected by South Africa: that of an outside-in, hit-and-run operation. The challenge to the apartheid regime does not come, by and large, from outside, but rather from social and political forces generated within the country and very much on the move there. Increasingly, the ANC finds itself well established on the ground and rooted in these forces. In consequence, it cannot be defeated in Mozambique. By attempting to export its own domestic contradictions into the region, South Africa has done nothing to erase this fundamental reality. It is also the case that the ANC has had no military bases in Mozambique (South African hints to the contrary notwithstanding); and the movement is to continue to have a diplomatic-cum-political presence in Maputo. Even having said this, however, there can be little doubt that Mozambique's decision, in conformity with its bargain with South Africa, to substantially reduce the ANC presence in Mozambique and to monitor and control its activities ever more tightly will have a negative impact upon the logistics of the movement's access to South Africa and upon its ability to act against the regime.

Nor, however unavoidable such an adjustment in its policy may have been, has Mozambique implemented it in an altogether comradely manner. Or so the ANC has felt. It had been kept in the dark about developments until the very last moment, it argued, and when, immediately after the signing of the Accord, Mozambique acted, there can be little doubt that the latter's security apparatus came down on ANC personnel in Maputo with a surprisingly heavy hand. In part such severity may have reflected a desire to dramatize to South Africa and the world the fact that Mozambique was conforming to the very letter of the Accord (to encourage South Africa, in turn, to do so); in part, perhaps, a Mozambican backlash against ANC's own sharp initial reaction to Nkomati (there was even an implied comparison made between Mozambique and South Africa's Bantustans in the ANC's first formal statement on the subject, for example). It has also been suggested that the ANC showed some initial reluctance to conform

404   A Difficult Road

with the agreement's terms by handing over their weapons voluntarily in response to FRELIMO requests. In any case, FRELIMO did apologize for excesses committed and, ultimately, things were smoothed over. Various members of the ANC leadership began publicly to express their sympathetic comprehension of the imperatives which had moved Mozambique toward some accommodation with the apartheid regime.* And Oliver Tambo figured prominently on the list of honored guests for the April meeting of Mozambique's People's Assembly and the country's Independence Day celebrations in June.

The matter is, in the end, a straightforward one. FRELIMO had decided, at independence, that there would have to be strict limits upon how far it could go in confronting the South African state. Recent events have shown these limits to be even narrower than had been anticipated and, in the end, the ANC has had to live with this fact. However, FRELIMO has tended to put a rather more elaborate gloss on its actions in this sphere, a gloss which has caused considerable controversy in its own right. For FRELIMO has suggested the existence of an important difference between itself and the ANC in terms of their definitions of the nature of the South African struggle. FRELIMO argues that other situations of white minority rule in the southern Africa region have been of a colonial character and, the question of decolonization being an international question, external intervention by Mozambique and others to resolve it was entirely legitimate. However, South Africa—the ANC's definitions of it as a "colonialism of a special type" or "internal colonialism" to the contrary notwithstanding—is a fully sovereign independent state (internationally recognized, its white population "permanent" and so on). Whereas the former situation has required an anticolonial national liberation struggle, the latter demands an *internal* transformation.[23]

It has been difficult for some observers to avoid seeing in this kind of word play something of an ex post facto rationalization for Mozambique's inability to back up the ANC from outside. Whether South Africa is considered a "sovereign state" or not, there can be little doubt that armed action must be one important dimension of the struggle to overthrow the unjust system there. And the existence of rear bases can be extremely important to the mounting of such action. Joe Slovo, a leading ANC militant and theoretician, may or may not have been correct when he sought, in a public

---

*Some also felt moved to acknowledge privately that the *relative* paucity of assistance to Mozambique by one of ANC's own major backers, the Soviet bloc, was an important factor in narrowing Mozambique's options.

lecture delivered in Maputo some months after the Nkomati Accord, to defend the "colonialism of a special type/internal colonialism" analytical construct. There was some point, however, to his comment that "whether or not you believe that Botha's regime is sovereign and independent, we all surely agree that at any rate it is not a legitimate representative of the South African people. What outsiders can do about that fact is for them a practical rather than a theoretical question." Point, too, to his crisp (if, in light of the extremely high price Mozambique has already paid for its support of the struggles in both Zimbabwe and South Africa, somewhat uncharitable) reminder: "One wonders whether we would be sitting here tonight without Tanzania's grant of exclusive and massive external rear base facilities for FRELIMO."[24]

Of course, behind the apparent legalism of Mozambique's position there is a hint of a more substantial, albeit no less controversial, argument: FRELIMO's sense that the ANC had become too set in its exile guerrilla mold and had thus far moved too slowly to root itself inside South Africa and in close interaction with the various oppositional forces which are exploding into life there. One prominent Mozambican observer, very close to the policymaking process in that country, hinted at this point when he argued at the time of Nkomati that the "ANC will have to rethink the new situation, which to a certain extent seems to have caught them by surprise. . . . [W]ith the creation of the People's Republics of Angola and Mozambique, a new situation has been created [in South Africa] since 1975 which has brought a rapid growth of organizations which now, legally, are taking up inside the country those principles advanced by the ANC." This has in turn given the ANC much more resonance inside the country, but the implication is that the movement has not yet moved effectively enough to consolidate this internal presence and build on such advance. After all, "FRELIMO cannot substitute for the ANC in the liberation of the people, since revolutions cannot be made by proxy."[25]

The latter statement seems uncharitable in its own right, since there is no evidence that the ANC has ever sought to carry the day "by proxy." As for the former point, it too could easily be overstated and brought far too close to the apartheid regime's own stereotype of the ANC as an "outside-in" operation. The ANC has been engaged in building up a more substantial political network inside the country—and it has been aware of its own shortfalls in this respect. Thus, even before Nkomati, it has scheduled an important national conference for 1985 designed to carry forward a discussion of how best to operate on the changing political-military terrain of South Africa. Surely it is Mozambique's own weakness vis-à-vis South Africa, rather than any weaknesses on the part of ANC, which best "justifies" FRELIMO's compromise with the apartheid regime. But one suspects that FRELIMO leaders understand this perfectly well.

One additional question arises, a question often posed by critics of the Nkomati Accord. Grant for the moment Mozambique's distinction, discussed earlier, between Rhodesia- or Namibia-type situations on the one hand and South Africa on the other. Just how revolutionary a brand of internally based transformation does Mozambique really see to be on the cards in the latter context? Certainly, some Mozambican statements have employed the distinction in a militant manner: "Since 1974 Mozambicans have always had the same conception regarding South Africa, one very different from our conception of Namibia and Rhodesia. . . . There exist international problems such as the decolonization process which permit Mozambican intervention. There exist national problems such as apartheid whose resolution is only possible *by means of a revolution.*"[26] Well and good. Despite the evidence of this kind of assertion, however, some observers have seen FRELIMO as running the risk of lapsing into a *reformist* perspective, a risk, even, of its reducing the struggle in South Africa to a mere question of "civil rights." This latter seems an unfair charge,[27] but it is the case that many of Samora Machel's speeches since Nkomati have tended to present South Africa, in fairly conventional anti-apartheid terms, as a problem of racial inequality rather than as a problem of racial capitalism.[28]

Similarly, when Machel addressed a meeting of the Socialist International, held in September to discuss international support for the front-line states, he did identify cogently the various impediments to progress which the apartheid regime has thrown up. But his speech found him emphasizing the need to facilitate "dialogue" in South Africa, rather than advocating, front and center, support for the revolutionary process (armed and class-based) which alone can create the conditions—very much further down the road—for real negotiations with the guardians of racial capitalism.[29] To many, the advocacy of dialogue seemed much too comfortable a message to be bringing to social-democratic politicians, as premature as Machel's apparent advocacy before the previously mentioned April meeting of the front-line states themselves of talks between Pretoria and the ANC. It is difficult to imagine that, in the end, FRELIMO would stray very far from the principle re-enunciated in the final communique of that meeting: "[T]he alternative to free negotiations within South Africa aimed at the ending of apartheid will inevitably be continued struggle against that system by other means, including armed struggle. This struggle . . . therefore receives and will continue to receive the full support of the peoples and the nations represented by the heads of state and government of the front line states."[30] Still, there could be costs involved in not being at once both perfectly clear and perfectly frank on the subject.

We cannot pursue the question of the South African revolution here. Time alone will tell how heavy have been the costs to that revolution exacted by the Nkomati Accord. However, we must say something further about the nature of the peace which Mozambique itself has purchased with that Accord. Unfortunately, this is not a straightforward question, not least because it is difficult to know, almost a full year after the signing, whether peace is actually on the agenda. In the immediate wake of Nkomati the scope and savagery of MNR activity actually intensified, in part because South Africa had taken the precaution of pushing a fresh wave of men and material across the border on the very eve of the agreement. Nor has the Botha government done all that it might have—certainly far less than FRELIMO has done vis-à-vis the ANC—in order to wind down MNR activities.[31] MNR trainees in South Africa have not been fully demobilized, much less repatriated to Mozambique, for example, and there are signs of some even more compromising continuing entanglements. Such facts may reflect mixed feelings on the part of South African decision-makers, a reluctance to give up the leverage which the stick provides, despite the fact that continued disruption must surely be a disincentive to South African investors and other bearers of economic carrots. Or they may reflect some differences of opinion—and practice—within the South African power structure itself; Botha seems, at least implicitly, to have hinted as much in recent months.

Nonetheless, South Africa does seem to have cut back on some of its support for the MNR. A look at the combat map suggests this to be the case, with the activities of the *bandidos* now less intense in the center of the country (where South African logistical support has been most important) and more so in the south and north, near the Swaziland and Malawi borders respectively. As this shift has occurred other MNR backers have taken on higher profiles than previously, most importantly various right-wing Portuguese elements, many of them with a history of previous involvement in the colonial economy and/or security system. Apparently such countries as Israel, the Comoros, and Oman have also joined more actively in the game. And there is another factor: the MNR has always been a fairly diffuse grouping, as much a collection of bandit-gangs as a coherent political instrument. Insofar as South African direction of it has been qualified, its bandit characteristics may have become even more pronounced. Lumpen elements, adrift and with no clear future in the devastated Mozambican economy, armed and brutalized by the nature of the combat they have waged heretofore, they continue to live off the land and the people, a formidable "security problem" by virtue of that fact alone.

Mozambique continues to press South Africa to fulfill its part of the bargain more effectively. And ongoing diplomatic negotiations with both Swaziland and Malawi gives some promise of weakening the MNR's rearguard in those countries. Paradoxically, however, the post-Nkomati situation appears, at least momentarily, to have given South Africa more leverage rather than less—as witness October's so-called Pretoria Declaration. By dint of skilled stage management South Africa—principal architect of the war in Mozambique—contrived on that occasion to present itself to the international media as peacemaker and "honest broker," holding the ring between FRELIMO on the one hand and the MNR on the other. An "implementation commission" was then established—comprised of all three parties!—to facilitate the ending of the war. FRELIMO insisted that what was involved here was merely a streamlining of the process of MNR surrender, but the leadership of the latter continues to outline the significant political, economic, and ideological concessions which are necessary on FRELIMO's part in order to bring the conflict to an end. In all of this, South Africa's own agenda remains somewhat unclear (as does the agenda of other relevant actors like the United States); there was even some talk of South Africa establishing a military presence inside Mozambique in order to help police the peace, although the precise status of this rather surprising proposal remains very unclear. Clearly leverage remains the name of the game, with South Africa apparently feeling it has sufficient advantage to press it and up the ante of required compromise. It is fortunate, therefore, that FRELIMO appears very far from being naive about the hazards of the current period. As Jacinto Veloso, a Mozambican minister and a central negotiator with the South Africans, has stated, "Military action must continue to be our main priority in the struggle against banditry in our country. What is considered in the diplomatic sphere is merely to support action on the ground."[32] Meanwhile, the war continues.

What of the supposed economic benefits to Mozambique of the Accord? We noted in Chapter 2 Mozambique's difficulties in attracting private investment, even as it has become more welcoming to it. South African capital seems unlikely to be any less concerned about the probable profitability of its projected investments.

Moreover, surpluses are tight in South Africa in the context of the present severe recession in that country. To be sure, the South African government has interpreted the Accord as potentially exemplifying a dramatic breakthrough for its cherished "Constellation of States" concept and the further integration of the southern Africa economy under South African hegemony; it also sees itself as becoming (along with Portugal) a privileged intermediary for the entry of international capital from outside the region. In consequence, Pretoria has shown signs of taking the initiative, beginning, for example, to turn the tap back on in Maputo harbor—having turned it off previously as one kind of pressure upon Mozambique—by suggesting that more transit traffic will be sent that way. In negotiations (which have also involved Portugal), Mozambique has been conceded more advantageous terms for the shipping to South Africa of Cabora Bassa power. And Botha and company have publicly encouraged South Africa's private sector to help nail down Mozambique's reintegration into the republic's regional grid by entering into that country's economy.

All this has had very mixed results, as noted. Although the South African firm Rennies has agreed to take an active role in the abovementioned effort to revitalize Maputo port, there has been, after an initial flurry of excitement, no great activity on the part of other large corporations. As Robert Davies has suggested, a number of smaller firms have been more alert to the possibilities in Mozambique but given the crisis in South Africa itself few are buoyant enough to contemplate anything very dramatic.[33] In any case, the sectors that do seem most attractive to South African capital are not self-evidently those most important to undergirding the project of "expanded socialist reproduction" geared to mass needs which we saw FRELIMO to be working toward in earlier chapters. For example, the development of tourist facilities is one of the few very prominent targets for investment, with some interest as well in agriculture (although more for export to South Africa than for serving local markets), but little enough in key industrial spheres. Again, it is much too early to predict outcomes with any confidence. Yet the fact remains that, to date, it is more the prospect of carrots that has been dangled before the noses of Mozambican economic decision-makers—the better to obtain further concessions, it would seem—than their delivery.

Indeed, as regards the economic tack, Mozambique has felt compelled to choose both vis-à-vis South Africa and vis-à-vis international capital more generally, and one sometimes gets the sense of a trap slowly swinging shut. Thus, Mozambique looks for short-term economic succour precisely by reinforcing many of the elements of economic subordination vis-à-vis South Africa that defined the structure of its colonial economy. Moreover, at the extreme, it has even been hinted (not least by David Rockefeller on a visit to Maputo) that at some point it would be a logical step for Mozambique to guarantee its access to the South African goods it requires by entering the Rand Monetary Zone! At the very least, it was asserted, Mozambique would need a formal investment code, the better to signal its good intentions to potential investors. And when just such a law on investment was promulgated in August, it was very far from being a restrictive one—even if one accepts that the actual import of deals struck with prospective investors will be primarily defined by the outcome of case by case negotiations.[34] In addition, much new aid—most notably that from the United States—has had very dangerous strings attached. For example, U.S. emergency food aid was made contingent upon Mozambique accepting, for purposes of its administration, the prominent presence in the rural areas of a range of right-wing "nongovernmental organizations," such as World Vision.[35] Other kinds of U.S. aid were exclusively earmarked to "revitalize and develop" the private sector, notably in the agricultural sphere. Finally, much promised credit—its foreign exchange crisis being Mozambique's most vulnerable economic front—was made contingent upon the country's coming to terms with the International Monetary Fund and the World Bank, which organizations Mozambique finally joined in September. Yet as debt-ridden Mozambique gets further drawn onto the terrain defined by such organizations, the terms of "IMF conditionality" could well begin to reinforce other pressures toward accepting the orthodoxy of dependency: the further reinforcing of the private sector, both local and international; the concentration of the state's activities in infrastructural development; even the cutting back of such "frills" as health and educational programs. This last would, of course, close the circle, marking international capital's assault on the spheres of FRELIMO's most salient, progressive, and popular accomplishments.

Beggars can't be choosers! This would be too bleak a summation of Mozambique's present plight, yet there can be little doubt that the country's projected transition to socialism has taken a frightful battering. The need to adjust rapidly to a deteriorating situation has also placed great strain on the progressive political alliance which FRELIMO had come to encapsulate in Mozambique— although the relevant political faultlines have cut across each other in diverse and often unpredictable directions. The MNR and its backers are unlikely, in and of themselves, to impose upon FRELIMO the kind of overt retreat from Marxism and socialism which MNR leaders now demand. Yet there are classes in Mozambique—"kulaks" and traders whose prospects are enhanced, at least in the short run, by the present Mozambican-style "New Economic Policy," as well as bureaucratically inclined "petty bourgeois" functionaries of party and state—who will be inclined, in their own interests, to make a virtue of the necessity of accommodation with regional and international centers of capital accumulation. Of course, it is also the case that denizens of the bureaucratic structures might have something to lose if an IMF package were eventually to cut back the role of the state sector too aggressively. Some of the latter group might instead opt for a much tougher line, begrudging the compromises of the NEP (even if temporarily on the defensive with respect to it), but doing so in the interests of a hard-nosed state-collectivist and "benignly authoritarian" vision of the future.

As we have already suggested in Chapter 2, steering a course through these extremes will be no easy task for those who seek to refurbish FRELIMO's project in a more progressive manner. Some of the tensions involved in so doing surfaced in June when, for the first time, two members of the Politburo were sacked from their ministerial postings (though not, be it noted, from the Politburo), in which they had responsibility for such crucial sectors as security and the interior (police). Although both were subsequently given new (if rather less central) postings, much speculation of a "Kremlinological" nature followed this event—were they for or against Nkomati?—but in this case at least the explanation seemed much more closely linked to the ongoing attempt to revitalize the revolution by pre-empting the kind of reversion to repression all too familiar in many other third world settings ("socialist" or otherwise). For the two ministers were identified as being responsible for the heavy-handed use and abuse of state power: "Here is [Armando] Guebuza. He is the one who arrests many people and just leaves them there. And this is Mariano [Matsinhe]. He detains many people and forgets them. And they are members of the Politburo!"[36] So Samora Machel introduced them to a public meeting in Maputo in the month before they were removed from office. It seemed that the Legality Offensive, begun in 1981, was to be refurbished in dramatic style, surely a positive sign.*

---

*The need to struggle against bureaucratic abuse and formation of any kind of state-class also continued to be emphasized for spheres beyond the police/security one. Thus, in his speech at the People's Assembly in April, the President "attacked state managers who used State property for their personal ends and who 'have a life-style that is not in our traditions.' Abuse and waste of state property, he stressed, 'is a crime against the people.' "

Other tensions are bound to surface on the new terrain. Perhaps their texture was anticipated in a recent controversy which saw peasants—some organized into cooperatives—from the green belt around Maputo complaining that the city council was arbitrarily licensing already occupied land to private farmers, many of them civil servants. Indeed, "one peasant women accused the new private farmers and their supporters in the state apparatus of being similar to the bandits of the MNR, but 'instead of guns they are armed with briefcases full of papers that order our eviction.'" Jorge Rebelo, the First Party Secretary for Maputo (and a Politburo member), in arbitrating this dispute criticized the city council, seeking, in doing so, to balance the claims of "the private sector, the peasant family sector, and the cooperatives."[37] But just how the latter, in particular, will be supported—not only in Maputo but throughout the country—continues to be an open question.

On another front in Maputo, Rebelo's initiatives have been much clearer, and much more successful, as with his efforts to breathe new life into grass-roots political institutions, at "ten-house group," *quarteirao* (block), *celula* (cell), and *bairro* (neighborhood) levels:

> "We must make democracy live from the base upward," said Jorge Rebelo. He criticized the way in which some heads of ten-family groups had been appointed from above, and stressed that it was essential that they should be chosen by, and known to, the families they were to represent. Mr. Rebelo denounced "bureaucratic methods, with no input by the people," which had occurred in the choice of some of these individuals.[38]

More generally, a critical review was made of the functioning of the first People's Assemblies, in preparation for a second set of elections. There had been problems, Marcelino dos Santos explained to the April meeting of the national People's Assembly, many caused by the MNR: "The bandits deliberately carry out criminal acts against the deputies who represent the people." But there was also "a confusion of functions and jobs between party and state organs, caused by the concentration of various responsibilities on the same people," as well as "irregularities committed by some deputies, including apathy, tacit abandonment of their mandate, failure to carry out tasks given to them, lengthy and unjustified periods of absence, and lack of contact with the people who elected them." Such problems would have to be overcome if the proposed efforts to redemocratize the revolution were to realize their promise. But at least "the advances we have made in the military field, linked to the conditions for peace resulting from the Nkomati Accord, make it possible for us to envisage the holding of the second general elections."[39] To be sure, some observers have felt that the fact that so dramatic a policy initiative as the Nkomati Accord could be introduced almost exclusively from the very top down suggested a continuing hyper-concentration of power that might not be entirely healthy. Nonetheless, the dialectic between leadership and mass action continues to be alive in Mozambique.

We have already had a great deal to say in this book regarding perils on the economic front. Have the weaknesses in planning capacity which scarred the apparatus set up around the ten-year *Plano Prospectivo Indicativo* (PPI) been made good by the disbanding of that apparatus and the ingestion of its powers into the President's office? Is there the strength and clarity of purpose required to control the proposed and novel expansion of the private sector along lines consistent with long-term socialist goals? The answers are far from clear, although the emergence of vigorous and self-critical debate around some of the most important questions to be raised regarding planning—past, present, and future—is another positive sign.[40] Even the proposed growth of South African tourism, possible bearer though it may be of distortions in the development process, could help relieve short-term foreign exchange constraints. It is fortunate, nonetheless, that there are instances of aid and trade agreements which seem better designed to drive that development process forward (Scandinavian assistance to the industrial sector, for example). Moreover, the range of partners—from East and West—is still a broad and diversified one.[41] There is some agricultural advance: cashew production is up this year, for example. And in service sectors various programs, referred to in previous chapters, are still scoring some successes (among other initiatives a number of adult literacy programs might be mentioned). Modest enough perhaps, but also signs that FRELIMO is regrouping, the better, after taking one step back, to take two forward!

In concluding a book of this nature it is difficult, and perhaps even inadvisable, to avoid a personal note. Like all the authors whose work is included in this volume, I have had a long history of close personal contact and involvement with the Mozambican revolution, an involvement which, in my case, stretches back nearly twenty years to a time when, in FRELIMO's dusty little office on Nkrumah Street in Dar es Salaam, I moonlighted from my university job and assisted the movement's Information Department in the preparation of English-language materials for overseas political work. I visited the liberated areas of Tete Province with FRELIMO guerrillas in 1972 during the time of the anticolonial war and I shared the joy of victory at the independence celebrations in 1975.

In subsequent years I was to visit independent Mozambique on numerous occasions and ultimately to work there for a more extended period as a *cooperante*. And I was to be a guest and observer at FRELIMO's important and dramatic Fourth Congress in 1983. I can remember dinners with Eduardo Mondlane, FRELIMO's first president, and long conversations with Marcelino dos Santos, over tea in his small house in one of the *bairros* of Dar es Salaam, occasions so important to my own political development. And I can remember Samora Machel visiting my house on University Hill in Dar on the back of Jorge Rebelo's motorcycle—to talk of the war, of information and support work, still a long way from victory but well on the road, a vibrant and inspiring figure. I remember the palpable feeling of "people's power" in the liberated areas of Fingoe, where women revelled in their ability to speak up publicly for the first time and all shared a sense of freedom; I remember the unrestrained emotion of the rain-soaked crowd as the new Mozambican flag went up in the National Stadium a few minutes after midnight, June 25, 1975, and I remember how moved I was later that day when, at the investiture, Machel and dos Santos, freshly installed in office, embraced in triumph; I remember the intense concentration of my students in the evening course on Marxism at FRELIMO's party school, cadres bone-tired after a full day's work but dedicated to mastering the tools which would help see a transition to socialism in their country; I remember the creative and self-critical atmosphere alive in the impressive new conference hall at the Fourth Congress as FRELIMO fought, against lengthening odds, to keep its revolution alive. I am, in short, *parti pris*.[42]

To have seen a people making its own history, freeing itself from a morally bankrupt and viciously oppressive colonialism and then launching an impressive project of humane and egalitarian social reconstruction, is a moving experience; to be allowed, as an outsider, to share in these struggles in some small way is more than moving, it is inspiring. Such experiences also challenge one's ability to remain objective. This is not entirely a negative thing, of course. While one must strive to be honest about registering failures of omission and commission on the part of FRELIMO, as has been the attempt in this book, one's anger at the callous, ruthless manner in which outside forces—South Africa in particular—have sought to destroy the Mozambican revolution can also sharpen perceptions. It can help one to grasp and underscore crucial aspects—in this case *the* crucial aspect—of the process which other analyses might touch upon only in passing as some kind of "external variable." Moreover, a committed posture can help the observer to identify deeper currents, currents which serve to contextualize the diverse and fluctuating eddies of the present and to point the way forward. Thus, it is impossible for those who have been close to developments in Mozambique over the years to "factor out" from the analysis of the present conjuncture a consideration of the historical process which has produced FRELIMO and grounded that movement in a popular revolution. The leadership cadre which launched that revolutionary process is still in place, frayed at the edges certainly, older (although, one suspects, wiser), girded for one further attempt to recast the foundations of its revolution. And the link—replete with tensions and contradictions but forged in struggle—which has joined FRELIMO to the popular classes in Mozambique also remains in place, stretched, perhaps, to the breaking point but in place nevertheless. Such assertions are not premised on mere faith; it is the analysis of the long arc of Mozambican development presented in earlier chapters which underpins them. Nor can there be any question of underestimating the odds against the successful attainment of FRELIMO's goals: they have jumped out at us at every turn in the present chapter. Moreover, there is one essential determinant of Mozambique's future which falls largely outside the orbit of the present book: the pace at which the revolutionary struggle advances in South Africa itself.[43] Whatever ground FRELIMO may be able to recoup in the years ahead, whatever the progress that may be made in Mozambique, it will certainly be much less than it might otherwise have been were apartheid South Africa not a looming presence, stick and carrots in hand. As that behemoth is dragged down from within by its own people, as will eventually be the case, a very much smoother path will open up to its neighbors. Yet, in the meantime, in Mozambique too—the phrase has worn thin through repetition, but is still true—*a luta continua*, the struggle continues.

Notes

1. "The Nkomati Accord," reprinted in Mozambique Information Office (MIO), *News Review* 25 (16 March 1984).
2. From a communique cited in Mozambique Information Agency (AIM), "Talks Between Mozambique and South Africa," *News Review* 21 (19 January 1984).
3. "Resumo da palestra de camarada (Jose Luis) Cabaço do bureau politico sobre o Acordo de Nkomati" (typescript, n. d.).
4. AIM, "President Machel Addresses the People's Assembly," *News Review* 28 (27 April 1984).
5. AIM, "1984 Plan Presented to People's Assembly," in ibid.
6. AIM, "President Machel Addresses People's Assembly."

7. See my article "Under Fire II: John Saul in Mozambique," *This Magazine* 18, no. 4 (December 1984).
8. Quoted in AIM, "People's Assembly Ratifies Nkomati Accord," *News Review* 28 (27 April 1984).
9. Samora Machel, "A Paz é essência propria do socialismo," speech to a "solemn session" *(sessâo solene)* held to hail the Nkomati Accord in Maputo, 5 April 1984, and published in *Tempo* (Maputo), 705 (15 April 1984): 43.
10. Quoted in AIM, "People's Assembly Ratifies Nkomati Accord."
11. Quoted from the English translation of the speech cited in n. 9, above, and published as Samora Machel, "Accord of Nkomati: A Victory for Peace," *Supplement to AIM Bulletin No. 94* (Maputo), pp. 6, 7, 8. A summary appears in *News Review* 26 (30 March 1984) under the evocative title (a quote from the speech), "We have turned off the tap."
12. Quoted in AIM, "People's Assembly Ratifies Nkomati Accord."
13. Quoted in Robert Davies and Dan O'Meara, "Total Strategy in Southern Africa: An Analysis of Regional Policy since 1978," paper presented to the 1984 *Review of African Political Economy* Conference, University of Keele, September 1984, pp. 13–14.
14. Quoted in ibid., p. 23, n. 48.
15. "Notes from a Meeting with Minister of Information José Luis Cabaço, 18 July 1983," unpublished manuscript, summarizing a meeting with Cabaço and a delegation from the Toronto Committee for the Liberation of Southern Africa (TCLSAC).
16. Machel, "Accord of Nkomati: A Victory for Peace," pp. 8–9.
17. Samora Machel, "Speech Following the Signing of the Accord of Nkomati, 16 March 1984," *Supplement to AIM Bulletin No. 93* (Maputo), p. 10.
18. Carlos Cardoso, "The Nkomati Accord and SADCC," *News Review* 26 (30 March 1984).
19. AIM, "South African Anglers at Inhaca Island," *News Review* 31 (14 June 1984).
20. AIM, "President Machel Addresses the People's Assembly."
21. Samora Machel, "Paz e cooperaçâo sâo indissociáveis," presentation to the Conference in Support of the Front Line States, organized by the Socialist International, September 1984, and reproduced in *Noticias* (Maputo), 11 September 1984.
22. AIM, "AIM Interviews Oliver Tambo," *News Review* 33 (12 July 1984).
23. Although FRELIMO claims a fundamental consistency in its position in this respect, this is not quite true. In an important speech delivered in the immediate aftermath of South Africa's aerial attack on Matola (a suburb of Maputo) in 1981, Samora Machel stated that "Apartheid is a form of colonialism. For this reason we understand profoundly the just struggle of the South African people." Moreover, "The ANC is one of the beacons in Africa that has inspired the national liberation struggle against racism and colonial domination, the fertile ground in which our own liberation struggle took root." See "Speech by President Samora Machel at a Mass Rally in Maputo, 14 February 1981, published as *Supplement to AIM Bulletin No. 56* (Maputo). It was in this

same speech that Machel coined the defiant phrase, "Que venham—" "Let the South Africans come"—an admirable boast but unfortunately one which it has been difficult to back up in practice.
24. Joe Slovo, "Second Ruth First Memorial Lecture," presentation at the University of Eduardo Mondlane, 24 August 1984 (mimeo).
25. "Vitoria da nossa soberania," interview with Professor Aquino da Bragança, *Tempo* 702 (25 March 1984).
26. "Resumo da palestra de camarada Cabaço."
27. Although this "civil rights" formulation has been attributed to FRELIMO by a number of critics, my own investigation suggests that the sole source cited for it is a South African radio report of an interview/press conference with Sebastiâo Mabote, Mozambique's vice-minister of defense. The source is a dubious one and the position it purports to convey not typical.
28. See, among other instances (speeches in Bulgaria and Ethiopia of about the same time period, for example), Samora Machel's speech at the official banquet in honor of the visiting Portuguese prime minister, reproduced in *Noticias*, 4 September 1984, under the headline "Soubemos ultrapassar em pouco tempo os traumas de uma guerra injusta."
29. Machel, "Paz e cooperaçâo sâo indissociáveis."
30. "Final Communique from a Meeting of Front Line Heads of State and Government Held in Arusha, Tanzania, 29 April 1984," *Supplement to AIM Bulletin No. 94* (Maputo).
31. On this and related matters see Robert Davies, "South African Strategy Toward Mozambique in the Post-Nkomati Period: A Critical Analysis of Effects and Implications," unpublished paper, Maputo, October 1984.
32. Quoted in AIM, "Implementation Commission: Talks Continue," *News Review* 39 (19 October 1984).
33. Davies, "South African Strategy."
34. Government of the People's Republic of Mozambique, "Law No. 4/84 of 18th August: Foreign Investment Law," mimeo, August 1984.
35. See Joseph Hanlon, "Stealing the Dream," *New Statesmen* (London), 19 October 1984.
36. Quoted in "Mozambique: A Parting of the Ranks," *African Confidential* 25, no. 16 (1 August 1984). The army's Sebastiâo Mabote was also singled out: "Mabote's men create secret prisons. They detain people and don't know what to do with them." See also Samora Machel's important speech on related matters in Nampula, 24 May 1984, entitled "Nossas Estruturas Nâo Devem Ser Refugio Para Incompetentes" and reproduced in *Tempo* 713 (10 June 1984).
37. The quotations in this paragraph are from AIM, "Land Problems Around Maputo," *News Review* 39 (19 October 1984).
38. Quoted in AIM, "Grass Roots Democracy—The Corner Stones of Our Society," *News Review* 19 (15 December 1983); see also AIM, "City Life: New Organizations Created," *News Review* 31 (14 June 1984).
39. The quotations in this paragraph are drawn from AIM, "People's Assembly: Elections Planned," *News Review* 29 (17 May 1984).

40. See, as one important example, the critical document prepared by the Secretary of State for Physical Planning and entitled *Plano, projecto, e planeamento fisico* (Maputo: Instituto Nacional do Planeamento Fisico, 1984).
41. See, for example, AIM, "Soviet Union Continues to Be 'Firm Friend,'" *News Review* 27 (12 April 1984).
42. I have recounted some of these experiences in my *The State and Revolution in Eastern Africa* (New York: Monthly Review Press, 1979); see, in particular, chaps. 2, 3, and 15.
43. I have explored this subject elsewhere: See *The Crisis in South Africa: Class Defense, Class Revolution* (New York and London: Monthly Review Press, 1981), which I co-authored with Stephen Gelb, and *South Africa: Apartheid and Africa* (Boulder: Westview Press, forthcoming). See also Rob Davies, Dan O'Meara, and Sipho Dlamini, *The Struggle for South Africa*, 2 vols. (London: Zed Press, 1984) and the first two numbers of *South African Review* (Johannesburg, 1983 and 1984 respectively).

Notes on Contributors

Carol Barker is a lecturer at the Nuffield Centre for Health Services Studies in Leeds, England, where she directs a postgraduate course in health planning and administration for health professionals in developing countries. She was the first Western *cooperante* to arrive at the Ministry of Health in Mozambique after independence, starting work there in April 1976. She was also a member of the Technical Committee for Therapeutics and Pharmacy and was involved in policy studies for that body. She returned to England at the end of 1979, but visited Mozambique again in August 1980, when she undertook the interviewing and archival work that forms the basis of her chapter.

Helena Dolny has been working in Mozambique since 1976. She spent four years as an agricultural economist in the Ministry of Agriculture, at first in the state-farm planning team, later with cooperatives. In 1981 she moved to the Centre of African Studies at the University of Eduardo Mondlane as one of a team of lecturers/researchers whose aim was to link teaching/fieldwork to questions of transition. She is currently a program coordinator for CUSO and SUCO, the two Canadian nongovernmental organizations in Mozambique.

Judith Marshall worked in the Ministry of Education in Mozambique from 1978 to 1984, in both the departments of adult education and international cooperation. She has been involved in southern African liberation support activities through the Toronto Committee for the Liberation of Southern Africa (TCLSAC) for many years and also worked for Oxfam-Canada in developing its southern Africa program from 1976 to 1978. She is presently working on her Ph.D. in education at the University of Toronto.

Barry Pinsky is a Canadian architect and community planner who first worked in Mozambique from 1977 to 1979 on a shantytown improvement project in Maputo. He returned in 1980 to study the development of urban government and in 1983 to work on guidelines for urban planning administration. When in Canada he is active in developing nonprofit housing cooperatives and in solidarity work. He is a research associate at the University of Toronto and a founding member of the Settlements Information Network Africa which is encouraging contact between grassroots housing activists.

John S. Saul first worked with the Front for the Liberation of Mozambique (FRELIMO) in Dar es Salaam, Tanzania, in the 1960s and in 1981–1982 taught in Maputo at the FRELIMO Party School liberation struggle there (1972). He has returned frequently since, and in 1981–1982 taught in Maputa at the FRELIMO Party School and at the Faculty of Marxism-Leninism, University of Eduardo Mondlane. He lives in Toronto where he teaches at Atkinson College, York University, and works with the Toronto Committee for the Liberation of Southern Africa (TCLSAC). His previous books for Monthly Review Press include *Essays in the Political Economy of Africa* (co-authored with Giovanni Arrighi, 1973), *The State and Revolution in Eastern Africa* (1979), and *The Crisis in South Africa* (co-authored with Stephen Gelb, 1981).

Peter Sketchley is a British systems analyst specializing in computerized production-control systems. He was one of the first *cooperantes* to arrive in independent Mozambique, in March 1977, and spent the following two and one-half years working in a steel rolling mill in Maputo.

Stephanie Urdang, a South African, is a journalist who has worked in the southern Africa support movement in the United States for many years. She is presently research director of the American Committee on Africa. She has written on the role of women in the liberation struggles and in post-independence societies in Africa, and on South Africa in general. She is author of *Fighting Two Colonialisms: Women in Guinea-Bissau* (Monthly Review Press, 1979) and co-author with Richard Lapchick of *Oppression and Resistance: The Struggle of Women in Southern Africa* (1981). She has visited Mozambique a number of times since 1980 to continue her research on women.